AF861393

QuickBooks®
in the Classroom

Instructor's
Resource Guide

Intuit Education Program

Copyright

Copyright 2003 Intuit Inc.

All rights reserved.

First printing: January 2003

Intuit Inc.

P.O. Box 7850

Mountain View, CA 94039-7850

ISBN 1-57338-099-7

STATEMENTS IN THIS DOCUMENT REGARDING THIRD-PARTY STANDARDS OR SOFTWARE ARE BASED ON INFORMATION MADE AVAILABLE BY THIRD PARTIES. INTUIT AND ITS AFFILIATES ARE NOT THE SOURCE OF SUCH INFORMATION AND HAVE NOT INDEPENDENTLY VERIFIED SUCH INFORMATION. THE INFORMATION IN THIS DOCUMENT IS SUBJECT TO CHANGE WITHOUT NOTICE.

Trademarks

Intuit, the Intuit logo, QuickBooks, QuickBooks Pro, Quicken, TurboTax, ProSeries, Lacerte, EasyStep, and QuickZoom, among others, are registered trademarks and/or registered service marks of Intuit Inc. or one of its subsidiaries in the United States and other countries. Other parties' trademarks or service marks are the property of their respective owners and should be treated as such.

The Sentry Spelling-Checker Engine Copyright © 1993 Wintertree Software Inc. This product includes code license from RSA Security, Inc. Some portions licensed from IBM are available at http://oss.software.ibm.com/icu4j/.

Important

Terms, conditions, features, service offerings, prices, and hours referenced in this document are subject to change without notice. We at Intuit are committed to bringing you great online services through QuickBooks. Occasionally, we may decide to update our selection and change our service offerings, so please check **www.quickbooks.com** for the latest information, including pricing and availability, on our products and services.

Table of contents

Introduction

This training guide introduces you to QuickBooks—Intuit's easy-to-use, powerful accounting systems for small businesses. The guide contains 15 lessons in addition to this chapter.

Many of the lessons in this guide can be performed with any QuickBooks Financial Software 2003 Edition. When a lesson or exercise requires QuickBooks Pro or QuickBooks Premier, that requirement is stated at the beginning of the lesson or exercise.

Important: Most of the step-by-step instructions and screen captures in this guide were created with QuickBooks Financial Software: Pro Edition 2003. Your screens may differ, and some instructions may vary slightly, if you are using QuickBooks Basic or Premier Editions instead of QuickBooks Pro. Screen captures for features available only in QuickBooks Premier Editions were created with QuickBooks Financial Software: Premier Edition 2003.

Course objectives

After completing this guide, your students should be able to do the following:

- Create a new QuickBooks company.
- Modify the preset chart of accounts to suit your needs.
- Add information to company lists, or edit information in company lists.
- Open and use registers for any QuickBooks balance sheet accounts.
- Reconcile a QuickBooks checking account.
- Track credit card transactions.
- Invoice customers.
- Create sales orders.
- Generate customer statements.
- Receive payments from customers and make bank deposits.
- Write QuickBooks checks and assign amounts to specific expense accounts.
- Work with asset and liability accounts in QuickBooks.
- Enter bills into QuickBooks accounts payable.
- Pay bills.
- Create and customize QuickBooks reports and graphs.
- Export QuickBooks reports to Microsoft Excel.
- Set up inventory and build finished good with QuickBooks.
- Track and pay sales tax.
- Understand QuickBooks payroll features.
- Create estimates and do progress invoicing.

- Track time and pay nonemployees for time worked.
- Customize QuickBooks sales forms.
- Write letters in Microsoft Word using QuickBooks data.

Hardware and software requirements

For all QuickBooks 2003 products

To use the 2003 version of any QuickBooks product, you need the following equipment and software:

- 200 MHz IBM compatible Pentium computer (350 MHz or higher recommended).
- A minimum of 64 MB (megabytes) of RAM (random access memory); 95 MB is recommended.
- Hard disk with the following amounts of free disk space:

Installation component	QuickBooks Basic	QuickBooks Pro	QuickBooks Premier and Premier: Accountant Edition
QuickBooks Financial Software	170 MB	175 MB	250 MB 280 MB
Microsoft Internet Explorer 6.0	70 MB	70 MB	70 MB
Additional for Timer	N/A	9 MB	9 MB

- 2x CD-ROM drive (double speed) or higher.
- 8-bit or 16-bit sound card if you want to use the sound features.
- 256-color VGA monitor, SVGA monitor, or better is recommended (minimum resolution of 800 x 600 using Small Fonts in your Windows Control Display settings).
- Either Windows 98, Me, 2000, XP, or NT 4.0 (with Service Pack 3, 4, or 6a).
- Internet access (with a connection speed of 28.8 or higher) is required for Payroll and all online features/services.
- QuickBooks for Windows installation CD-ROM.
- Printer supported by Windows 98, Me, 2000, NT 4.0, or XP.

For QuickBooks Pro, Premier, and Premier: Accountant Edition only

- Microsoft® Word 97, 2000, or 2002 if you plan to use the QuickBooks Letters feature. (More RAM enhances the use of this feature.)
- Microsoft® Excel 97, 2000, or 2002 if you plan to use the features in QuickBooks Pro and Premier that integrate with Microsoft Excel. (More RAM enhances the use of these features.)
- Either Microsoft® Outlook (version 97, 98, 2000, or 2002), Symantec ACT! version 3.0.8, 4.0.2, OR Interact 2000 if you want to synchronize with contact management software.

Network requirements

QuickBooks 2003 network requirements are the same whether you are sharing a company file or printing to a network printer:

- Windows 2000 Server, Windows XP Server, Windows NT 4.0 Server (with Service Pack 3, 4, or 6a), or NetWare Network File Server 3.12.

  OR

- Peer-to-peer network, using either Windows NT 4.0 (with Service Pack 3, 4, or 6a), or Windows 98, 2000, Me, or XP.

Important: Intuit recommends you have the latest Service Pack or update for your operating system or network software. If you are uncertain whether you have the latest Service Pack or update, contact Microsoft, Novell, or your network administrator.

About the exercise file

An exercise file is included with this guide. Install the file on the CD-ROM to your computer's hard disk as described below. You'll use a copy of this file to complete the lessons in this guide.

We recommend that you make a copy of the exercise file and store it in a safe place in case the original becomes damaged.

Using the exercise file in each lesson

For each lesson in this guide, except for lessons 1 and 2, you'll restore a new copy of the exercise file **qblesson.qbb**, and use that file to complete the lesson. The qblesson.qbb file you copy into the QBtrain directory on your hard disk is a QuickBooks backup copy. This means that at the start of each lesson, you'll be restoring a new qblesson file. Instructions on how to restore the file are given at the start of each lesson.

Installing the exercise file

To install the exercise file on your hard disk:

1 From the Windows Start menu, choose Run.

2 Type ***Explorer***, and then click OK.

3 From Windows Explorer, select your hard disk (usually c:).

4 From the File menu, choose New, and then choose Folder.

5 Type ***QBtrain***, and then press Enter.

6 Select your CD-ROM drive containing the exercise file (usually d: or e:).

7 Select qblesson.qbb.

8 Drag qblesson.qbb to the QBtrain folder on your hard disk.

9 Remove the CD-ROM from your CD-ROM drive.

Your exercise file is now installed in the QBtrain folder on your hard disk.

Exercise transaction dates

The exercise file for use with this guide was created in QuickBooks Pro 2002 with the date set to 12/15/2003. When you open the exercise file in QuickBooks, QuickBooks automatically sets the sample data file date to 12/15/2003. When you close the exercise file, use your own QuickBooks company file, or exit QuickBooks, your date will return to the current date.

Teaching methodology and methods

This course is divided into 15 lessons and combines lectures with hands-on student participation. We encourage you to pick and choose lessons to fit the needs of your students, or to fit your own teaching objectives.

Each lesson begins with a list of student objectives, handout materials needed, and instructor preparation. Appendix A includes a brief demonstration of QuickBooks to be presented by the instructor. The demo introduces students to QuickBooks and provides them with a road map of what they will learn in the course.

Most lessons in this course include one or more handouts. We encourage you to use the handouts provided with a lesson; they summarize or illustrate the main points of your lecture, and are helpful for students to refer to later. If you choose not to distribute a copy of each handout to all your students, you can display the handouts on an overhead projector as you explain the basic concepts.

A copy of each handout is bound into the back of this guide and we've included an electronic copy on the CD-ROM that accompanies this guide so that you can edit and print the handouts as desired. See Appendix C for copies of the handouts.

To maximize hands-on practice with QuickBooks, a computer lab with one computer per student is ideal. If this is unavailable, you can teach the course with up to three students sharing a computer. However, sharing computers lengthens the course and reduces the effectiveness of student learning.

Each lesson contains special notes that help you present the material. These notes are printed *in italics* and appear at key places in the lessons.

Finally, you'll find a brief student test and review section at the end of each lesson. The text for each section is available electronic format file on the CD-ROM that accompanies this guide.

Instructor's preparation

To gain a quick overview of what will be presented in the course, you may want to run through the QuickBooks demonstration in Appendix A. If you are new to the latest version of QuickBooks and want to see a list of new features, search the onscreen Help index for *new features*. (From the QuickBooks Help menu, choose Help Index.) Or see the summary of new features in Appendix B.

An important supplement to this instructor's manual is the QuickBooks *User's Guide*, which provides conceptual explanations of QuickBooks features. You can look up common business situations and find suggestions on how to handle those situations in QuickBooks. We suggest you have a guide available for reference during the course.

Student prerequisites

No knowledge of finances or accounting is needed to use QuickBooks. Students should however, have a basic knowledge of the computer operating system and know how to move files around, create folders or directories, copy files to and from disks, and run applications.

Evaluating the guide

We are interested in your evaluation of the course guide. What would you like to see changed, added, or deleted?

We are particularly interested in the following:

- The type of course you're teaching.
- The number of days or hours the course takes (i.e., five weeks, one day).
- Do you give quizzes or tests?
- What other material do you use when teaching this course?

There is a form in the back of this guide for you to complete and mail or fax to us.

LESSON 1 Getting started

Lesson objectives

- To gain an overview of the course and the topics to be covered
- To know how QuickBooks works and how you can get around in QuickBooks
- To learn common business terms used by QuickBooks
- To see how to exit QuickBooks

Handout materials

- Handout 1: Course syllabus
- Handout 2: Record your daily transactions on QuickBooks forms
- Handout 3: Information stored in the Customer list
- Handout 4: Register for an accounts receivable account
- Handout 5: The QuickBooks chart of accounts
- Handout 6: About assets, liabilities, and equity
- Handout 7: Sample balance sheet
- Handout 8: Sample profit and loss statement

Instructor preparation

- **Make sure you've read the sections on "Teaching methodology and methods" and "Instructor's preparation" in the introduction to this guide.**
- Install QuickBooks Pro onto your computer's hard disk. (See the *User's Guide* for instructions.)
- Copy the qblesson.qbb file from your *QuickBooks in the Classroom* CD-ROM onto the computer's hard drive. (See "Installing the exercise file" in the Introduction to this guide.)
- Run through the "Instructor demo of QuickBooks features on page 306 of this guide to make sure you're familiar with the material.
- Have Handouts 1 through 8 ready for distribution.

Course introduction

Distribute copies of Handout 1, "Course syllabus," to the students.

This course is an introduction to QuickBooks. Its main objective is to introduce you to the basic features in QuickBooks and give you an opportunity for hands-on practice. You'll learn about the types of information you need to track in your business, and you'll see how to enter that information and track it in QuickBooks. By the time you complete the course, you'll have a good idea of all that QuickBooks offers, you'll be familiar with the most common tasks, and you'll know where to find information about more advanced features.

Depending on the size of your class, you may want to spend a little time inquiring about your students' backgrounds—whether they own a business or are the bookkeeper for a small business, for example, or whether any of them have experience with accounting. This information can help you gear the course towards your students' particular needs.

Introducing QuickBooks

Before you begin your demonstration of QuickBooks (see Appendix A), students may find it helpful to hear an introduction to the basic features in QuickBooks.

Although most small business owners are worried about revenue, running a business involves a lot of other tasks. Depending on the type of business, you need to invoice customers, record payments from customers, pay your own bills to outside vendors, manage inventory, and—in your "spare time"—analyze your financial data to see where you need to focus your next efforts. QuickBooks is a tool you can use to automate the tasks you're already performing as a business owner.

Tell your students that they will see a demonstration of how QuickBooks works in a few minutes so they can get an overall view of the program. But first, here's an overview of some of the basic features they'll be seeing in the demo.

When you're working in QuickBooks, you'll spend most of your time using a form, a list, or a register. Since these are so basic to QuickBooks, we're going to spend a few minutes introducing them.

Using forms

You record most of your daily business transactions on a QuickBooks form, which looks just like a paper form. Here's an example of the form you use when you want to record a bill from and write a check to one of your vendors.

Refer to Handout 2, "Record your daily transactions on QuickBooks forms."

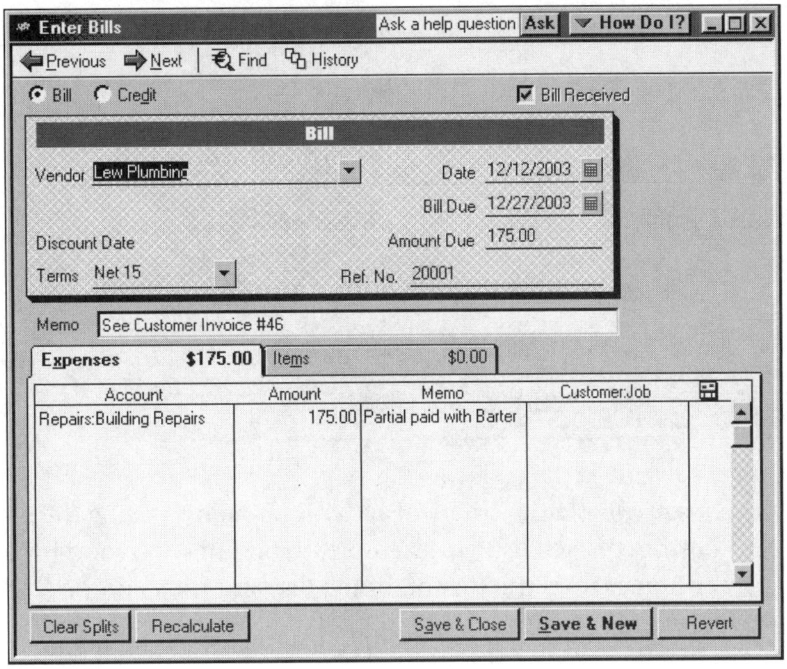

The form is intuitive—you already know how to fill out a form. But after you provide the information on a QuickBooks form, QuickBooks does the accounting for you in the background. For example, when you record a bill and then write a check (using the Pay Bills window) to pay for the business expense, QuickBooks enters transactions in your accounts payable register to show the expense you incurred and the payment you made. (*Accounts payable* is the money owed by your business to vendors.) It also records the check in your checking account, keeping your records up to date, and providing a running balance of what you owe at any time.

Using lists

The list is another basic QuickBooks feature. You fill out most QuickBooks forms by selecting entries from a list.

On Handout 2, point out that these fields all have lists from which you can choose an item: Bank Account, Pay to the Order of and, at the bottom of the form, the Account and Customer:Job fields.

QuickBooks has lists where you can store information about customers, vendors, employees, items or services you sell, and so on. Lists save you time and help you enter information consistently and correctly.

When you're filling out an invoice form and you select a customer name from the Customer:Job list, QuickBooks not only fills in the name but also fills in the address, the payment terms, and the customer's sales tax.

Refer to Handout 3, "Information stored in the Customer list."

Here's an example of the Customer:Job list.

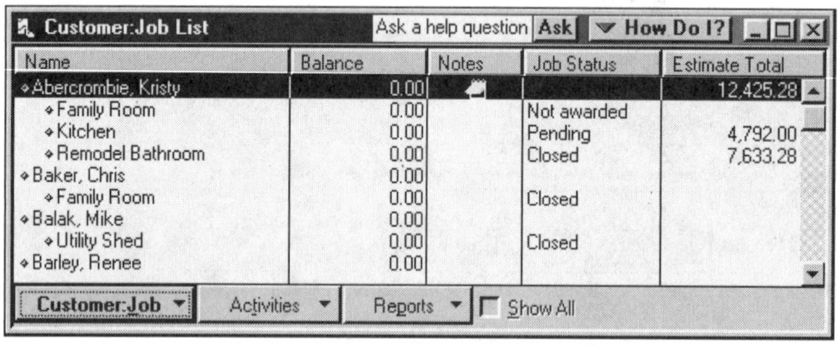

QuickBooks lets you complete a variety of activities from lists, using the menu buttons located at the bottom of each list. For example, to fill out an invoice for a customer, first select the customer from the Customer:Job list, and then choose Create Invoices from the Activities menu button.

Using registers

In addition to forms and lists, you'll also work with registers in QuickBooks. Just as you use your paper checkbook register to see a record of all the transactions in your checking account—checks you've written, other withdrawals you've made from your account, and deposits—a QuickBooks register contains a record of all the activity in one account. Almost every QuickBooks account has its own register.

Refer to Handout 4, "Register for an accounts receivable account."

You may want to explain to students that accounts receivable is the record of money owed to a business, that is, the outstanding invoices for which a business has not received payment.

Here's an example of the register for an accounts receivable account.

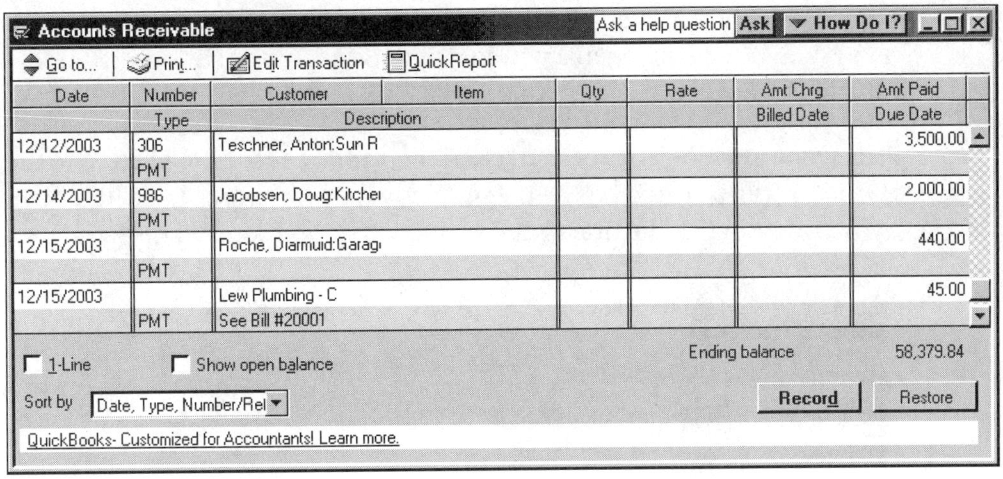

The register shows information about invoices written to customers—the date of the invoice, the date it's due, the name of the customer, and the amount. It also shows payments you've received against your invoices. The right column of the register gives you a running balance of all your accounts receivable, so you always know how much you're owed.

Getting around in QuickBooks

QuickBooks maximizes your work space and gives you quick access to the features and reports that you use most. In this section, you'll learn how to do the following:

- Find information to help you get started using QuickBooks
- Manage your open windows
- Compare windows side by side
- Customize navigation features

Finding information to help you get started

If you're **new to QuickBooks**, the Getting Started window displays when you open a company file. This window guides you through the steps you need to complete after you've set up your company file. To display the Getting Started window, choose Getting Started from the Help menu.

If you're **upgrading from a previous version**, QuickBooks displays the New Features window. This window contains information about new features and explains how to find what you need to start working with the latest version. To display the New Features window, choose New Features from the Help menu.

Managing your open windows

To give you more room to work on the task at hand, QuickBooks displays one window at a time. When you open a window, it appears in front of other windows that you previously opened.

The Open Window list keeps track of the windows that are open. Use the Open Window list to switch between windows while you work. To switch to another open window, just click the title of the window that you want to display.

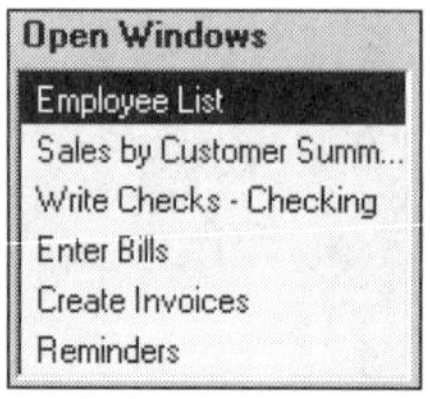

To show or hide the Open Window list:

- From the View menu, choose Open Window List.

  If the list is currently displayed, a checkmark appears to the left of the menu item.

For comparison purposes, you may wish to display more than one window at a time. You can easily switch between viewing one window at a time and viewing multiple windows. When you choose Multiple Windows from the View menu, QuickBooks tiles the windows in the main area. You can then move and resize the windows as needed.

To view multiple windows:

- From the View menu, choose Multiple Windows.

Using the menu bar

You can find all of the QuickBooks commands on the menu bar.

Many commands available on the menu bar can be added to the Icon Bar.

Using the Icon Bar

Another feature that makes it easy to get around in QuickBooks is the Icon Bar. It comes preset with shortcuts to several windows, such as Create Invoices and Enter Bills. By including the features and reports you use most, you can manage your business more quickly than ever.

In addition to deciding which features to add to the Icon Bar, you can add or remove icons, change the order in which the icons display, insert spaces between icons, and edit icons by changing the icon text, graphic, or tooltip.

For instructions on how to customize the Icon Bar, search the onscreen Help for *Icon Bar,* and then choose "Customizing the Icon Bar" from the list of topics that displays.

Using the Shortcut list

The QuickBooks Shortcut list groups together related lists and forms in an easy-to-follow format that helps you work more efficiently. The Shortcut list displays vertically and is an alternative to the Icon Bar.

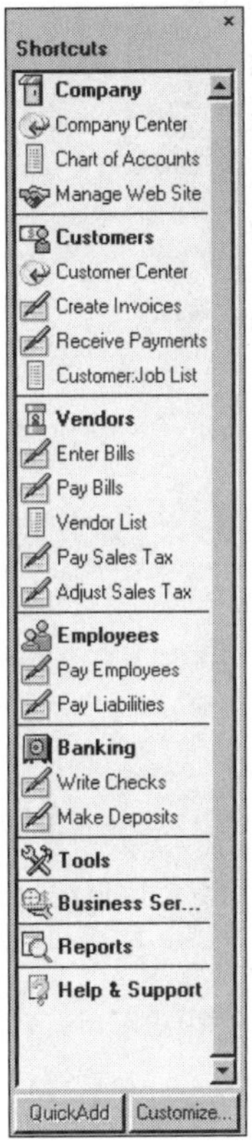

QuickBooks is preset to display the Icon Bar, but you can display the Shortcut list instead of, or in addition to, the Icon Bar.

To show or hide the Shortcut list:

- From the View menu, choose Shortcut List.

Like the Icon Bar, the Shortcut list can be customized, so you can add the forms, lists, and registers that you use frequently, and remove those that you don't use.

For instructions on how to customize the Shortcut list, search the onscreen Help for *shortcuts, Shortcut list.* Then, double-click the topic "Customizing the Shortcut list."

Making navigators your starting point

QuickBooks navigators provide a graphical representation of the workflow for a particular area of the product. For example, the Customers Navigator window has icons for important activities that are common to working with customers and making sales (such as, creating invoices, receiving payments, and making deposits). It looks like the following.

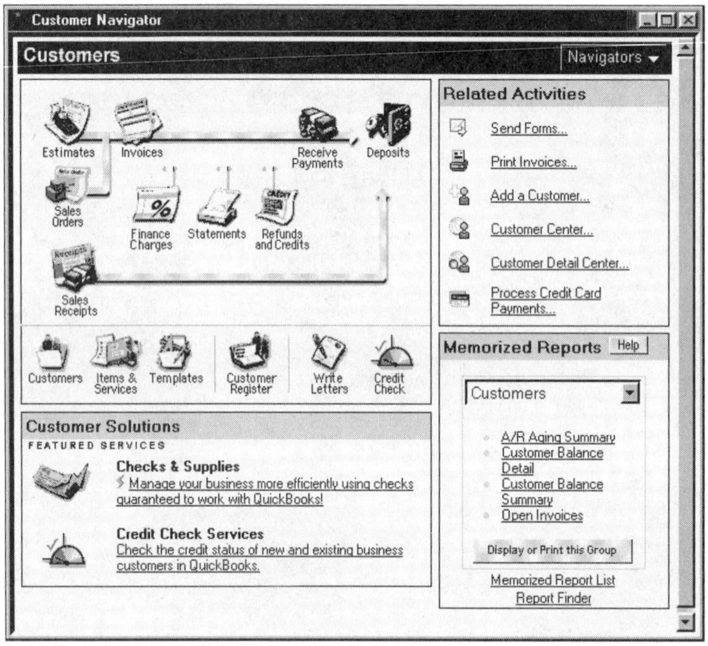

The navigators let you access features, reports, and solutions for the major areas of QuickBooks.

- Flow charts guide you in performing tasks in the correct order.
- Related Activities and Memorized Reports let you analyze your data and take action.
- Customer Solutions help you find features and services that you can use to manage your business.

To display a navigator, select its name from the Navigator list.

All the accounting you need to know

QuickBooks doesn't require users to learn or understand accounting jargon. However, it does use some common business terms.

Your chart of accounts

Refer to Handout 5, "The QuickBooks chart of accounts."

When you keep books for a company, you want to track where your income comes from, where you put it, what your expenses are for, and what you use to pay them. You track this flow of money through a list of accounts called the chart of accounts.

To display the chart of accounts:

1 From the Lists menu, choose Chart of Accounts.

QuickBooks displays the chart of accounts for Rock Castle Construction Company.

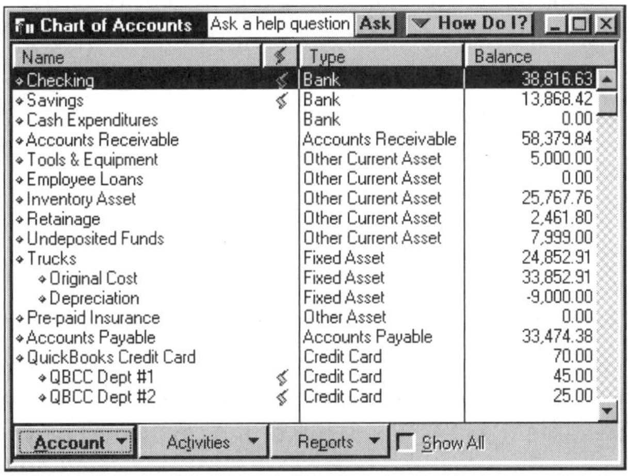

2 Scroll through the Rock Castle Construction chart of accounts. Notice that the list displays balance sheet accounts first, followed by income accounts and expense accounts.

About assets, liabilities, and equity

Refer to Handout 6, "About assets, liabilities, and equity."

Assets

Assets include both what you have and what other people owe you. The money people owe you is called your accounts receivable, or A/R for short. QuickBooks uses an accounts receivable account to track the money owed you.

The rest of your company's assets may include checking accounts, savings accounts, petty cash, fixed assets (such as equipment or trucks), inventory, and undeposited funds (money you've received from customers but haven't yet deposited in the bank).

When setting up your company file in QuickBooks, please note that even though checking, savings, and petty cash are all company assets, you'll set them up as "bank" type accounts in QuickBooks.

Liabilities

Liabilities are what your company owes to other people. The money you owe for unpaid bills is your accounts payable, or A/P for short. QuickBooks uses an accounts payable account to track the money you owe different people for bills.

A liability can be a formal loan, an unpaid bill, or sales and payroll taxes you owe to the government.

When setting up your company file in QuickBooks, please note that even though unpaid bills are liabilities, you'll set them up as accounts payable type accounts in QuickBooks.

Equity

Equity is the difference between what you have (your assets) and what you owe (your liabilities):

Equity = Assets – Liabilities

If you sold all your assets today, and you paid off your liabilities using the money received from the sale of your assets, the leftover money would be your equity.

Your equity reflects the health of your business, since it is the amount of money left after you satisfy all your debts. Equity comes from three sources:

- Money invested in the company by its owners

- Net profit from operating the business during the current accounting period
- Retained earnings, or net profits from earlier periods that haven't been distributed to the owners

Of course, you as the owner can also take money out of the business. Such withdrawals, called owner's draws, reduce the business equity.

If you have a sole proprietorship (where the existence of the business depends solely on your efforts), you can check the value of your owner's equity by creating a QuickBooks balance sheet.

Cash versus accrual bookkeeping

When you begin your business, you should decide which bookkeeping method to use. The bookkeeping method determines how you report income and expenses on your tax forms. Check with your tax advisor or the Internal Revenue Service (IRS) before choosing a bookkeeping method for tax purposes.

Cash basis

Many small businesses record income when they receive the money and expenses when they pay the bills. This method is known as bookkeeping on a cash basis. If you've been recording deposits of your customers' payments but haven't been including the money customers owe you as part of your income, you've been using cash basis. Similarly, if you've been tracking expenses at the time you pay them, rather than at the time you first receive the bills, you've been using cash basis.

Accrual basis

In accrual-basis bookkeeping, you record income at the time of the sale, not at the time you receive the payment. Similarly, you enter expenses when you receive the bill, not when you pay it.

Most accountants feel that the accrual method gives you a truer picture of your business finances.

How your bookkeeping method affects QuickBooks

Whether you use the cash or accrual method, you enter transactions the same way in QuickBooks.

QuickBooks is set up to do your reports on an accrual basis. For example, it shows income on a profit and loss statement for invoices as soon as you record them, even if you haven't yet received payment. It shows expenses as soon as you record bills, even if they're unpaid.

You can see any report (except transaction reports) on a cash basis by changing the reporting preference. (From the Edit menu, choose Preferences. In the Preferences window, click Reports & Graphs in the left scroll box, and then click the Company Preferences tab.)

Important: When you create reports in QuickBooks, you can switch between cash and accrual reports at any time, regardless of which bookkeeping method you have chosen for tax purposes.

Measuring business profitability

Two of the most important reports for measuring the profitability of your business are the balance sheet and the profit and loss statement (also called an income statement). These are the reports most often requested by CPAs and financial officers. (For example, banks request both documents when you apply for a loan.)

The balance sheet

Refer to Handout 7, "Sample balance sheet."

If you had not planned to include hands-on student participation in this first lesson, complete these steps on your own computer while the students observe.

A balance sheet is a financial snapshot of your company on one date. It shows:

- What you have (assets)
- What people owe you (accounts receivable)
- What your business owes to other people (liabilities and accounts payable)
- The net worth of your business (equity)

To see an example of a balance sheet:

1. From the Reports menu, choose Company & Financial.
2. From the submenu, choose Balance Sheet Standard.

The profit and loss statement

Refer to Handout 8, "Sample profit and loss statement."

A profit and loss statement, also called an income statement, shows your income, expenses, and net profit or loss (equal to income minus expenses). The QuickBooks profit and loss statement summarizes the revenue and expenses of your business by category (first income, then expenses).

To see a profit and loss report:

1. From the Reports menu, choose Report Finder.
2. From the Select a type of report drop-down list, choose Company & Financial.
3. In the Select a report list, click Profit & Loss Standard.

4 Click Display.

5 Scroll the report window to see all parts of the report.

The statement of cash flows

Another report that your accountant may be interested in is the statement of cash flows report. A statement of cash flows shows your receipts and payments during a specific accounting period.

To see a sample statement of cash flows report:

1 From the Reports menu, choose Report Finder.

2 From the Select a type of report drop-down list, choose Company & Financial.

3 In the Select a report list, click Statement of Cash Flows.

4 Click Display.

Exiting QuickBooks

Unlike most other Windows programs, QuickBooks doesn't require you to save your data before exiting. It does an automatic save while you're working with QuickBooks and every time you leave the program.

To exit QuickBooks:

- From the File menu, choose Exit.

If no other applications are open, QuickBooks returns you to the Windows desktop.

To prevent or minimize data loss, you should make regular backup copies of your QuickBooks company data. In the event of a data loss you can restore your data from the backup copy. To make a backup copy, from the File menu, choose Back Up.

For more information about the recommended backup routine, see Chapter 8, "Protecting your data," in the QuickBooks *User's Guide*.

Moving between company files

If you work with several companies, you'll be working with multiple QuickBooks company files. You can change from one company file to another at any time, but you can have only file open at a time.

QuickBooks provides an easy way to find and open a company file that you've worked with before.

To open a previously opened file:

1 From the File menu, choose Open Previous Company.

2 From the submenu, choose the company file you want to open.

You can increase the number of company files that QuickBooks will display in the submenu.

To increase the number of company files displayed:

1 From the File menu, choose Open Previous Company.

2 Choose "Set number of previous companies."

3 Enter the number of company files you want QuickBooks to display (up to 20).

4 Click OK.

Student test and review

1 List the three main ways you enter data in QuickBooks.

Forms, lists, registers

2 List three ways to access features in QuickBooks.

Menu bar, Icon Bar, Shortcut list, Navigators

3 What bookkeeping method does QuickBooks use to create most reports?

Accrual, but you can see any report (except transaction reports) on a cash basis by changing the reporting preference.

LESSON 2 Setting up QuickBooks

Lesson objectives

- To discuss some of the decisions you need to make before using QuickBooks, such as your QuickBooks start date and the number of QuickBooks companies you should create
- To create a new QuickBooks company using the EasyStep Interview
- To set QuickBooks preferences in the Interview
- To record the opening balance for a checking account
- To practice using the QuickBooks Help tools

Handout materials

- Handout 9: Setting up QuickBooks
- Handout 10: How to choose a start date

Instructor preparation

- Review this lesson, including the examples, to make sure you're familiar with the material.
- Install a copy of QuickBooks onto each student's computer. (For installation instructions, see the *User's Guide*.)

Creating a QuickBooks company

A QuickBooks company contains all the financial records for a single business. Before you can use QuickBooks, you need to tell QuickBooks about your business so that it can set up your company file.

Explain to students that if they've been using Quicken or an older version of QuickBooks to keep their company's financial records, they don't need to create a new company; QuickBooks can convert their data for them. However, in this lesson, you'll be showing them how to create a new QuickBooks company.

How many companies should you set up?

If you operate a business enterprise, the IRS expects you to clearly show all sources of income and to document any business expenses you claim as deductions. For tax purposes, therefore, it's usually best to set up a separate QuickBooks company for each business enterprise you report on your tax forms.

About the EasyStep Interview

As you walk students through the process of creating a QuickBooks company, you may want to have Handout 9 displayed on an overhead projector. It shows the steps involved in setting up QuickBooks, and helps students keep track of where they are in the procedure.

The EasyStep Interview walks you through the process of setting up your entire business on QuickBooks. The Interview is broken down into sections. You must complete the required General section first. If you are not sure how to answer a question, you can always go back and change your answer later. A few questions ask you to make a decision that's not easily reversed. When this is the case, you'll see this symbol.

The EasyStep Interview has five sections:

General—Lets you enter company information, choose a chart of accounts appropriate for your business, decide on QuickBooks preferences, and specify a business start date.

Income & Expenses—Lets you review the income and expense accounts on your business's chart of accounts, and lets you enter new accounts.

Income Details—Lets you specify whether your business income is from services and/or products you sell. Based on the information provided, QuickBooks determines which parts of the income and accounts receivable features you will be using.

Opening Balances—Lets you enter information about the customers who owe you money as of your start date, vendors to whom you owe money as of your start date, and balances in your balance sheet accounts as of your start date.

What's Next—This section describes some common tasks in QuickBooks that you may want to complete after you've gone through the other sections of the Interview.

Each major section of the Interview is divided into topics that are displayed as tabs at the top of the EasyStep Interview window. After you complete a topic or section, QuickBooks displays a checkmark on that tab.

Navigating through the Interview

- Click Next to display the next window in the Interview.
- Click Prev to display the previous window in the Interview.
- When a window has a More button (in the lower right corner), click it to see more detailed information about the question being asked in the Interview. After you read the detailed information, you can click OK to return to the Interview.

- Click Leave to leave the Interview and return to QuickBooks. You can return to the Interview later by opening your company file and then choosing EasyStep Interview from the File menu. QuickBooks remembers the information you have already entered.

Starting the EasyStep Interview

To begin adding a new company:

1 Start QuickBooks.

2 Select "Create a new company" or choose New Company from the File menu.

QuickBooks displays the EasyStep Interview window.

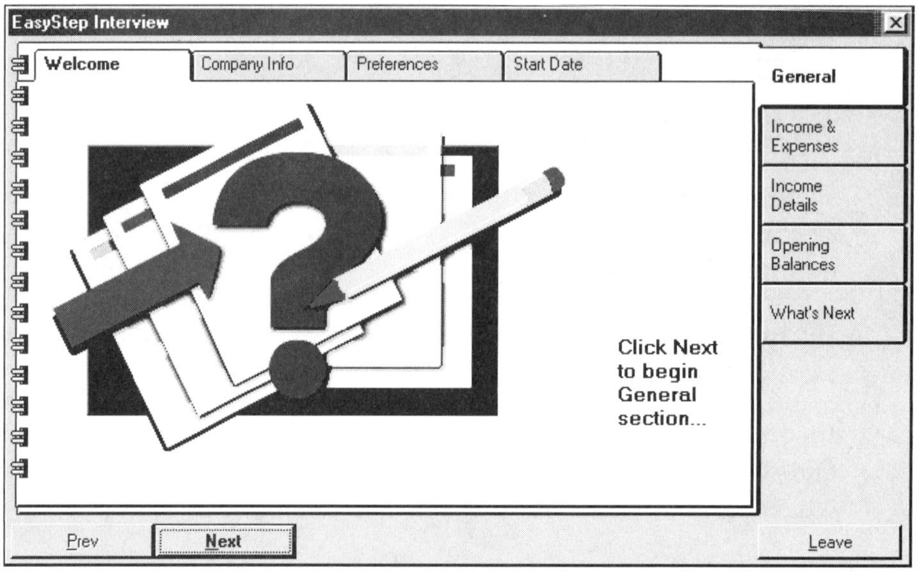

Entering company info

When you use the EasyStep Interview to create a new QuickBooks company, QuickBooks asks you questions about the type of business you own. It uses your answers to get you started quickly, by setting up the appropriate accounts and lists.

In this lesson, you'll create a new QuickBooks company for a business named Lockhart Design. Margaret Lockhart is the sole proprietor of this interior design firm. Most of her income comes from consulting services, but she also sells products such as fabrics and room accessories to clients.

To create a new QuickBooks company file:

1 At the first Welcome window for the Interview, click Next to begin.

2 Keep clicking Next, reading the information presented on the Welcome windows, until you have completed the Welcome section.

When you finish the section, QuickBooks places a checkmark on the Welcome tab.

3 Click Next until you come to the "Your company name" screen on the Company Info tab.

4 In the Company Name field, type ***Lockhart Design*** and press Tab.

When you press Tab, QuickBooks automatically enters the same name you typed into the Legal Name field. QuickBooks uses the company name on all reports.

5 Click Next.

6 Type the following information in the Your company information window.

1239 Bayshore Road

Middlefield, CA 94432

QuickBooks prints this company address on checks, invoices, and other forms.

7 Now enter the following information in the Phone # and FAX # fields:

Phone #: ***650-555-1234***

Fax #: ***650-555-5678***

8 Next enter the email and Web addresses for Lockhart Design.

Email: ***margaret@samplename.com***

Web Site: ***lockhart_design@samplename.com***

Your screen should resemble the following.

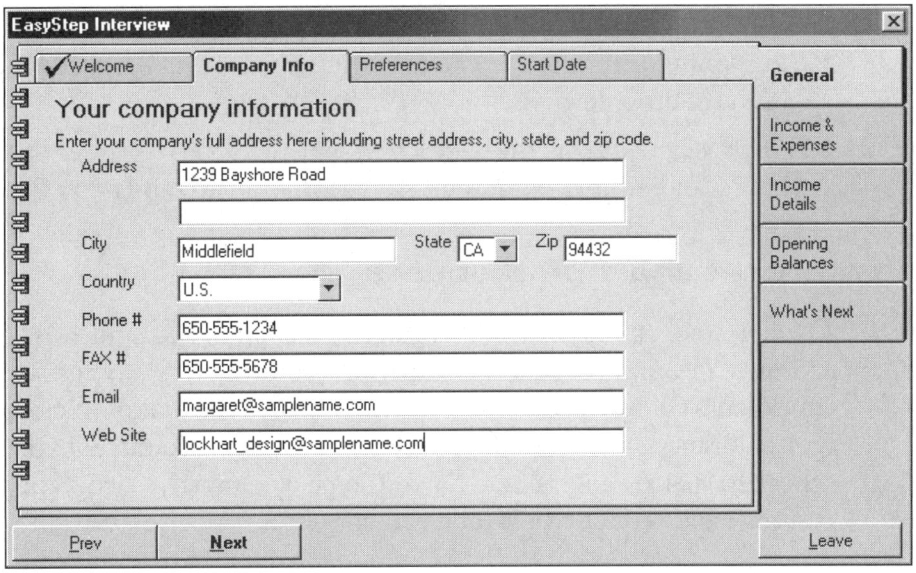

9 Click Next.

10 In the Other company information window, enter the following information:

- Tax identification number: ***94-1234567***
- Make sure January is selected for the first month of the income tax year and first month of the fiscal year.

Your screen should match the following.

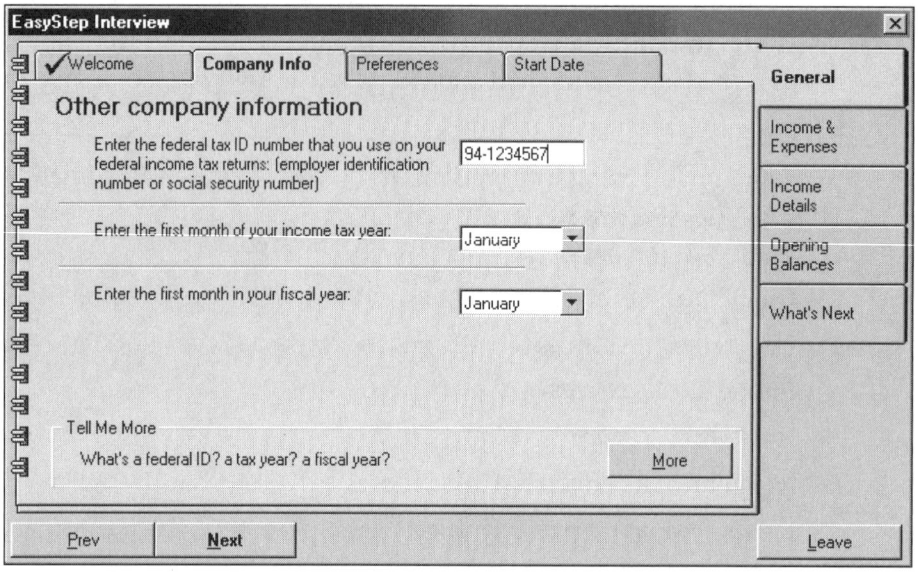

11 Click Next.

QuickBooks uses the financial year you choose to create year-to-date reports.

12 In the Your company income tax form screen, select Form 1040 (Sole Proprietor) from the drop-down list.

13 Click Next to display the next screen, where select the type of business you are in. Your choice in this window affects the chart of accounts that QuickBooks sets up.

Using a preset chart of accounts

As you learned in Lesson 1 of this guide, the chart of accounts lists balance sheet accounts, income accounts, and expense accounts. When you create a new QuickBooks company, you can select a company type that most closely matches your type of business, and QuickBooks sets up a chart of accounts for you. It also sets up other lists that are appropriate for your type of company, such as payment methods, customer and vendor types, and payment terms.

Even if you own a type of company that isn't specifically listed, you should select the one that's closest and get a head start on creating your own chart of accounts. Once QuickBooks creates a chart of accounts for you, you can modify it however you want.

To create a chart of accounts:

1 In the Select your type of business screen, select Retail from the Industry list.

Although Lockhart Design receives most of its income from consulting, not from retail sales, the Retail company type will give us most of the accounts we need. We'll need to modify the chart of accounts later to include an income account for Consulting Income.

2 Click Next three more times to get to the Save As window.

3 Make sure that QuickBooks is set to save the file in the QBtrain folder you set up in the introduction to this guide.

4 In the Save As window, click Save to accept the default filename of "Lockhart Design."

QuickBooks creates the company file and then displays a list of the income and expense accounts available in the preset chart of accounts for retail businesses.

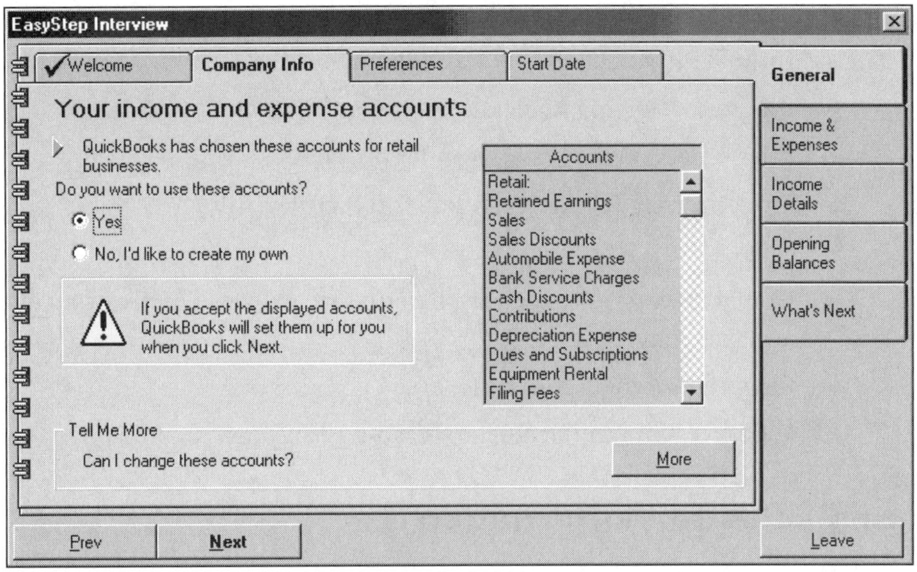

5 Scroll through the preset income and expense accounts to get an idea of what is included, and then click Yes (that you want to use these accounts).

6 Click Next to go to the next window.

7 In the Accessing your company window, leave the number of people who need to have access to the QuickBooks files at 0 and click Next.

Margaret Lockhart is the only one who needs access to the company file.

8 Click Next until you move from the Company Info section to the Preferences section.

Setting up QuickBooks preferences

The Preferences section of the EasyStep Interview is where you indicate whether you want to use certain features of the QuickBooks program. From the Interview you can choose to use:

- Inventory (whether turned on)

  Turning on inventory from the EasyStep Interview is not available for all industries. When this is the case for your industry, you can turn it on from the Preferences window. (From the Edit menu, choose Preferences. Click Purchases & Vendors in the left scroll box. Click the Company Preferences tab, and then click the "Inventory and purchase orders are active" checkbox.)
- Sales tax
- The invoice format you want to use
- Payroll (whether turned on)
- Estimates (QuickBooks Pro and Premier only)
- Progress invoicing (QuickBooks Pro and Premier only)
- Sales orders (QuickBooks Premier only)
- Time tracking (QuickBooks Pro and Premier only)
- Classes
- How you want to enter bills: by entering checks directly or by entering bills first, and then payments
- Reminders (whether to turn on)
- Whether you want accrual- or cash-basis reports

Entering sales tax information

This part of the Preferences section asks whether you charge sales tax. You should turn the sales tax preference off only if you *never* charge sales tax. Margaret Lockhart typically charges sales tax, so we'll turn on sales tax in her company file.

To set up QuickBooks to track sales tax:

1. Click Next to move to the Sales tax screen in the Preferences section of the Interview.
2. At the Sales Tax window, click Yes for the question, "Do you collect sales tax from your customers?" Then click Next.
3. Select "I collect single tax rate paid to a single tax agency."

   Margaret Lockhart collects one sales tax for one tax district, paid to only one tax agency. If your customers are from different states, you should click "I collect multiple tax rates or have multiple tax agencies."

4 Click Next.

QuickBooks automatically creates a current liability account, called Sales Tax Payable, that keeps track of the sales tax you collect in your business.

5 Fill out the Sales Tax Information window as shown below.

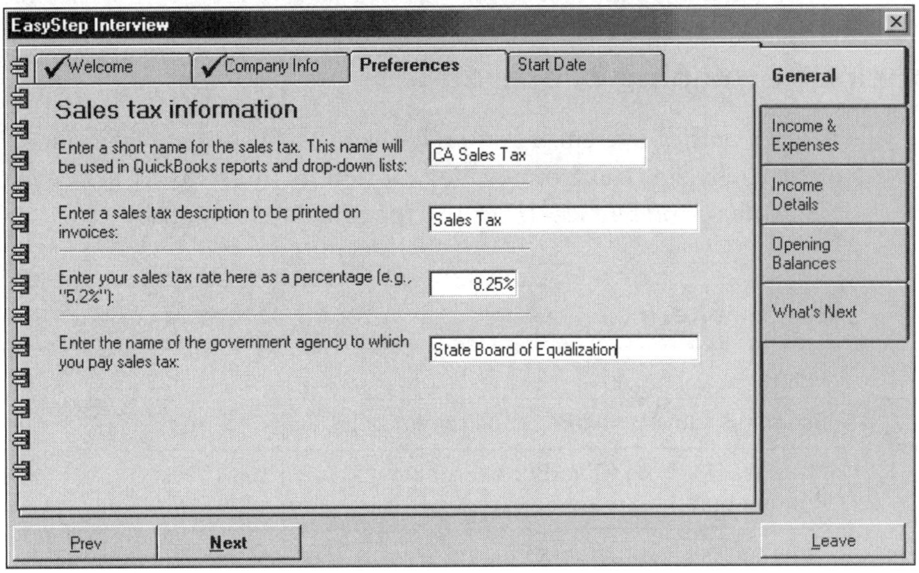

6 Click Next.

Choosing an invoice format

QuickBooks offers four different formats for invoices: Product, Professional, Service, and Custom. The type you choose affects the look of your invoices.

- The **Product invoice** is for businesses that sell parts or products and need fields relevant for shipping (for example, a retail store).
- The **Professional invoice** is for businesses that sell services and need a lot of room for descriptions of their services (for example, a public relations consultant).
- The **Service invoice** is for businesses that primarily provide services, but that also sell some goods (for example, an interior design firm).
- The **Custom invoice** is for businesses that want to create their own invoice format.

You can also customize any of these formats to suit your needs. You'll see how to do that in Lesson 15 of this guide. For Lockhart Design, which primarily sells consulting services, but also sells the occasional product, we'll choose the Service invoice format.

To select the invoice format for Lockhart Design:

- In the Interview window leave Service selected, and then click Next.

Tracking sales orders

If you use a QuickBooks Premier Edition product, QuickBooks asks if you want to track sales orders. If you do, click Yes, and then click Next.

If you are using QuickBooks Basic or QuickBooks Pro, you will not see this preference.

Choosing remaining preferences

The rest of the Preferences section is a series of "yes or no" questions. Simply click Yes or No, then click Next to move forward in the Interview. For Lockhart Design, complete the preferences by giving the following responses:

For this item...	Do this...
Payroll	Click Yes.
Estimates (QuickBooks Pro and Premier only)	Click Yes.
Progress invoicing (QuickBooks Pro and Premier only)	Click Yes.
Time tracking (QuickBooks Pro and Premier only)	Click Yes.
Classes	Click Yes.
How to deal with bills and payments	Select "Enter the bills first and then enter the payments later"
How often would you like to see your Reminders list	Select "At start up"
Type of reports you want to create	Select "Accrual-based reports"

This completes the Preferences portion of the EasyStep Interview. All that remains of the General section is to specify a start date.

Choosing a start date

Before you start entering your company's financial data, you need to choose a QuickBooks start date. This is the starting point you want to use for all your QuickBooks accounts. The start date is the date for which you give QuickBooks a financial snapshot of your company assets and liabilities.

Once you decide on a start date, you enter all your company's transactions *since* that date. That's why you should choose a start date that's not too far back in the past for you to handle. Many business owners like to use the last day of a financial period as their start date, such as the end of last fiscal year, last quarter, or last month. You need to enter all historical transactions from the day *after* your start date up through today.

For example, if you decide on a start date of March 31, you'd enter your historical transactions from April 1 up through today.

Continue clicking Next as you move through the Start Date section of the Interview. When you get to the Choose your company start date window, enter 12/31/2002 as Lockhart Design's start date, and click Next.

Refer to Handout 10, "How to choose a start date," and explain the tips given there.

Setting up income and expense accounts

Because you chose an industry from the list earlier in the Interview, QuickBooks has already created income and expense accounts for your company. The Income & Expenses section of the EasyStep Interview lets you view the preset income and expense accounts and add new income or expense accounts from within the Interview.

To streamline the Interview process, you won't add income or expense accounts in this lesson. You'll see how to add new accounts to the chart of accounts in Lesson 3, "Working with lists."

For now, move through this portion of the Interview by answering "No" to the following questions:

- Do you want to add an income account now?
- Would you like a more detailed explanation of expense accounts and subaccounts?
- Do you want to add an expense account now?

Click Next until you get to the Income Details section.

Providing details about your income

The Income Details section of the EasyStep Interview is where you specify whether you track accounts receivable, set up QuickBooks items to track the services you provide or products you sell, and set up inventory items if you plan to track inventory in QuickBooks.

You should complete the Introduction tab of the Income Details section because that tells QuickBooks whether you need the accounts receivable feature and whether you need statement charges (for businesses that send regular monthly statements showing past due, current balance, and so on).

To complete the Income Details section:

1. In the Income Details Introduction window, click Next two times.
2. For the question, "Do you receive full payment at the time (or before) you provide a service or sell a product?" make sure "Sometimes" is selected and then click Next.
3. For "Statement charges," select No, and then click Next two more times.
4. In the Items section, click No when asked if you want to set up service items, non-inventory part items, or other charge items.

   You'll see how to set up a new service item in Lesson 6, "Entering sales and invoices."
5. Click Next two times.
6. Select "Skip inventory items" to complete the Inventory tab.

Entering opening balances

The Opening Balances section of the EasyStep Interview is where you enter the amounts currently owed you by customers as of your start date, the amounts you currently owe vendors as of your start date, and the balances in your balance sheet accounts as of your start date. We recommend that you provide the opening balances from within the Interview; that makes it easier when you're ready to use QuickBooks for your daily business transactions.

The balance sheet accounts in the QuickBooks chart of accounts start with an opening balance of zero. Before you begin working in QuickBooks, you need to enter an opening balance for each balance sheet account as of your start date.

The opening balance is important because QuickBooks can't give you an accurate balance sheet (what your company owns and what it owes) without it. An accurate balance sheet gives you a true picture of your company's finances. Also, if you start with an accurate balance as of a specific date, you can reconcile your QuickBooks bank accounts with your bank statements, and your QuickBooks checking accounts will show the actual amount of money you have in the bank.

The easiest way to determine an account's opening balance is to work from an accurate balance sheet. If you have a balance sheet as of your start date, you can take the opening balance from there.

Let's assume Margaret Lockhart wants to enter an opening balance for her checking account. The opening balance for a QuickBooks bank account is the dollar amount you have in the bank on your start date. You can determine this amount in two ways: you can use the ending balance on the last bank statement on or immediately prior to your start date, or you can use your bank account balance from a balance sheet prepared by your accountant. Margaret has a recent bank statement for this account, so she'll use that method.

To enter the checking account opening balance:

1 Click the Accounts tab in the Opening Balances section of the Interview and click Next. (Skip the Customers and Vendors tabs.)

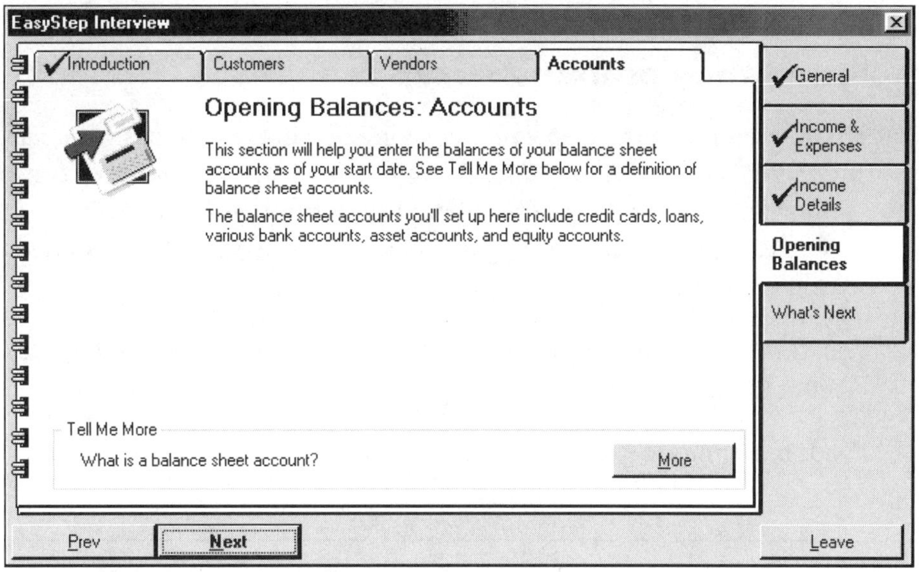

2 Click No when QuickBooks asks if you want to set up credit card accounts, lines of credit, and liability accounts.

3 For "Would you like to set up a bank account?", make sure Yes is selected and then click Next.

4 Type ***Checking*** as the name of the account and then click Next.

5 For Statement Ending Date, enter the same date you used for Lockhart Design's start date (12/31/2002).

6 In the Statement Ending Balance field, type ***8359.00*** and then click Next.

7 When QuickBooks asks if you want to add another bank account, click No. Then click Next.

The rest of the Opening Balances section lets you add asset and equity accounts. In the interest of time, we won't be adding any other accounts from within the Interview.

Finishing the Interview

The final section in the EasyStep Interview is What's Next. This is not an essential item for initial setup, so we will not cover it in this lesson.

- To leave the EasyStep Interview and save your changes, click Leave.

After you have completed the EasyStep Interview, Intuit recommends that you not use the Interview to make changes to your company file. Instead, use the information in the help options described in the next section of this chapter to help you make changes and adjustments to your company file.

Completing the company setup process

When you are setting up your own company in QuickBooks, you may want to use the Getting Started window to help you finish setting up your own company file. The information provided there will guide you through the rest of the setup process and help you get started using QuickBooks. To display the Getting Started window, choose Getting Started from the Help menu.

If you have upgraded from an earlier version of QuickBooks, choose New Features from the Help menu.

For more information, choose Help & Support from the Help menu.

Getting help while using QuickBooks

QuickBooks provides extensive help in various formats. When you have questions, QuickBooks provides:

- Step-by-step instructions. These are available via the onscreen Help and How Do I menu.
- A search engine that provides you with a list of topics related to the word or phrase you enter in the Ask field.
- Conceptual explanations of how to apply QuickBooks to your particular business situation.

Finding a topic in the onscreen Help Index

Suppose you want to find out how to add a new customer. You can type what you're looking for in the Help index, and QuickBooks displays a list of topics.

To find a topic in onscreen Help:

1. From the Help menu, choose Help Index.
2. Type ***customers***.

   QuickBooks selects the first occurrence of the word "customers" in the index. You can see there is a topic for "customers, adding new."
3. Double-click "customers, adding new."

   QuickBooks displays the topic in the screen to the right.

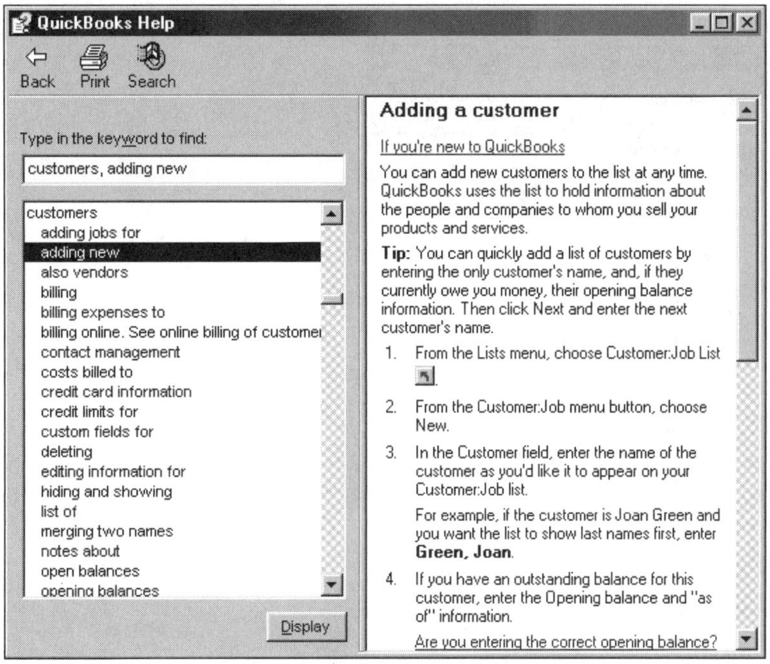

4. Close the Help window.

Finding answers from the How Do I menu

Throughout QuickBooks, you'll find windows with a drop-down menu called How Do I. This menu provides quick access to information and instructions for the current window.

To use the How Do I menu:

1 From the Customers menu, choose Create Invoices.

QuickBooks displays the Create Invoices window.

2 From the How Do I menu, choose "Reformat and print invoices." Then choose "Add my logo."

QuickBooks displays a Help window on how to add a company logo to an invoice form.

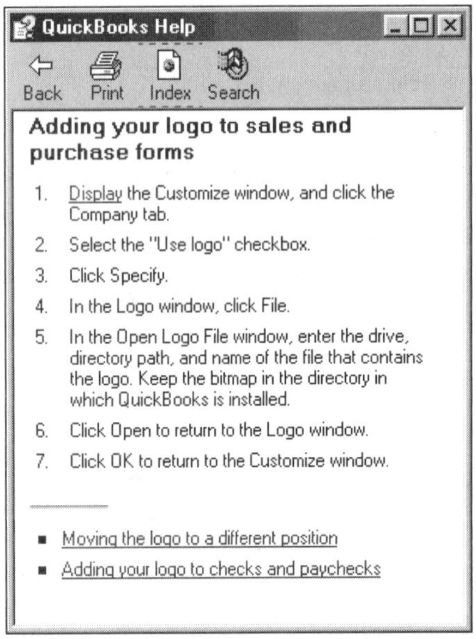

3 Close the Help window and the invoice.

Finding industry-specific information

QuickBooks includes a collection of information that has been customized for various industries. In these documents, you'll find specific information about how to set up and use QuickBooks for your type of business.

To find industry-specific information:

1 From the QuickBooks Help menu, choose Using QuickBooks for Your Type of Business.

2 In the list of business types, click the industry you want to see.

3 Select the topic that interests you.

4 (Optional) Print a topic by choosing Print on the toolbar.

Student test and review

1 The _________________ section of the EasyStep Interview is where you indicate whether you want to use certain QuickBooks features.

Preferences

2 Search the onscreen Help index for information on how to turn on the inventory feature in QuickBooks.

LESSON 3 Working with lists

Lesson objectives

- To edit the company chart of accounts
- To add a new customer to the Customer:Job list
- To add a new vendor to the Vendor list
- To learn about custom fields, and to practice adding custom fields
- To see how to manage lists in QuickBooks

Handout materials

- Handout 11: QuickBooks balance sheet accounts

Instructor preparation

- Review this lesson, including the examples, to make sure you're familiar with the material.
- Ensure that all students have a copy of qblesson.qbb on their computer's hard disk.
- Have Handout 11 ready for distribution.

To start this lesson

Before you perform the following steps, make sure you have installed the exercise file (qblesson.qbb) on your hard disk. See "Installing the exercise file" in the Introduction to this guide if you haven't installed it.

The steps that follow will restore the exercise file to its original state so that the data in the file matches what you see on the screen as you proceed through each lesson.

To restore the exercise file (qblesson.qbb):

1. From the File menu in QuickBooks, choose Restore.

   QuickBooks displays the Restore Company Backup window.
2. In the "Get Company Backup From" section of the window, click Browse and select your c:\QBtrain directory.
3. Select the qblesson.qbb file, and then click Open.
4. In the "Restore Company Backup To" section of the window, click Browse and select your c:\QBtrain directory.
5. In the File name field of the Restore To window, type ***lesson 3*** and then click Save.
6. Click Restore.

Using QuickBooks lists

QuickBooks lists organize a wide variety of information, including data on customers, vendors, inventory items, and more. Lists save you time by helping you enter information consistently and correctly. When you store information on a list, you enter it once and never need to retype it. Think about how much information you use more than once in your business:

- Names, addresses, and other information about customers who purchase from you on a regular basis
- Contact information for vendors from whom you purchase your supplies
- Descriptions and prices for products or services you sell again and again

Simply enter repetitive information into a list once, and then use it over and over on checks, on invoice forms, and other daily transactions. You don't have to enter all the information for your company lists before you begin working with QuickBooks. You can add information to lists as you go along.

Editing the chart of accounts

The chart of accounts is your most important list because it shows how much your business has, how much it owes, how much money you have coming in, and how much you're spending. When you set up your own company in QuickBooks, the EasyStep Interview lets you choose a chart of accounts designed especially for your type of business. However, not every business has the same needs; you'll want to make a few changes to the list.

To display the chart of accounts:

1 From the Lists menu, choose Chart of Accounts.

QuickBooks displays the chart of accounts for Rock Castle Construction.

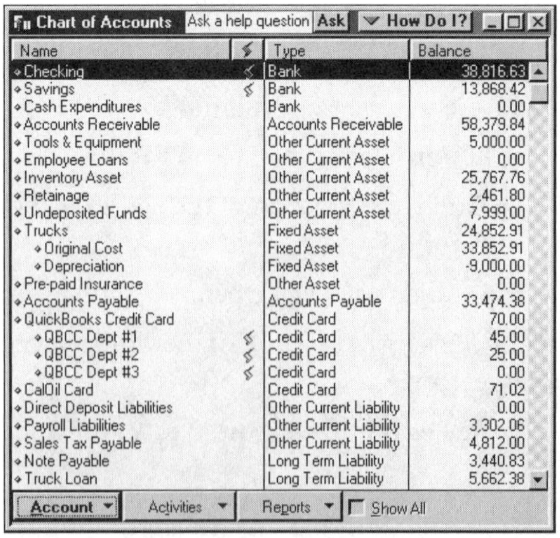

Chart of Accounts · Ask a help question · Ask · How Do I?

Name	$	Type	Balance
Checking	$	Bank	38,816.63
Savings	$	Bank	13,868.42
Cash Expenditures		Bank	0.00
Accounts Receivable		Accounts Receivable	58,379.84
Tools & Equipment		Other Current Asset	5,000.00
Employee Loans		Other Current Asset	0.00
Inventory Asset		Other Current Asset	25,767.76
Retainage		Other Current Asset	2,461.80
Undeposited Funds		Other Current Asset	7,999.00
Trucks		Fixed Asset	24,852.91
Original Cost		Fixed Asset	33,852.91
Depreciation		Fixed Asset	-9,000.00
Pre-paid Insurance		Other Asset	0.00
Accounts Payable		Accounts Payable	33,474.38
QuickBooks Credit Card		Credit Card	70.00
QBCC Dept #1	$	Credit Card	45.00
QBCC Dept #2	$	Credit Card	25.00
QBCC Dept #3	$	Credit Card	0.00
CalOil Card		Credit Card	71.02
Direct Deposit Liabilities		Other Current Liability	0.00
Payroll Liabilities		Other Current Liability	3,302.06
Sales Tax Payable		Other Current Liability	4,812.00
Note Payable		Long Term Liability	3,440.83
Truck Loan		Long Term Liability	5,662.38

Account · Activities · Reports · Show All

2 Scroll through the list. The chart of accounts displays balance sheet accounts first, followed by income and expense accounts.

Refer to Handout 11, "QuickBooks balance sheet accounts," as you explain each account type and the kinds of transactions you can use it for.

Editing an account

If any of the accounts don't suit your needs, you can edit or delete them. In the next exercise, you'll edit Rock Castle Construction's Checking account to provide the account number.

To edit an account:

1 In the chart of accounts, select Checking.

2 Click the Account menu button (at the bottom of the window), and then select Edit.

QuickBooks displays the Edit Account window.

3 In the Description field, type ***Great Statewide Bank***.

4 In the Bank Acct. field, type ***555-333-2222***.

Your window should look like this.

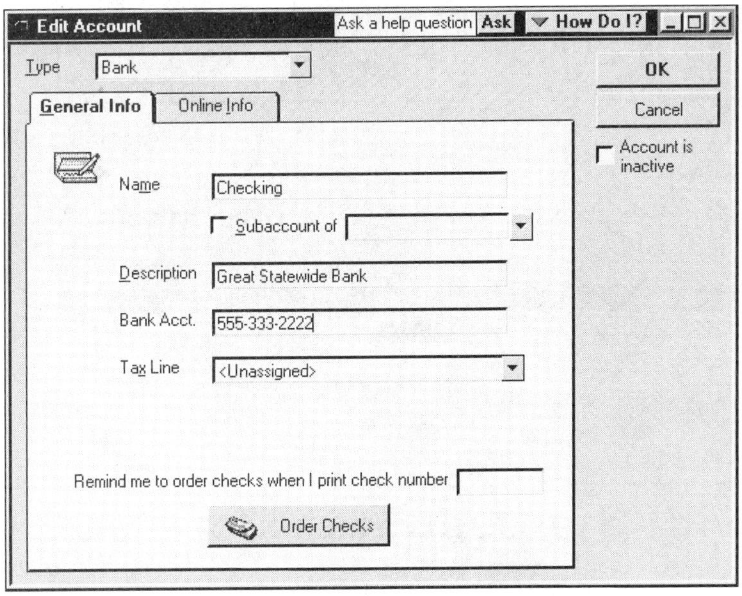

5 Click OK.

Adding subaccounts

The Dues and Subscriptions expense account has one subaccount called Union Dues. Rock Castle Construction wants to add a second subaccount for trade publications.

To add a subaccount:

1 In the chart of accounts, click the Account menu button and then choose New.

QuickBooks displays the New Account window.

2 In the Type field, select Expense from the drop-down list.

3 In the Name field, type ***Trade Pubs.***

4 Select the "Subaccount of" checkbox, and then select Dues and Subscriptions in the drop-down list.

5 In the Description field, type ***Trade Publications.***

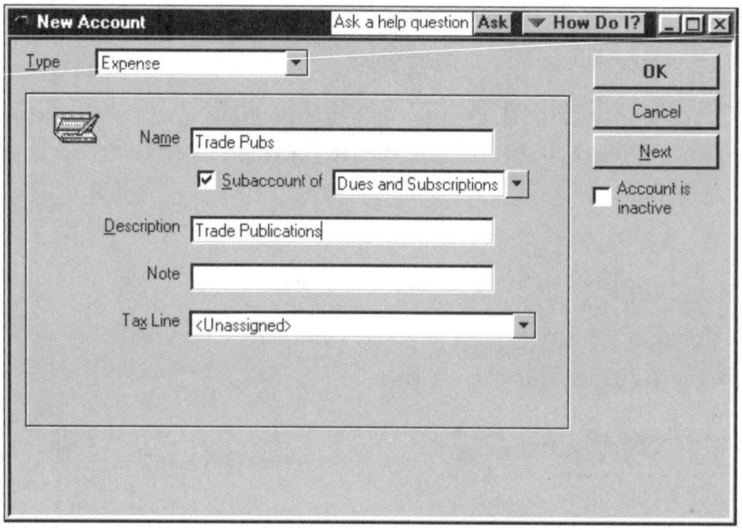

6 Click OK.

QuickBooks displays the new subaccount in the chart of accounts list.

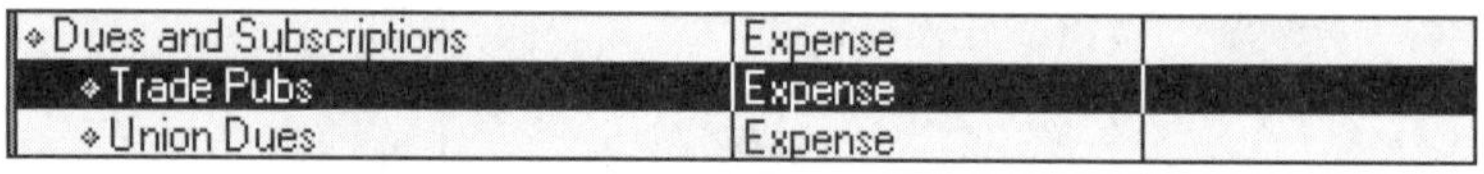

7 Close the chart of accounts.

Working with the Customer:Job list

The Customer:Job list stores names, addresses, and other information about your customers. It also holds information about the jobs or projects you may want to track for each customer.

Adding new customers

In this exercise, you'll add a new customer to the Customer:Job list.

To add a new customer:

1 From the Customers menu, choose Customer:Job List.

QuickBooks displays the Customer:Job list.

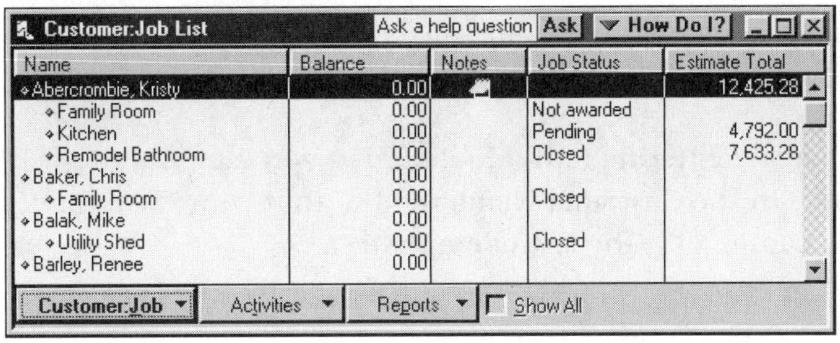

The Customer:Job list lets you add, edit, and get reports on your customers. Each customer in the list can have multiple jobs (you may call them projects or accounts). Notice that this Customer:Job list already has quite a few entries.

2 Click the Customer:Job menu button (at the bottom of the list window), and select New.

QuickBooks displays the New Customer window.

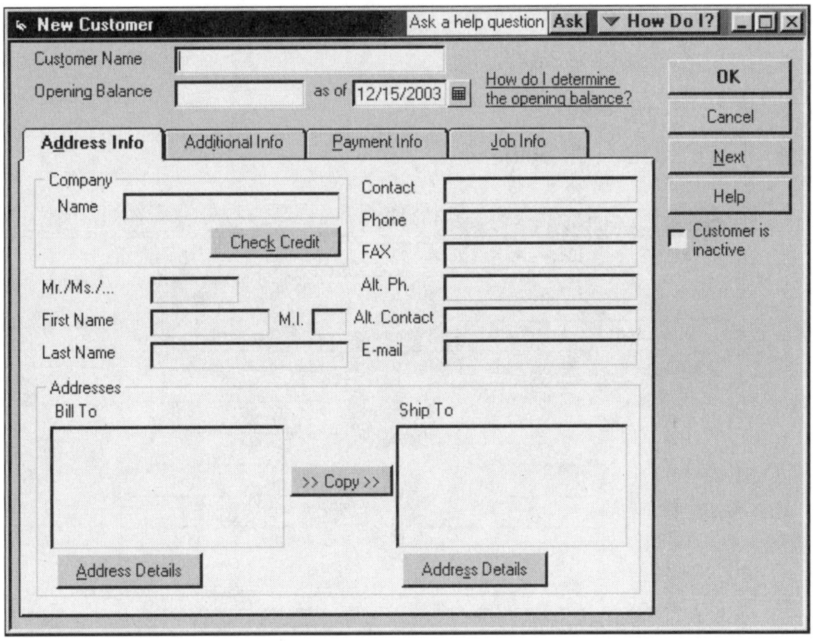

The New Customer window is where you enter all the information about a new customer, including billing and shipping addresses, contacts, credit limit, and payment terms. QuickBooks uses the information you enter to complete invoices, bills, and receipts. When you're setting up your company file, you use this window to record customers' opening balances.

3 In the Name field in the Company section, type ***Godwin Manufacturing,*** and then press Tab.

Notice that QuickBooks fills in the Customer Name field and the first line of the Bill To field with the information you typed in the Company Name field.

QuickBooks displays the name listed in the Customer Name field in the Customer:Job list. By default, QuickBooks sorts the list alphabetically.

Tip: **If you are entering individual names, you may want to use last name, first name in the Customer Name field so that your Customer:Job list displays the names with the last name first.**

4 In the Bill To field, click the line below the company name. Type ***376 Pine Street***, and then press Enter.

Notice that you press Tab to move between fields, but you press Enter to move from one line to the next within a field.

5 On the next line of the Bill To field, type ***Bayside, OR 64326***.

6 Click Copy to have QuickBooks copy the billing address to the Ship To field.

7 Continue filling out the customer information by providing the following information:

- Contact: ***John Godwin***
- Phone: ***325-555-9841***
- Fax: ***325-555-0012***
- Alt Contact: ***Tracy Heldt***

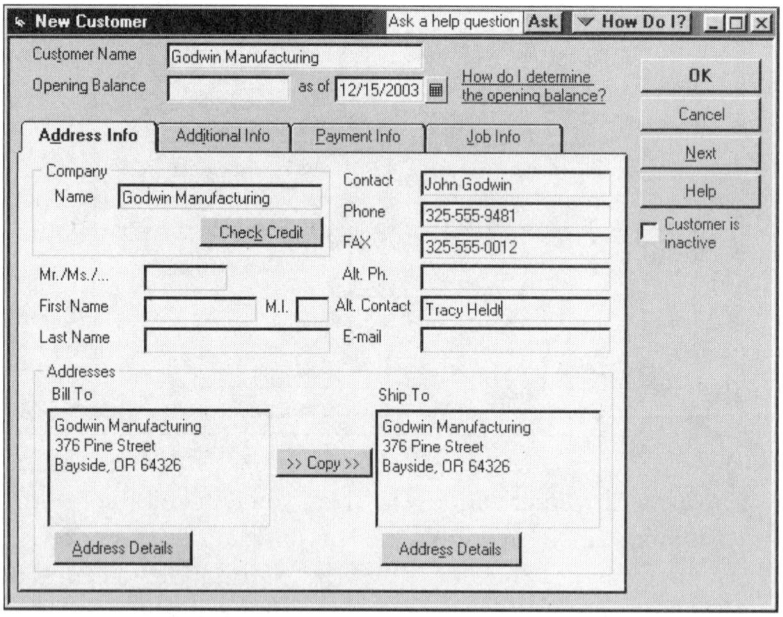

Note: **If you use plan to e-mail invoices or statements to customers using the Send Forms feature, use this window to enter your customers' e-mail addresses.**

Providing additional customer information

You've just completed the Address Info tab for a new customer. The Additional Info tab is where you can provide other important information, such as customer type (if you want to categorize your customers in some way), payment terms, and sales tax information.

To add additional information to a customer record:

1 Click the Additional Info tab.

QuickBooks displays the Additional Info tab of the New Customer window.

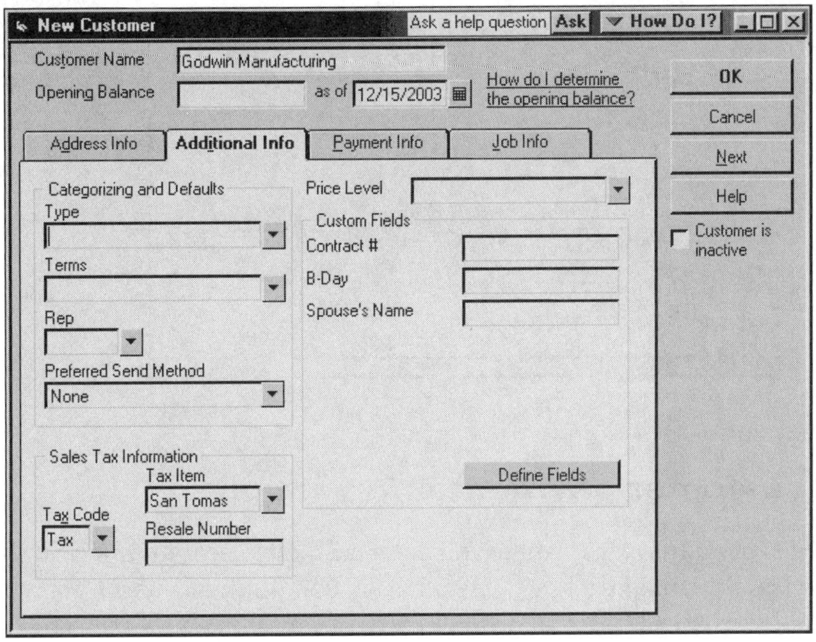

2 In the Type field, type ***Industrial***.

The Type field lets you track customers in any way that is meaningful for your business. For example, if you run ads on television, radio, and in print, and you want to know which advertising method brings you the most customers, you can assign customers a "type" (TV, Radio, or Print) and run reports that tell you which referral source is most effective. Rock Castle Construction uses the Type field to categorize customers by the type of service provided.

3 Press Tab.

QuickBooks tells you that Industrial is not currently on the Customer Type list and asks if you wish to add it.

4 Click the Quick Add button to add the customer type to the list.

Quick Add lets you set up the item with a minimum amount of data. If you click Set Up, you can enter more detailed information, but that interrupts the process of creating a new customer.

5 In the Terms field, type ***Net 30***.

6 In the Tax Code field, select Non from the drop-down list.

7 In the Tax Item drop-down list, select Out of State.

Your screen should now look like this.

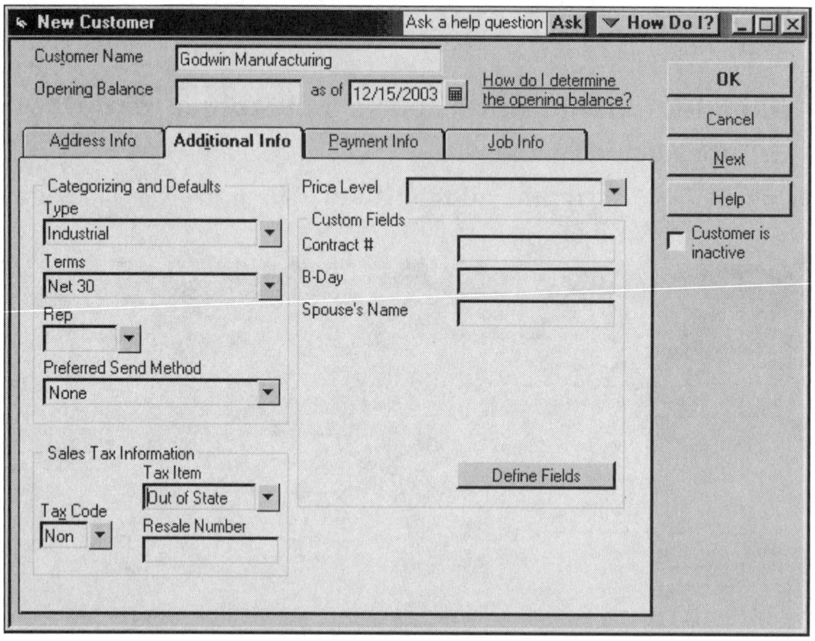

Providing customer payment information

The Payment Info tab is where you enter customer account numbers and credit limits. QuickBooks remembers each customer's credit limit and warns you when a customer is about to exceed it. You can also record information about each customer's preferred payment method. For customers who pay by credit card, you can enter credit card numbers and expiration dates.

To add payment and credit information to a customer record:

1 Click Payment Info.

2 In the Credit Limit field, type ***2000***.

3 In the Preferred Payment Method drop-down list, choose Check.

When you finish, your window should look like this.

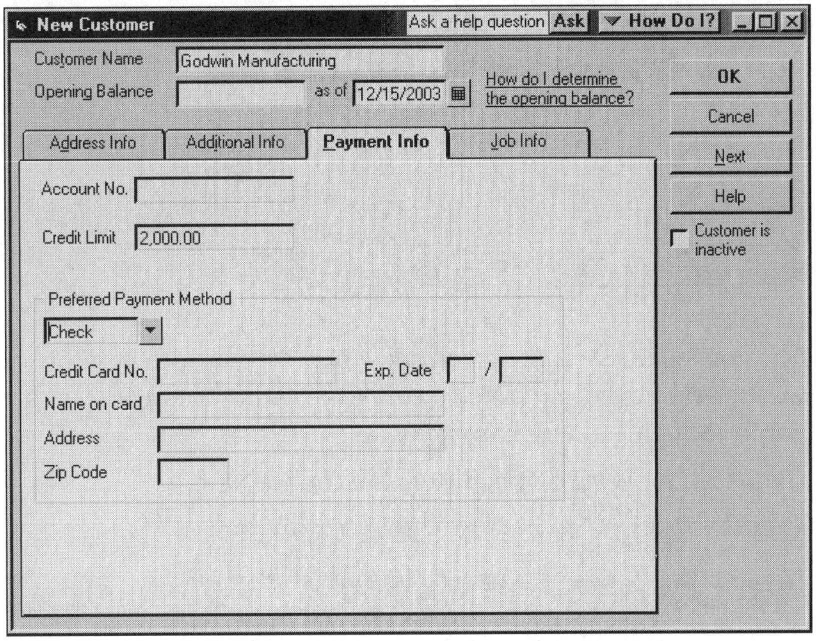

4 Click OK to add the customer and close the New Customer window.

QuickBooks displays the Customer:Job list with Godwin Manufacturing added.

5 Close the Customer:Job list.

Working with the Employee list

The Employee list stores information about your employees such as name, address, and social security number. It also stores information QuickBooks needs to calculate your employee paychecks (if you are using QuickBooks for payroll). You'll learn how to enter employee payroll information later in this course. For now, enter only the basic employee information.

QuickBooks uses the information you enter in the Employee list to track sales and fill in information on checks and other forms.

Adding new employees

Suppose that Rock Castle Construction has hired a new employee and you want to add her information to the Employee list.

1 From the Employees menu, choose Employee List.

QuickBooks displays the Employee list.

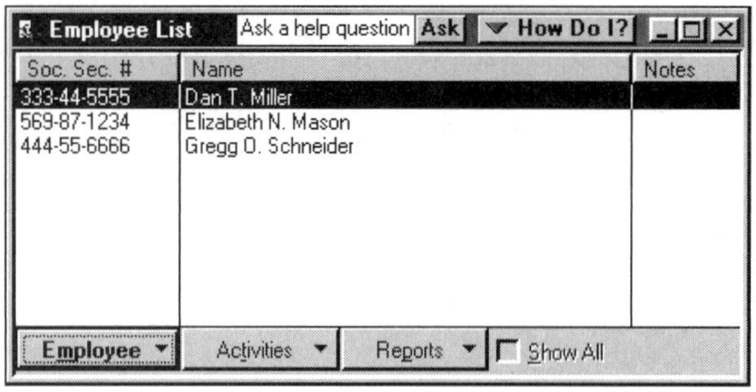

The Employee list is where you add a new employee, edit information for an existing employee, or delete an employee name (as long as you have not used the employee name in any transactions).

2 Click the Employee menu button and choose New.

QuickBooks displays the New Employee window.

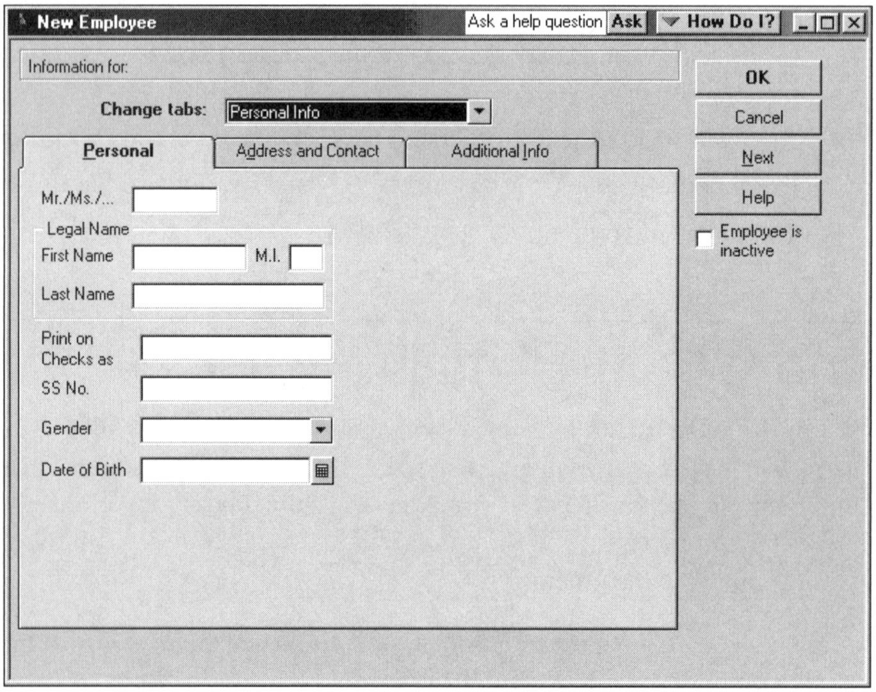

The Personal tab is where you enter basic information about the employee, such as name, Social Security Number, and date of birth.

3 In the First Name field, type ***Marlene***.

4 In the Last Name field, type ***Duncalf***.

Notice that QuickBooks fills in the Print on Check as field with the information you entered in the name fields. You can enter a different name if you wish.

5 In the Social SS No. field type ***123-45-6789***.

6 In the Gender field, select Female from the drop-down list.

7 In the Date of Birth field, type ***7/18/82***.

The Personal tab should look like this.

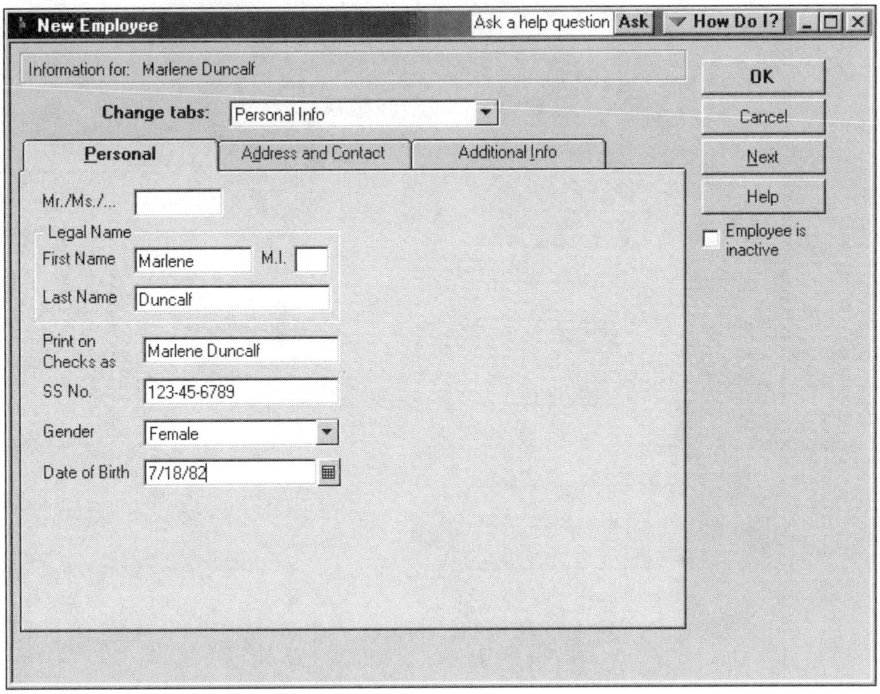

8 Click the Address and Contact tab.

9 In the Address field, type ***195 Spruce Avenue, #202***.

10 For the City, State, and Zip fields, type ***Bayshore, CA 94326***.

11 In the Phone field, type ***415-555-1111***.

When you finish, the window should look like this.

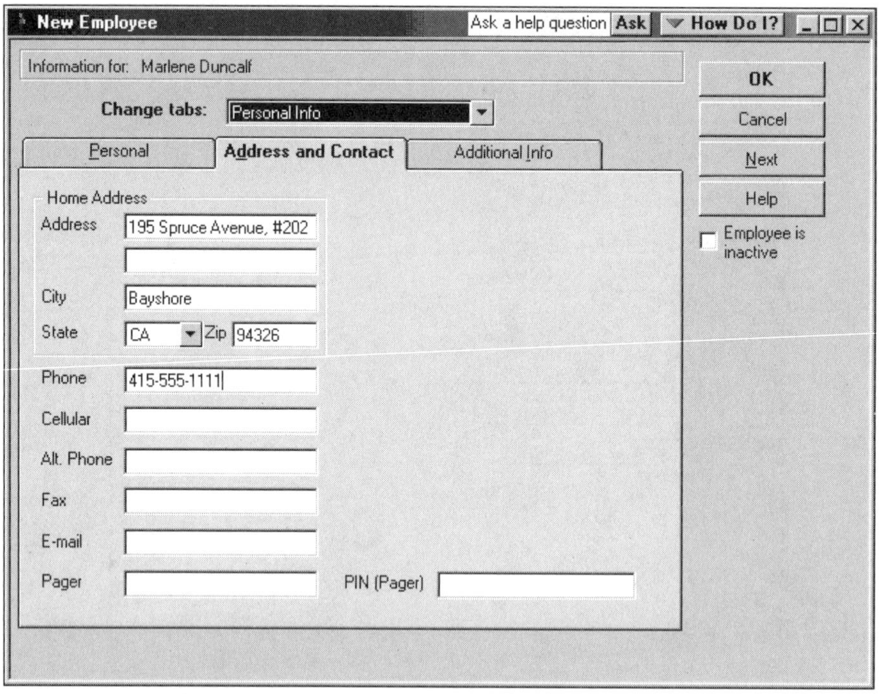

12 In the Change tabs field, select Employment Info from the drop-down list.

13 In the Hire Date, type 11/25/2003.

14 Click OK.

15 When QuickBooks asks if you want to set up payroll information, click Leave As Is.

You learn how to set up payroll in Le sson12.

16 QuickBooks updates and displays the Employee list with the new employee's name added.

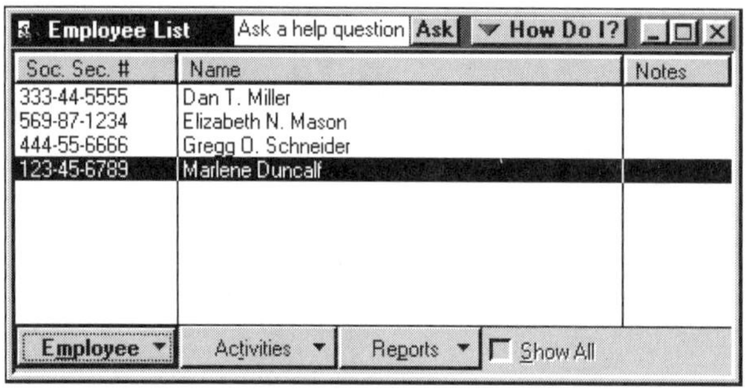

17 Close the Employee list.

Working with the Vendor list

The Vendor list is where you record information about the companies or people from whom you buy goods or services. QuickBooks uses the data in the Vendor list to fill in purchase orders, receipts, bills, and checks as you receive and pay for goods and services.

Adding new vendors

In this exercise, you'll add a new vendor to the Vendor list. Suppose Rock Castle Construction is working with a new subcontractor, and it needs to add information about the new vendor to its QuickBooks Vendor list.

1 From the Vendors menu, choose Vendor List.

QuickBooks displays the Vendor list.

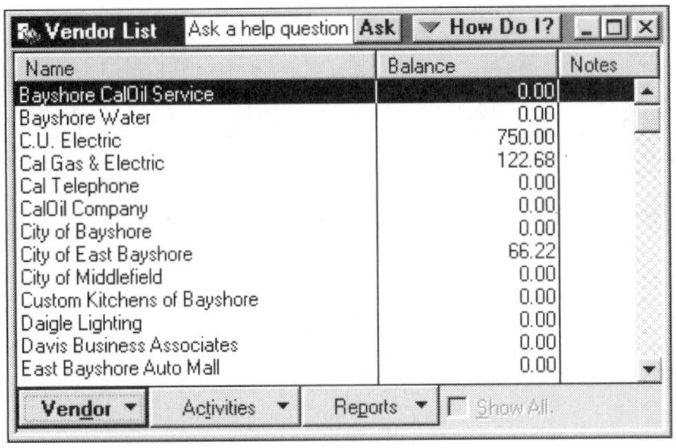

2 Click the Vendor menu button, and then choose New.

QuickBooks displays the New Vendor window.

The New Vendor window is where you enter all of the information regarding a new vendor, such as name, phone, contact, address, and opening balance. Just as when you add a new customer, you start by providing basic information on the Address Info tab.

3 In the Vendor Name field, type ***Hughes Electric***.

This is the name QuickBooks displays for this vendor in the Vendor list. If the vendor is an individual, you may wish to enter the last name first, then the first name.

4 In the Company Name field, type ***Hughes Electric***.

5 Click in the Address field, below the company name displayed on the first line.

Notice that QuickBooks displays the company name on the first line of the Address field.

6 On the second line of the Address field, type ***P.O. Box 2316***.

7 Press Enter to move to the next line.

8 Type ***Middlefield, CA 94432***.

9 In the Contact field, type ***David Hughes.***

10 In the Phone field, type ***510-555-6666.***

11 In the FAX field, type ***510-555-6667.***

When you finish, your window should look like this.

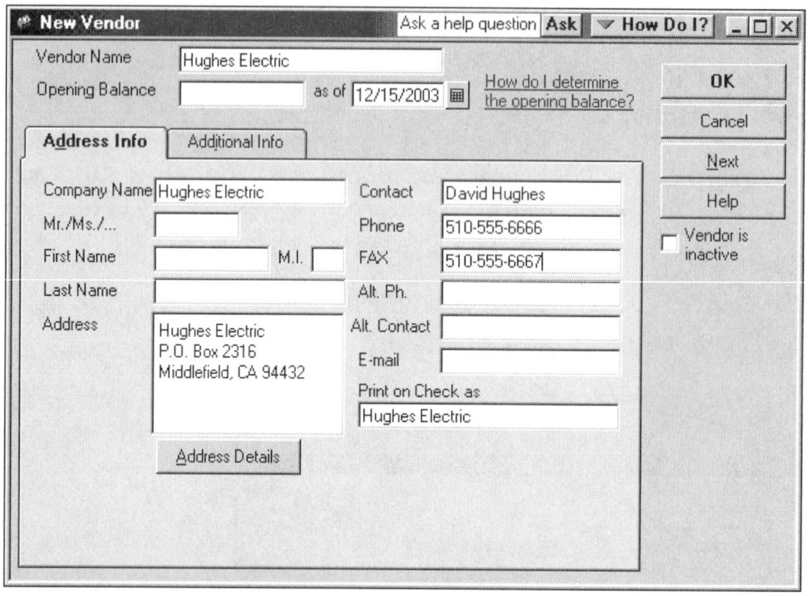

Providing additional vendor information

The Additional Info tab in the New Vendor window is where you can enter a vendor type (if you want to categorize your vendors), payment terms, your credit limit, the vendor's tax identification number, whether this vendor is eligible for a 1099 form, and your opening balance. You'll add this information now for Hughes Electric.

To add information to a vendor record:

1 Click the Additional Info tab.

QuickBooks displays the Additional Info tab of the New Vendor window.

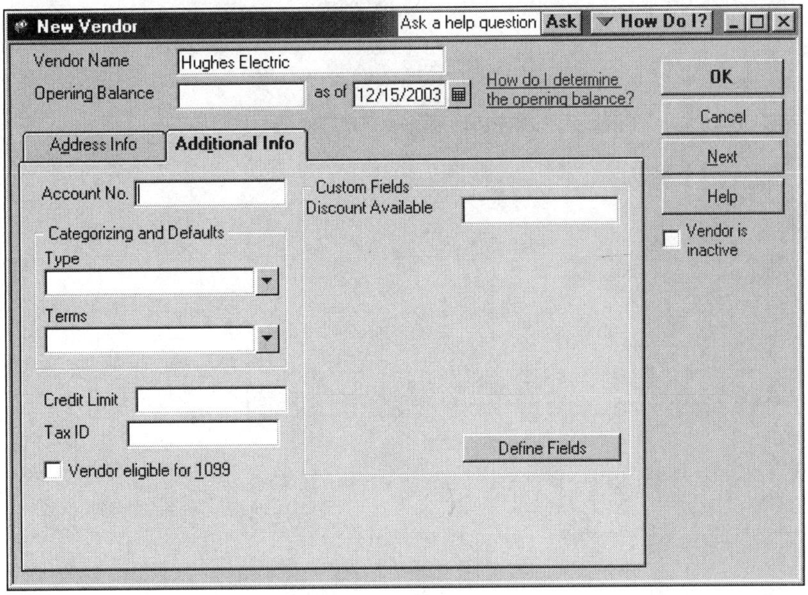

2 In the Account No. field, type ***123-445***.

3 In the Type field, type ***Subcontractors***.

Notice that when you type "sub," QuickBooks fills in the rest.

4 In the Terms field, choose 2% 10 Net 30 from the drop-down list.

5 In the Credit Limit field, type ***2000*** and press Tab.

Your New Vendor window should resemble the figure below.

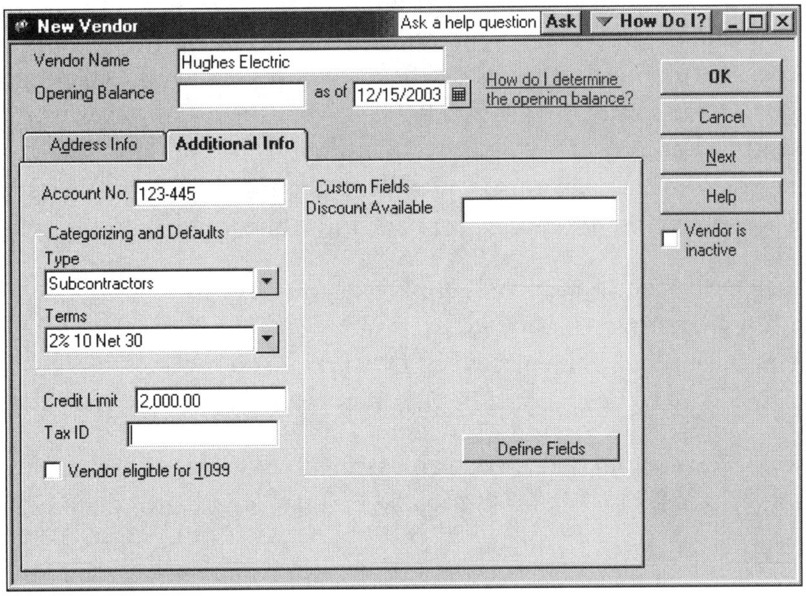

6 Click OK.

QuickBooks adds the vendor and displays the updated Vendor list.

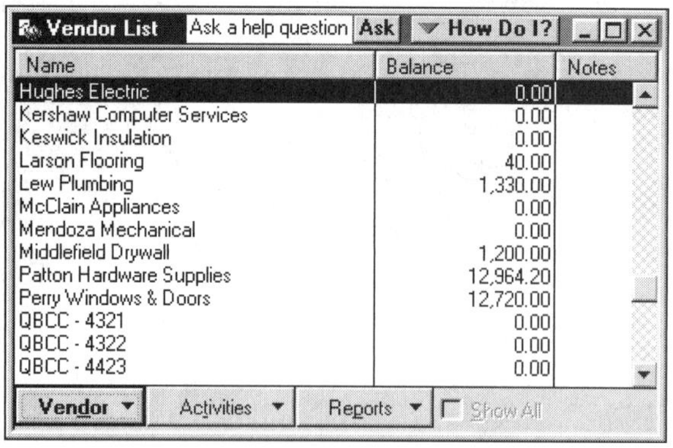

Notice that Hughes Electric has been added to the list.

7 Close the Vendor list.

Adding custom fields

QuickBooks lets you add custom fields to your Customer:Job, Vendor, Employee, and Item lists. Custom fields give you a way to track additional information specific to your business. For example, you can add a field for pager numbers to your Vendor and Employee lists, a field for customers' birthdays to your Customer:Job list, and fields for units of measurement, color, and size to your Item list.

When you add the custom fields to your sales forms or purchase orders, the fields are prefilled with the information for that specific customer, employee, vendor, or item (if you specified a value for the custom field when you added the customer, for example). You don't have to add the custom fields to your forms, however; you can also use custom fields as a way to record information just for your use, such as a credit rating for each customer. QuickBooks remembers the information you entered in the custom fields when you import and export data and when you memorize transactions.

For each customer, vendor, and employee, you can add up to seven custom fields, including fields that overlap. For example, if you add a custom birthday field for customers, vendors, and employees, QuickBooks counts it as one field used for each. You can add up to five custom fields for each item your company sells.

After you add custom fields, you can use them on invoices, credit memos, sales receipts, estimates (QuickBooks Pro and Premier only), and purchase orders.

Adding custom fields for customers, vendors, and employees

You can enter information in the custom fields only through the New or Edit windows (for example, the New Customer or Edit Customer windows). You can display information from the custom fields on form as well as add custom fields to reports.

First, look at the custom fields that Rock Castle Construction has already added to its Customer:Job, Vendor, and Employee lists. Then, you'll add two new custom fields.

To add custom fields:

1. From the Customers menu, choose Customer:Job List.

   QuickBooks displays the Customer:Job list.
2. In the Customer:Job list, select Cook, Brian.
3. Click the Customer:Job menu button, and then choose Edit.

   QuickBooks displays the Edit Customer window.

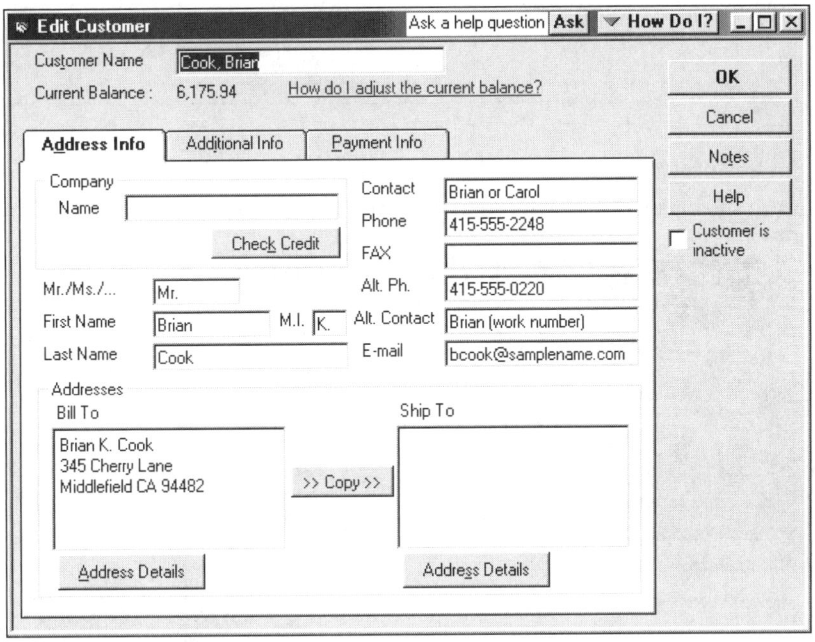

4. Click the Additional Info tab.

QuickBooks displays the Additional Info tab in the Edit Customer window.

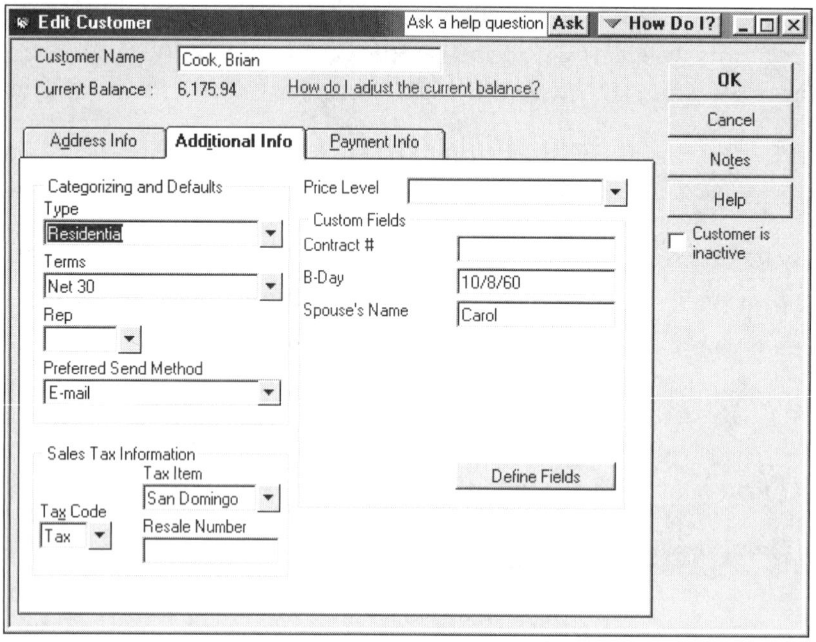

5 Click Define Fields.

QuickBooks displays the Define Fields window.

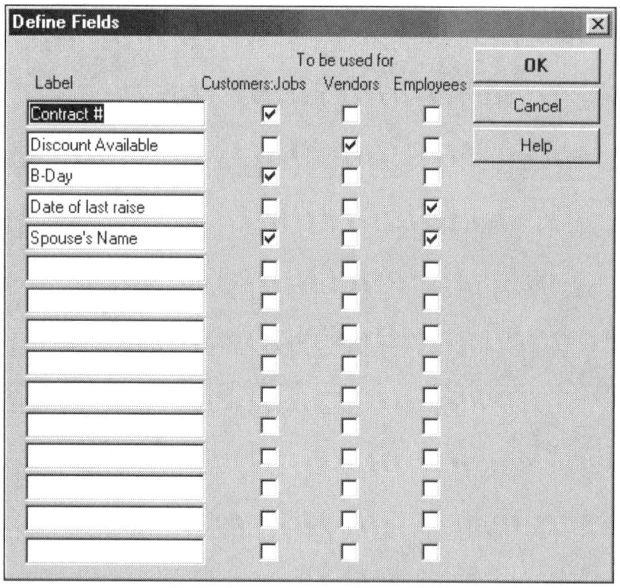

Notice that Rock Castle Construction has already set up custom fields in the Customer:Job list for contract number, birthday, and spouse's name. In the Vendor list, they have set up a custom field for discount available. In the Employee list, they have set up custom fields for the date of last raise and spouse's name.

Now, you'll add a custom field for pager numbers to the Customer:Job and Vendor lists. You'll also add a custom field to the Employee list that tracks the date of each employee's last review.

6 In the first blank Label field, type ***Pager Number.***

7 Click the Customers:Jobs checkbox to select it.

8 Click the Vendors checkbox to select it.

9 In the next blank Label field, type ***Date of last review.***

10 Click the Employees checkbox to select it.

Your Define Fields window should now look like this.

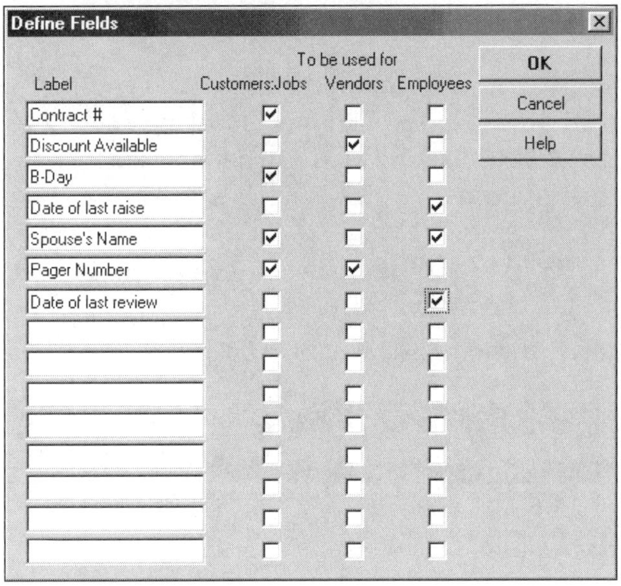

11 Click OK.

12 If you see an informational message about using the custom fields in transactions by turning them on in your custom templates, click OK.

QuickBooks has added the Pager Number field to the Edit Customer window.

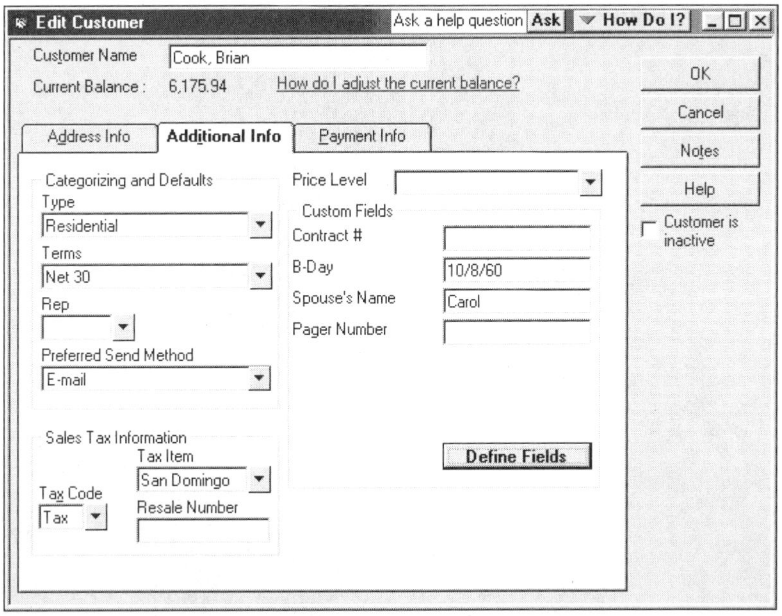

13 In the Pager Number field, type ***415-555-9876***.

If you customize your sales forms to display the Pager Number field, this number displays whenever you create a form for this customer. It also displays on reports modified to display the Pager Number column.

14 Click OK to close the Edit Customer window.

15 Close the Customer:Job list.

Adding custom fields for items

Now suppose that Rock Castle Construction wants to add another custom field to its Item list. The company purchases several types of locking doorknobs. The Item list already has custom fields for Color and Material, but now Rock Castle wants to add an additional field to track Style.

To add custom fields for items:

1 From the Lists menu, choose Item List.

QuickBooks displays the Item list, as shown below.

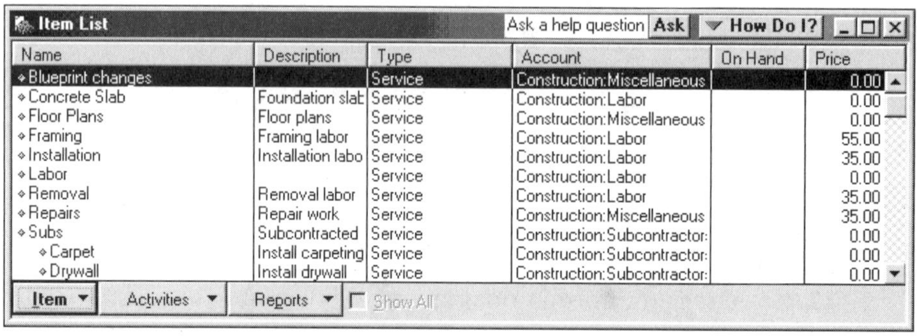

2 In the Item list, select Lk Doorknobs (a sub item of Hardware).

3 Click the Item menu button, and then choose Edit.

QuickBooks displays the Edit Item window.

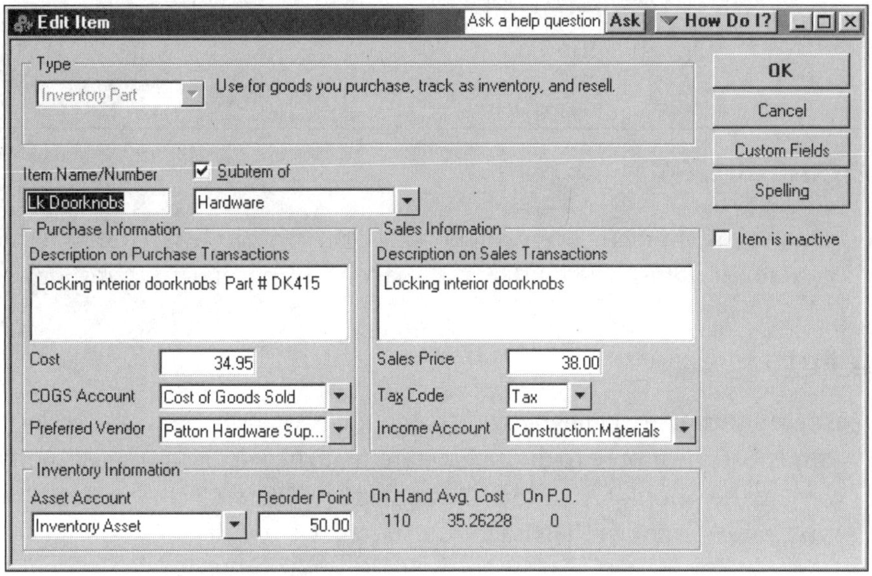

4 Click Custom Fields.

QuickBooks displays the custom fields already defined for this item.

5 Click Define Fields.

QuickBooks displays the Define Custom Fields for Items window.

6 Under Use, click the first blank checkbox to select it. Then type ***Style*** in the Label field.

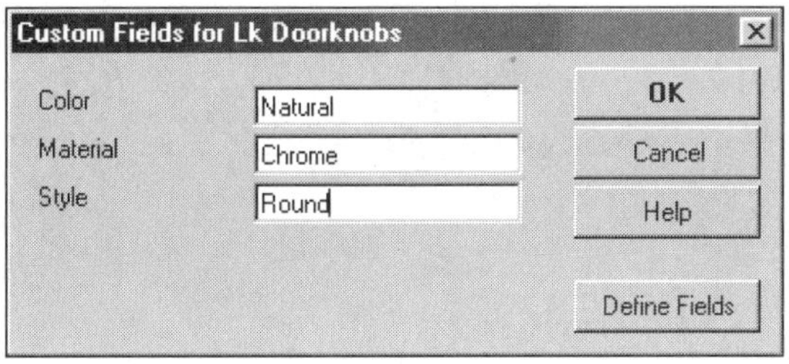

7 Click OK to close the window.

8 If you see an informational message about using the custom fields in transactions by turning them on in your custom templates, click OK.

9 In the Custom Fields for Lk Doorknobs window, type ***Round*** in the Style field.

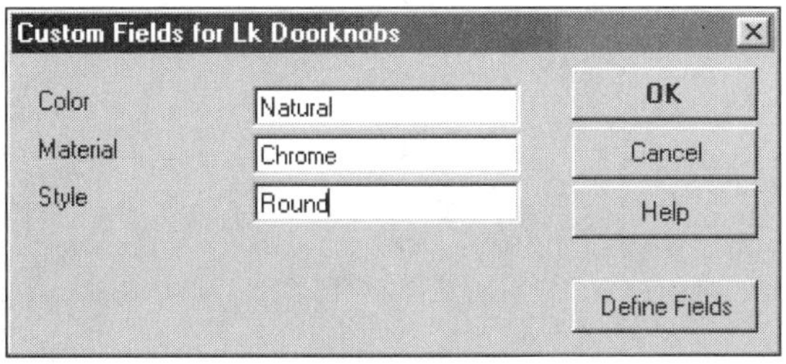

10 Click OK to close the Custom Fields for Lk Doorknobs window, and then click OK to close the Edit Item window.

11 Close the Item list.

Managing lists

Lists are easy to manage in QuickBooks. You can sort lists, combine (merge) list items, rename list items, delete list items, make list items inactive, and print lists.

Sorting lists

You can sort many QuickBooks lists manually or alphabetically. To sort a list manually, simply use the mouse to drag a list item to its new location. Lists that you can sort this way are the Chart of Accounts, Customer:Job, Class, Customer Type, Vendor Type, Job Type, and Memorized Transaction lists.

If you have changed the order of a list by dragging items and then decide you'd rather have an alphabetically sorted list, QuickBooks has a Re-sort List command. In the chart of accounts, the Re-sort List command sorts alphabetically within account type; in the Item list, the Re-sort List command sorts alphabetically within item type.

Sorting lists manually

In this exercise, you'll sort a list manually, and then re-sort it to put it back in alphabetical order.

To sort a list manually:

1 From the Lists menu, choose Chart of Accounts.

QuickBooks displays the chart of accounts for Rock Castle Construction.

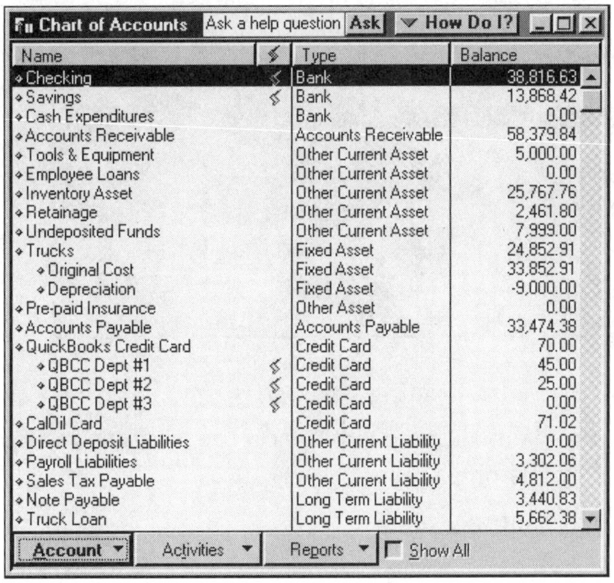

2 Click the diamond to the left of the Owner's Draw subaccount of Owner's Equity.

The mouse pointer becomes a four-directional arrow.

3 Click and hold the mouse button, and drag the pointer upward until you see a dotted line directly below Owner's Equity.

4 Release the mouse button to drop the account in the new position.

The Owner's Draw account is now directly under the Owner's Equity account.

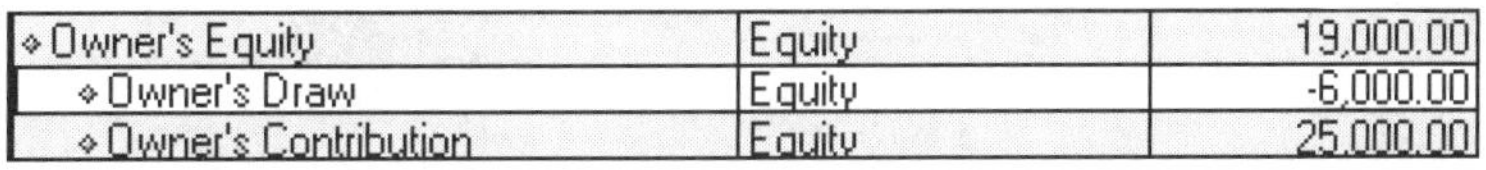

Now you can use the Re-sort List command to return the list to alphabetical order.

5 To re-sort the list alphabetically, click the Account menu button, and select Re-sort List.

QuickBooks asks you to confirm that you want to return the list to its original order.

6 Click OK.

QuickBooks re-sorts the chart of accounts alphabetically by account type.

7 Close the chart of accounts.

Sorting lists in ascending or descending order

Depending on the type of business you have, you may want to order your list entries in a certain way. For example, perhaps you'd like to see people who owe you money at the top of your Customer:Job list. In this exercise, you'll learn how to sort the Customer:Job list in descending order by customer balance.

To sort a list in descending order:

1 From the Lists menu, choose Customer:Job List.

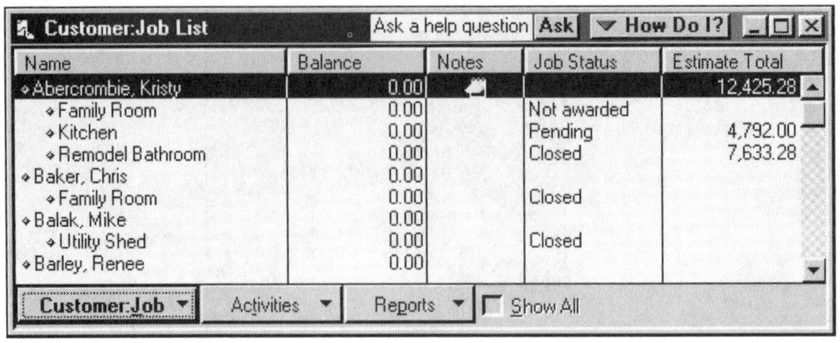

2 Click the Balance column heading.

Notice that an arrow pointing up appears on the heading and the list is sorted in ascending order by customer balance.

3 Click the column heading again.

Notice that the arrow now points down and the list is sorted in descending order with the customers with the highest balances at the top of the list.

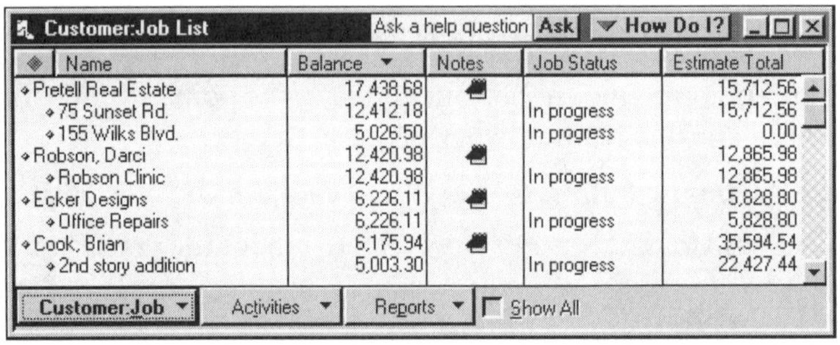

4 To return to the order you started with, click the large diamond to the left of the Name column heading.

5 Close the Customer:Job list.

Merging list items

In most lists, you can combine two list items into one. For example, you may find that you've been using two customers (because of different spellings) when you really need only one on your Customer:Job list. You can merge list items in the Chart of Accounts, Item, Customer:Job, Vendor, Employee, and Other Names lists.

Important: After you merge list items, you cannot separate them. When working in your own company file, we recommend that you back up your data before merging list items.

In this exercise, suppose you want to merge Hughes Electric (the vendor you added earlier in the lesson) with C.U. Electric. To merge them, you edit the incorrect name to match the spelling of the correct name.

To merge items on a list:

1 From the Vendors menu, choose Vendor List.

QuickBooks displays the Vendor list.

2 Select Hughes Electric.

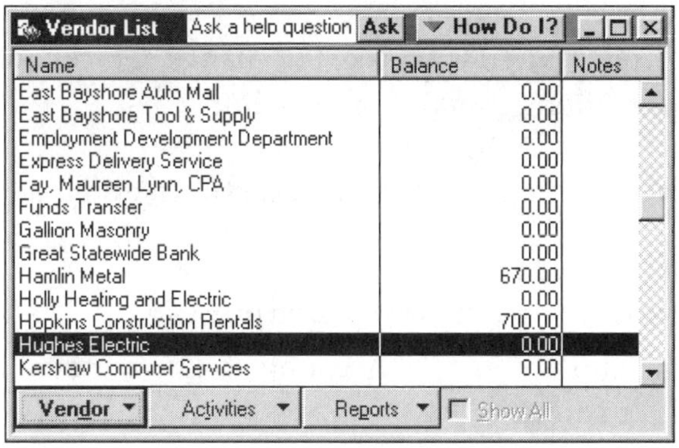

3 Click the Vendor menu button, and then choose Edit.

QuickBooks displays the Edit Vendor window.

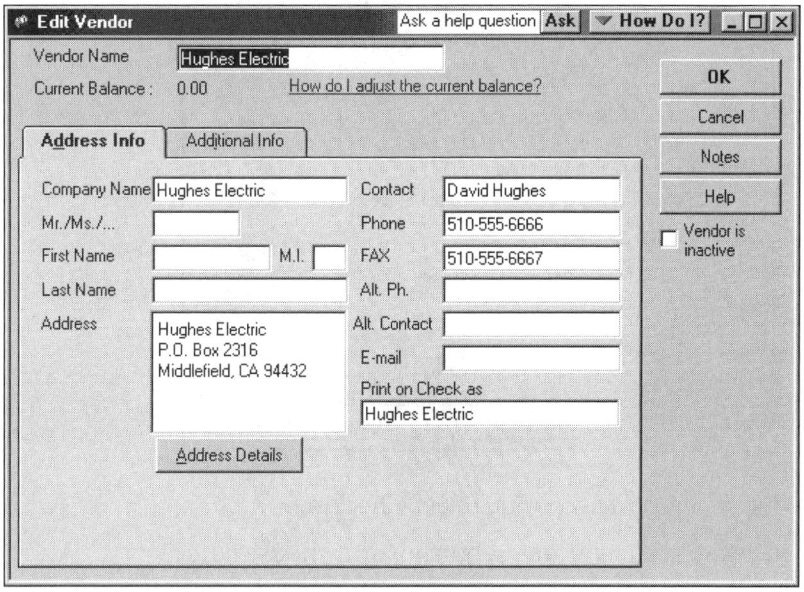

4 In the Vendor Name field, type ***C.U. Electric***. (This is the vendor name you want to merge with.)

5 Click OK.

QuickBooks asks if you would like to merge the names.

6 Click Yes.

QuickBooks merges the two names, and you now have only C.U. Electric in the Vendor list.

7 Close the Vendor list.

Note: **If you use assembly items in QuickBooks Premier Edition products, you cannot merge them with other assembly items or with any other type of item.**

Renaming list items

You can rename any list item. When you make the change, QuickBooks automatically modifies all existing transactions containing the item.

Tip: **If you don't want to change existing transactions, add a new name or item instead.**

To rename a list item in the chart of accounts:

1 From the Lists menu, choose Chart of Accounts to display the chart of accounts for Rock Castle Construction.

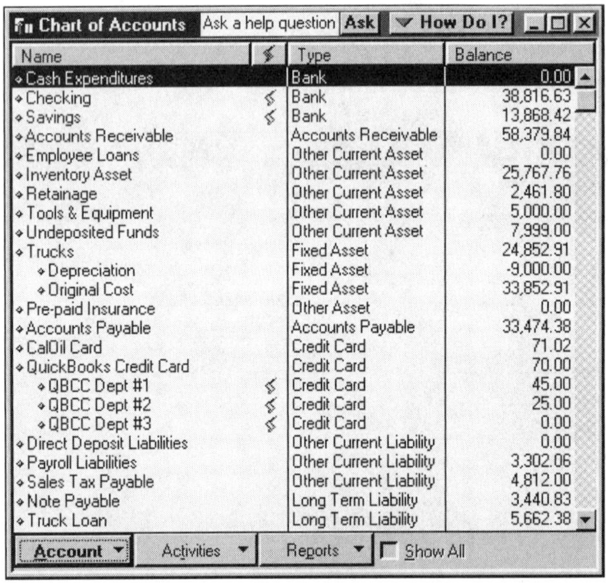

2 In the chart of accounts, select Checking.

3 Click the Account menu button, and choose Edit.

QuickBooks displays the Edit Account window.

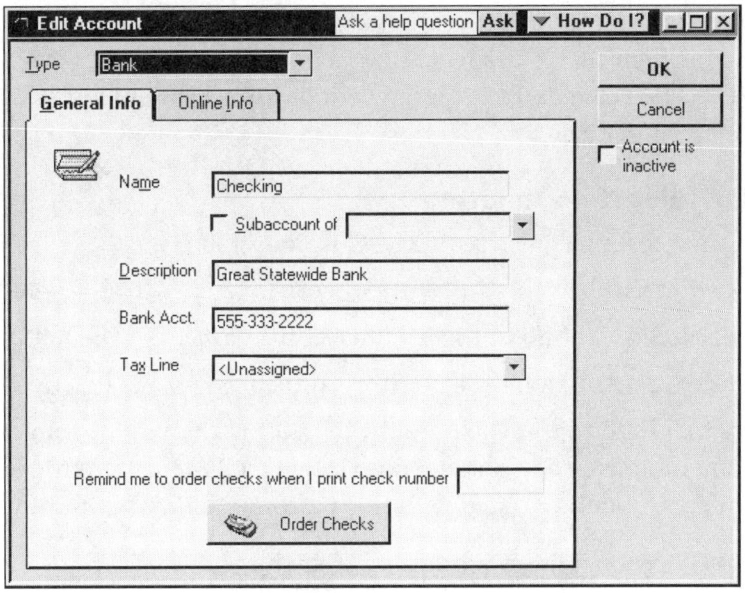

4 In the Name field, type ***Master Checking Account***.

5 Click OK.

QuickBooks changes the account name in the chart of accounts.

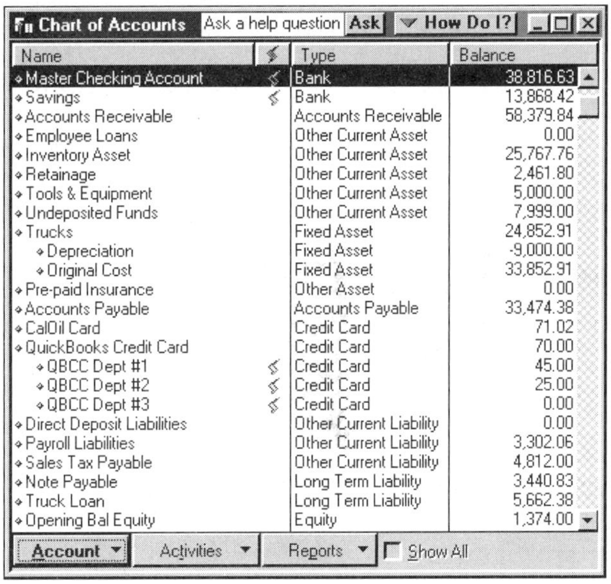

6 Close the chart of accounts.

Deleting items and making list items inactive

You can delete list items only if you have not used them in any transactions. If you try to delete a list item that is used in a transaction, QuickBooks displays a warning that the item can't be deleted. If you don't want to use a list item but you can't delete it, you can make it inactive.

To make a list item inactive:

1. From the Customers menu, choose Customer:Job List.

   QuickBooks displays the Customer:Job list.

2. Select Natiello, Ernesto in the list. (Select his name, not the job.)
3. Click the Customer:Job menu button, and choose Make Inactive.

   Notice that Ernesto Natiello (and the job for his kitchen) no longer appears on the Customer:Job list. (The customer:job item is only removed from the list—transactions associated with this customer:job will still show in reports.)

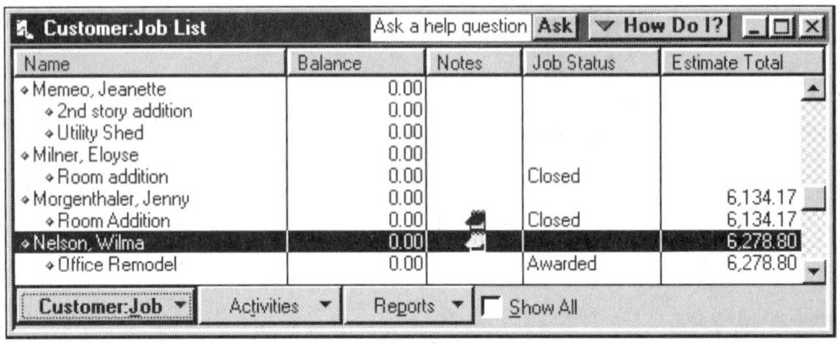

4. To see inactive list items, select the Show All checkbox in the list window.

   QuickBooks displays all the list items again, but the Xs signify that this customer is still inactive.(You make the customer active again by choosing Make Active from the Customer:Job menu button.)

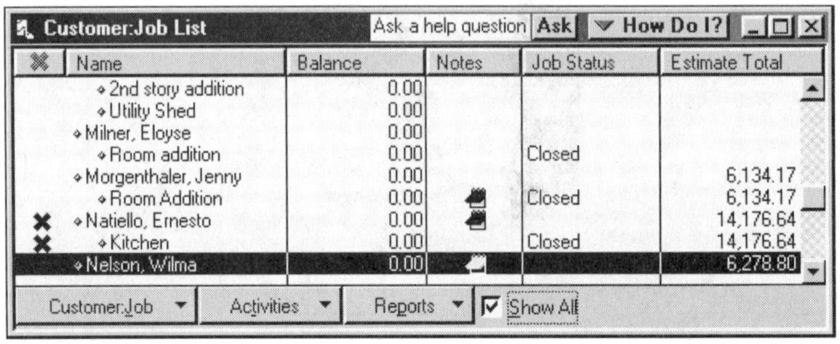

5. Leave the Customer:Job list open, you'll print it in the next exercise.

Printing a list

You can print a QuickBooks list for reference, or you may print a list to a file to use in your word processor or spreadsheet.

To print a list of customers:

1 Click the Customer:Job menu button, and then choose Print List.

QuickBooks displays a message telling you that you can also print list information from the Reports menu.

2 Click OK to bypass the List Reports message.

QuickBooks displays the Print Lists window, which displays the name of your printer and printer port.

You can select to print to a printer or to a file.

3 Click Print.

Note: This is a fairly long list, so if you don't want to print it now, click Cancel.

4 Close the Customer:Job list.

Let students know that if they want to print the list to a file (so that they can use it in their word processing, spreadsheet, or database program), they can select File and select the appropriate file format from the drop-down list. They can also create a list report, which they can filter and print as necessary.

Student test and review

1 Match the information on the left with the appropriate QuickBooks list on the right.

1. A subcontractor	A. Customer:Job list
2. Someone who purchases the goods or services you sell	B. Chart of accounts
3. A new hire	C. Vendor list
4. Checking account	D. Employee list

2 Add the following customer using the data below:
- Customer Name: Alla Rozenvasser
- Opening Balance: $234.00
- Company Name: Rozenvasser Advertising
- Contact: Alla Rozenvasser
- Bill to: 300 Main Street, Suite #3, Middlefield, CA 94432
- Phone: 415-555-6767
- Fax: 415-555-9090
- Alt. Contact: Shannon Stubo
- Type: Commercial
- Credit Limit: $2500
- Terms: Net 15
- Tax Item: San Domingo

3 Add a new vendor using the data below:
- Vendor: Martin Drywall
- Contact: Sean D. Martin
- Address: P.O. Box 76, Middlefield, CA 94432
- Phone: 555-5432
- Fax: 555-6565
- Account: 082-4343
- Type: Subcontractors
- Terms: Net 30
- Credit Limit: 1,000.00

LESSON 4 Working with bank accounts

Lesson objectives

- To learn how to work with the registers for QuickBooks bank accounts
- To demonstrate how to open a register
- To learn the features common to all registers
- To learn when and how to make entries directly in the register
- To demonstrate how to reconcile a QuickBooks bank account

Handout materials

- Handout 12: Registers associated with QuickBooks windows
- Handout 13: Using the keyboard to move around a register

Instructor preparation

- Review the lesson, including the examples, to make sure you're familiar with the material.
- Ensure that all students have a copy of qblesson.qbb on their computer's hard disk.
- Have Handouts 12 and 13 ready for distribution.

To start this lesson

Before you perform the following steps, make sure you have installed the exercise file (qblesson.qbb) on your hard disk. See "Installing the exercise file" in the Introduction to this guide if you haven't installed it.

The steps that follow will restore the exercise file to its original state so that the data in the file matches what you see on the screen as you proceed through each lesson.

To restore the exercise file (qblesson.qbb):

1. From the File menu in QuickBooks, choose Restore.

   QuickBooks displays the Restore Company Backup window.
2. In the "Get Company Backup From" section of the window, click Browse and select your c:\QBtrain directory.
3. Select the qblesson.qbb file, and then click Open.
4. In the "Restore Company Backup To" section of the window, click Browse and select your c:\QBtrain directory.
5. In the File name field of the Restore To window, type ***lesson 4*** and then click Save.

6 Click Restore.

Writing a QuickBooks check

You can enter checks directly into the check register by using the QuickBooks Write Checks window. When you enter a check at the Write Checks window, you can see the address information and easily allocate the check between multiple accounts.

Suppose that you need to write a check to pay Rock Castle Construction's telephone bill.

To write a check:

1 From the Banking menu, choose Write Checks.

QuickBooks displays the Write Checks window.

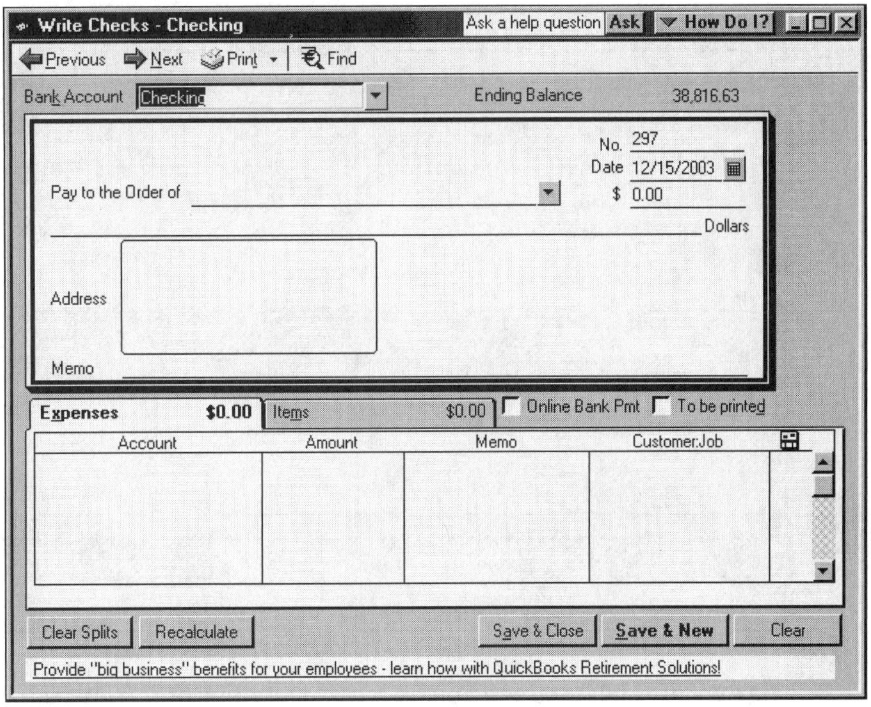

The Bank Account field shows the account from which you are writing this check. QuickBooks displays the current date in the Date field. (The sample data is set to display December 15, 2003 as the current date.) You can change either of these values if you wish, but they are fine for our example.

2 Select the "To be printed" checkbox.

QuickBooks displays a checkmark in the checkbox.

3 In the Pay to the Order of field, type ***Cal Telephone***.

4 Press Tab to move to the Amount field.

Tip: QuickBooks has an AutoRecall feature that fills in the amount from the last transaction with a payee. This is convenient when you have recurring payments of the same amount. **You can turn on AutoRecall by choosing Preferences from the Edit menu.** Click General, and then select the checkbox for "Automatically recall last transaction for this name" on the My Preferences tab.

5 Type ***156.91*** (the amount of the telephone bill), and then press Tab.

Notice that QuickBooks spells out the amount of the check for you on the line below the payee.

6 Click in the Account column on the Expenses tab, and then choose Utilities:Telephone from the drop-down list.

Your screen should resemble the following figure.

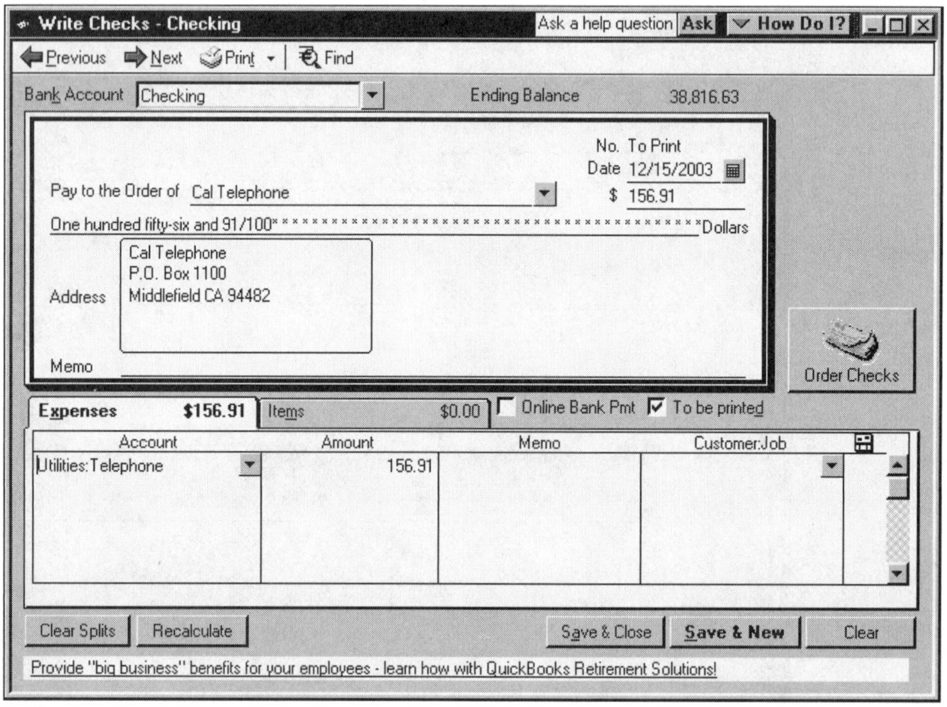

The Expenses tab is where you assign the amount of the check to one of the expense accounts on your company's chart of accounts. In this case, Rock Castle Construction assigns the check to its Utilities account and the Telephone subaccount. You use the Items tab only when purchasing items you plan to stock in inventory.

7 Click Save & Close.

8 From the Banking menu, choose Use Register.

Rock Castle Construction has more than one type of bank account, so QuickBooks displays the Use Register window and asks you to specify the account you want.

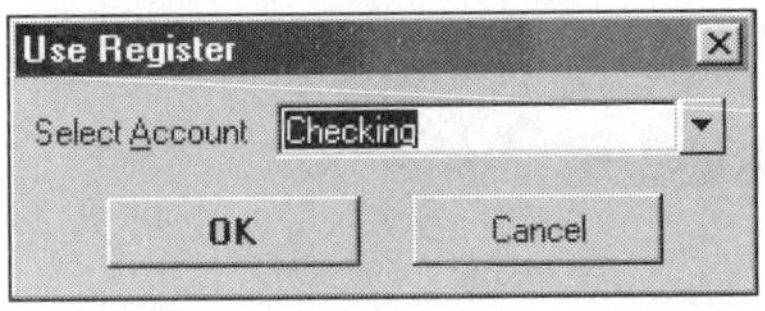

9 Click OK to accept Checking as the account whose register you want to see.

QuickBooks opens the Checking register.

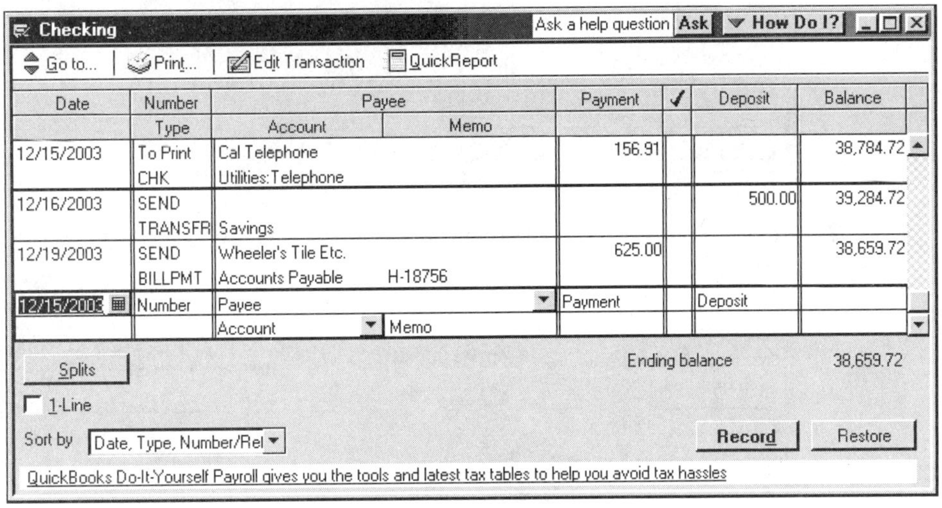

Notice that the check you just wrote is listed in the register as a check that needs to be printed.

10 Close the Checking account register.

Using bank account registers

When you work in QuickBooks, you often use forms, such as a check or an invoice, to enter information. But behind the scenes, QuickBooks records your entries in the appropriate account register. Each balance sheet account listed on the chart of accounts has a register associated with it (except the Retained Earnings account).

Refer to Handout 12, "Registers associated with QuickBooks windows."

Opening a register

When you have a QuickBooks form displayed on your screen, you can view its account register by choosing Use Register from the Banking menu, or by double-clicking the account name in the chart of accounts.

To open a register (when no form is open):

1 From the Lists menu, choose Chart of Accounts.

QuickBooks displays the Chart of Accounts window.

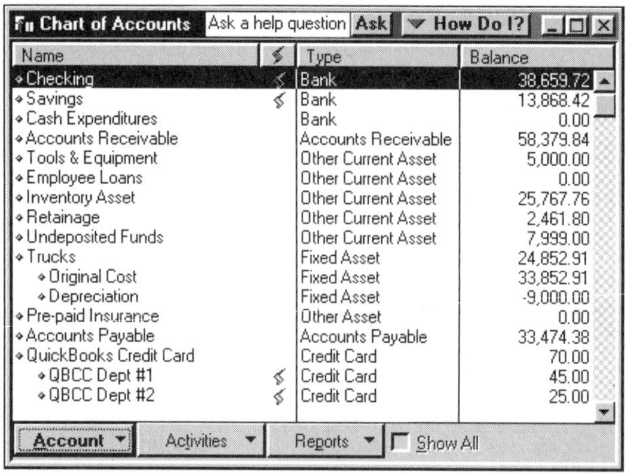

2 In the chart of accounts, double-click the Savings account.

QuickBooks opens the register for Rock Castle Construction's Savings account.

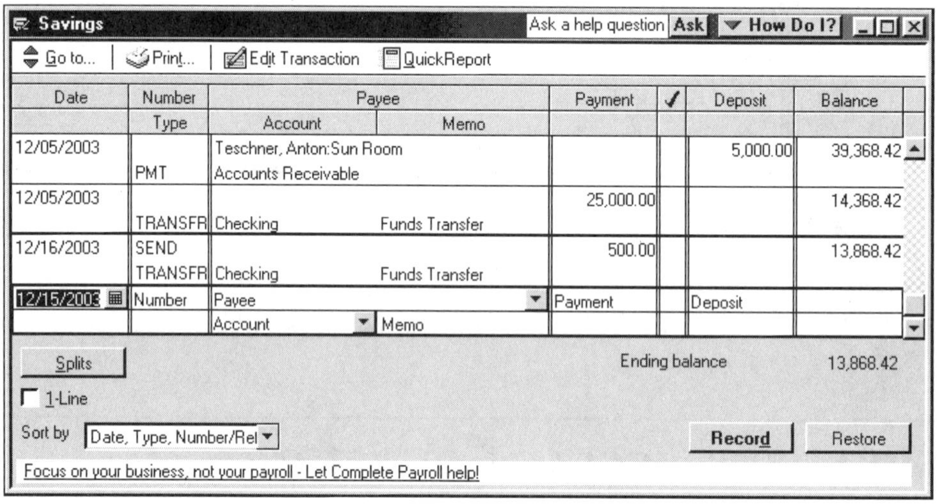

Common features of QuickBooks registers

All QuickBooks registers work the same way, regardless of the accounts with which they are associated. Here are some common features of all QuickBooks registers:

- The register shows every transaction that affects an account's balance and lists them in chronological order (though you can change the order by choosing a different option from the Sort by drop-down list). For example, in a checking account, the register shows checks you've written (either with QuickBooks or by hand), deposits to the account, and withdrawals from the account.
- The columns in the register give specific information about the transaction. The first column is the date. The second column shows a reference number (a check number or a vendor's P.O. number) and a type (to tell you whether the transaction represents a check or a bill payment, for example). The next column lists the payee, the account to which you've assigned the transaction, and any descriptive memo you choose to type. The final columns for a bank account show the transaction amount (either in the Payment or Deposit column) and whether the transaction has cleared the bank (indicated by a checkmark in the column).
- On every transaction line, QuickBooks shows the account's running balance. The bottom of the register window shows the account's ending balance—the balance takes into account all the transactions entered in the register, including checks you haven't yet printed.

Refer to Handout 13, "Using the keyboard to move around a register."

To complete the exercise:

1 Close the Savings register window.

2 Close the chart of accounts.

Entering a handwritten check

Sometimes you need to write a check on the spot for items you did not plan to purchase. QuickBooks lets you write the check, and then enter it later in the checking account register or on the check form.

Suppose that while picking up supplies one day, you stop at Bayshore Office Supply and find a new office chair on sale for $99.95. The sale ends today, so you write a check on the spot. You'll have to enter it in QuickBooks later.

To enter a handwritten check in the checking account register:

1 From the Banking menu, choose Use Register.

QuickBooks displays the Use Register window.

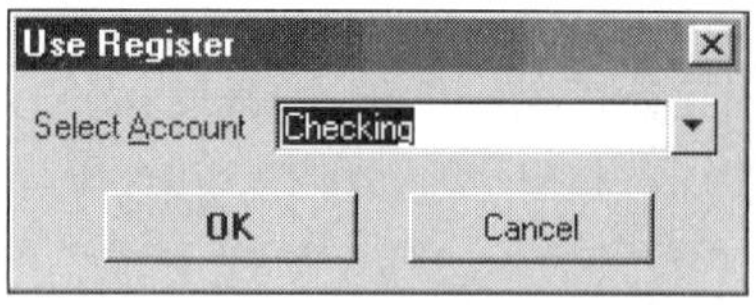

2 Click OK to accept Checking.

QuickBooks displays the register for the Checking account.

3 Click in the Number field in the blank transaction at the bottom of the register, then double-click to highlight the number that QuickBooks prefills.

4 Type ***1204***, and then press Tab.

5 In the Payee field, type ***Bayshore Office Supply***, and then press Tab.

QuickBooks displays a message telling you that Bayshore Office Supply is not on the Name list.

6 Click Quick Add.

QuickBooks displays the Select Name Type window.

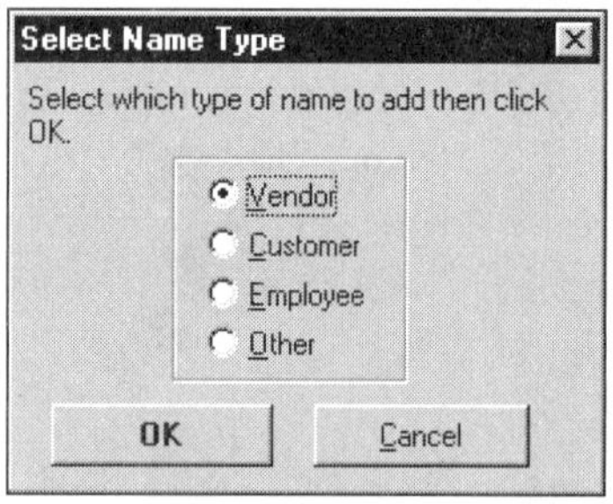

Bayshore Office Supply is a vendor, so you can accept the displayed choice.

7 Click OK.

QuickBooks adds the new vendor to the Vendor list.

8 In the Payment field, type ***99.95***, and then press Tab.

9 In the Account field, type ***Of***, and then press Tab.

QuickBooks fills in Office Supplies.

10 In the Memo field, type ***Office chair.***

The Checking account register on your screen should resemble the following figure.

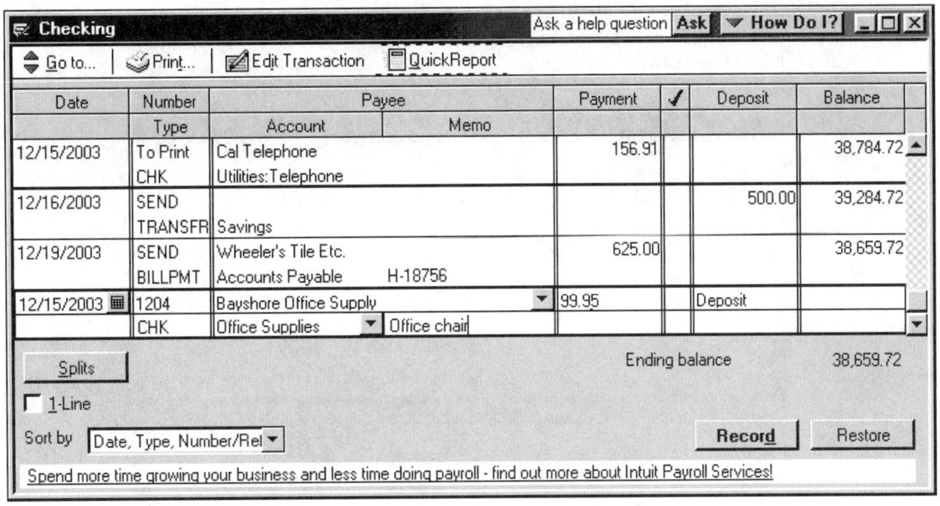

11 Click Record.

12 Close the Checking account register.

Transferring money between accounts

You can easily transfer money to different accounts using the QuickBooks Transfer Funds Between Accounts window. Rock Castle Construction wants to transfer $5,000.00 from checking to savings.

To transfer money:

1 From the Banking menu, choose Transfer Funds.

QuickBooks displays the Transfer Funds Between Accounts window.

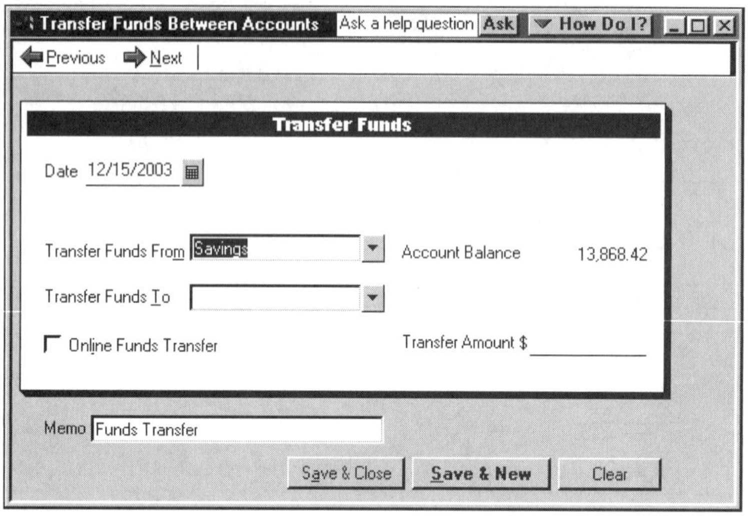

Notice that QuickBooks displays the current balance for the Savings account.

2 In the Transfer Funds From field, choose Checking from the drop-down list.

3 In the Transfer Funds To field, choose Savings from the drop-down list.

4 In the Transfer Amount field, type ***5000***.

Your screen should resemble the following figure.

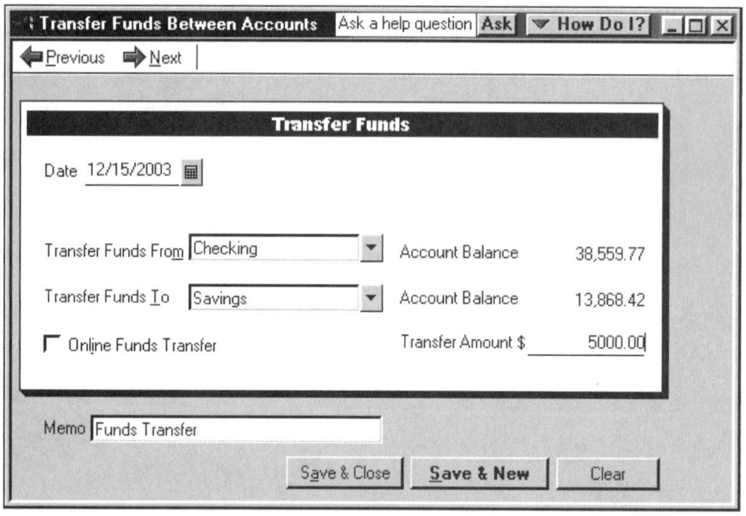

5 Click Save & Close.

QuickBooks decreases the balance in the checking account by $5,000 and increases the balance in the savings account by $5,000.

Reconciling checking accounts

Reconciling is the process of making sure that your checking account record matches the bank's record.

An overview of reconciliation

When you keep your records with QuickBooks, you don't have to worry about addition or subtraction errors like you do when you're using a paper check register. Even so, it is important to get in the habit of reconciling your QuickBooks bank accounts on a monthly basis. This helps you avoid overdraft charges for bad checks, gives you a chance to spot possible bank errors, and helps you keep more accurate financial records.

Your bank sends you a statement for each of your accounts each month. The statement shows all the activity in your account since the previous statement:

- The opening balance for your bank account (amount in your account as of the previous statement)
- The ending balance for your bank account (amount in your account as of the closing date for the statement)
- The amount of interest, if any, you've received for this statement period
- Any service charges assessed by the bank for this statement period
- Checks that have cleared the bank
- Deposits you've made to the account
- Any other transactions that affect the balance of your account (for example, automatic payments or deposits or automatic teller machine (ATM) withdrawals or deposits)

When you receive a statement from your bank or from a credit card company, you need to reconcile the statement with your QuickBooks records. You can reconcile any QuickBooks bank account, including accounts for savings and money market funds. The goal of reconciling is to make sure that your QuickBooks records and the bank's statement agree about your account balance.

Marking cleared transactions

To begin reconciling an account, you need to tell QuickBooks which account you want to reconcile. Then you can provide information from the top part of your bank statement.

To reconcile your account:

1 From the Banking menu, choose Reconcile.

QuickBooks displays the Begin Reconciliation window.

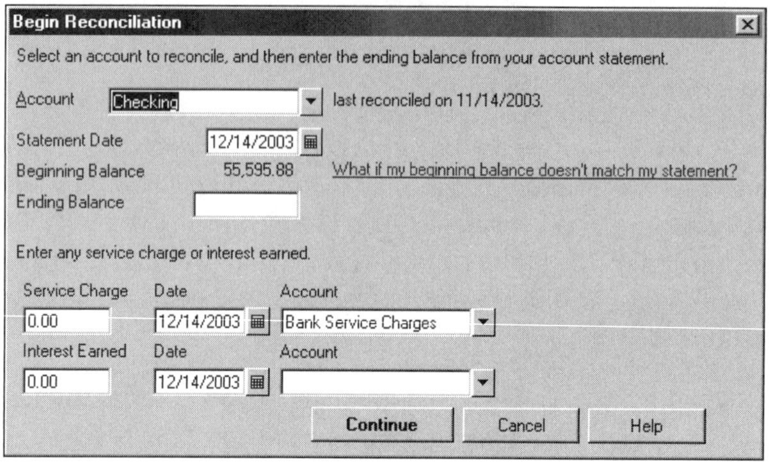

2 In the Account field, make sure Checking is selected.

3 In the Ending Balance field, type ***52,881.88***.

4 In the Service Charge field, type ***14.00***.

Your screen should resemble the following.

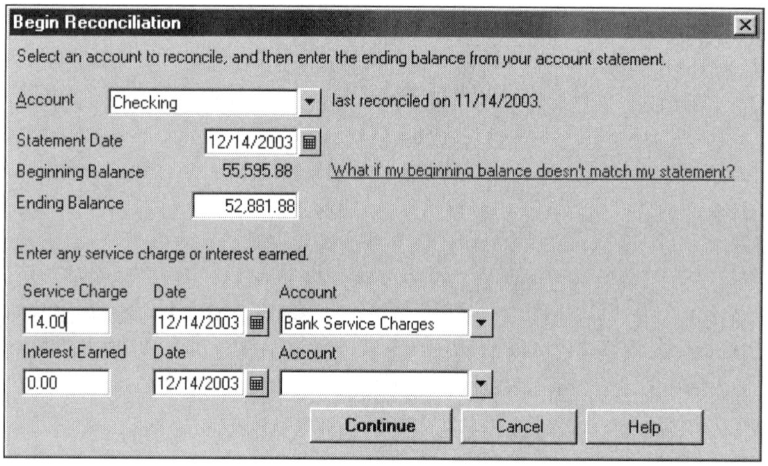

5 Click Continue.

QuickBooks displays the Reconcile - Checking window.

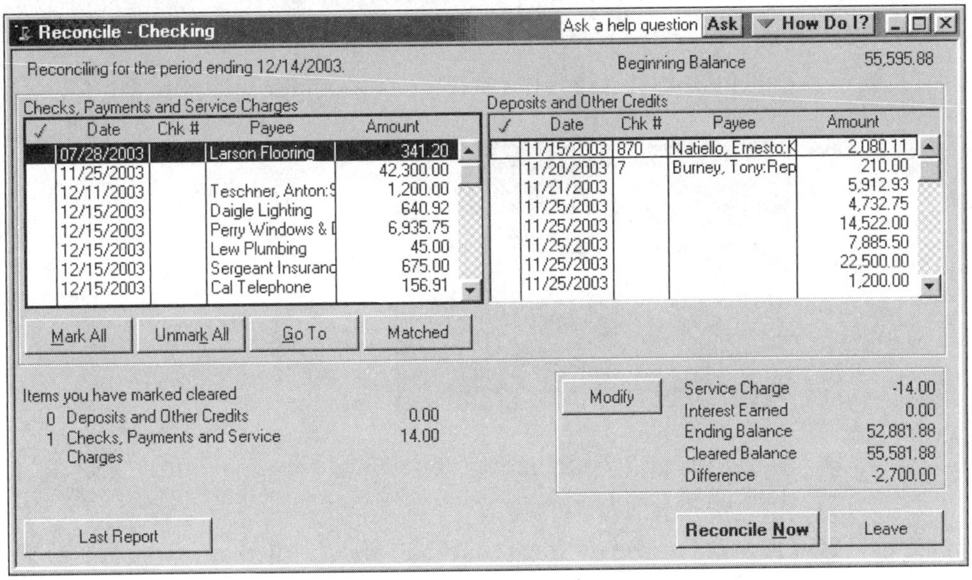

6 In the Checks, Payments and Service Charges section, select Check # 265 from Reyes Properties for $1,200.00, and Check #266 from Larson Flooring for $2,700.00.

QuickBooks places a checkmark to the left of both items.

7 In the Deposits and Other Credits section, select the 12/03/03 deposit from Anton Teschner for $1,200.00.

Your screen should resemble the following figure.

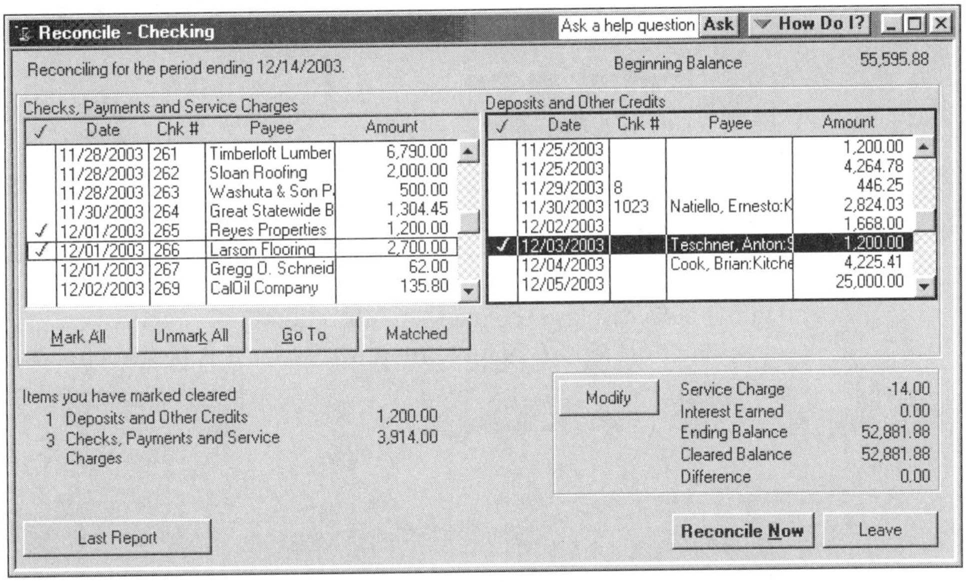

Tip: The Go To button allows you to select a transaction that needs a correction, jump to the actual transaction in the register to make an adjustment, and then return to the reconciliation window.

8 Click Reconcile Now.

QuickBooks displays the Select Reconciliation Report window.

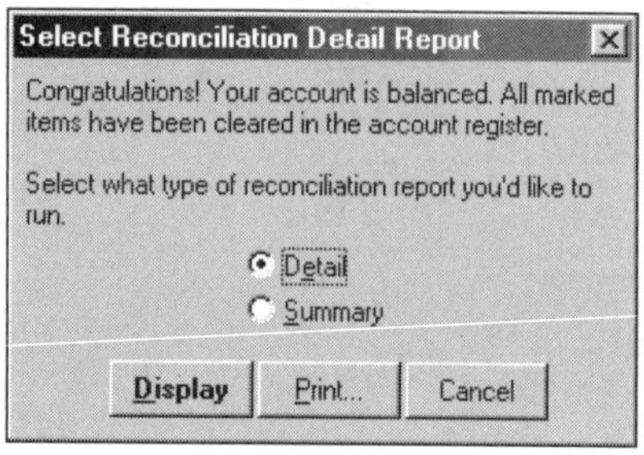

9 In the Select Reconciliation Report window, make sure "Detail" is selected, and then click Display.

10 Click OK at the message that QuickBooks displays.

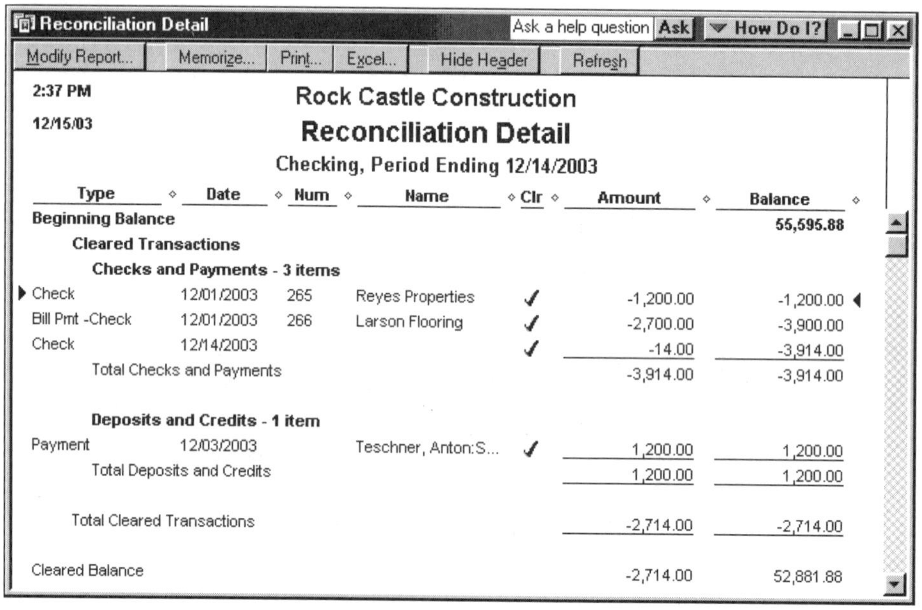

2:37 PM
12/15/03

Rock Castle Construction
Reconciliation Detail
Checking, Period Ending 12/14/2003

Type	Date	Num	Name	Clr	Amount	Balance
Beginning Balance						55,595.88
Cleared Transactions						
Checks and Payments - 3 items						
Check	12/01/2003	265	Reyes Properties	✓	-1,200.00	-1,200.00
Bill Pmt -Check	12/01/2003	266	Larson Flooring	✓	-2,700.00	-3,900.00
Check	12/14/2003			✓	-14.00	-3,914.00
Total Checks and Payments					-3,914.00	-3,914.00
Deposits and Credits - 1 item						
Payment	12/03/2003		Teschner, Anton:S...	✓	1,200.00	1,200.00
Total Deposits and Credits					1,200.00	1,200.00
Total Cleared Transactions					-2,714.00	-2,714.00
Cleared Balance					-2,714.00	52,881.88

QuickBooks displays the reconciliation detail report. It's a good idea to print each reconciliation report, but for the purposes of this lesson viewing the report is sufficient.

Because QuickBooks Basic and QuickBooks Pro only store information for the latest reconciliation, you may want to print the report to a file if you think you will want to print the reconciliation report again. QuickBooks overwrites the previous reconciliation report with data from the latest reconciliation.

If you're using QuickBooks Premier, you can print the reconciliation reports for all previous reconciliations.

In addition, if you're using QuickBooks Premier, you have two additional report options: the reconcile discrepancy report and the reconciliation summary report. The reconcile discrepancy report lists the transactions that have changed since you last reconciled an account. This report is useful when the beginning balance that QuickBooks shows is different than the ending balance from the bank statement for the previous period. The reconciliation summary report provides a quick look at the overall totals for deposits/credits and checks/payments for a reconciliation period.

11 Close the report window.

Now you know that the balance in your QuickBooks check register is accurate as of the latest bank statement. The next time you look at the check register, you'll see a checkmark in the Cleared column next to each reconciled transaction.

If the Difference amount is not zero, your account does not balance for the current bank statement period. Advise students that, in this situation, they can have QuickBooks record an adjustment transaction that modifies their QuickBooks balance so it agrees with the bank statement. Or, they can find the difference between the check register and the bank statement and correct it. For more information, search the onscreen Help index for reconciling, adjusting for differences.

Viewing cleared checks in the register

Open the Checking account register to see the cleared checks.

To viewed cleared checks in the register:

1 From the Banking menu, choose Use Register.

QuickBooks displays the Use Register window.

2 Click OK to accept Checking.

3 Scroll through the register to view the cleared items (checks numbered 265 and 266).

Your register should resemble the figure below.

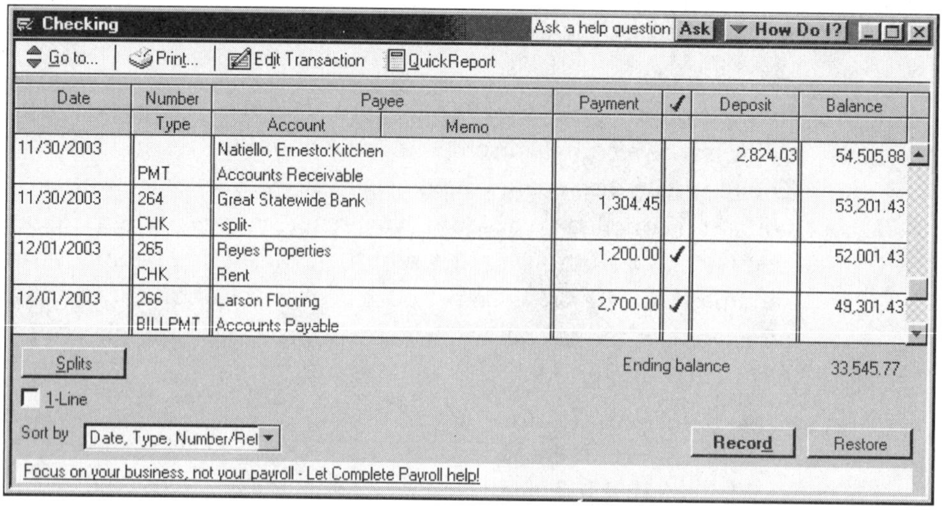

Notice that QuickBooks displays a checkmark next to all cleared items.

4 Close the Checking account register.

Student test and review

1 Use the checking account register to enter a handwritten check for $76.95. Use the next available check number and make the check payable to Express Delivery Service, for delivery of a new sign. Assign the check to the Freight & Delivery expense account.

2 Write a QuickBooks check to Bayshore Water for $143.87 to pay this month's water bill. Assign the check to the Utilities:Water expense account.

LESSON 5 Using other accounts in QuickBooks

Lesson objectives

- To introduce the other account types available in QuickBooks
- To learn how to track credit card transactions in QuickBooks
- To reconcile a credit card account
- To see how to make a credit card payment
- To discuss the different types of asset and liability accounts you can create and see how to track assets and liabilities in QuickBooks
- To introduce the subject of equity and QuickBooks equity accounts

Handout materials

- Handout 14: Determining the value of a fixed asset
- Handout 15: Tracking asset cost and depreciation
- Handout 16: Understanding QuickBooks equity accounts

Instructor preparation

- Review the lesson, including the examples, to make sure you're familiar with the material.
- Ensure that all students have a copy of qblesson.qbb on their computer's hard disk.
- Have Handouts 14 through 16 ready for distribution.

To start this lesson

Before you perform the following steps, make sure you have installed the exercise file (qblesson.qbb) on your hard disk. See "Installing the exercise file" in the Introduction to this guide if you haven't installed it.

The steps that follow will restore the exercise file to its original state so that the data in the file matches what you see on the screen as you proceed through each lesson.

To restore the exercise file (qblesson.qbb):

1. From the File menu in QuickBooks, choose Restore.

   QuickBooks displays the Restore Company Backup window.
2. In the "Get Company Backup From" section of the window, click Browse and select your c:\QBtrain directory.
3. Select the qblesson.qbb file, and then click Open.

4 In the "Restore Company Backup To" section of the window, click Browse and select your c:\QBtrain directory.

5 In the File name field of the Restore To window, type ***lesson 5*** and then click Save.

6 Click Restore.

Using other account types in QuickBooks

In this lesson, you'll learn about these types of QuickBooks accounts:

- **Credit card accounts**—Used to track transactions you pay for with a credit card.
- **Asset accounts**—Used to track both current assets (those assets you're likely to convert to cash or use up within one year, such as inventory on hand) and fixed assets (such as long-term notes receivable and depreciable assets your business owns that aren't liquid, such as equipment, furniture, or a building).
- **Liability accounts**—Used to track both current liabilities (those liabilities scheduled to be paid within one year, such as sales tax, payroll taxes, and short-term loans) and long-term liabilities (such as loans or mortgages scheduled to be paid over terms longer than one year).
- **Equity accounts**—Used to track owner's equity, including capital investment, draws, and retained earnings.

Tracking credit card transactions

In your business, you sometimes pay for expenses with a credit card rather than a check. For travel expenses especially, a credit card is invaluable because it gives a detailed listing of each charge. You can track your credit card transactions in QuickBooks just as easily as you track expenses you pay for by check.

You should set up a QuickBooks credit card account for each credit card you use in your business. Like any QuickBooks account, a credit card account has its own register. The register lists all the charges and credits you've recorded, as well as payments you've made.

The way you open and scroll through a credit card register is the same way you open and scroll through any QuickBooks account register.

Entering credit card charges

QuickBooks lets you choose when you enter your credit card charges. You can enter credit card charges when you charge an item or when you receive the bill. Your choice depends on whether you like to enter information into QuickBooks incrementally or all at once. The advantage to entering charges when you charge an item is that you can keep close track of how much you owe. In addition, if the charge is for a particular job, you can keep track of how much you're spending on that job.

Suppose you have a $30 gasoline charge you want to enter into QuickBooks. The form you use is the Enter Credit Card Charges form.

To enter a credit card charge:

1 From the Banking menu, choose Enter Credit Card Charges.

QuickBooks displays the Enter Credit Card Charges window.

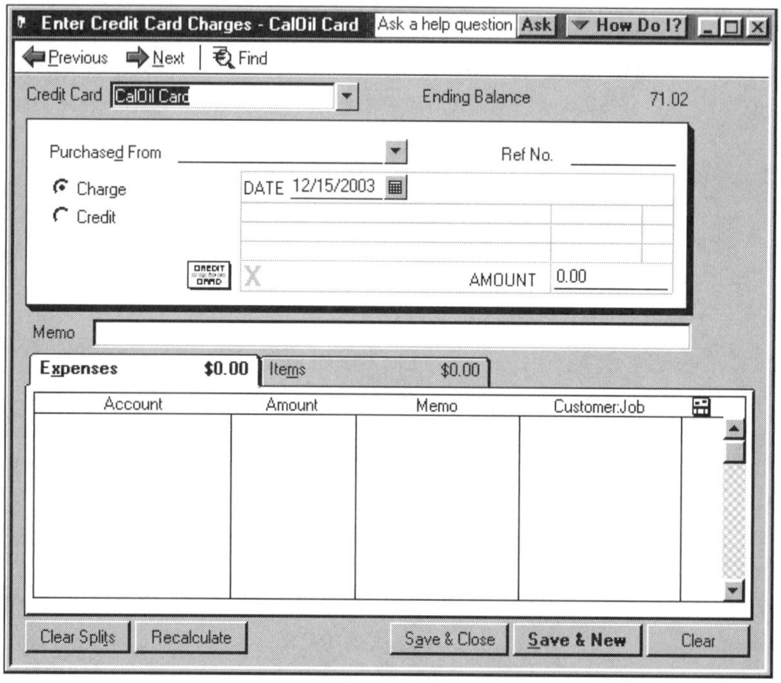

This is the window where you enter your charges. Notice that the form at the top of the window looks just like a familiar credit card charge slip.

2 In the Credit Card field, select CalOil Card from the drop-down list (if it's not already selected).

3 In the Purchased From field, select Bayshore CalOil Service from the drop-down list.

The next field is called Ref No. Most credit card receipts have some sort of transaction number near the top, which exists for identification and tracking purposes. Entering this number from a credit card receipt gives you additional information for the credit card charge, but you don't have to use it. You don't need to enter one for this example.

4 Click in the Amount field, and then double-click to select the entire amount.

5 Type ***30*** and then press Tab.

6 Click the Expenses tab.

7 In the detail area, click in the Account column and assign the charge to the Automobile:Fuel expense account, as shown in the figure below. (Automobile is the account; Fuel is the subaccount.)

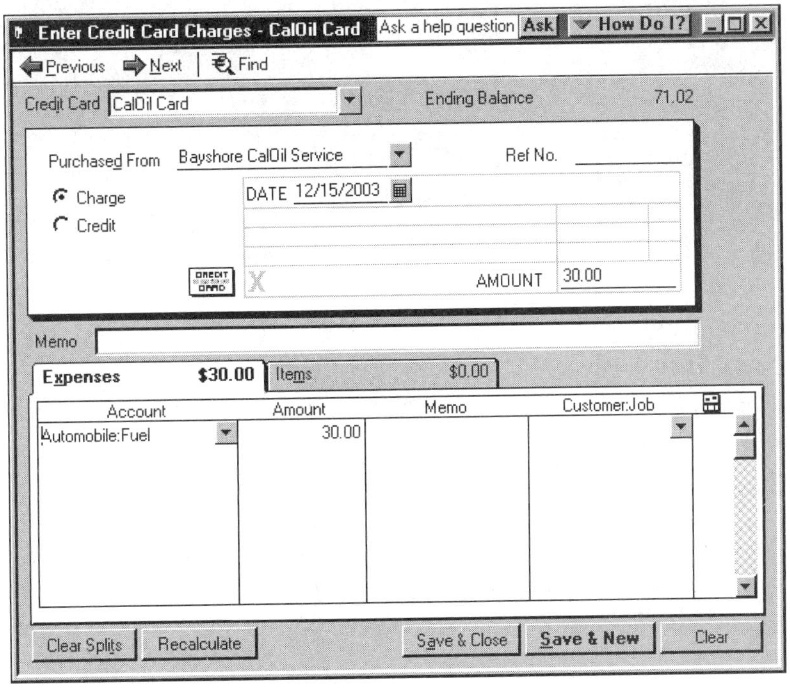

8 Click Save & Close to record the transaction and close the window.

After you record this credit card charge, QuickBooks adds a $30 transaction to the credit card account register (increasing the liability by $30). It also adds $30 to the Automobile:Fuel expense account. (You will see the increase when you create reports on their expense accounts.)

Reconciling a credit card statement

Just as we reconciled a bank account in the previous lesson, you should compare your credit card receipts with your statement and reconcile your credit card statement. Reconciling a credit card account is almost identical to reconciling a bank account.

To reconcile a credit card statement:

1 From the Company menu, choose Chart of Accounts.

QuickBooks displays the chart of accounts.

2 Click CalOil Card in the list once to select it.

3 Click the Activities menu button, and then choose Reconcile Credit Card.

QuickBooks displays the Begin Reconciliation window.

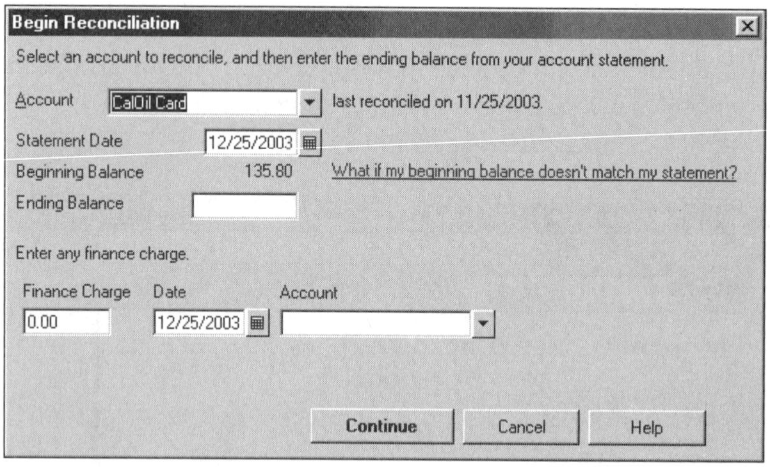

In the Opening Balance field, QuickBooks displays the balance of all cleared transactions in the credit card register. To reconcile a credit card statement, all you have to do is enter the ending balance and check off each transaction listed on your statement.

4 In the Statement Date field, enter 12/15/2003.

5 In the Ending Balance field, type ***101.02***.

Note: When the opening balance is different from the previous month's ending balance, check for cleared transactions that are now showing as uncleared.

6 Press Continue.

QuickBooks displays the Reconcile Credit Card window.

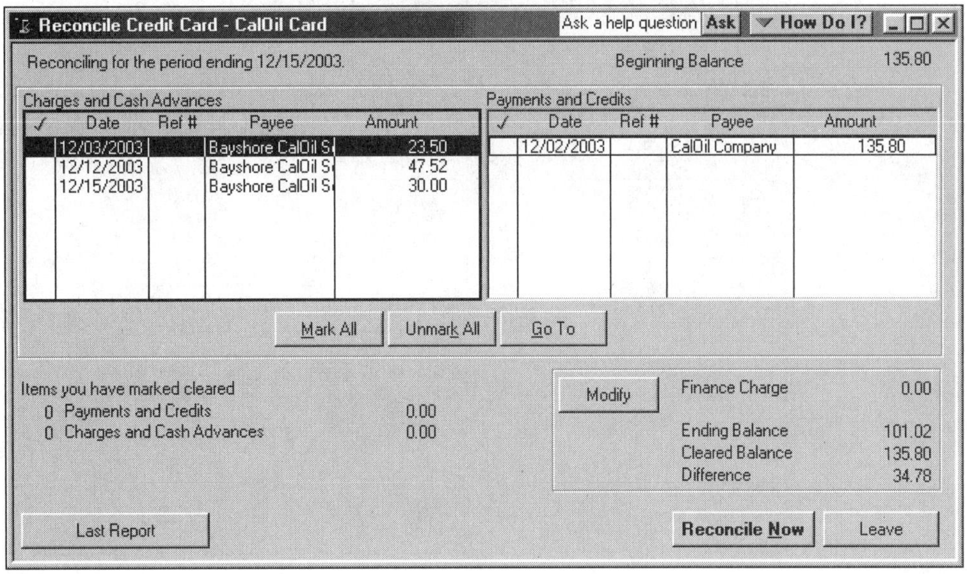

The Reconcile Credit Card window shows all the transactions for the credit card account that have not yet cleared. You'll use this window to check off the transactions listed on your statement.

Marking cleared transactions

To mark the transactions as cleared:

1 In the Charges and Cash Advances section of the window, select all three charges.

2 In the Payments and Credits section of the window, select the 12/02/03 payment for $135.80.

QuickBooks places a checkmark in the column to the left of each transaction you select. Your Reconcile Credit Card window should resemble the following figure.

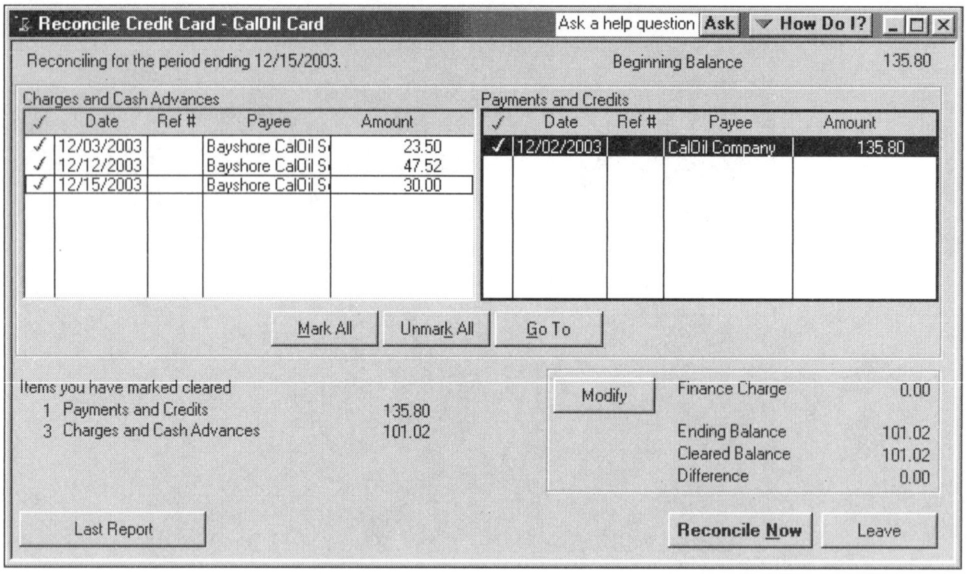

3 Click Reconcile Now.

QuickBooks displays the Make Payment window.

When you've finished reconciling a credit card account, QuickBooks gives you a chance to pay part or all of the balance due on your credit card.

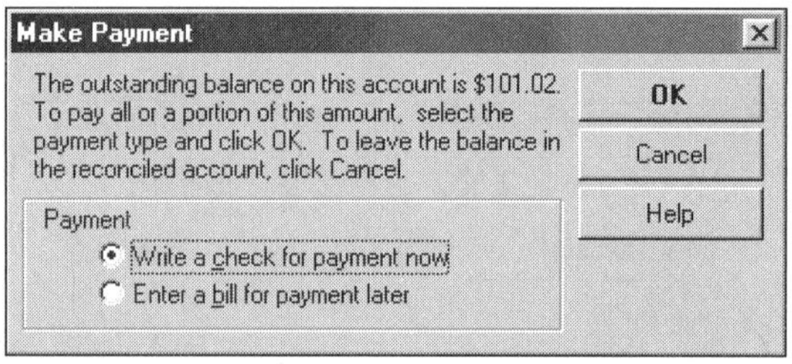

4 For this exercise, you want to write a check for payment now, so leave that option selected and click OK.

QuickBooks displays the Select Reconciliation Report window.

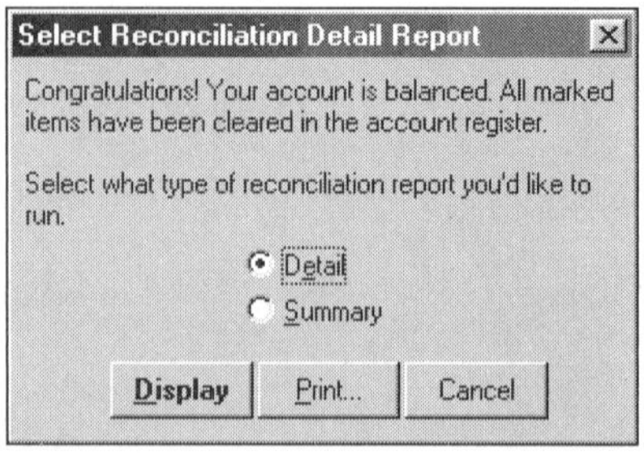

5 In the Select Reconciliation Report window, make sure Detail is selected and then click Display. (If you wanted to keep a copy of the reconciliation report, you would click Print, but you don't need to print the report for this lesson.)

6 Click OK at the message that QuickBooks displays.

7 Close the report.

Paying a credit card bill

To write a check for the bill now:

1 In the Write Checks window, make sure Checking is listed as the bank account.

Notice that QuickBooks has already filled in the amount of the payment for you, and has assigned the expense to the CalOil Card account. (If you change your mind and decide you only want to make a partial payment, you can change the amount here.)

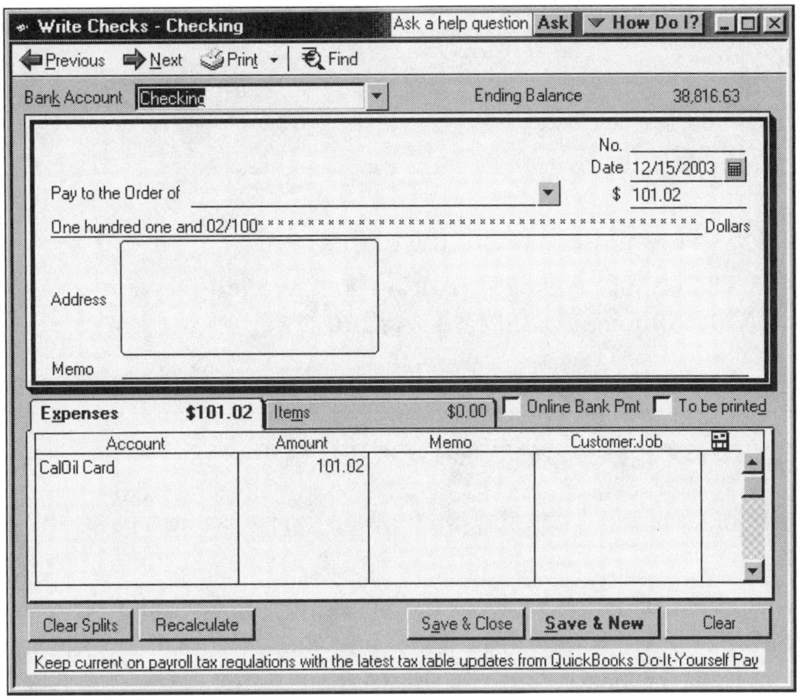

2 Click in the Pay to the Order of field and select CalOil Company as the name of the credit card company from the drop-down list.

3 Click in the "To be printed" checkbox to put a checkmark in it.

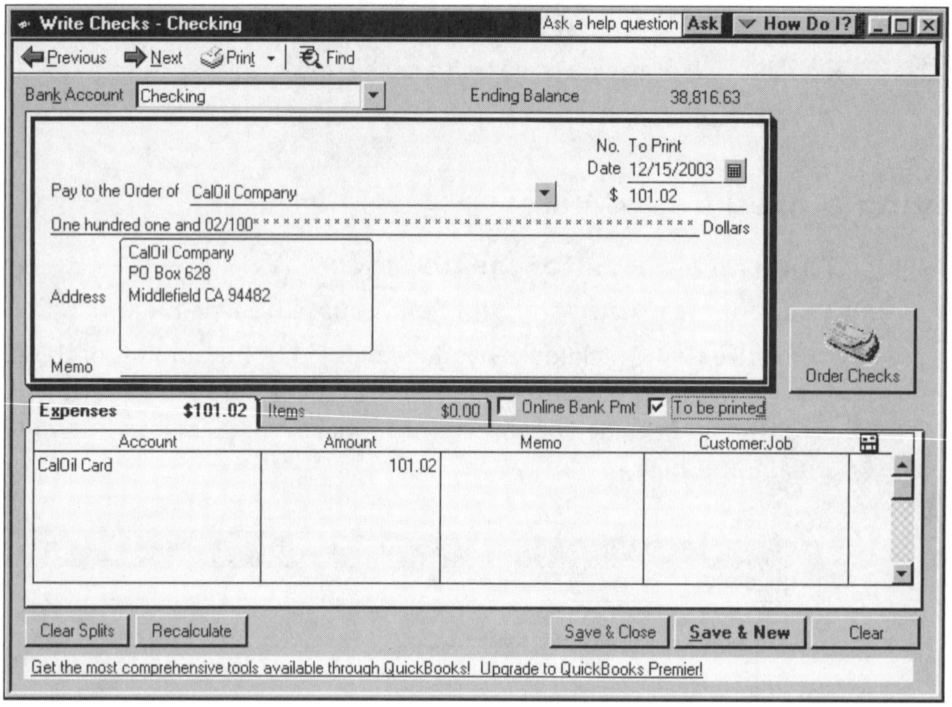

4 Click Save & Close to record the transaction.

QuickBooks subtracts $101.02 from your checking account and also subtracts that amount from your credit card account.

Working with asset accounts

QuickBooks has two account types for tracking the value of your short- and long-term assets:

- An Other Current Asset account tracks assets that are likely to be converted to cash or used up within one year. If you buy and sell inventory, the value of all your inventory on hand is usually shown in an Other Current Asset account called something like "Inventory Asset." Other current assets might include treasury bills, certificates of deposit, prepaid expenses (amounts already paid for services your business has yet to receive), prepaid deposits (which will be returned to you at a later date), reimbursable expenses, and notes receivable (if due within one year).

  Make sure you explain to students that some additional examples of other current assets are accounts receivable, bank accounts, and cash. QuickBooks provides three types of current asset accounts for you to use as you create asset accounts for your company: **bank account** *(to track each bank account as well as petty cash),* **accounts receivable** *(to track money owed to your business), and* **other current asset**.

- A Fixed Asset account tracks assets your business owns that are *not* likely to be converted into cash within a year. A fixed asset is usually something necessary for the operation of your business, like a truck, cash register, computer, or photocopier.

Setting up an Other Current Asset account

Suppose you need an Other Current Asset account to track a prepaid expense for rent. (The landlord requires a six-month advance payment.)

1 In the chart of accounts, click the Account menu button, and then choose New.

QuickBooks displays the New Account window.

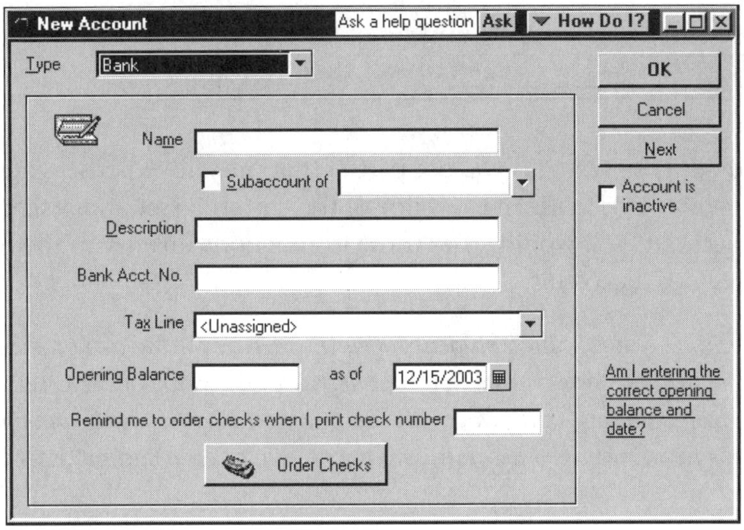

2 For the Type, choose Other Current Asset from the drop-down list.

3 In the Name field, type ***Prepaid rent.***

4 In the Opening Balance field, type ***6000.***

5 Click OK.

QuickBooks displays the new account in the chart of accounts.

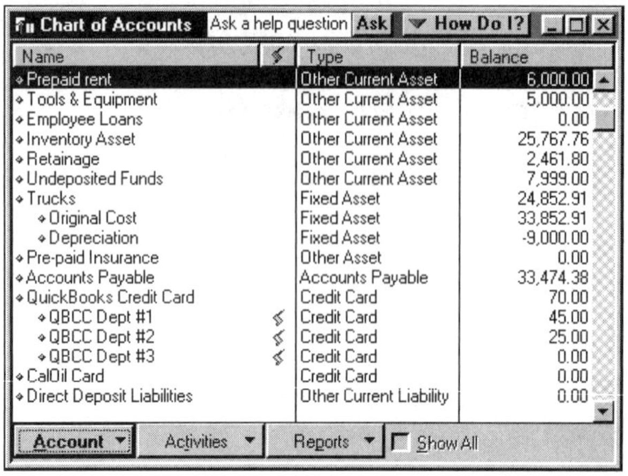

As each month goes by and you use part of that prepaid expense, you can enter each month's rent as a decrease in the value of the current asset and assign it to the rent expense account. You would enter those transactions directly in the register for the Prepaid rent asset account.

If you have time, you can have students open the register for the current asset account, and show them how to enter a transaction that decreases the value of the asset. If you don't feel you have time to do this, don't worry: the next section gives students an opportunity to enter transactions in a fixed asset account, and the procedure for a current asset is very similar.

Setting up asset accounts to track depreciation

There is more than one way to keep track of depreciation; this is just one suggested method. If you have students who are keeping track of asset depreciation in other ways, assure them that they can continue using their own method.

Refer to Handout 14, "Determining the value of a fixed asset," for this discussion.

Fixed assets are equipment or property your business owns that are not for sale. Since they last a long time, you don't completely charge their cost to the year in which you buy them. Instead, you spread their cost over several years. But because fixed assets wear out or become obsolete, their value declines constantly from the day you purchase them. The amount of this decline in value is called depreciation.

To determine the estimated value of a fixed asset at any point in time, you need to subtract its accumulated depreciation (total amount of depreciation since the asset's purchase) from its original cost.

Usually, you'll want your balance sheet to show the original cost of an asset (plus any subsequent improvements) on one line, with the accumulated depreciation subtracted from the original cost on a second line, and the current value (net) on a third line. The method you'll learn in this lesson lets you see each asset's cost and its accumulated depreciation separately on your balance sheet. You set up a separate fixed asset account for each asset, and two subaccounts under each fixed asset account: one for cost and one for accumulated depreciation.

You may want to have Handout 15, "Tracking asset cost and depreciation," displayed on an overhead projector as students go through the sample exercise.

In the next exercise, you'll set up an asset account to track depreciation on a new trailer purchased by Rock Castle Construction.

To set up asset accounts to track depreciation:

1. In the chart of accounts window, click the Account menu button, and then choose New.

   QuickBooks displays the New Account window.

2. In the Type field, choose Fixed Asset from the drop-down list.
3. In the Name field, type ***Trailer***.
4. Leave the opening balance blank, and click OK.

   QuickBooks displays the new fixed asset account in the chart of accounts.

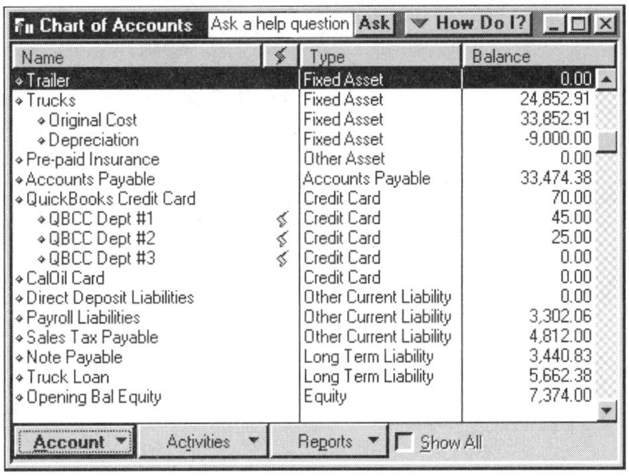

Now you need to add two subaccounts—one for the asset's cost, and the other for depreciation.

To add subaccounts:

1. In the chart of accounts window, click the Account menu button, and then choose New.
2. In the Type field, choose Fixed Asset from the drop-down list.
3. In the Name field, type ***Cost***.

4 Select the "Subaccount of" checkbox, and then select ***Trailer*** as the parent account.

5 Leave the opening balance blank.

Tip: **The opening balance is the original cost of the asset, if you purchased the asset before your QuickBooks start date.** If you're buying the asset now, as the owner of Rock Castle Construction is, you leave the opening balance for the Cost account blank. When you enter information about the loan Rock Castle Construction takes out to pay for the truck (later in this lesson), you'll update the Cost account with the truck's original cost.

Your screen should resemble the following figure.

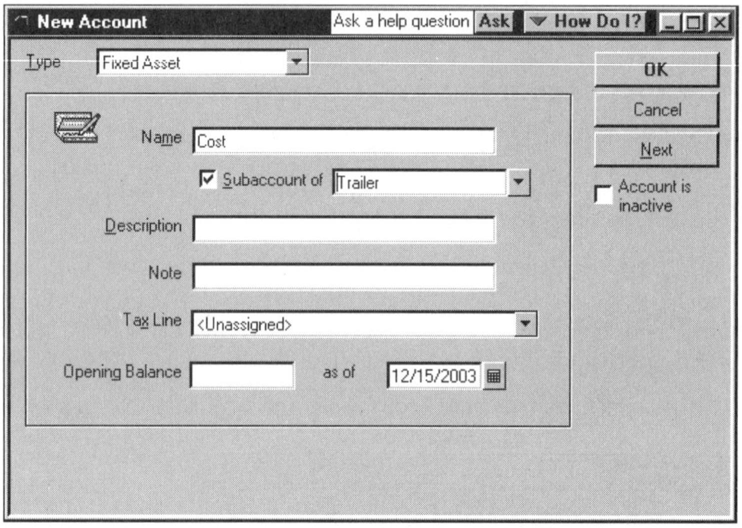

6 Click OK.

7 Repeat the previous steps to add a second subaccount to the Trailer fixed asset account. Call the subaccount "Accumulated Depreciation," and leave the opening balance blank.

The New Account window should look like this.

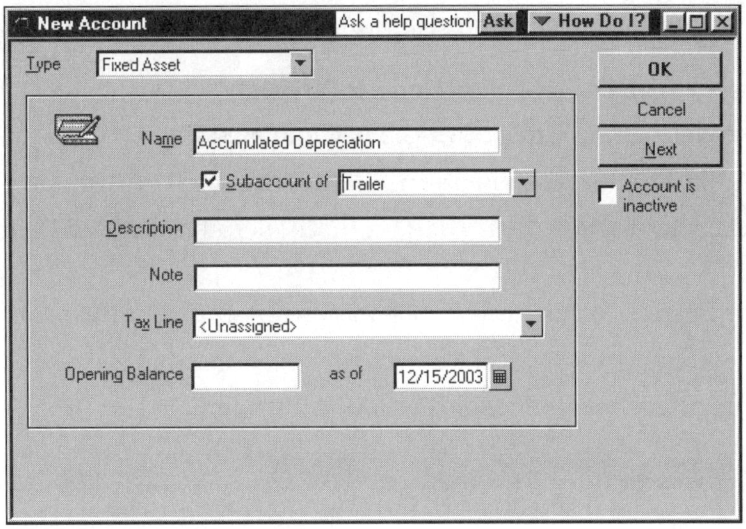

When you complete these steps, your chart of accounts should look like this.

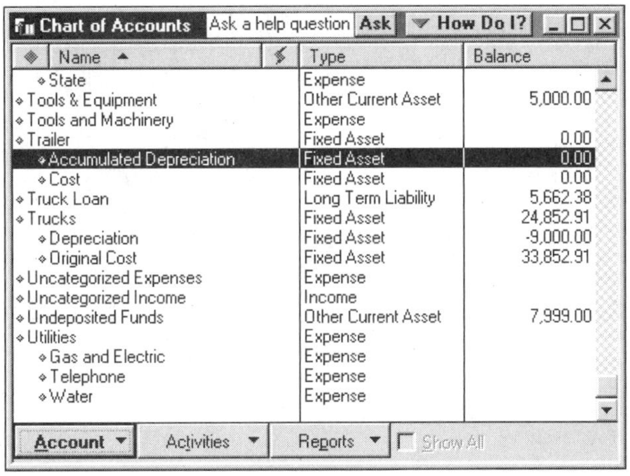

Note: **The amount you enter as the opening balance depends on whether you acquired the asset after or before your QuickBooks start date.** If you acquired the asset after your QuickBooks start date, you don't enter an opening balance. If you acquired the asset before your QuickBooks start date, you enter the accumulated depreciation of the asset as of the start date—entered as a negative number.

Entering depreciation transactions

When it's time to enter depreciation for an asset, you can use the register for the asset's accumulated depreciation account.

Determining the amount of depreciation to deduct can be a complex process, and the IRS rules on the subject change often. Students should ask a competent advisor for help in figuring actual depreciation amounts for tax purposes.

To enter a transaction for depreciation:

1 In the chart of accounts, select the Accumulated Depreciation subaccount.

2 Click the Activities menu button, and then choose Use Register.

QuickBooks displays the register for the Trailer:Accumulated Depreciation asset account.

3 In the Decrease column, type ***1300*** and press Tab. This is the depreciation amount.

4 In the Account field, select Depreciation Expense from the drop-down list.

Your register should resemble the following figure.

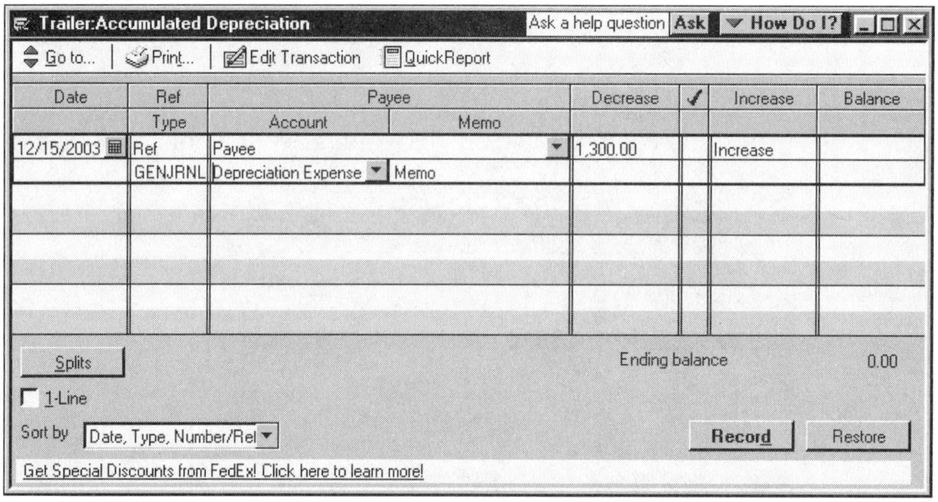

5 Click Record.

6 Close the register window.

When you record the transaction, QuickBooks does the following:

- Subtracts the depreciation amount from the current value of the asset in the asset's fixed asset account.
- Enters the depreciation amount as an increase to your company's depreciation expense in the expense account that tracks depreciation.

Working with liability accounts

QuickBooks has two account types for tracking the value of your short- and long-term liabilities:

- An Other Current Liability account tracks liabilities that your company expects to pay within a year. Other current liabilities might include short-term loans or a line of credit.

  Make sure you explain to students that some additional examples of other current liabilities are accounts payable, credit card accounts, accrued sales tax, and accrued payroll. QuickBooks provides three types of current liability accounts for you to use as you create liability accounts for your company: credit card, (to track credit card charges and payments), accounts payable (to track money owed by your business), and other current liability.

- A Long-term Liability account tracks debts that your business is *not* likely to pay off within a year. The most common long-term liabilities are loans that you expect to pay off in more than one year.

Tracking a loan with a long-term liability account

You've already added an asset account to track the value of the new trailer. Because the trailer loan is not going to be paid off in a year or less, you need to add a long-term liability account.

To add a long-term liability account:

1. In the chart of accounts, click the Account menu button, and then choose New.
2. In the New Account window, select Long Term Liability in the Type drop-down list.
3. In the Name field, type ***Trailer Loan***.

4 Leave the Opening Balance field blank.

Your screen should resemble the figure below.

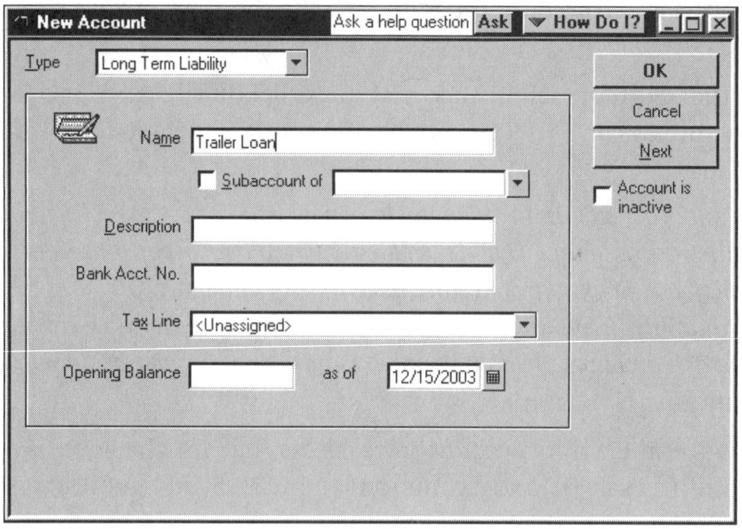

5 Click OK.

QuickBooks displays the new liability account in the chart of accounts.

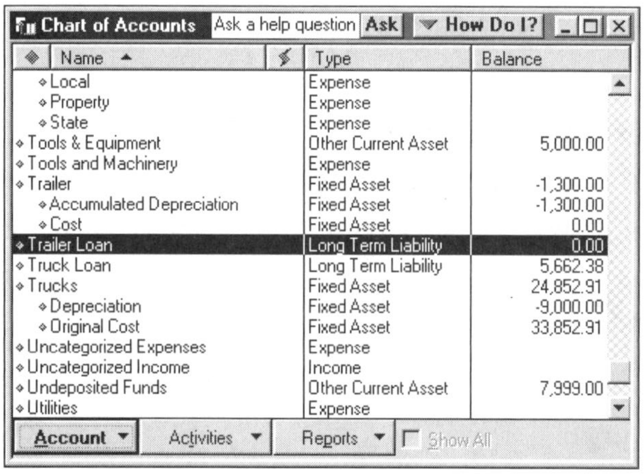

Because this is a new loan, you are either receiving money to deposit in your bank account or receiving a new asset. In this example, you received an asset (the new trailer), so you need to show an increase in the asset's Cost account.

To record an increase in the asset's Cost account:

1 In the chart of accounts, double-click the Trailer:Cost subaccount.

QuickBooks displays the Trailer:Cost register.

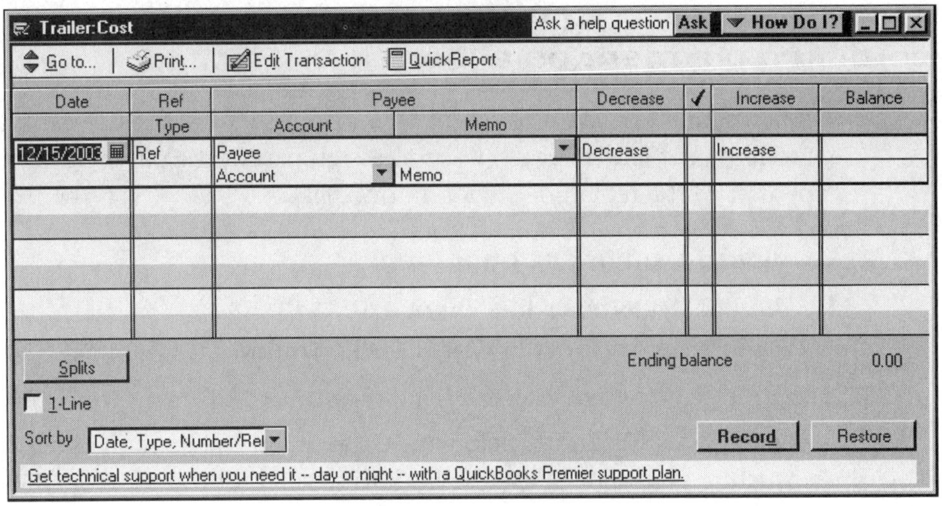

2 In the Increase field, type ***30,000***.

3 In the Account field, select the Trailer Loan liability account from the drop-down list.

Make sure that you select the Trailer Loan long-term liability account, not the Trailer fixed asset account.

Your screen should resemble the following.

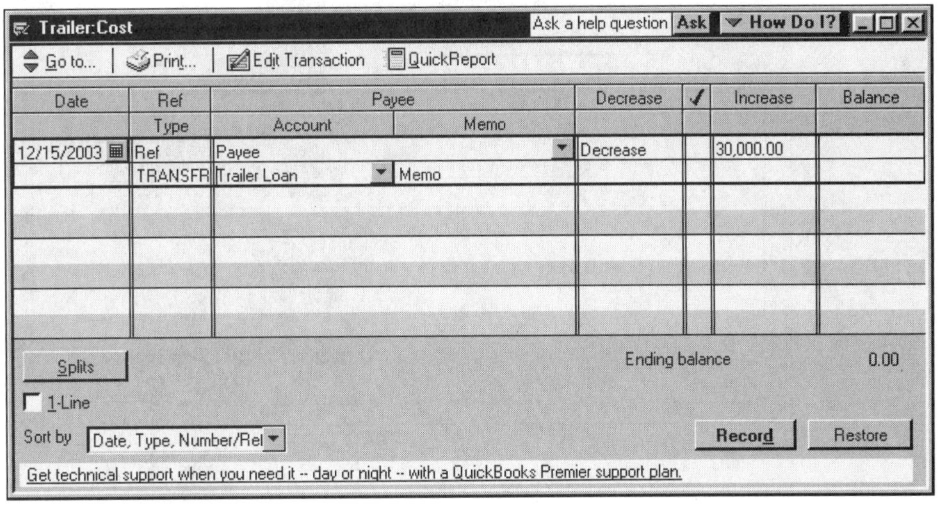

4 Click Record.

5 Close the register window.

6 Close the chart of accounts.

When you complete these steps, QuickBooks increases the value of your Cost asset account to 30,000. (This effectively sets the opening balance.) It also enters a liability of 30,000 in the liability account you use to track the loan. (Again, this sets the opening balance.)

Recording a payment on a loan

When it's time to make a payment on a loan, use the Write Checks window to record a check to your lender. You'll want to assign part of the payment to a loan interest expense and the remainder to loan principal.

To record a payment on a loan:

1 From the Banking menu, choose Write Checks.

QuickBooks displays the Write Checks window.

2 In the "Pay to the Order of" field, type ***Great*** and then press Tab.

QuickBooks fills in the field with Great Statewide Bank. If QuickBooks asks whether you want to use the last transaction for this vendor, click No.

3 For the dollar amount of the check, type ***500.00***.

4 Click the Expenses tab, and then click in the Account column and choose the Interest Expense:Loan Interest expense account from the drop-down list.

5 In the Amount column highlight the amount that QuickBooks prefilled and then type ***225.00***.

6 Assign the remainder of the expense (275.00) to the Trailer Loan liability account.

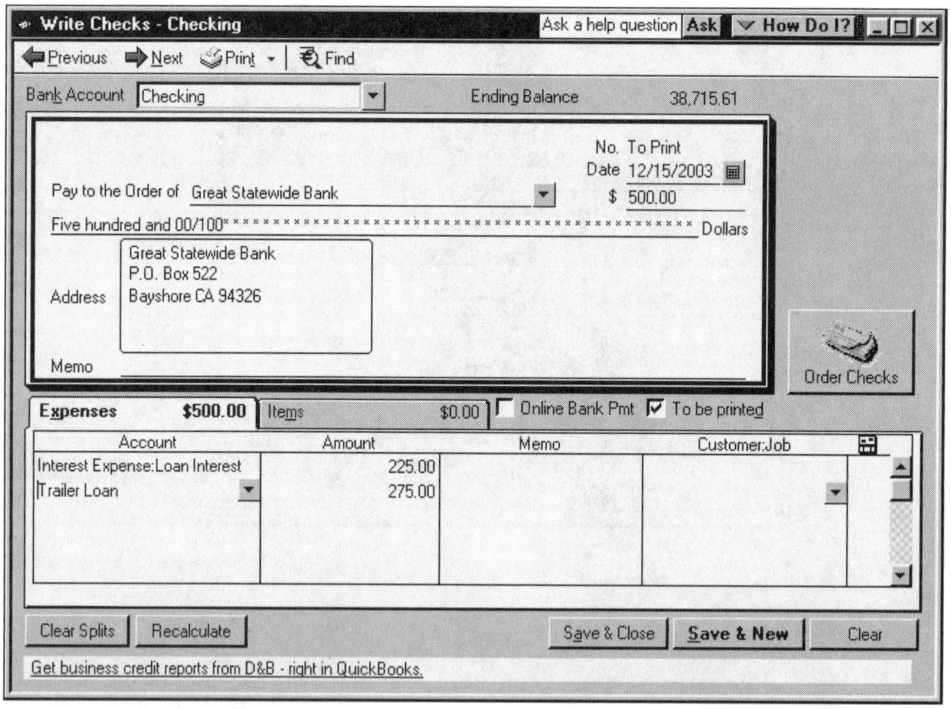

7 Click Save & Close to record the payment.

When you record the transaction, QuickBooks automatically updates the accounts affected by this transaction:

- In your checking account, QuickBooks subtracts the amount of the check from your balance.
- In the expense account that tracks interest, QuickBooks enters the interest amount as an increase to your company's interest expense.
- In the Trailer Loan liability account, QuickBooks subtracts the principal amount from the current value of the liability (reducing the amount of your debt).

Understanding equity accounts

Many students will see the equity accounts QuickBooks automatically adds for them, and wonder what equity is all about. Equity can be a complicated subject, especially for newer business owners, and a complete discussion of it is not the focus of this lesson. This section introduces the subject of equity, and helps students understand why QuickBooks creates the two default equity accounts.

Refer to Handout 16, "Understanding QuickBooks equity accounts," as you lead this discussion.

If you want to teach equity in more detail, see the discussion in the QuickBooks User's Guide.

Equity is the difference between what you have (your assets) and what you owe (your liabilities). If you sold all your assets today and paid off your liabilities using the money received from the sale of your assets, the money you'd have left would be your equity.

A balance sheet shows your company assets, liabilities, and equity on a particular date. Because equity is the difference between total assets and total liabilities, it's also true that total assets equal the sum of total liabilities and equity.

As you enter the opening balances of your assets and liabilities, QuickBooks calculates the amount of equity and records it in an equity account called Opening Bal Equity (Bal stands for Balance).

In addition to the Opening Bal Equity account, QuickBooks sets up another type of equity account for you called Retained Earnings. This account tracks your company's net income from previous fiscal years. QuickBooks automatically transfers your profit (or loss) to Retained Earnings at the end of each fiscal year.

If your company is a sole proprietorship (an unincorporated company with only one owner), you don't have to add any more equity accounts to your chart of accounts. All the equity belongs to the company's sole owner.

You can get as involved in tracking equity as you wish. Some people like to track owner investments, owner's draws, and retained earnings prior to their QuickBooks start date by putting them in separate equity accounts. If your business is a partnership, you'll probably want to set up separate equity accounts for each partner.

To learn more about equity and to learn how to set up equity accounts for your business, search the onscreen Help index for *equity*.

Student test and review

Assume that the owner of Rock Castle Construction has taken out a loan and purchased a computer system for $15,000. He wants to track the accumulated depreciation and cost of the system in two separate fixed asset accounts.

1. Create a fixed asset account called Computer System and two subaccounts—one for Cost and one for Accumulated Depreciation.
2. Create a long-term liability account to track the loan.

   Enter the amount of the loan as an increase in the asset's Cost account. Assign the transaction to the loan liability account.

LESSON 6 Entering sales and invoices

Lesson objectives

- To learn about the different formats available for sales forms
- To practice creating a new invoice
- To learn the purpose and use of the QuickBooks Item list
- To see how QuickBooks records the information you enter on sales forms
- To memorize an invoice transaction for reuse
- To add a new item to the Item list
- To add a new price level to the Price Level list
- To associate a price level with a customer
- To generate customer statements
- To create sales orders

Handout materials

- Handout 17: Create Invoices window
- Handout 18: Enter Sales Receipts window
- Handout 19: Choosing a format for sales forms
- Handout 20: Types of QuickBooks items

Instructor preparation

- Review this lesson, including the examples, to make sure you're familiar with the material.
- Ensure that all students have a copy of qblesson.qbb on their computer's hard disk.
- Have Handouts 17 through 20 ready for distribution.

To start this lesson

Before you perform the following steps, make sure you have installed the exercise file (qblesson.qbb) on your hard disk. See "Installing the exercise file" in the Introduction to this guide if you haven't installed it.

The steps that follow will restore the exercise file to its original state so that the data in the file matches what you see on the screen as you proceed through each lesson.

To restore the exercise file (qblesson.qbb):

1. From the File menu in QuickBooks, choose Restore.

   QuickBooks displays the Restore Company Backup window.
2. In the "Get Company Backup From" section of the window, click Browse and select your c:\QBtrain directory.
3. Select the qblesson.qbb file, and then click Open.
4. In the "Restore Company Backup To" section of the window, click Browse and select your c:\QBtrain directory.
5. In the File name field of the Restore To window, type ***lesson 6*** and then click Save.
6. Click Restore.

Using sales forms in QuickBooks

Any time you make a sale in your business, you record it in QuickBooks on a sales form. A sales form can be an invoice (when you expect payment to come later), a sales receipt (when you expect payment at the time you make the sale), or a credit memo.

You use a credit memo when a customer returns merchandise for which you've already entered a payment or a cash sale. This lesson shows students how to use invoices and sales receipts.

When to use different types of sales forms

The type of sales form you use depends on whether you expect payment in the future or at the time of the sale.

For payment in the future

If you expect to receive payment at some future date, you enter an invoice. The invoice lists the customer's name and address, along with an itemized list of how much that customer owes.

Refer to Handout 17, "Create Invoices window."

To display a completed invoice form in QuickBooks:

1. From the Customers menu, choose Create Invoices.

   QuickBooks displays the Create Invoices window.

2 Click Previous to display the previously created invoice.

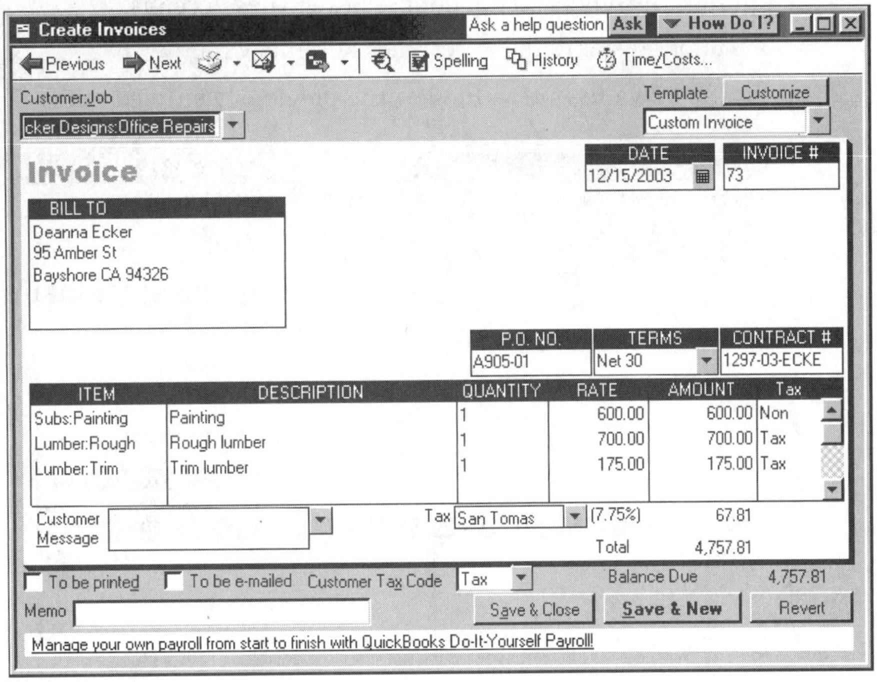

If you own a business that sells products, like Rock Castle Construction, your invoice lists the products purchased by the customer, the amount charged for each item, and any sales tax you need to apply. Notice that Rock Castle Construction's invoice charges for both products and services (such as labor).

A business that sells mainly services, such as a consulting firm, might use a different type of sales form than the one shown above. QuickBooks lets you choose from three different preset formats for your sales forms, or you can create your own customized forms.

3 Close the Create Invoices window.

For payment at the time of sale

Refer to Handout 18, "Enter Sales Receipt window."

If you receive payment at the time you make a sale—either by cash, check, or credit card—you fill out a sales receipt instead of an invoice. Like the invoice, the QuickBooks sales receipt includes information about the items or services purchased, but it also includes information about how payment was made.

To display a completed sales receipt in QuickBooks:

1. From the Customers menu, choose Enter Sales Receipts.

   QuickBooks displays the Enter Sales Receipts window.

2. Click the Previous button to view the previously entered sale.

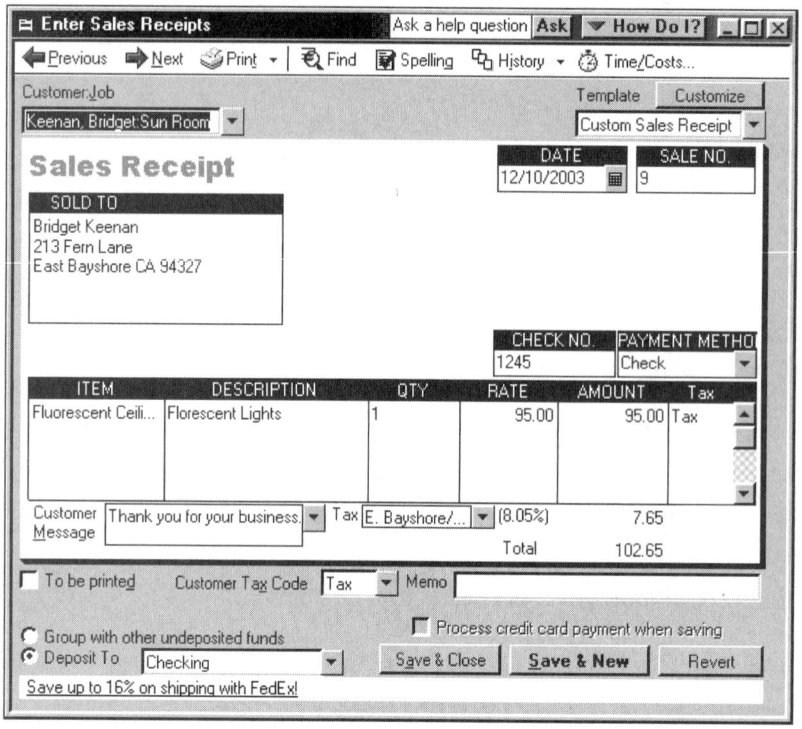

   The sales receipt is similar to the invoice—both forms display customer information and describe the items and services purchased. However, because payment is made at the time of sale, the sales receipt has deposit information at the bottom of the window.

3. Close the Enter Sales Receipts window.

Choosing a format for sales forms

Refer to Handout 19, "Choosing a format for sales forms."

QuickBooks has four different formats for invoices: Service, Professional, Product, and Custom.

- Use the Service format if you primarily sell services but occasionally sell goods.
- Use the Professional format if you sell services and need a lot of room for descriptions of your services.
- Use the Product format if you sell parts or products and need fields relevant to shipping.
- Use the Custom format if you want to tailor a form to your type of business.

As you review Handout 19 with students, ask them to give you examples of the types of businesses that fit the description given in the table. (You may want them to describe their own businesses and choose the format that best applies.)

Here are some examples: A typical business that would use the Service format is an interior design firm, because it sells both consulting services and products (such as fabric or furniture). A typical business that would use the Professional format is a law office or a medical/dental office. A retail store or mail-order business would be a typical user of the Product format.

Each format has an onscreen version and a printed version. This lets you record all the sales detail you need, but print only what you want customers to see. For example, if you use the Professional format, the onscreen version shows the number of hours you're billing the client as well as your hourly rate; the printed version shows only the Description and the Amount fields.

You'll learn how to customize forms in Lesson 15, "Customizing forms and writing QuickBooks Letters."

Filling in a sales form

Suppose Rock Castle Construction wants to bill a customer for a portion of a kitchen remodeling job. Because they expect payment to be made in the future (rather than cash on the spot), they need to create an invoice.

Filling in the customer information

Filling in an invoice is just like filling in a paper form; you enter the customer information first, followed by a description of the charges.

To enter customer information on an invoice:

1. From the Customers menu, choose Create Invoices.

   Notice that the new invoice already has the current date (12/15/2003 in the sample file) entered in the Date field, and the next invoice number assigned in the Invoice # field.

2. In the Customer:Job field, click the arrow next to the drop-down list.

   QuickBooks shows you a list of Rock Castle Construction's existing customers and jobs.

3 Choose Jacobsen, Doug:Kitchen for the customer and job.

Because this name has already been entered on the Customer:Job list, QuickBooks knows the billing name, the address, and the payment terms. It provides this information for you on the top half of the form.

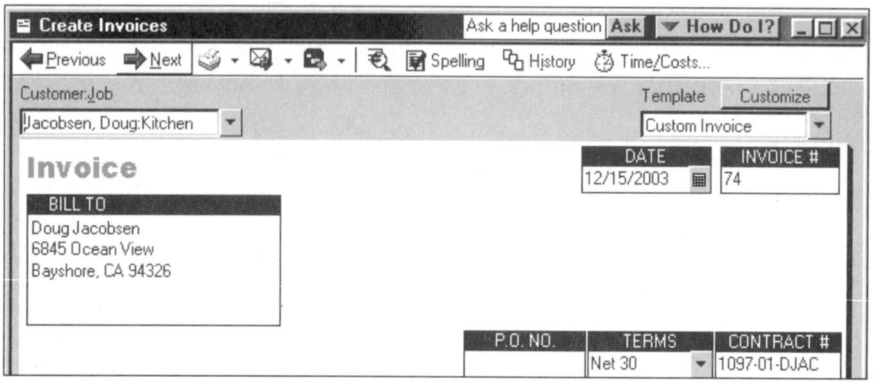

Filling in the line item area

On the bottom half of the invoice, you list each service or product you're selling on its own line, along with the amount the customer owes for that item. Because information about individual items is on separate lines, the lines are called line items.

In QuickBooks, you enter line items using the Item list, so you don't have to type and retype lines for services or products you sell frequently. For example, an architect would have one item for design and another for construction supervision.

But items are not just products you sell or services you provide to clients. Line items can be anything you might want to put in the detail area of an invoice, like a discount, a subtotal line, a markup, or a sales tax calculation.

Refer to Handout 20, "Types of QuickBooks items," as you explain the types of information stored in the QuickBooks Item list.

Rock Castle Construction has already entered the items for which it bills customers on its Item list.

To complete the line item area of an invoice:

1 In the Item field, type the letters ***rem*** (for Removal).

QuickFill is an alternative to choosing from a list. Whenever you're in a field where you'll use a list item, you can start typing the first letter or two of the list item you want, and QuickBooks fills in the field with the item that matches the letters you're typing.

2 Press Tab.

When you press Tab to accept a QuickFill entry, QuickBooks fills in other information about the item, like its description and rate. In this case, QuickBooks displays "Removal labor" in the Description column and a rate of $35 per hour. All you have to do is enter the number of hours.

3 Press Tab again and type ***40*** in the Quantity column.

4 Press Tab to have QuickBooks update the invoice total.

ITEM	DESCRIPTION	QUANTITY	RATE	AMOUNT	Tax
Removal	Removal labor	40	35.00	1,400.00	Non

Completing the sales form

You may want to let students know that Intuit has preprinted invoices they can purchase. The invoices are designed especially for use with QuickBooks and present a professional, easy-to-read image.

If you want to check the form before you print it, you can use the print preview feature in the Create Invoices window.

To complete and record the invoice:

1 On the Create Invoices window toolbar, click the Print drop-down arrow, and then choose Preview.

QuickBooks displays the invoice page as it will look when printed.

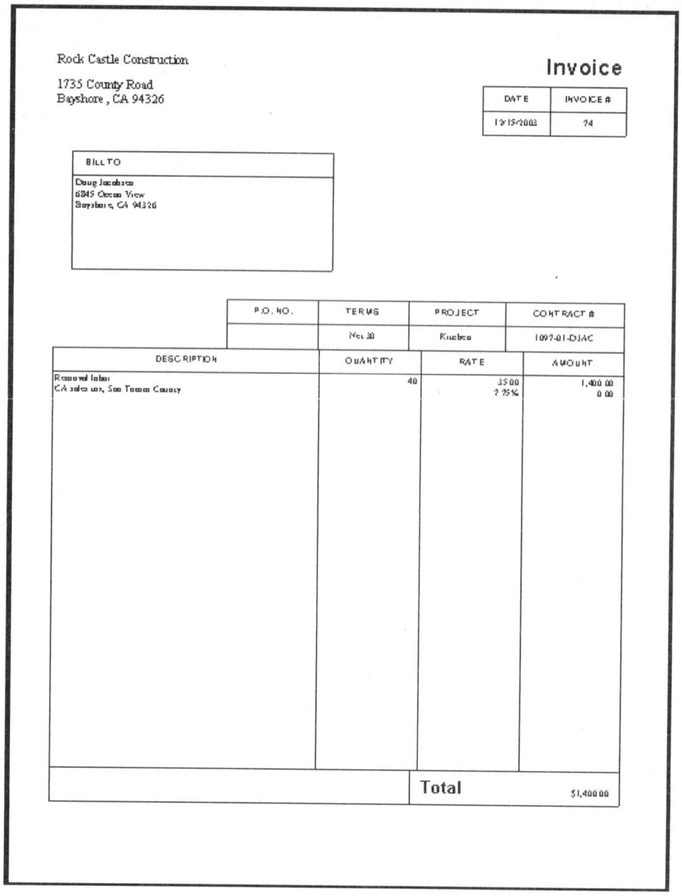
Rock Castle Construction

1735 County Road
Bayshore , CA 94326

Invoice

DATE	INVOICE #
12/15/2003	24

BILL TO

Doug Jacobsen
6845 Ocean View
Bayshore, CA 94326

P.O. NO.	TERMS	PROJECT	CONTRACT #
	Net 30	Kitchen	1097-01-DJAC

DESCRIPTION	QUANTITY	RATE	AMOUNT
Removal labor	40	35.00	1,400.00
CA sales tax, San Tomas County		7.75%	0.00
		Total	$1,400.00

2 Click Zoom In and use the scroll bars to see the invoice items at greater magnification.

3 Click Close.

4 In the Create Invoices window, record the sale by clicking Save & Close.

QuickBooks records the invoice in your accounts receivable register. If this were a sales receipt, QuickBooks would record the sale in your Undeposited Funds account until you deposit the money at the bank, or record a deposit in the bank account you specified in the Enter Sales Receipts window.

The accounts receivable register keeps track of how much money your customers owe you.

To see the Accounts Receivable register:

1 From the Company menu, choose Chart of Accounts.

QuickBooks displays the chart of accounts.

2 In the chart of accounts, double-click the Accounts Receivable account.

QuickBooks displays the accounts receivable register.

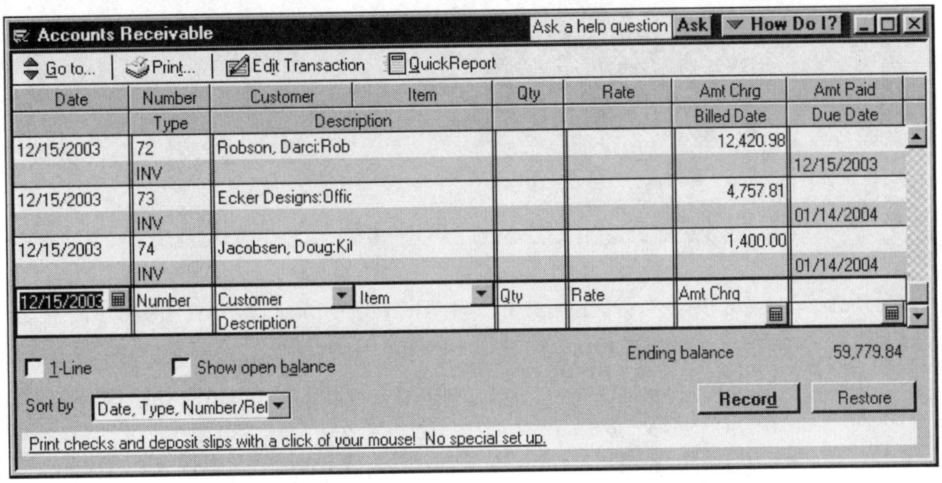

3 Select the sale we just recorded in the register (for Doug Jacobsen).

4 Double-click the entry.

When you double-click an entry in a register, QuickBooks displays the original form (in this case, the invoice).

5 Keep the invoice window open, you'll use it in the next exercise.

Make sure students keep this invoice displayed on the screen. You'll show them how to memorize it in the next section.

Memorizing a sale

Many of the sales you make in your business are ones you repeat again and again. For example, you may have a standing monthly order from a customer, or you may perform essentially the same services for more than one client. QuickBooks lets you memorize sales forms so that you don't have to retype the information.

To memorize the invoice:

1 Make sure you have the invoice you want to memorize displayed on your screen.

2 From the Edit menu, choose Memorize Invoice.

QuickBooks displays the Memorize Transaction window.

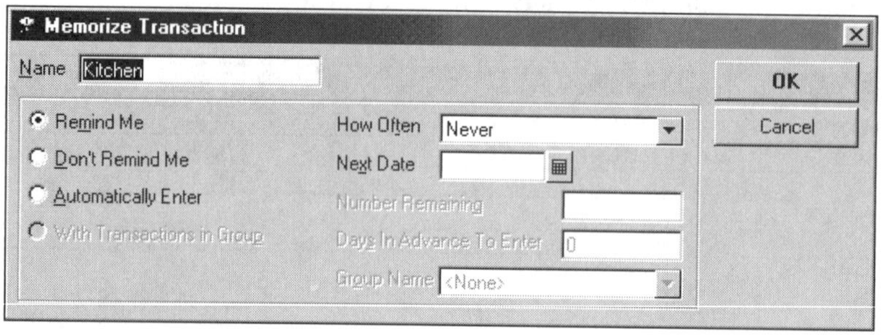

3 Type a description that helps you recognize the memorized invoice, or keep the default description QuickBooks has provided.

You can enter any description you like. Notice that you can also have QuickBooks remind you when to use the memorized transaction (for an invoice you always send at the end of the month, for example).

4 Click OK.

5 From the Window menu, choose Close All.

When you memorize an invoice, QuickBooks adds it to the Memorized Transaction list.

To recall a memorized sale:

1 From the Lists menu, choose Memorized Transaction List.

QuickBooks displays the Memorized Transaction List window.

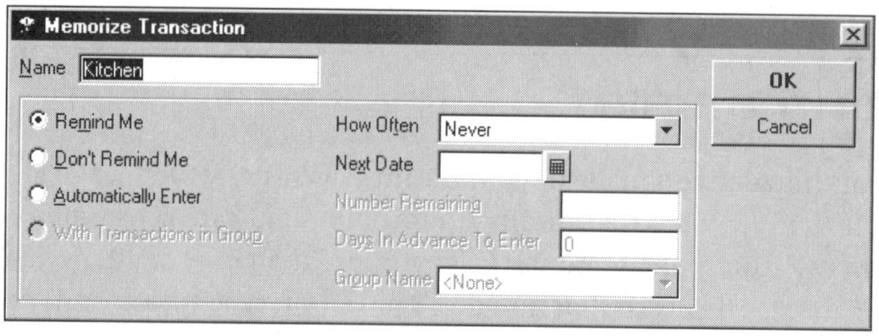

2 Double-click the transaction you just added.

QuickBooks displays the Create Invoices window, with the information you memorized displayed on the form. It gives you a new invoice number and displays the current date. You can modify the information as you wish, or just save the invoice as is.

3 Click Save & Close to record the invoice.

4 Close the Memorized Transaction list.

Entering a new service item

When you begin using your own QuickBooks company file, you'll need to create your own line items to include on your invoices. In the next exercise, you'll see how to add information to the Item list.

Rock Castle Construction already has a service item called Repairs that it uses when it wants to charge for general repair work. Suppose Rock Castle wants to add a subitem for plumbing repairs to the Item list. (The company charges a higher rate for plumbing repairs, so it wants a separate item for it on its Item list.)

Have students refer to Handout 20 for a review of the types of items you can add to the Item list.

To create a new service item:

1 From the Customers menu, choose Item List.

QuickBooks displays the Item list for Rock Castle Construction.

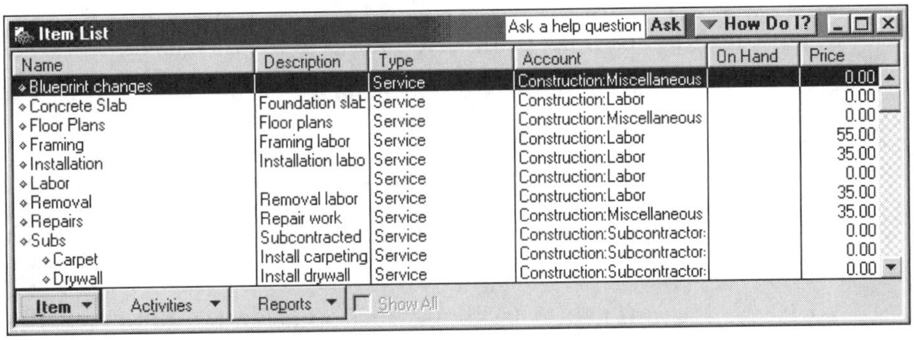

2 Click the Item menu button, and then choose New.

QuickBooks displays the New Item window.

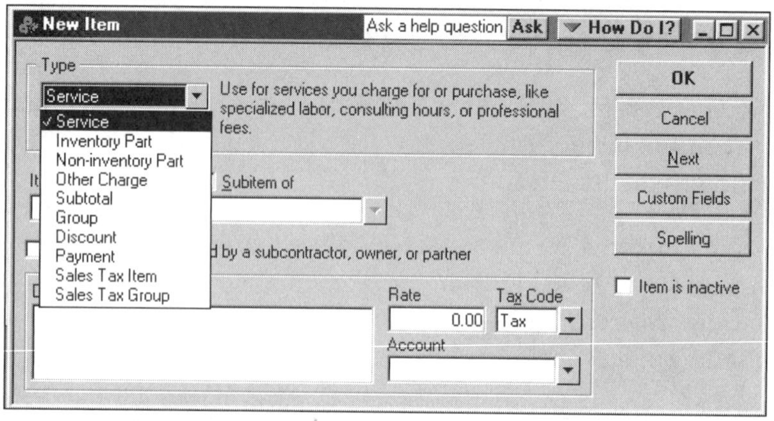

If you're using a QuickBooks Premier product, you'll also see Assembly Item listed as an item type.

3 In the Type field, select Service from the drop-down list.

4 In the Item Name/Number field, type ***Plumbing***.

5 Click the "Subitem of" checkbox to select it.

6 In the drop-down list below the "Subitem of" field, select Repairs.

7 In the Description field, type ***Plumbing repairs and maintenance*** and Press Tab.

8 In the Rate field, type ***55***.

9 In the Tax Code drop-down list, select Non.

Now you need to assign this line item to one of Rock Castle Construction's income accounts.

10 In the Account field, select Construction:Labor from the drop-down list.

Your screen should look like the following figure.

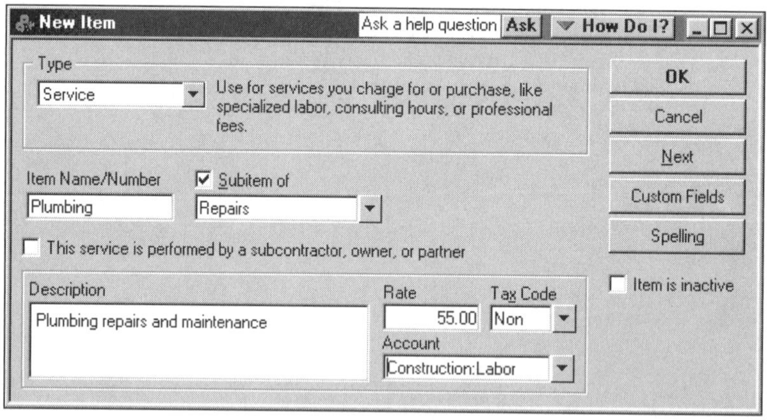

11 Click OK to add the new item to Rock Castle Construction's Item list.

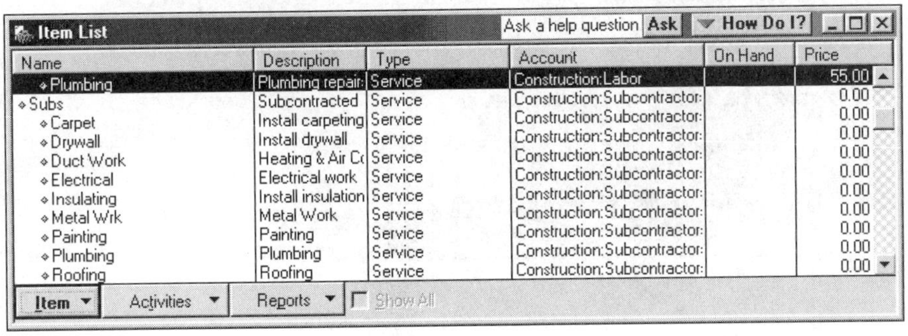

12 Close the Item list.

Now that the new item is on the Item list, Rock Castle Construction can invoice for plumbing repairs separate from its general repair work. It can also create sales reports that show sales for general repairs separate from sales for plumbing repairs.

Using multiple price levels

In the last exercise, you set up a new service item for Rock Castle construction and assigned a price to that item. Sometimes businesses want to vary an item's price based on who they are selling to. For example, Rock Castle Construction charges different prices depending on whether it is selling to a residential or a commercial customer.

You can associate price levels with specific customers so that each time you create an invoice (or other sales form) for that customer, QuickBooks uses the appropriate price level when calculating rates and amounts on the form. Price levels make it easy to use different rates on sales forms without having to calculate percentage amounts manually. Price levels affect amounts for service, inventory, and non-inventory part items only.

In this section, you'll create a new price level, associate it with one of Rock Castle's customers, and then create an invoice for that customer.

Note: **The ability to create multiple price levels is not available in QuickBooks Basic. You must be using QuickBooks Pro or Premier to complete the rest of this lesson.**

Creating new price levels

Rock Castle Construction charges its residential customers the base sales price it set up on its Item list. The company charges its commercial customers 10 percent less than the base sales price. In this exercise, you'll create a new price level for Rock Castle Construction to use to reduce the sales amount for its commercial customers.

For each price level you create, you assign a name and percentage increase or decrease to the item's base sales price. You can create up to 20 price levels to use on invoices, sales receipts, and credit memos.

To create a new price level:

1 From the Lists menu, choose Price Level List.

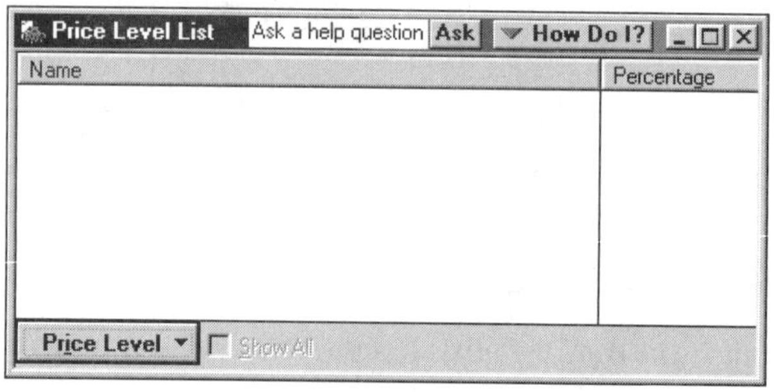

2 From the Price Level menu button, choose New.

3 In the Price Level field type ***Commercial***.

4 Make sure the "Reduce sales price by" checkbox is selected, and then type ***10*** in the Percentage field.

Always enter the percentage as a positive number.

5 Click OK.

Your screen should now resemble the following.

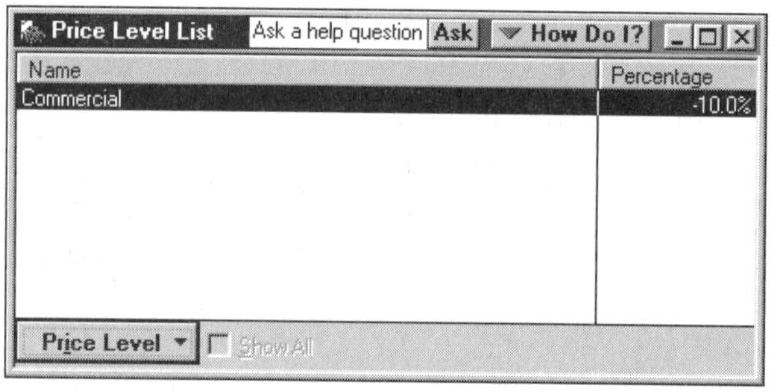

6 Close the Price Level list.

Associating price levels with customers

When you assign price levels to customers, QuickBooks calculates rates and amounts on sales forms based on the price level associated with that customer.

To associate a price level with a customer:

1 From the Customers menu, choose Customer:Job List.

2 From the Customer:Job drop-down list, choose Lew Plumbing - C.

3 From the Customer:Job menu button, choose Edit, and then click the Additional Info tab.

4 From the Price Level drop-down list, choose Commercial.

Your screen should look like this.

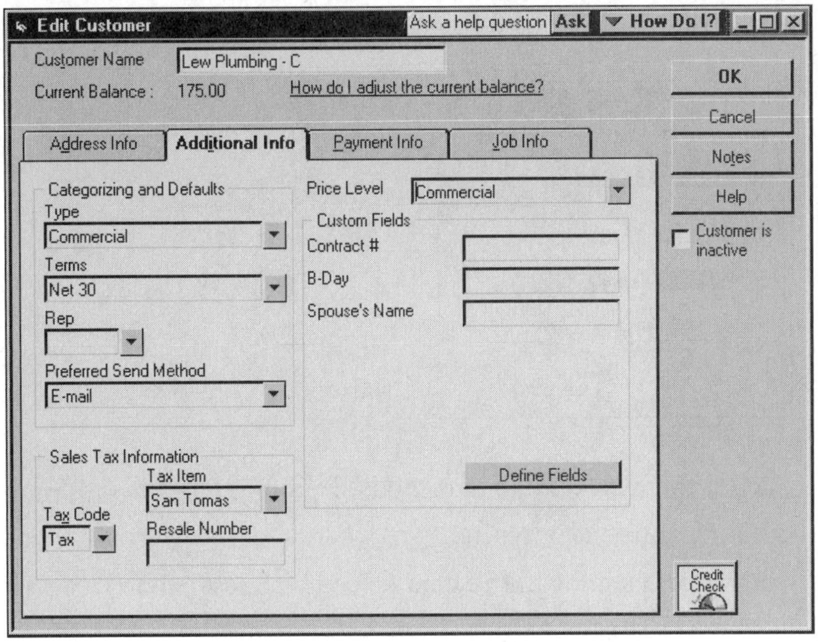

5 Click OK to close the Edit Customer window and save your changes.

6 Close the Customer:Job list.

Using price levels on sales forms

In this section, you'll create an invoice for the customer with whom you just associated the Commercial price level to see how the price level affects amounts on the form.

To use a price level associated with a customer:

1 From the Customers menu, choose Create Invoices.

2 From the Customer:Job drop-down list, choose Lew Plumbing - C.

Notice that QuickBooks displays the name of the price level associated with this Customer:Job in parentheses above the Customer:Job drop-down list. (This information will not be printed on the form.)

3 Click in the Item column and choose Framing from the drop-down list.

4 In the Quantity field, type ***8***.

5 Click below Framing in the Item field and choose Wood Door:Exterior from the drop-down list.

6 In the Quantity field, type ***2***.

Your screen should look like this.

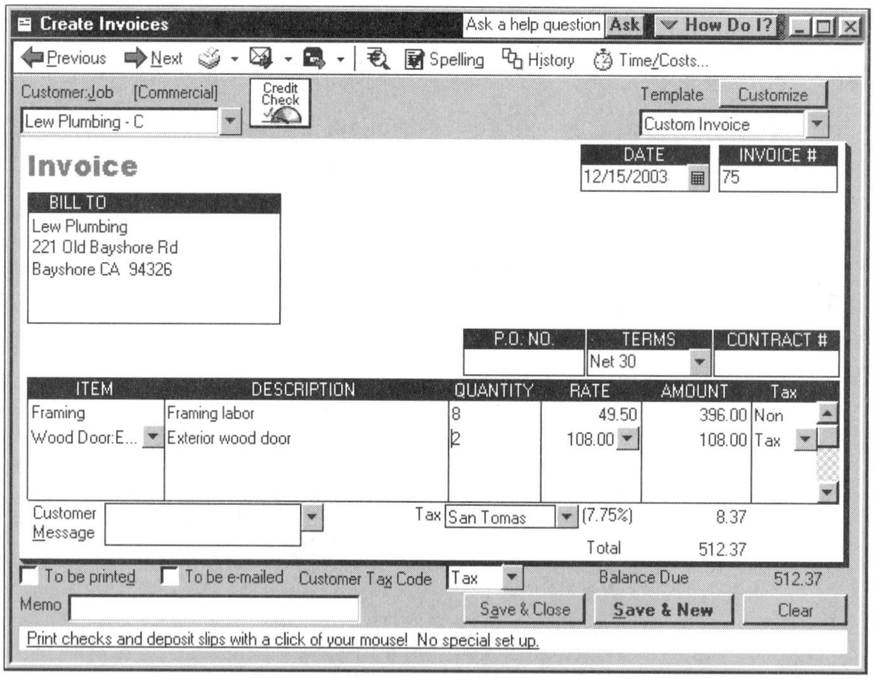

7 Keep the invoice open and choose Item List from the Lists menu.

8 In the Item list, go to Framing. Note that the price for framing is $55.00, but the rate on the invoice is $49.50—10 percent less than the base sales price. QuickBooks has automatically reduced the rate on the invoice by 10 percent.

Note: You can set up QuickBooks to round rates up to the next whole dollar. From the Edit menu, choose Preferences. Choose Sales & Customers from the scroll list and then click the Company Preferences tab. Click the "Round all sales prices up to the next whole dollar" checkbox and click OK.

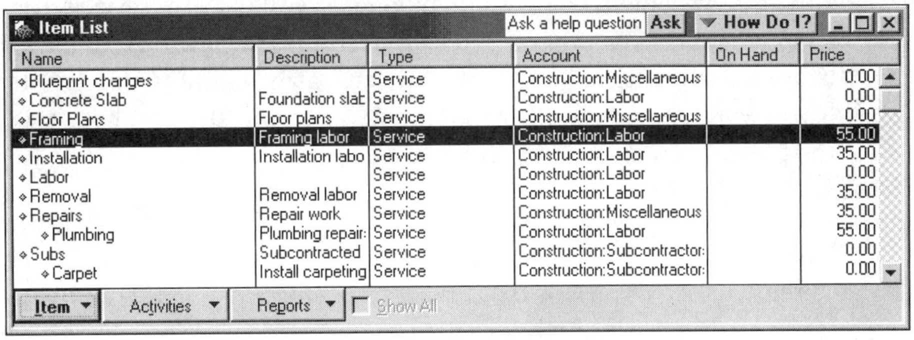

9 Scroll to the Wood Door:Exterior item and note that the base sales price is $120—10 percent greater than the rate listed on the invoice using the Commercial price level.

10 Close the Item list.

11 Record the invoice by clicking Save & Close.

Assigning price levels to individual line items

In addition to associating price levels with customers, you can also use price levels on an individual basis on sales forms. The following are some examples of when you might want to do this.

- You've associated a price level with a customer, but want to charge the base sales price for an item on a sale to that customer.
- You want to use a price level for one or more items, but you don't want to assign a price level to the customer for whom you're recording the sale.

To apply a price to a single line item:

- Click in the Rate column and select the price level you want to use from the drop-down list that displays.

  When you move out of that field on the form, QuickBooks recalculates the amount and balance due.

Using statements to bill customers

Another option for billing customers is to send statements. Statements are ideal if you want to accumulate charges before requesting payment, or if you assess a regular monthly charge. *Billing* statements list the charges a customer has accumulated over a period of time.

You enter statement charges one by one, as you perform services for the customer. Later, you print a billing statement that shows the previous balance, details of all new charges, payments received, and the new balance. Billing statements are appropriate if you want to send monthly statements that show the detail of new charges as well as the previous balance and payments received.

If you bill the same charge to a group of customers on a regular basis, you can set up QuickBooks to enter the charges automatically when it's time to send out your statements. Any business that bills a recurring charge on statements can use this feature. For more information, search the onscreen Help index for *memorized transactions, for statement charges*.

Reminder statements summarize a customer's account with your company by listing recent invoices, credit memos, and payments received. You use reminder statements when you bill through invoices but want to remind your customers about delinquent payments.

Reminder statements are different than other "forms" in QuickBooks such as invoices, sales receipts, or checks. Because QuickBooks already has all the information you need to create reminder statements, you don't have to fill them out. Instead, you review the information that will appear on each statement, decide whether to add finance charges, and print them.

Understanding statement limitations

In QuickBooks, statements have the following limitations:

- You can't record sales tax, percentage discounts, payment items, or group items as a separate charge on a billing statement. To bill for any of these, you must use an invoice.
- You cannot group related charges together and subtotal them (you can group and subtotal charges on an invoice).
- A charge on a billing statement can represent only one item (in contrast, an invoice can represent many items). This means you must enter a separate statement charge for each service or product you sell.
- You cannot add custom fields (for lists or items) to the statement form.

Customer statements are available in all QuickBooks editions, however, QuickBooks Pro and Premier editions have additional functionality. For example, in QuickBooks Pro and Premier editions, you can include invoice detail on statements and include all open transactions as of a certain date.

Note: **To complete the following exercises, you must be using QuickBooks Pro or Premier.**

Generating customer statements

Rock Castle uses invoices to bill its customers, but it sends reminder statements to customers with overdue invoices. In this exercise, you generate statements to send to customers with outstanding balances.

Rock Castle wants to send reminder statements to all customers who have balances more than 30 days past due.

To generate reminder statements:

1 From the Customers menu, choose Create Statements.

QuickBooks displays the Create Statements window.

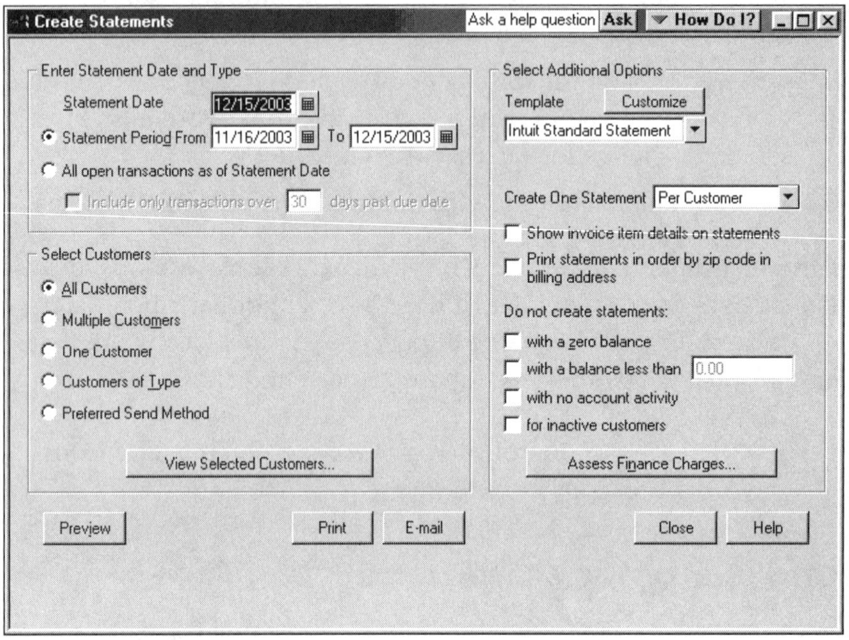

2 In the Enter Statement Date and Type section of the window, select the "All open transactions as of Statement Date" option.

3 Click to select the "Include only transactions over" checkbox.

4 Leave the number of days past due field entry at 30.

5 In the Select Customers section, leave "All Customers" selected.

6 In the Select Additional Options section, click to select the "Show invoice item details on statements" checkbox.

Your screen should look like the following graphic.

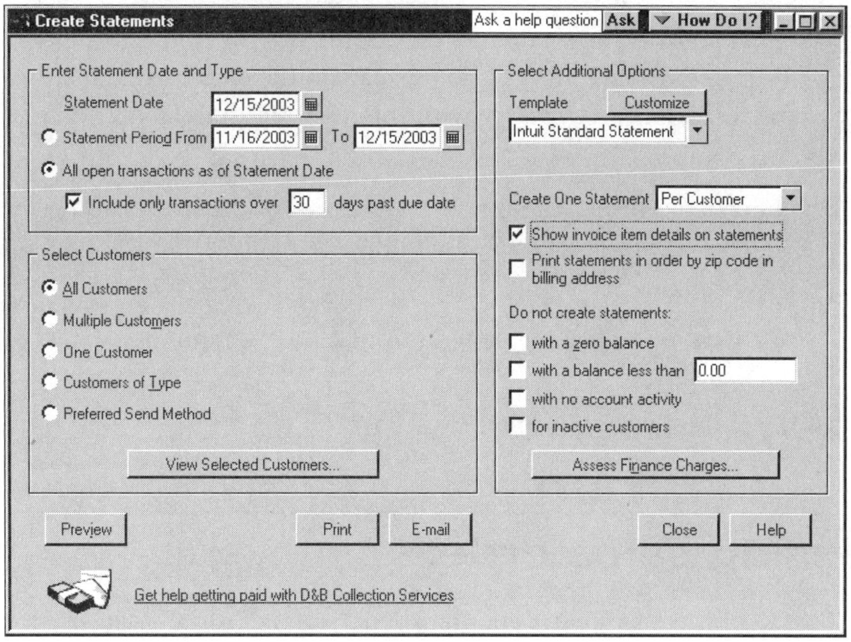

7 Click Assess Finance Charges.

QuickBooks displays the Assess Finance Charges window.

8 Click Unmark All.

9 In the Assess column, click to put a checkmark in the row for the 155 Wilks job for Pretell Real Estate (finance charges were assessed against Brian Cook on 12/11/03).

Your screen should look like the following graphic.

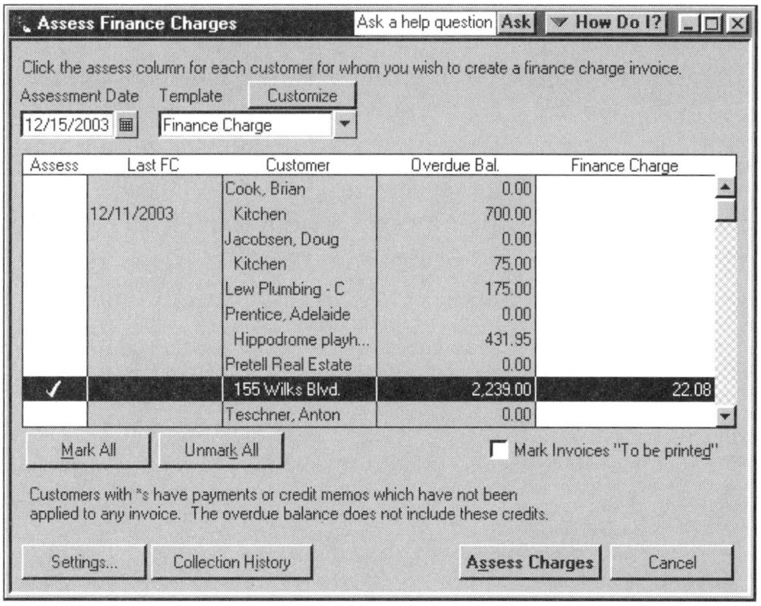

10 Click Assess Charges.

11 Answer Yes when QuickBooks displays the message telling you that finance charges have already been assessed today.

QuickBooks creates a finance charge invoice Pretell Real Estate in the amount of $22.08. This amount does not display on the current statement, but you can send the finance charge invoice with the reminder statement.

12 Click Preview.

QuickBooks displays reminder statements for the two customers who balances are 30 days or more past due—including the details from the original invoices.

13 Click Close.

At this point you could generate and send the reminder statements to your customers.

14 Close the Create Statements window.

Processing sales orders

The sales order feature lets you track orders from customers and "set items aside." You can also use sales orders to track back orders when a customer orders something and you are out of stock. Using this feature, you can track the orders you need to fill without affecting accounts receivable. Sales orders affect only inventory quantities—not values—until you actually sell the items.

When inventory items come in, you can create an invoice directly from the sales order. If only some of the items have come in, you can invoice for those items, and use the sales order to create invoices for the remaining items later. Once all items have been received and invoiced for, QuickBooks Premier closes the sales order.

Note: **Sales orders are available only in QuickBooks Premier editions.** To proceed through this exercise, you must be using a QuickBooks Premier product.

Creating sales orders

A customer calls Rock Castle to order some door frames. The employee who took the call checks inventory and realizes that they don't have enough items on hand to fill the customer's order. Create a sales order to track the customer's order.

To create a sales order:

1 From the Customers menu, choose Create Sales Orders.

QuickBooks displays the Create Sales Orders window.

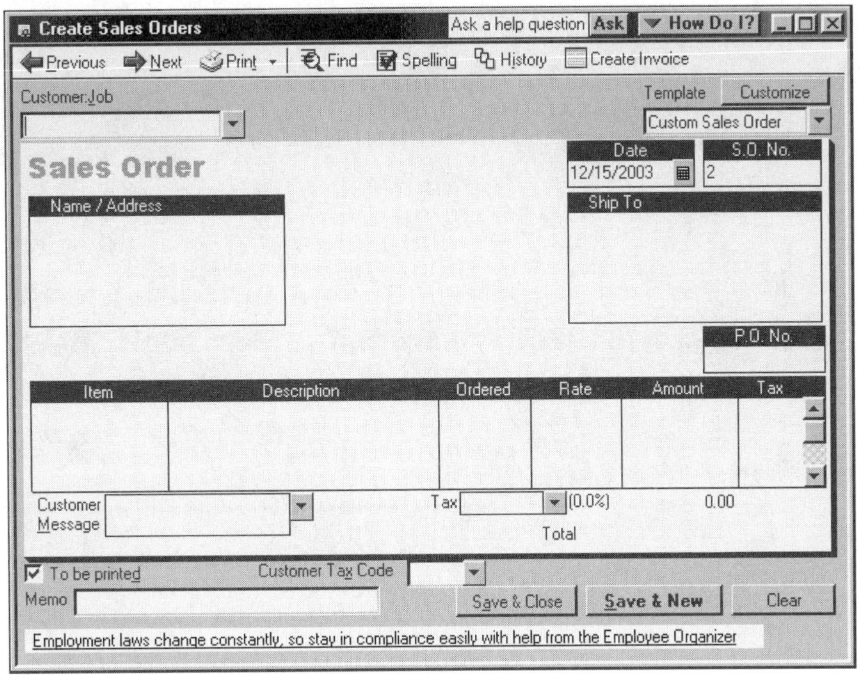

2 In the Customer:Job drop-down list, select Roche, Diarmuid:Room Addition.

3 Click in the Item column and select Frame from the drop-down list.

4 Press Tab twice to move to the Ordered column.

5 Type ***4***.

6 Press Tab, and then type ***25.00*** in the Rate column.

7 Press Tab again.

The sales order should look like the following graphic.

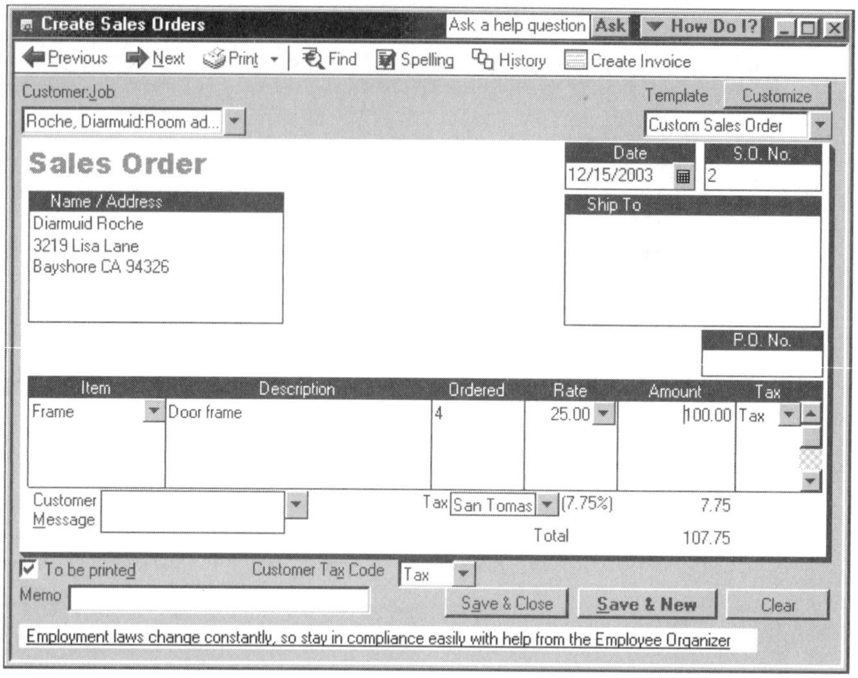

8 Click Save & Close.

If the inventory items are not already on order, create a purchase order. When the items arrive, enter them into inventory as usual, and then invoice the customer.

Checking stock status

If you want to see how sales orders affect inventory quantities, run the stock status by item report.

The following graphic shows the Frame item before the sales order for Diarmuid was created.

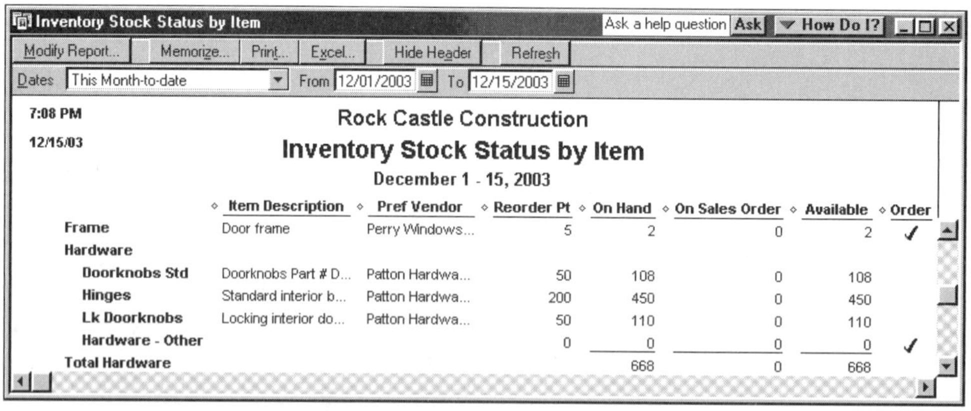

This graphic shows the Frame item after the sales order was created. Notice that QuickBooks tracks the items listed on sales orders.

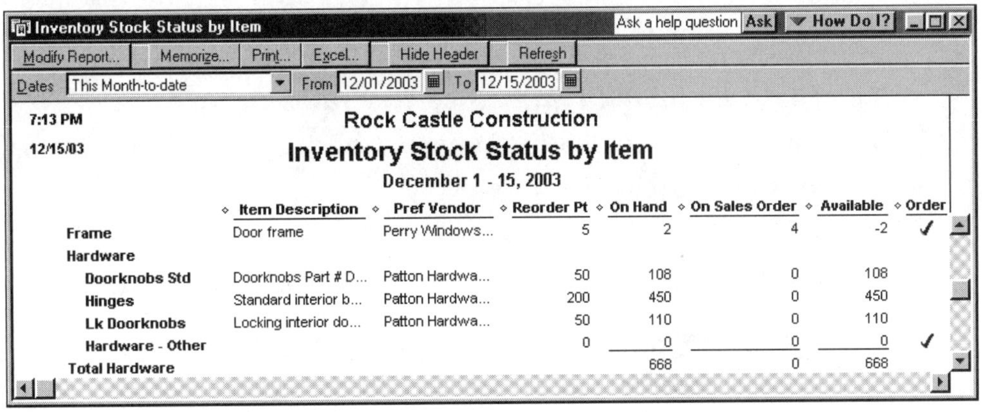

Invoicing against sales orders

Rock Castle recently received several deliveries and an employee has entered the items into inventory. He wants to find out if any of these items have been ordered for customers, so he runs the open sales order by item report.

To run the sales order by item report:

1. From the Reports menu, choose Sales.
2. Choose Open Sales Orders by Item from the submenu.

   QuickBooks displays the report.

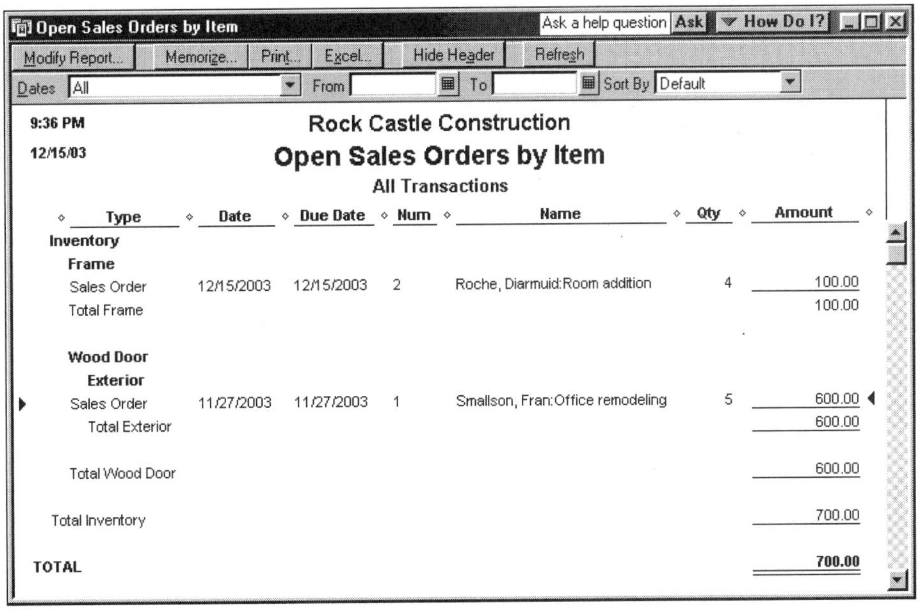

In addition to the sales order you just entered, the report shows that there is an open sales order for Exterior wood doors for Fran Smallson. Rock Castle now has sufficient quantity on hand to fill the customer's order, so you can close the sales order and invoice the customer.

To create an invoice and close the sales order:

1 Double-click on the line in the report window for Sales Order #1 for Fran Smallson.

QuickBooks opens the sales order.

2 In the Create Sales Orders window, click Create Invoice on the toolbar.

QuickBooks displays the Create Invoice Based On Sales Order window.

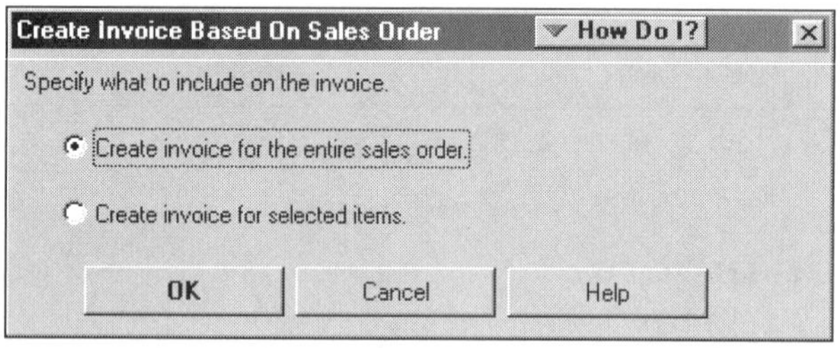

3 Leave the "Create invoice for the entire sales order" option selected, and click OK.

QuickBooks creates an invoice for the customer.

In this case, all of the items the customer order arrived, so you can close the sales order. If only some of the items had come in, you could invoice for only those items and keep the sales order open until any remaining items arrived. QuickBooks tracks which items are still open.

4 In the Create Invoices window, click Save & Close.

5 Close the report window.

Student test and review

1 From which list (or lists) does QuickBooks get the information for A, B, and C in the graphic below?

- *A: Customer:Job list*
- *B: Customer:Job list (if associated terms with the customer); Terms list*
- *C: Item list*

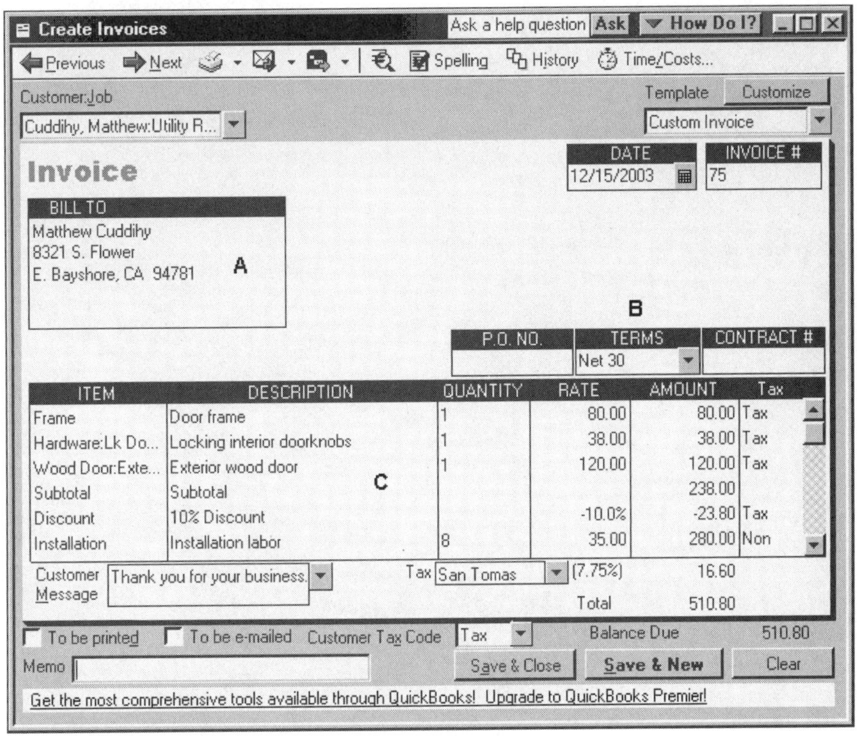

2 List the item types used in the line item area of the invoice above.

Inventory Part, Subtotal, Discount, and Service.

3 Create an invoice for Rock Castle Construction that uses the new Repairs:Plumbing line item. Create the invoice for a new customer by adding information to the Customer list "on the fly."

4 Filling out a sales receipt is similar to filling out an invoice form. Create a sales receipt for a customer of Rock Castle Construction. After you create the sales receipt, open the Undeposited Funds account register to see the transaction QuickBooks created automatically.

LESSON 7 Receiving payments and making deposits

Lesson objectives

- To learn how to record customer payments in QuickBooks
- To learn how to handle customer discounts, partial payments, overpayments, or down payments
- To see how to record a deposit in QuickBooks, and learn how QuickBooks treats the deposit behind the scenes
- To learn how to enter cash back from a deposit in QuickBooks

Handout materials

- Handout 21: Receive Payments window
- Handout 22: Make Deposits window

Instructor preparation

- Review the lesson, including the examples, to make sure you're familiar with the material.
- Ensure that all students have a copy of qblesson.qbb on their computer's hard disk.
- Have Handouts 21 and 22 ready for distribution.

To start this lesson

Before you perform the following steps, make sure you have installed the exercise file (qblesson.qbb) on your hard disk. See "Installing the exercise file" in the Introduction to this guide if you haven't installed it.

The steps that follow will restore the exercise file to its original state so that the data in the file matches what you see on the screen as you proceed through each lesson.

To restore the exercise file (qblesson.qbb):

1. From the File menu in QuickBooks, choose Restore.

   QuickBooks displays the Restore Company Backup window.
2. In the "Get Company Backup From" section of the window, click Browse and select your c:\QBtrain directory.
3. Select the qblesson.qbb file, and then click Open.

4. In the "Restore Company Backup To" section of the window, click Browse and select your c:\QBtrain directory.
5. In the File name field of the Restore To window, type ***lesson 7*** and then click Save.
6. Click Restore.

Recording customer payments

If you're receiving payment at the time of a sale, and you fill out a sales receipt, QuickBooks records a customer payment. When you invoice a customer, and you receive payment later, you enter the payment in the QuickBooks Receive Payments window.

The Receive Payments window lets you match up payments you receive with invoices you've written. You'll be working with the Receive Payments window in this lesson.

Distribute Handouts 21 and 22, "Receive Payments window" and "Make Deposits window."

Recording a payment in full for a single job

The simplest case is when a customer has one outstanding invoice for one job and sends you a payment for the full amount. Suppose that Rock Castle Construction receives a check for $4735.73 from Mike Violette for his workshop. Here's how you'd enter the payment.

To record a payment in full:

1 From the Customers menu, choose Receive Payments.

QuickBooks displays the Receive Payments window.

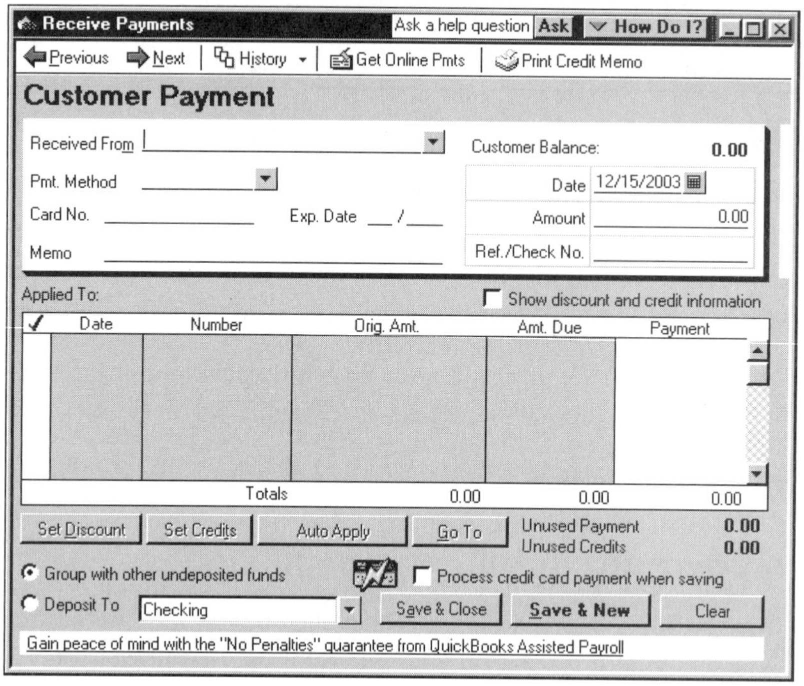

The first step is to enter the name of the customer from whom you've received a payment.

2 In the Received From field, select Violette, Mike:Workshop from the drop-down list.

QuickBooks displays the outstanding invoice for Mike Violette in the Applied To section of the window.

3 Press Tab twice to move to the Amount field.

4 In the Amount field, type ***4735.73*** and press Tab.

QuickBooks changes the Total to Apply to 4735.73, and applies the payment to the one outstanding invoice.

5 In the Ref./Check No. field, type ***6745*** and then press Tab.

6 In the Pmt. Method field, select Check from the drop-down list.

7 Click "Group with other undeposited funds" if it is not selected already.

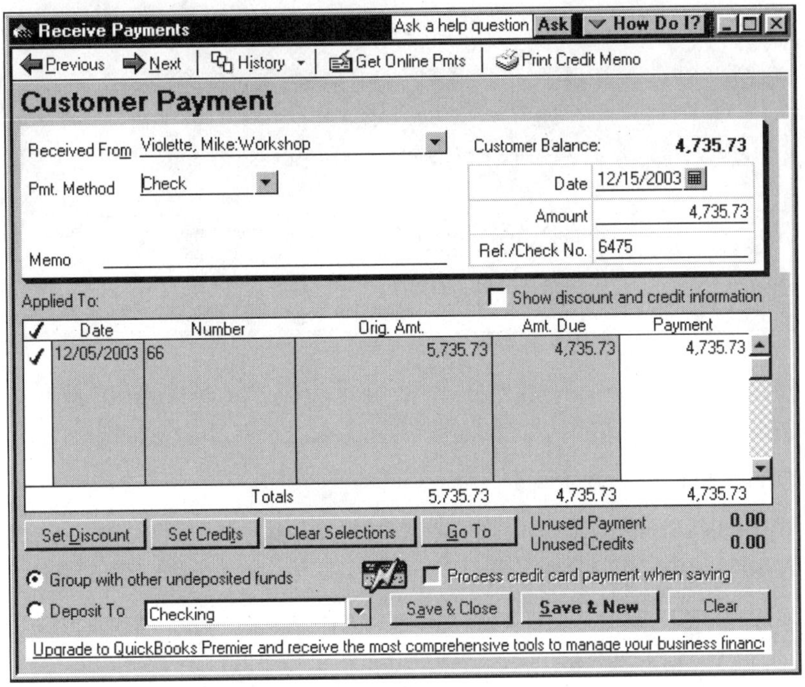

8 Click Save & New.

This records the payment and clears the window so you can enter another one.

Entering a partial payment

Rock Castle Construction has also received a check for $1,000 from Ecker Designs. Ecker Designs has two outstanding invoices and owes more than $6,000.

To enter a partial payment:

1 In the Received From field, select Ecker Designs:Office Repairs from the drop-down list.

In the middle of the window, QuickBooks shows you the invoices still outstanding for the job. In this case, there are two. Next, you need to enter the amount of the payment in the Amount field.

2 Press Tab twice to move to the Amount field, and then type ***1000***. Then press Tab again.

QuickBooks automatically applies the payment you've entered to Ecker Design's oldest invoice.

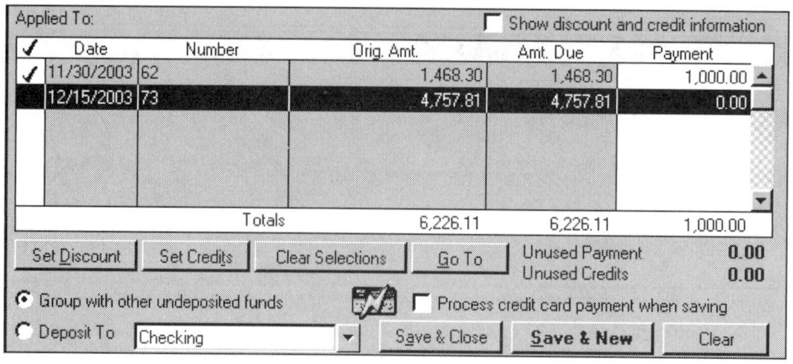

If you want to choose which invoice a payment applies to, rather than having QuickBooks apply it to the oldest one, you can click Clear Selections.

3 Click Clear Selections.

4 In the Payment column, type ***1000*** as the amount you want to apply to the second invoice, and then press Tab.

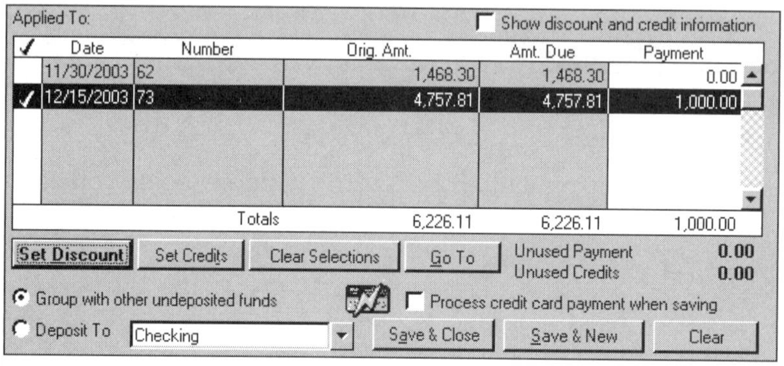

5 In the Pmt. Method field, select Check from the drop-down list.

6 Make sure that "Group with other undeposited funds" is selected.

7 Click Save & New to record the partial payment and clear the window.

Applying one payment to multiple jobs

Rock Castle Construction is working on several jobs for a customer, Brian Cook. Brian has payments outstanding for four invoices. He wants to write one check to cover all outstanding payments.

In this exercise, you'll apply this single payment to invoices for multiple jobs.

To apply one payment to multiple jobs:

1 In the Receive Payments window, select Cook, Brian from the Received From drop-down list.

QuickBooks lists the open invoices for all of the jobs associated with Brian Cook.

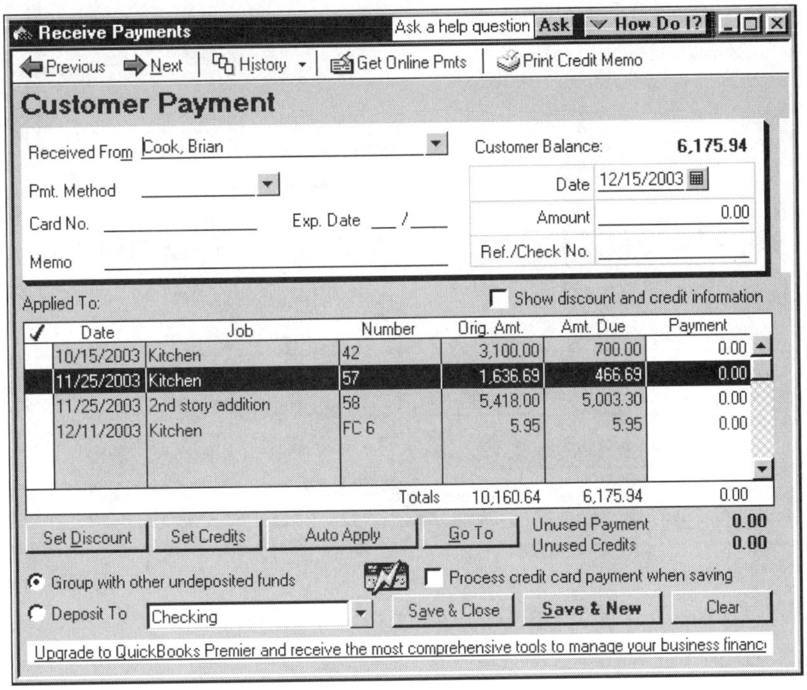

2 Press Tab twice to move to the Amount field.

3 In the Amount field, type ***6175.94*** and then press Tab.

Notice that QuickBooks applies the payment to all outstanding invoices.

4 In the Ref./Check No. field, type ***575*** and then press Tab.

5 In the Pmt. Method drop-down list, select Check.

Your window should look like this.

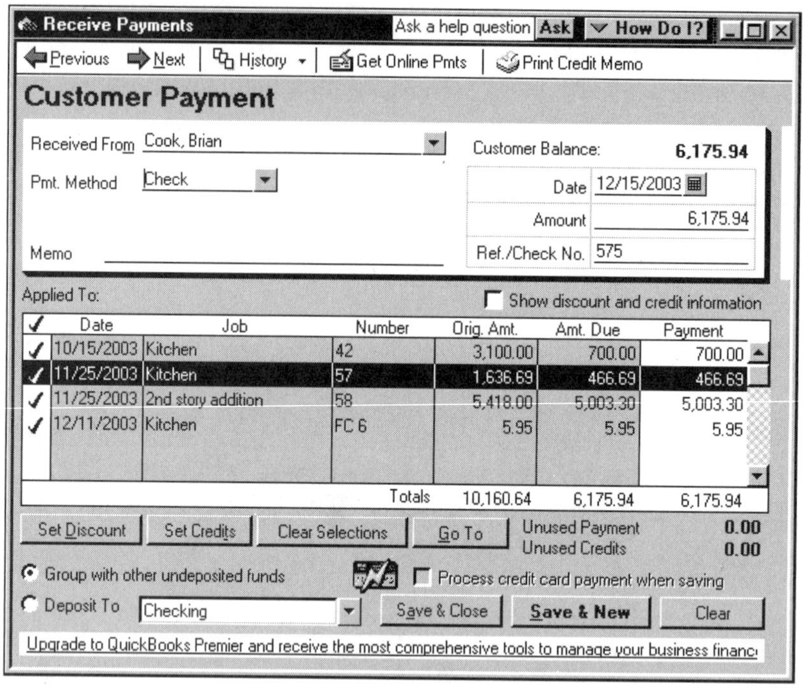

6 Make sure that "Group with other undeposited funds" is selected.

7 Click Save & New.

Entering overpayments

If a customer sends you an overpayment, you simply enter the amount in the Receive Payments window, and QuickBooks keeps track of the additional payment. When the customer has future invoices, you can apply the overpayment to those amounts.

Suppose that Rock Castle Construction has received a payment of $12,500.00 from Pretell Real Estate for the 75 Sunset Rd. job. The outstanding invoice for that job is $12,412.18.

To enter the payment:

1 In the Received From field of the Receive Payments window, select Pretell Real Estate:75 Sunset Rd. from the drop-down list.

QuickBooks displays an invoice dated 12/01/2003 for $12,412.18.

2 Press Tab twice and type ***12500*** in the Amount field.

3 Press Tab again.

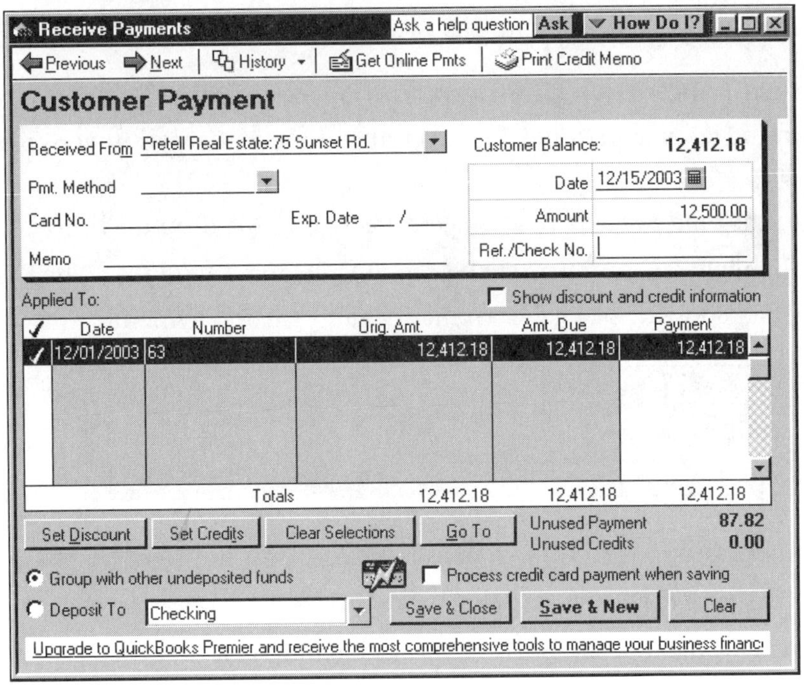

QuickBooks shows an Unused Payment amount of $87.82. QuickBooks keeps track of the overpayment amount for you, and you can apply it to any future invoices for the customer. The next time you invoice Pretell Real Estate and receive a payment, the Receive Payments window will show $87.82 in unused credits.

4 Select Check from the drop-down list in the Pmt. Method field.

5 Make sure "Group with other undeposited funds" is selected.

If you wanted to print a credit memo to the customer, acknowledging the amount you owe, you would click the Print Credit Memo button at the top of the window.

6 Click Save & New.

7 When QuickBooks displays a message telling you that the customer will have a credit if you proceed, click OK.

Handling down payments or prepayments

If a customer makes a payment before you've invoiced him for services (for example, he may be making a down payment or paying a retainer fee), you can still record the payment at the Receive Payments window. However, because you don't have any invoices to which to apply the payment, QuickBooks records the payment as an unused payment (just like an overpayment).

QuickBooks holds the unapplied amount with the customer's name. The next time you enter that customer in the Receive Payments window, QuickBooks displays the credit amount in the Unused Credits area. The customer's balance also reflects the credit amount.

Suppose Kristy Abercrombie wants Rock Castle Construction to do a kitchen remodeling job for her. She's sent Rock Castle Construction a check for $1,000 as an initial payment, but the company hasn't invoiced her yet.

To enter the down payment you've received:

1 In the Received From field, select Abercrombie, Kristy:Kitchen from the drop-down list.

2 In the Pmt. Method field, select Check from the drop-down list.

3 Highlight the numbers in the Amount field and type ***1000***. Then press Tab.

QuickBooks displays the payment as an Unused Payment.

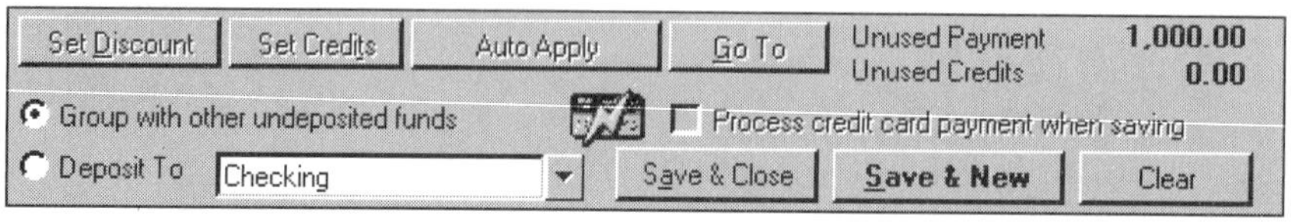

4 Click "Group with other undeposited funds" if it is not selected already.

5 Click Save & Close.

6 When QuickBooks displays a message telling you that the customer will have a credit if you proceed, click OK.

Later, Rock Castle Construction is ready to prepare its invoices and needs to invoice Kristy for the labor the workers have already completed on the job.

To create an invoice for a customer who made a down payment:

1 From the Customers menu, choose Create Invoices.

QuickBooks displays the Create Invoices window.

2 In the Customer:Job field, select Abercrombie, Kristy:Kitchen from the drop-down list.

3 If you have QuickBooks Pro or Premier, QuickBooks displays the Available Estimates window. You don't want to create the invoice from the estimate listed, so click Cancel.

4 Click in the Item column, select Removal from the Item drop-down list, and then press Tab twice.

5 In the Quantity column, type ***40*** and press Tab.

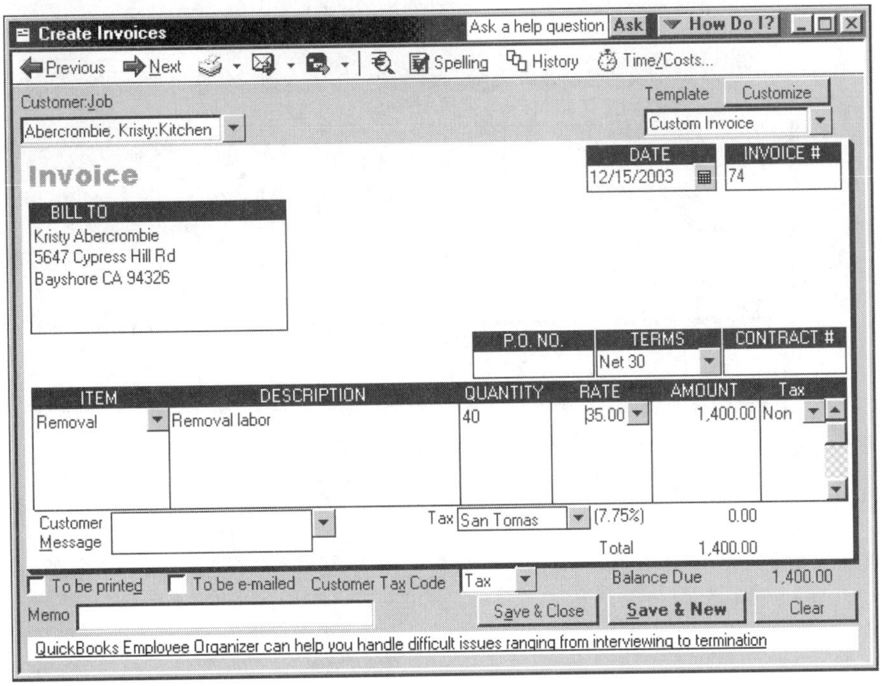

6 Click Save & Close to record the invoice and to close the Create Invoices window.

Now you can go to the Receive Payments window and see how QuickBooks applies the payment Kristy made earlier.

To view a down payment:

1 From the Customers menu, choose Receive Payments.

2 In the Received From field, select Abercrombie, Kristy:Kitchen from the drop-down list.

QuickBooks shows Unused Credits of $1,000.

3 Click in the Payment column, and then Click Set Credits.

In the Discounts and Credits window, notice that QuickBooks has applied the full credit amount to the invoice, which is what you wanted. If there were other invoices to which you wanted to apply part of the credit amount, you would use this window to apply the credits to the appropriate invoices.

4 Click Done.

QuickBooks applies the existing credit to the new invoice.

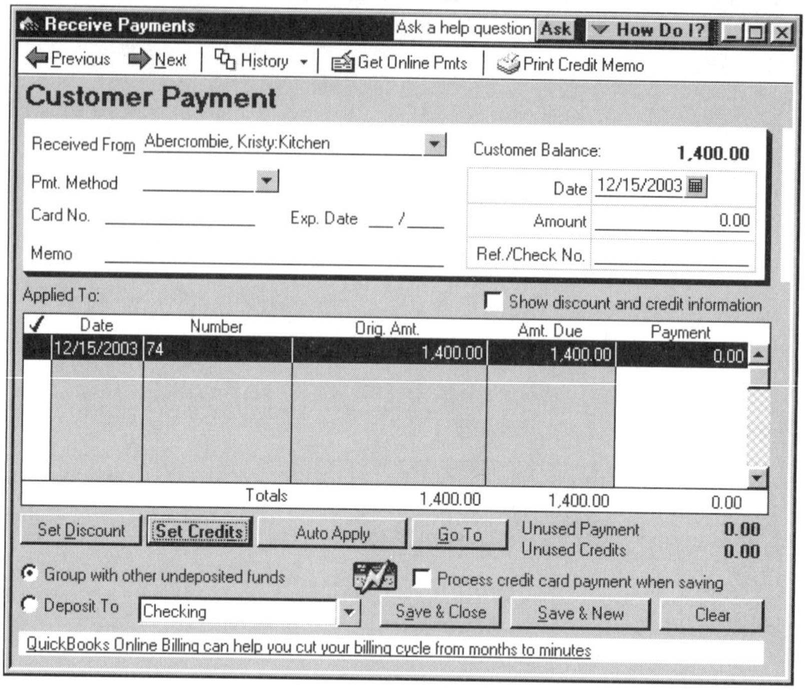

5 Click Save & Close to record the payment.

Making deposits

When you use the Enter Sales Receipt window (for a sales receipt where you receive payment on the spot), the Receive Payments window (for payments on invoices), or a payment item on an invoice, QuickBooks keeps track of the money you've received until you deposit it in the bank.

Selecting payments to deposit

At your office, you might hold payments in a locked cash drawer or a cash register until you can get to the bank; QuickBooks holds the amount in an asset account called Undeposited Funds. When you're ready to take your payments to the bank, you can record the deposit in QuickBooks, print a deposit slip to bring with you, and enter cash back amounts.

To select payments to deposit:

1 From the Banking menu, choose Make Deposits.

QuickBooks displays the Payments to Deposit window, which lists the payments you have not yet deposited.

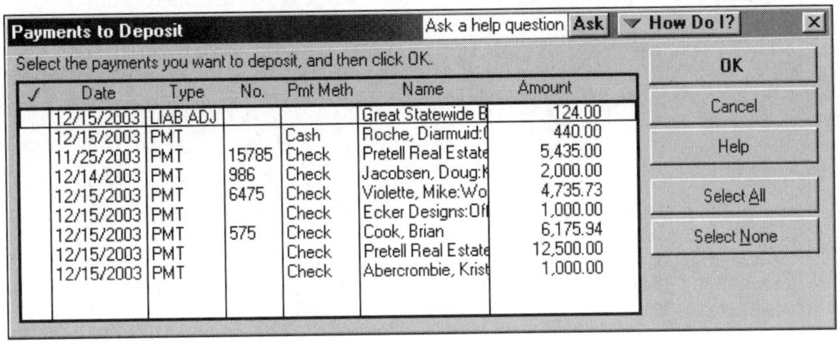

2 Click to select the payments you want to bring to the bank.

For this exercise, select the payments you recorded from Mike Violette, Brian Cook, Ecker Designs, Pretell Real Estate, and Kristy Abercrombie. Notice that there are two payments from Pretell Real Estate; select both of them.

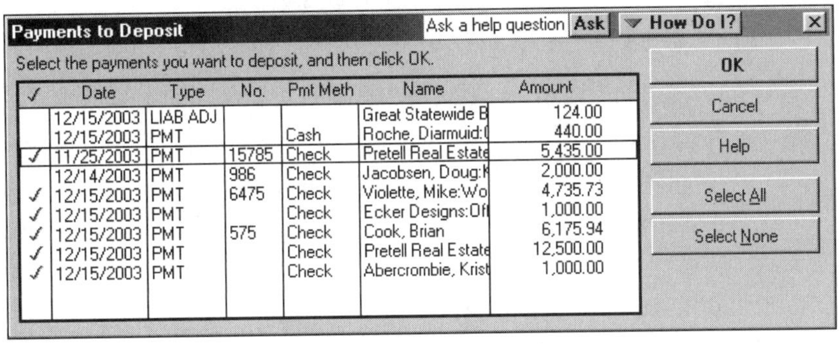

3 Click OK.

QuickBooks displays the Make Deposits window, which shows the payments you just selected.

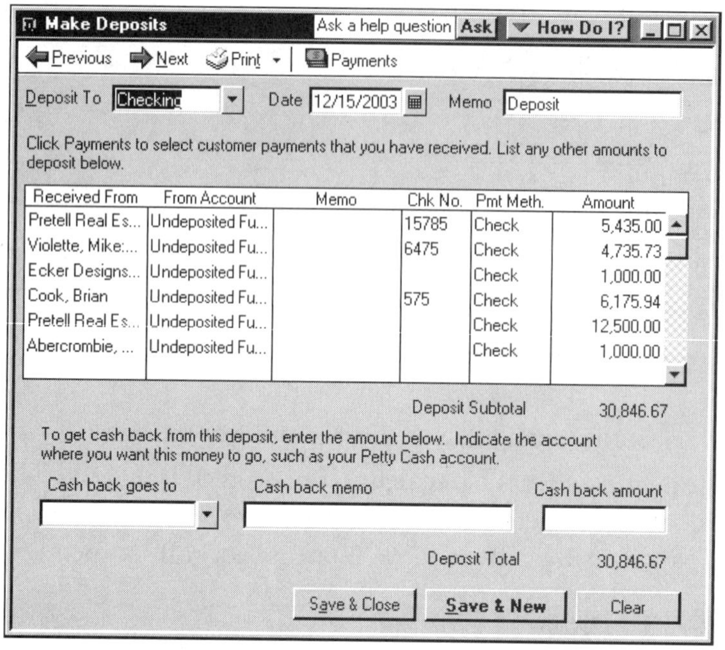

4 In the Deposit To field, make sure that Checking is selected.

Note: If you have money to deposit that is not the result of a payment you received for a sale, you can enter it in the detail area of the window. For example, if you received a premium refund from your insurance vendor, you would enter it here.

QuickBooks updates the deposit total at the bottom of the window automatically. If you wanted to print a deposit slip to take to the bank, you would click Print. The Printable Deposit Slips that you can order to work with QuickBooks work only with deposits of cash and checks.

5 Click Save & Close to record the deposit.

How QuickBooks handles the deposit

QuickBooks updates the Undeposited Funds account to show that you've made a deposit. It also adds the deposit to your checking account register.

To view the Undeposited Funds account:

1 From the Lists menu, choose Chart of Accounts.

2 In the chart of accounts, double-click the Undeposited Funds account.

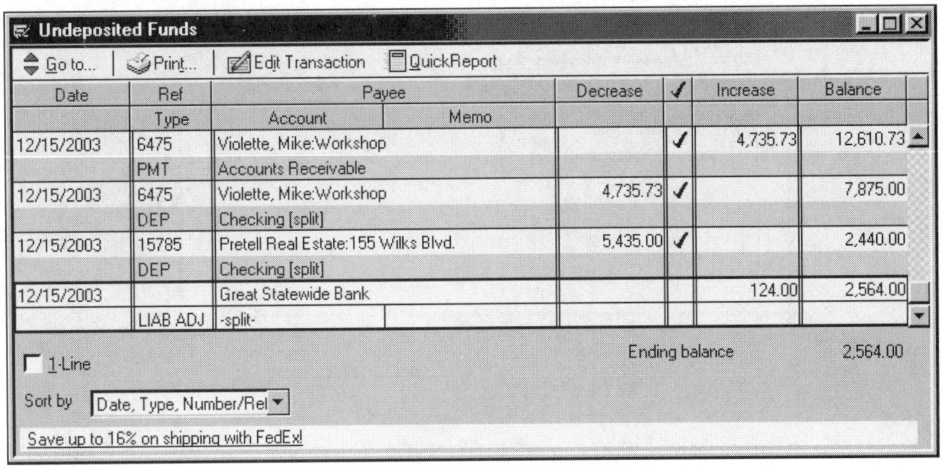

QuickBooks displays your deposits and reduces the balance in the account by the amount of the deposits.

3 Close the account register window.

Now you can look at the deposit transaction in the checking account.

4 In the chart of accounts, double-click the checking account.

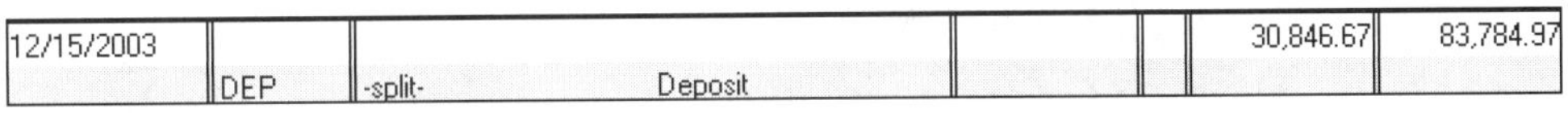

QuickBooks has entered the deposit as a transaction in the checking account register and has updated the balance of your checking account.

5 Close the checking account register and the chart of accounts.

Getting cash back from a deposit

In the Make Deposits window, you can enter information about any cash you took out of the deposit when you are recording the deposit.

To record getting cash back from a deposit:

1 From the Banking menu, choose Make Deposits.

QuickBooks displays the Payments to Deposit window. Notice that the deposits you made in the last exercise are no longer listed.

2 In the Payments to Deposit window, select the payment from Doug Jacobsen.

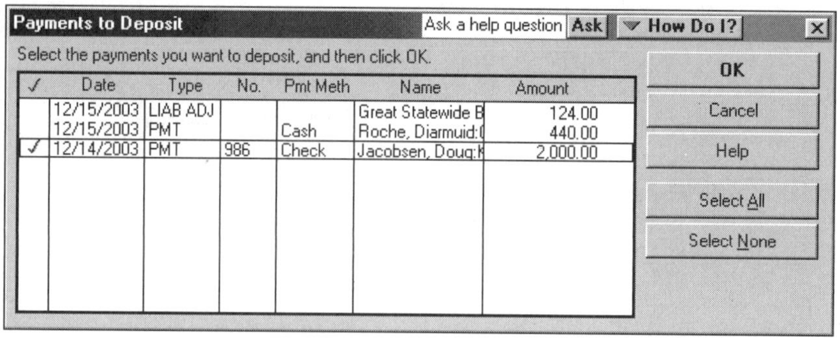

3 Click OK.

4 In the Make Deposits window, type ***Petty Cash*** in the "Cash back goes to" field and press Tab.

5 When QuickBooks displays a message telling you that Petty Cash is not on the account list, click Set up.

QuickBooks displays the New Account window with the name preset to Petty Cash.

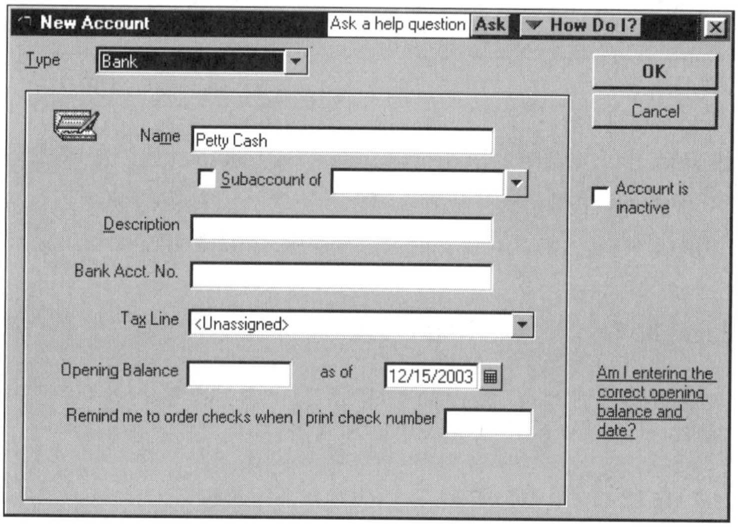

6 Make sure Bank is selected in the Type drop-down list, and then click OK to return to the Make Deposits window.

7 In the "Cash back amount" field, type ***200*** and press Tab.

QuickBooks displays the deposit subtotal amount ($2000.00) and the total less the cash back amount ($1800.00).

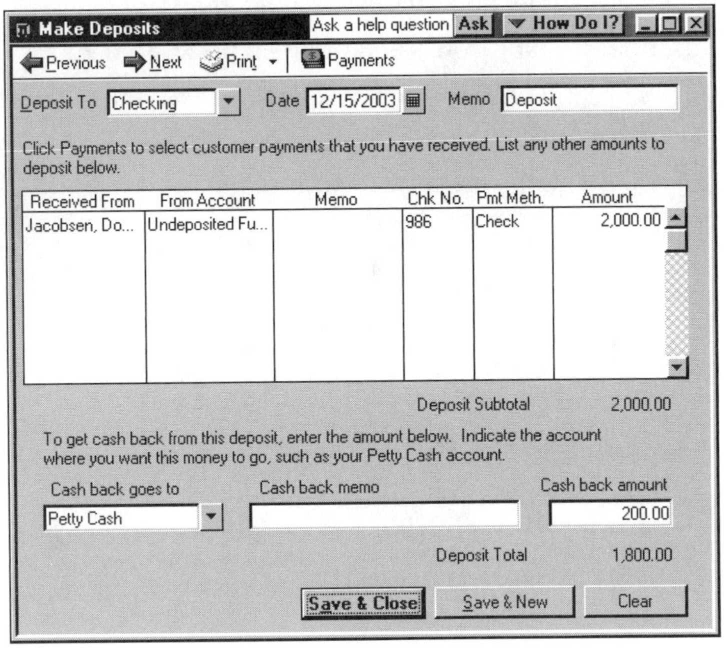

8 Click Save & Close.

QuickBooks records the Deposit Total amount in your checking account and the cash back amount in your Petty Cash account.

9 To see the effect on these accounts, choose Chart of Accounts from the Lists menu.

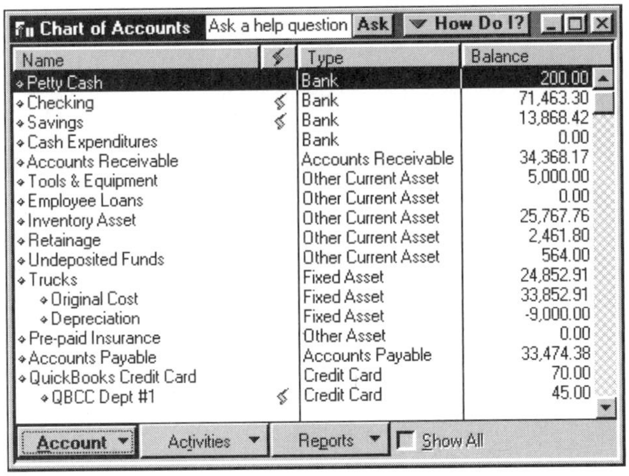

10 Close the chart of accounts.

Student test and review

1. Create an invoice for Bryan Ruff's utility shed job.

   Add items to Rock Castle Construction's Item list as needed.

2. After you invoice Bryan, record a payment from him in the Receive Payments window.

3. Record Rock Castle Construction's deposit of the payment.

LESSON 8 Entering and paying bills

Lesson objectives

- To discuss the different ways you can handle bills in QuickBooks
- To learn how to enter a bill in QuickBooks
- To use the Pay Bills window to pay a bill in QuickBooks
- To learn how to enter a discount on a bill from a vendor

Handout materials

- Handout 23: Handling expenses in QuickBooks

Instructor preparation

- Review the lesson, including the examples, to make sure you're familiar with the material.
- Ensure that all students have a copy of qblesson.qbb on their computer's hard disk.
- Have Handout 23 ready for distribution.

To start this lesson

Before you perform the following steps, make sure you have installed the exercise file (qblesson.qbb) on your hard disk. See "Installing the exercise file" in the Introduction to this guide if you haven't installed it.

The steps that follow will restore the exercise file to its original state so that the data in the file matches what you see on the screen as you proceed through each lesson.

To restore the exercise file (qblesson.qbb):

1. From the File menu in QuickBooks, choose Restore.

   QuickBooks displays the Restore Company Backup window.
2. In the "Get Company Backup From" section of the window, click Browse and select your c:\QBtrain directory.
3. Select the qblesson.qbb file, and then click Open.
4. In the "Restore Company Backup To" section of the window, click Browse and select your c:\QBtrain directory.
5. In the File name field of the Restore To window, type ***lesson 8*** and then click Save.
6. Click Restore.

Handling bills in QuickBooks

Refer to Handout 23, "Handling expenses in QuickBooks," as you discuss the following points.

When you have a business expense, you can handle it in one of the following ways:

- You can write a check manually and enter the information into a QuickBooks check register later. This doesn't take advantage of features in QuickBooks, but sometimes it's necessary. For example, if you purchase supplies at a retail store, they expect payment on the spot, and you may not know the amount in advance.
- You can use QuickBooks to write and print a check. When you receive a bill for which you want to make immediate payment, you can write a QuickBooks check more quickly and accurately than you can by hand, and you receive an additional advantage: QuickBooks makes the entry in your checking account register for you.
- You can use the QuickBooks accounts payable feature to track the amounts you owe to vendors, track your cash flow needs, and handle bills you want to pay later.
- You can pay by credit card and enter the credit card receipt into QuickBooks later.

Lesson 4, "Working with bank accounts," shows you how to enter a handwritten check and a QuickBooks check. In Lesson 5, "Using other accounts in QuickBooks," you learn about credit card accounts. This lesson shows you how to use QuickBooks for accounts payable.

Using QuickBooks for accounts payable

Some business owners, especially if they own smaller, home-based businesses, pay their bills when they receive them. Most business owners, however, find it more convenient to pay bills less often. (They also like keeping the cash in the company for as long as possible.) If you don't plan on paying your bills right away, QuickBooks can help you keep track of what you owe and when you owe it.

The money you owe for unpaid bills is called *accounts payable*. QuickBooks uses the Accounts Payable account to track all the money you owe. Like any QuickBooks balance sheet account, the Accounts Payable account has a register where you can view all your bills at once.

To see the Accounts Payable register:

1 From the Lists menu, choose Chart of Accounts.

QuickBooks displays the chart of accounts.

2 Double-click Accounts Payable in the list to open the register.

QuickBooks displays the Accounts Payable register.

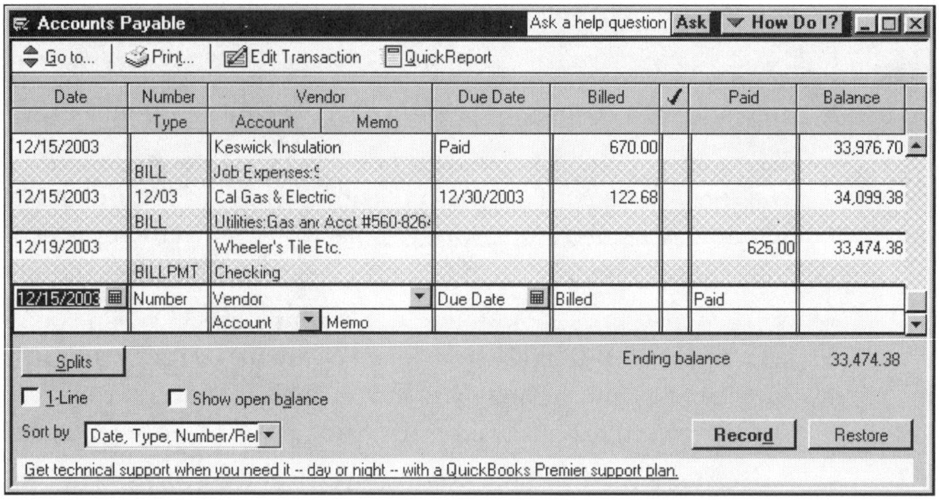

The register keeps track of each bill you have entered, shows you the due date, and keeps a running balance of all the bills you owe. As a business owner, this helps you forecast your cash flow, and the QuickBooks reminder system helps you pay your bills on time.

3 Press Esc twice to close the open windows.

Using accounts payable to pay your bills involves two steps: entering the bill and paying the bill. You'll practice both steps in this lesson.

Entering bills

When you receive a bill from a vendor, you should enter it into QuickBooks as soon as you can. This keeps your cash flow forecast reports up to date and doesn't give you the chance to set aside a bill and forget about it.

Rock Castle Construction received a bill from the company that created its new brochures. The bill includes a charge for courier delivery. Rock Castle Construction doesn't plan to pay the bill until close to its due date, but the company wants to keep an eye on the accounts payable total, so it enters the bill now.

To enter a bill:

1 From the Vendors menu, choose Enter Bills.

QuickBooks displays the Enter Bills window.

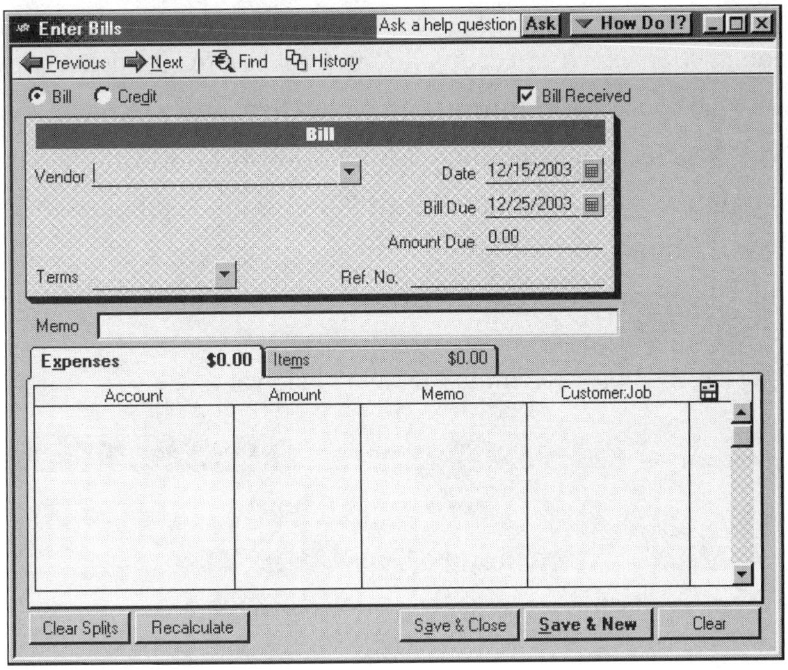

The top half of the window is where you enter the bill. The bottom half is the detail area where you can assign the bill amount to different expense accounts, customers, or jobs.

Notice that the Bill Received checkbox has a checkmark. The only time the Bill Received checkbox should be cleared is if you're using QuickBooks for inventory and you want to record items you've received that you haven't actually been billed for yet.

2 In the Vendor field, type ***Willis Advertising***, and then press Tab.

3 When QuickBooks displays a message telling you that Willis Advertising is not on the Vendor list, click Quick Add.

4 In the Amount Due field, type ***1500***.

5 Click in the Bill Due field.

Notice that QuickBooks supplies a date for you in the Bill Due field. The date displayed is ten days from the date in the Date field. You can change the date if you wish. If your Vendor list had payment terms entered for this vendor, QuickBooks would have used those terms to calculate the bill's due date.

6 Click in the Account column on the Expenses tab and type ***Printing***.

QuickFill completes the entry for you, and displays Printing and Reproduction as the account. QuickBooks lets you assign transactions to more than one account, so you can keep close track of where your company spends its money. Rock Castle Construction wants to assign the majority of this bill to a printing and reproduction expense account, and the rest to a freight delivery expense account.

7 Press Tab to accept Printing and Reproduction as the account.

8 Type ***1450*** to change the amount from 1,500 to 1,450.

9 Click in the Account column below Printing and Reproduction.

10 From the drop-down list, choose Freight & Delivery.

QuickBooks automatically assigns the remainder of the bill amount ($50.00) to Freight & Delivery.

Your screen should resemble the figure below.

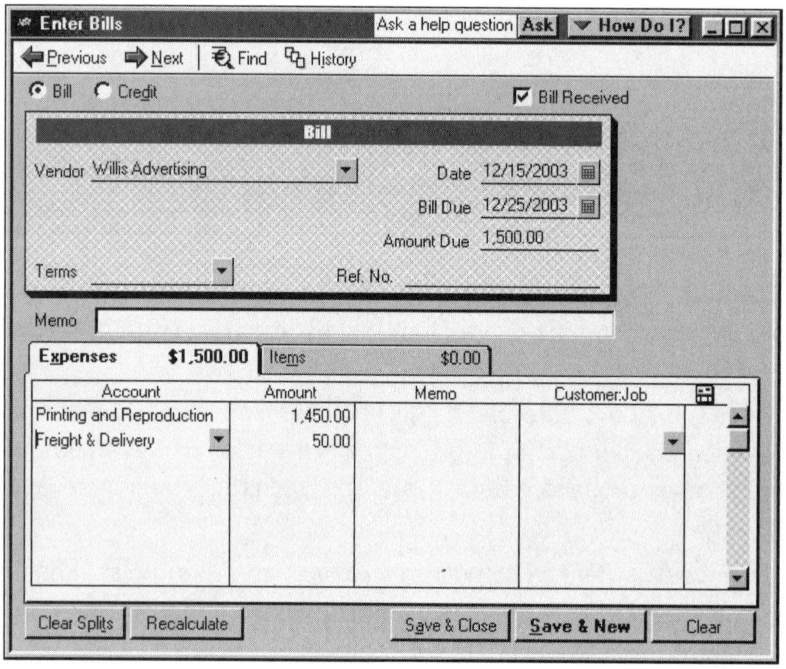

11 Click Save & Close to record the bill.

Paying bills

When you start QuickBooks or open a QuickBooks company file, a Reminders window appears that tells you if you have transactions to complete, such as bills to pay or money to deposit.

Tip: **If you don't see the Reminders window when you start QuickBooks, you can turn it on by choosing Preferences from the Edit menu.** Click Reminders, click the My Preferences tab, and select "Show Reminders List when opening a Company file."

When QuickBooks tells you that you have bills due, you can display the Pay Bills window and select the bills you want to pay.

To pay a bill:

1 From the Vendors menu, choose Pay Bills.

QuickBooks displays the Pay Bills window.

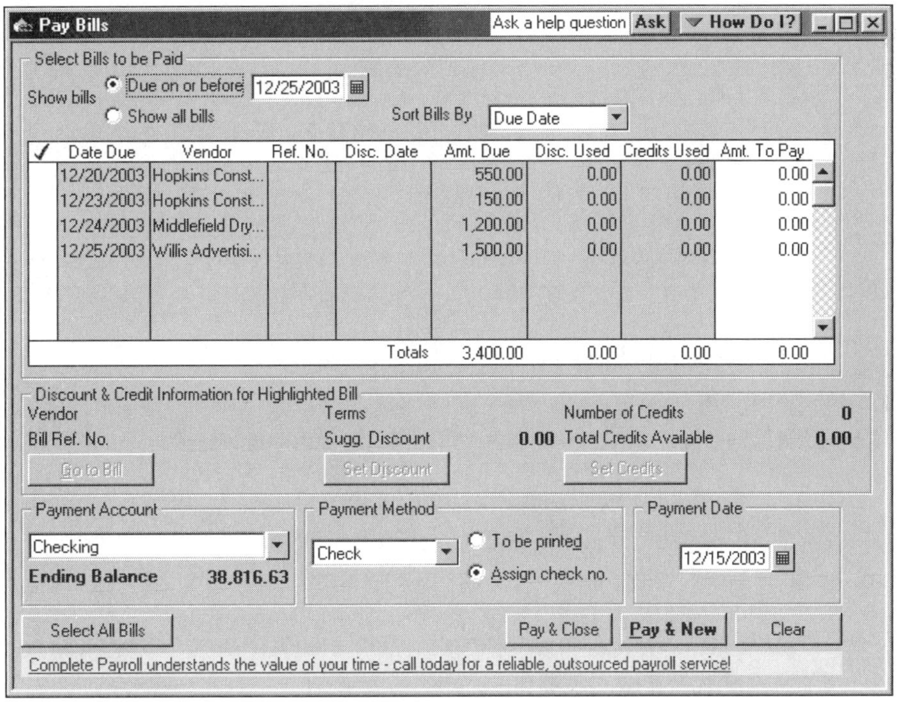

The Pay Bills window shows your unpaid bills as of any date you enter. You can pay by check, credit card, or with an online payment (if you are set up to make online payments).

For this exercise, you'll pay a bill using a QuickBooks check (rather than a handwritten one).

2 Select the "To be printed" option.

By selecting this option, you are telling QuickBooks that you will print this check later.

3 Select the Willis Advertising bill by clicking in the column to the left of the bill.

QuickBooks displays a checkmark next to the bill and changes the amount in the Ending Bank Balance to reflect a payment of $1,500.00. If you want to make a partial payment, you can enter the amount you want to pay in the Amt. To Pay column.

Your screen should resemble the figure below.

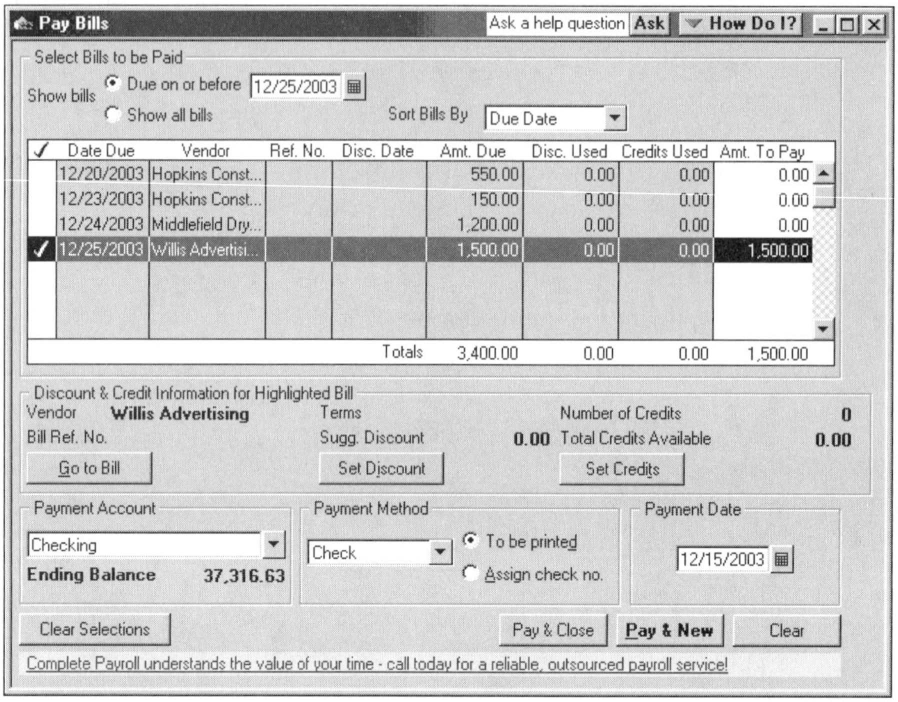

4 Click Pay & Close.

How QuickBooks records your bill payment

When you pay a bill through the Pay Bills window, QuickBooks makes an entry in the accounts payable register, showing a decrease of $1,500 in the total payables. It also creates a check from your checking account to pay the bill.

To see the entry in the accounts payable register:

1 From the Company menu, choose Chart of Accounts.

QuickBooks displays the chart of accounts.

2 In the chart of accounts, double-click the Accounts Payable account.

QuickBooks displays the accounts payable register.

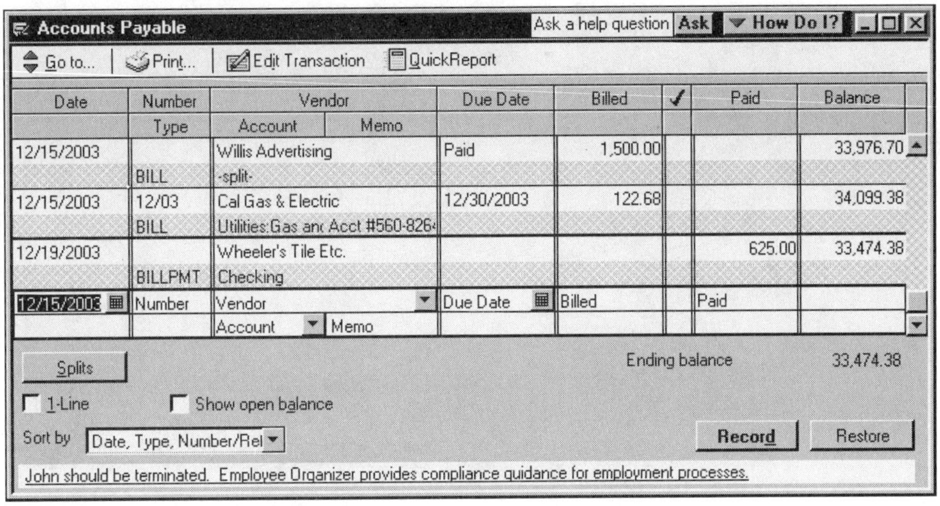

The register now shows the bill payment to Willis Advertising.

3 Close the accounts payable register.

At the same time QuickBooks recorded the entry in your accounts payable register, it made an entry in your Checking account.

To see the entry:

1 In the chart of accounts, double-click Checking.

QuickBooks displays the checking account register.

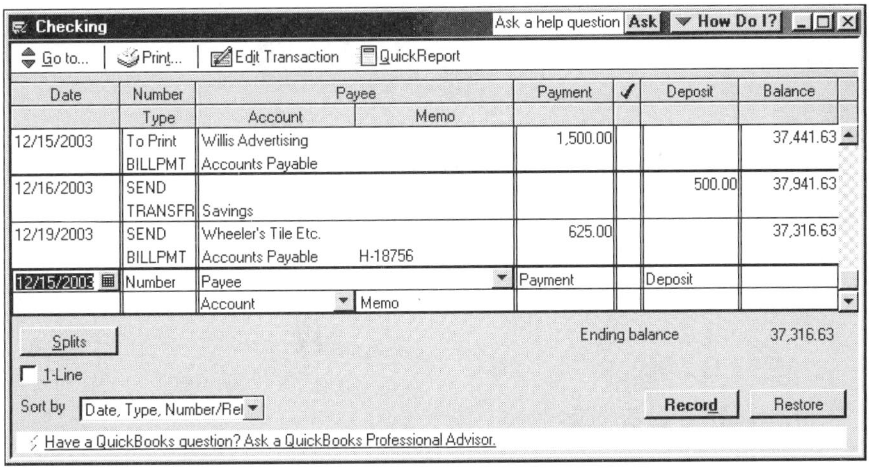

Notice that the third to the last entry in the register is the check for the payment to Willis Advertising.

2 Select the Willis Advertising transaction.

QuickBooks highlights the Willis transaction with a thick border to show that it is selected.

3 On the toolbar, click Edit Transaction.

QuickBooks displays the Bill Payments (Check) window.

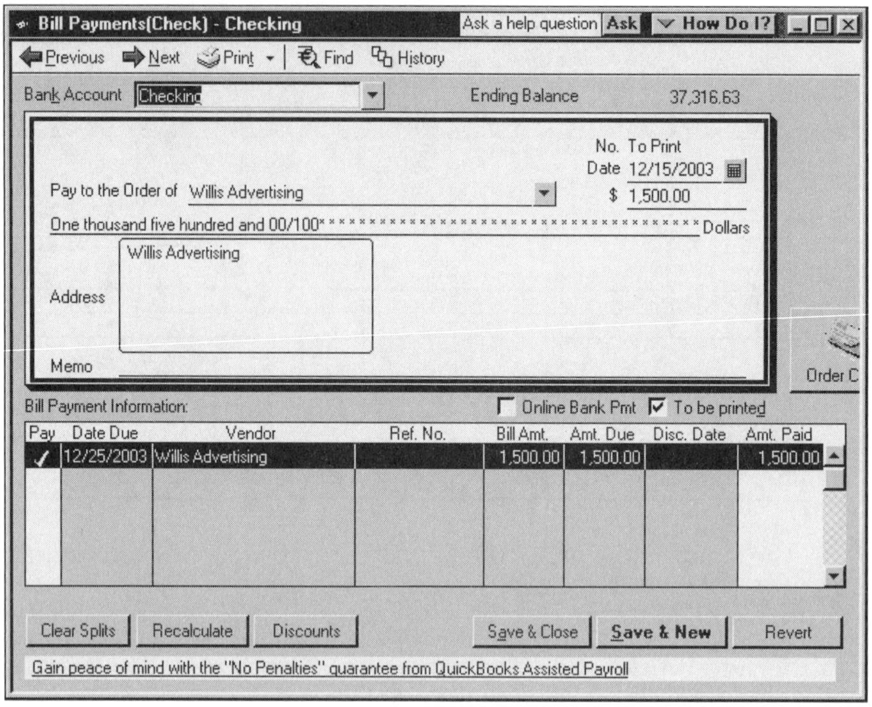

This check is called a "Bill Payment Check" and differs from the check form that you use to enter checks directly into the checking account. (That form shows expenses directly on the check voucher portion, while the bill payment form shows the bills paid by the check.)

4 Press Esc to close the Bill Payment Check window.

5 From the Window menu, choose Close All to close all the open QuickBooks windows.

Applying vendor discounts to bill payments

If you take advantage of discounts for early payment offered by some vendors, you can record the discounts directly in the Pay Bills window. You can set up QuickBooks to track the discount amounts.

In this section, you'll apply a discount for early payment to one of Rock Castle Construction's vendors.

To apply a discount for early payment:

1 From the Vendors menu, choose Pay Bills.

QuickBooks displays the Pay Bills window.

2 In the "Due on or before" field, type 1/16/04 and press Tab.

QuickBooks displays all of Rock Castle Construction's bills due on or before 1/16/04.

3 From the Sort Bills By drop-down list, choose Discount Date.

Your screen should look like this.

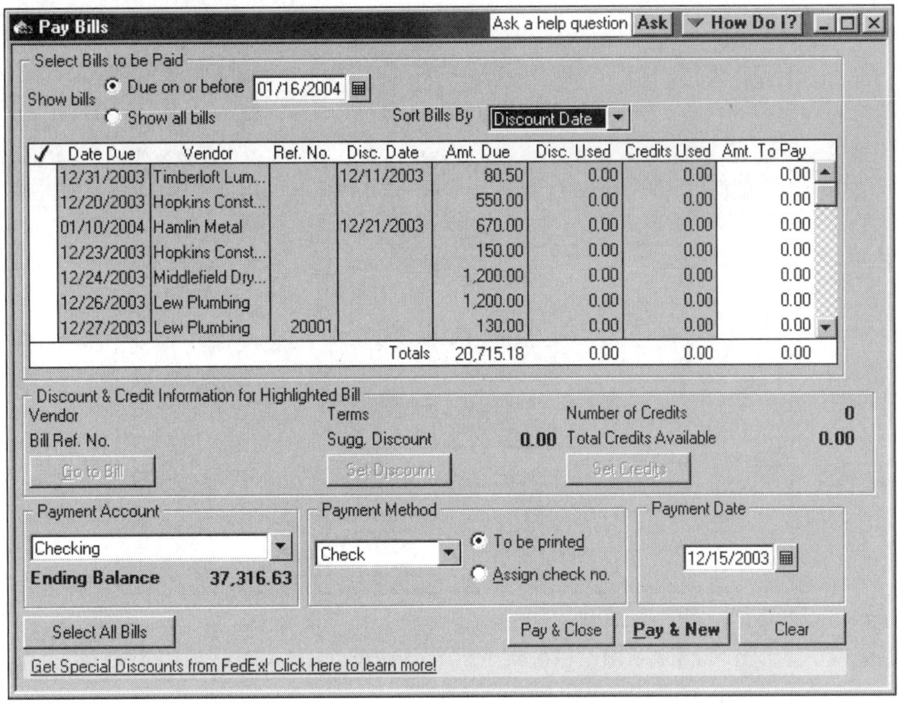

4 Click to put a checkmark next to the bill for Hamlin Metal with a due date of 1/10/04.

QuickBooks displays the discount and credit information for Hamlin Metal.

5 Click Set Discount.

6 QuickBooks displays the Discount and Credits window prefilled with information about Rock Castle's terms with Hamlin Metal, and the amount of the discount based on those terms (in this case, two percent of $670.00, or $13.40).

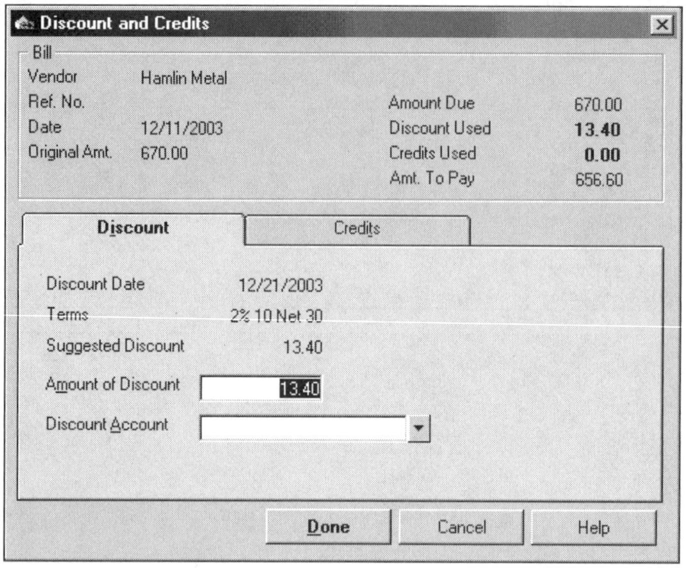

7 From the Discount Account drop-down list, choose Construction:Discounts given to track the discount amount.

8 Click Done.

9 Click Pay & Close.

Note: You can set up QuickBooks to always use discounts and credits from vendors. If you always track discounts from vendors in the same account, you can set up a default account. From the Edit menu, choose Preferences. Click Purchases & Vendors, and then click the Company Preferences tab. Select the "Automatically use discounts and credits" checkbox and choose the account in which you want QuickBooks to track the discounts you receive from vendors.

Student test and review

1 Write a check to a vendor, assigning the amount to more than one expense account.

2 Enter a bill in the Enter Bills window, and then view the bill transaction in the accounts payable register.

3 Pay the bill using the Pay Bills window.

LESSON 9 Analyzing financial data

Lesson objectives

- To discuss some of the tools QuickBooks gives you for analyzing financial data: QuickReports, preset reports, and graphs
- To create a QuickReport
- To add a column to a report
- To learn how to move a column in a report
- To learn about the types of preset reports QuickBooks offers
- To practice creating reports and viewing them onscreen
- To customize a report by changing how it looks and the data it covers (filtering)
- To learn how to process reports in batches
- To learn how to export a report to Microsoft Excel
- To practice filtering reports in Microsoft Excel
- To learn about the types of graphs QuickBooks offers
- To create and customize several graphs

Handout materials

- Handout 24: Creating a QuickReport from a list, register, or form
- Handout 25: Preset report types in QuickBooks
- Handout 26: Seeing more of an onscreen report
- Handout 27: QuickInsight graph types

Instructor preparation

- Review the lesson, including the examples, to make sure you're familiar with the material.
- Ensure that all students have a copy of qblesson.qbb on their computer's hard disk.
- Have Handouts 24 through 27 ready for distribution.

To start this lesson

Before you perform the following steps, make sure you have installed the exercise file (qblesson.qbb) on your hard disk. See "Installing the exercise file" in the Introduction to this guide if you haven't installed it.

The steps that follow will restore the exercise file to its original state so that the data in the file matches what you see on the screen as you proceed through each lesson.

To restore the exercise file (qblesson.qbb):

1. From the File menu in QuickBooks, choose Restore.

   QuickBooks displays the Restore Company Backup window.
2. In the "Get Company Backup From" section of the window, click Browse and select your c:\QBtrain directory.
3. Select the qblesson.qbb file, and then click Open.
4. In the "Restore Company Backup To" section of the window, click Browse and select your c:\QBtrain directory.
5. In the File name field of the Restore To window, type ***lesson 9*** and then click Save.
6. Click Restore.

Reports and graphs help you understand your business

So far, you've been learning ways to track your data in QuickBooks. In this lesson, you'll work with two of the most valuable tools in QuickBooks: reports and graphs. Reports and graphs give you insight into your finances; they're two of the most important benefits of tracking your data in QuickBooks.

Often, people's perceptions of their business profitability don't match the facts. If you enter your data in QuickBooks, but don't take the time to analyze the data, your business decisions are based on incomplete knowledge. Reports let you summarize your financial data so you make decisions based on analysis of the numbers.

Reports give you the bottom line—you can see exactly how profitable your business is. If it's not doing as well as you'd hoped, you can create reports that show you which areas need improvement. QuickBooks has dozens of preset reports, but if you have specific reporting needs, you can customize any QuickBooks report to show exactly the data you want. And if you're interested in getting quick information, you can use a QuickReport that lets you summarize information from your lists, forms, or registers with one click of a button.

Some people find it easier to see a visual picture of their financial data. If you're interested in learning more about trends or patterns in your business data (for example, what proportion of your income comes from consulting services as compared to product sales), QuickBooks offers six types of QuickInsight graphs.

Creating QuickReports

One of the fastest ways to see a report on your QuickBooks data is to create a QuickReport. QuickReports are predesigned reports that give you information about the items you're currently viewing onscreen. Whenever you have a list, a register, or a form displayed, you can click a button to have QuickBooks create a QuickReport.

When to use a QuickReport

Suppose you're viewing the Vendor list, and you want to see a history of all transactions for a certain vendor. Select the vendor's name, click the Report menu button, and then select QuickReport. You'll see a report listing information about each bill for that vendor.

Refer to Handout 24, "Creating a QuickReport from a list, register, or form."

Suppose that Rock Castle Construction wants to see what it owes to Patton Hardware.

To see what you owe a vendor:

1 From the Lists menu, choose Vendor List.

QuickBooks displays the Vendor list.

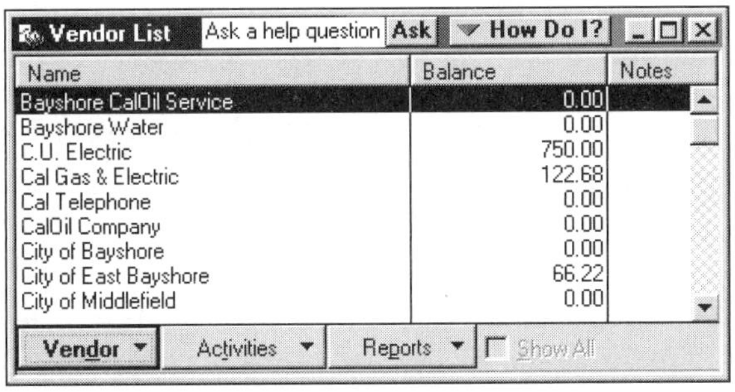

2 Select Patton Hardware Supplies.

3 Click the Reports menu button, and then select QuickReport:Patton Hardware Supplies.

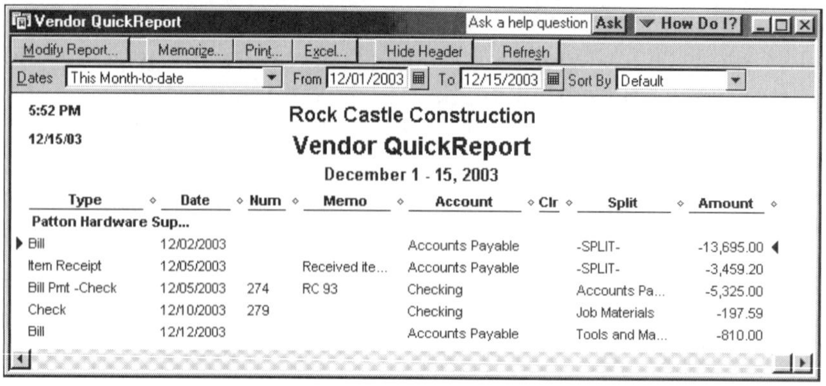

A vendor QuickReport shows all transactions for this month to date for the selected vendor, Patton Hardware Supplies. The transactions shown can include purchase orders, item receipts, bills, bill payments, and credits received from the vendor.

Note: If you want to see only unpaid bills and unapplied credits for the selected vendor, select Open Balance from the Reports menu button on the Vendor list.

Zooming in on a QuickReport

All QuickReports contain a summary of individual transactions. To help you better understand the information presented in reports, QuickBooks lets you trace report data to the individual transaction level using QuickZoom.

When you position the mouse pointer over a number in a report and you see the QuickZoom symbol (a magnifying glass with a Z in it), you can double-click the number to display the original transaction in QuickBooks.

Suppose you want more detail about the item receipt shown in the report. (You use an item receipt in QuickBooks when you want to record that you've received inventory items, but you haven't yet received a bill.)

To see more detail about an item:

1 Position the mouse pointer over the item receipt dated 12/05/03.

The arrow pointer turns into a magnifying glass with the letter Z (z for zoom).

2 Double-click the item receipt.

QuickBooks displays the Create Item Receipts window for the selected transaction.

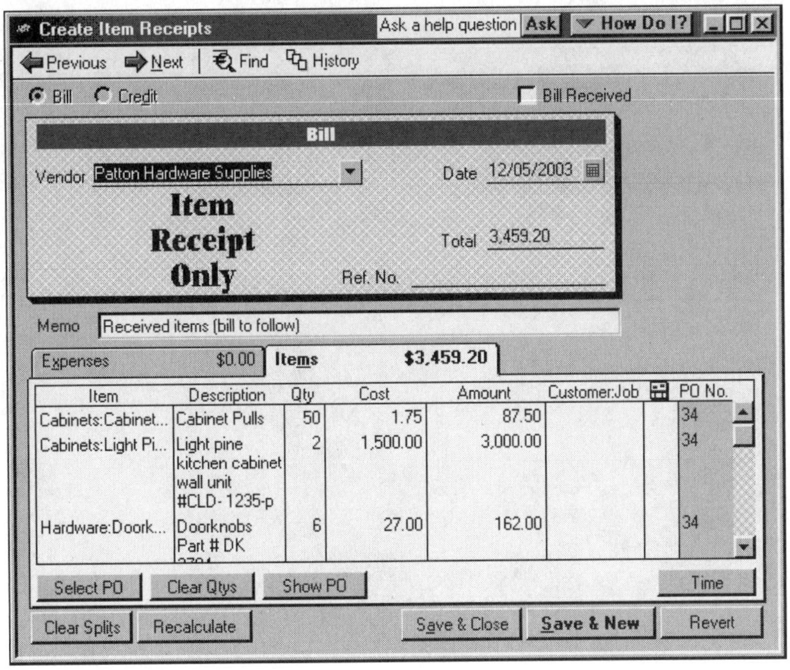

3 Click Save & Close to close the window.

QuickBooks returns you to the QuickReport.

Customizing QuickReports

Each QuickReport window has a buttonbar at the top of the report for customizing report content and layout.

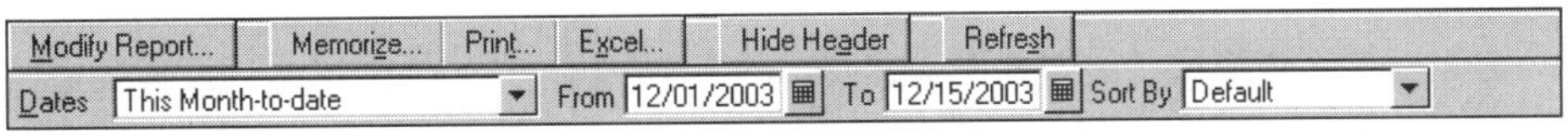

In this exercise, you'll customize the QuickReport you just created to display transaction numbers in the report.

To add a column to a report:

1 In the QuickReport window, click Modify Report.

QuickBooks displays the Modify Report window.

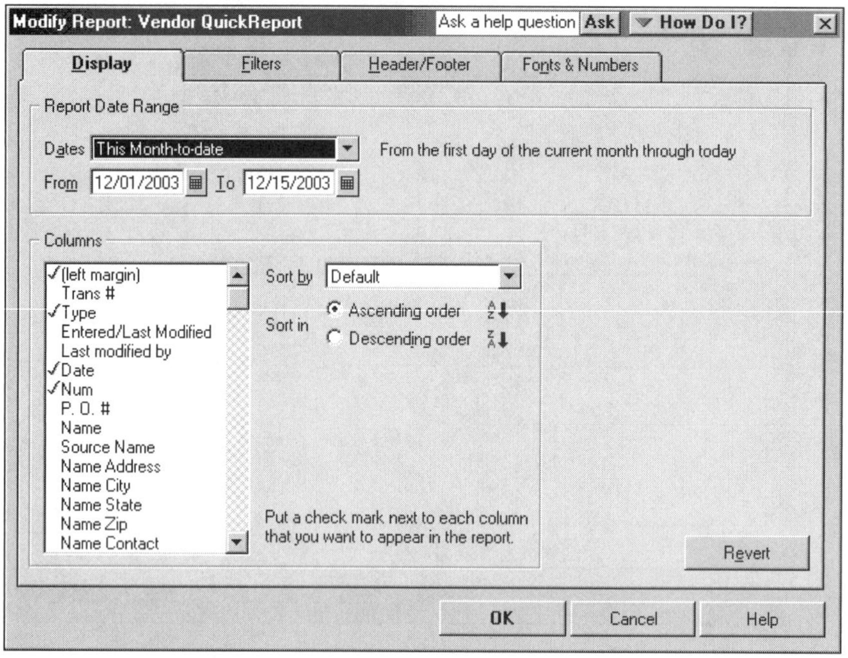

Use the Display tab of the Modify Report window to select the columns to include in the report and the date range of the report.

2 In the Columns list, select Trans #.

QuickBooks displays a checkmark next to Trans # to indicate that it's selected.

3 Click OK to accept the changes.

QuickBooks displays the customized vendor QuickReport.

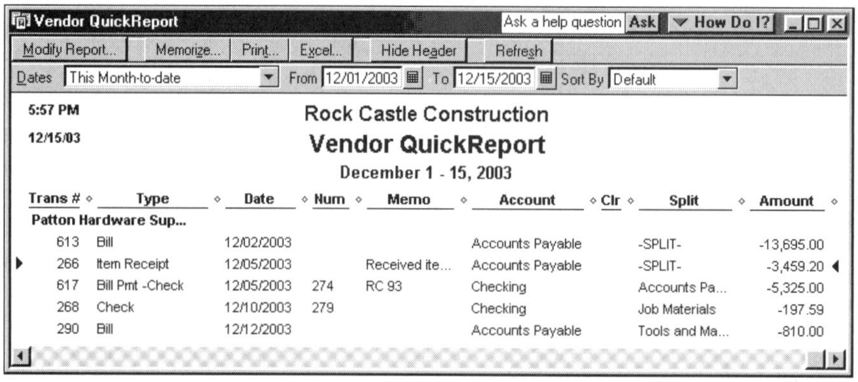

Notice that the item receipt from Patton Hardware Supplies is now listed as Transaction #266.

Next, you'll move the Trans # column to a new position in the report.

To move a report column:

1 Position your mouse pointer over the Trans # column that you added to the QuickReport.

  The mouse pointer changes shape to look like a hand.

2 Hold down the left mouse button and drag the Trans # column to the right until you see an arrow between the Date Column and the Num column.

3 Release the mouse button.

  QuickBooks places the Trans # column between the Date column and the Num column.

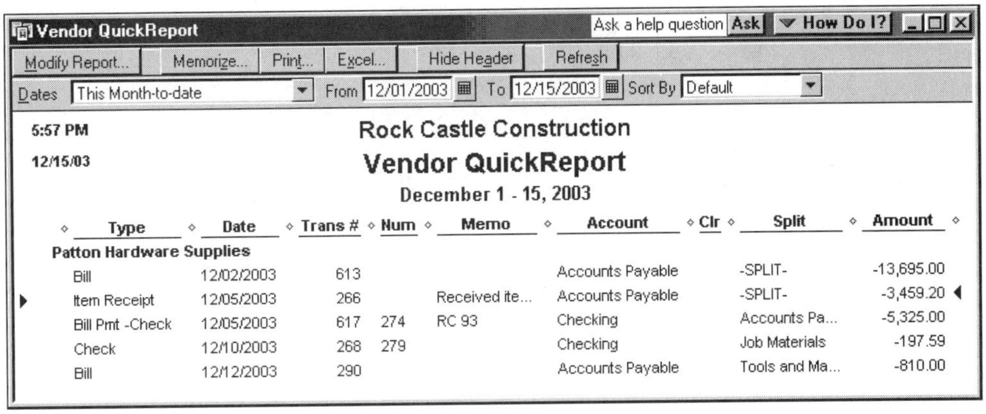

Next, you'll use the QuickReport buttonbar to customize the report header.

To change information in the report heading:

4 In the QuickReport window, click Modify Report, and then click the Header/Footer tab.

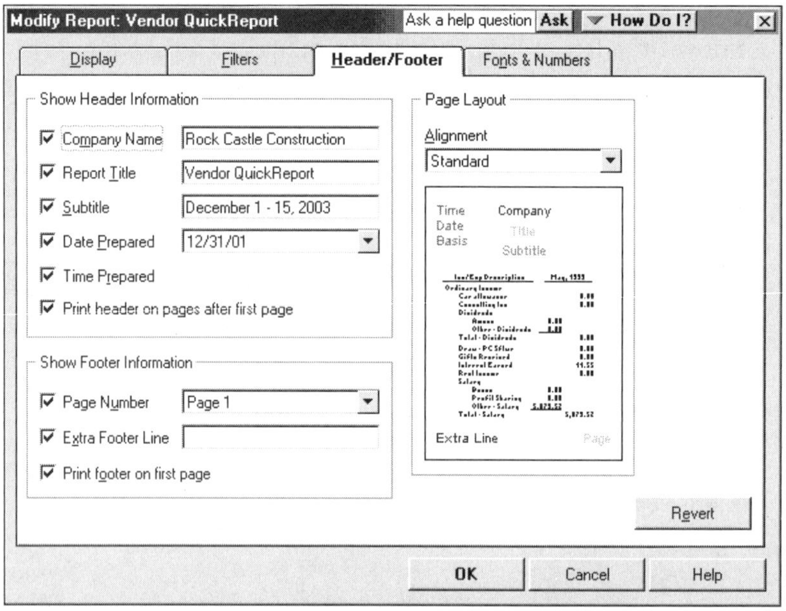

On the Header/Footer tab, you can change the company name, report title, subtitle, and date and time prepared. You can also specify whether to print the header on all pages or on just the first page. The Header/Footer tab is the same for all QuickBooks reports.

Use this window to change the report title from Vendor QuickReport to Vendor History Report.

5 In the Report Title field, select the text for "Vendor QuickReport," and type ***Vendor History Report*** to replace the title.

6 Click OK to close the Modify Report window.

QuickBooks changes the title of the report and displays the new report.

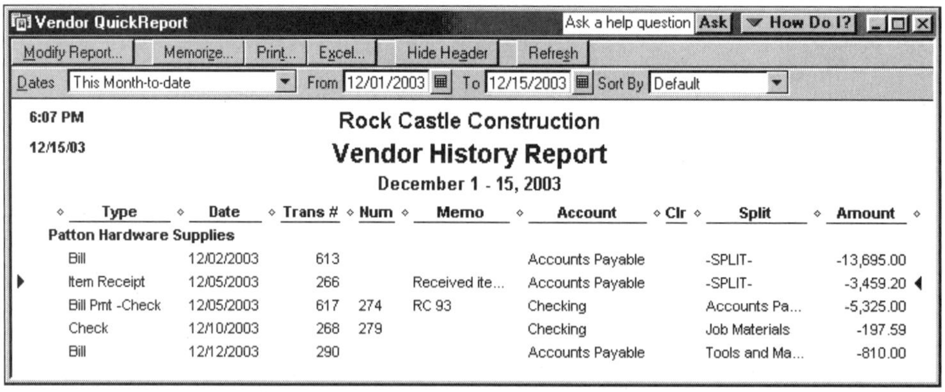

7 Close the QuickReport window.

8 Close the Vendor list.

Creating and customizing preset reports

In addition to QuickReports, QuickBooks has dozens of preset report formats. You can create profit and loss reports, balance sheet reports, accounts receivable reports, sales reports, accounts payable reports, inventory reports, and many other types of reports.

Refer to Handout 25, "Preset report types in QuickBooks," for this discussion.

The Reports menu categorizes the preset reports into 12 major categories:

Company & Financial reports include the following:

- Profit and loss reports give you a global view of your company's income, expenses, and net profit or loss over a specific period of time.
- Balance sheet reports show the financial position of your business by listing assets, liabilities, and equity.
- Statement of cash flows reports show the net change in your cash during a period of time.

Customers & Receivables (accounts receivable) reports give you information about the receivables side of your business: which invoices are due (or overdue), how much each customer owes your company, and so on.

Sales reports give you information about what you have sold and to whom.

Jobs & Time reports (QuickBooks Pro only) give information about the status and profitability of the jobs/projects you track in QuickBooks.

Vendors & Payables (accounts payable) reports give you information about the payables side of your business, including which bills are due, your sales tax liability, and your current balance with each vendor.

Purchases reports give you information about your purchases.

Inventory reports give you information about status (such as the quantities you have on hand or on order) and the value of your inventory.

Employees & Payroll reports summarize the information you need to pay your current payroll liabilities and fill out your tax forms. QuickBooks has these payroll reports: summary, employee earnings, liabilities, item detail, transaction detail, and transactions by payee.

Banking reports include check detail, deposit detail, and missing check reports.

Accountant & Taxes reports include income tax summary, income tax detail, general ledger, trial balance, journal, transaction journal, and audit trail reports.

Budget reports show how your income and expenses compare to the budgets you've set up.

List reports let you report on any information stored in a QuickBooks list.

Creating a balance sheet comparison report

The balance sheet comparison report compares the current year against the previous year in both dollar amount and percentage.

To create a balance sheet comparison report for Rock Castle Construction:

1 From the Reports menu, choose Company & Financial. Then choose Balance Sheet Prev Year Comparison.

The report on your screen should resemble the following figure.

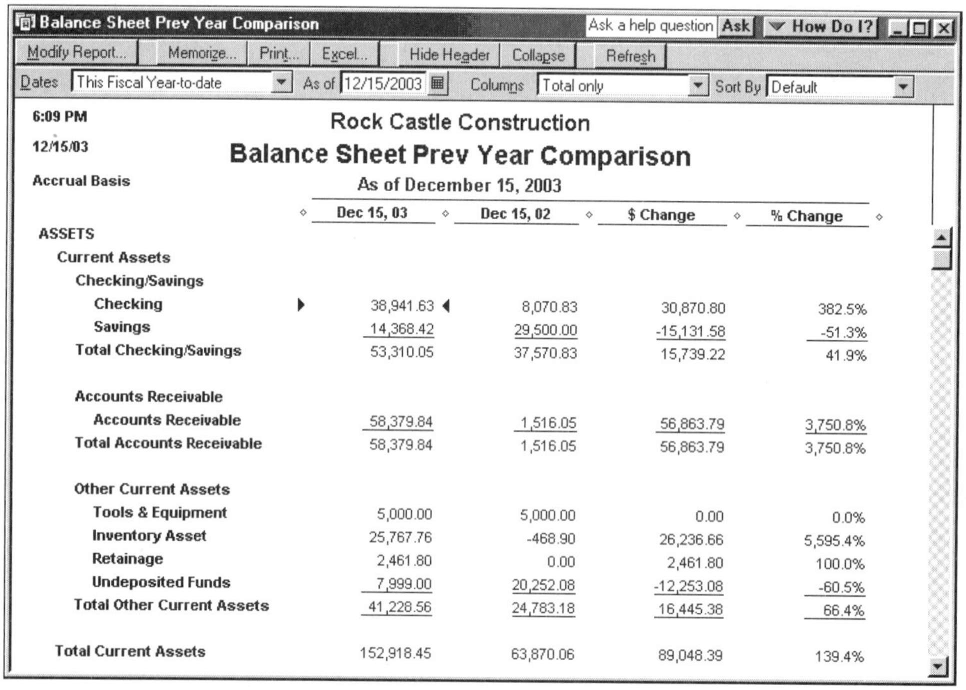

6:09 PM
12/15/03
Accrual Basis

Rock Castle Construction
Balance Sheet Prev Year Comparison
As of December 15, 2003

	Dec 15, 03	Dec 15, 02	$ Change	% Change
ASSETS				
Current Assets				
Checking/Savings				
Checking	38,941.63	8,070.83	30,870.80	382.5%
Savings	14,368.42	29,500.00	-15,131.58	-51.3%
Total Checking/Savings	53,310.05	37,570.83	15,739.22	41.9%
Accounts Receivable				
Accounts Receivable	58,379.84	1,516.05	56,863.79	3,750.8%
Total Accounts Receivable	58,379.84	1,516.05	56,863.79	3,750.8%
Other Current Assets				
Tools & Equipment	5,000.00	5,000.00	0.00	0.0%
Inventory Asset	25,767.76	-468.90	26,236.66	5,595.4%
Retainage	2,461.80	0.00	2,461.80	100.0%
Undeposited Funds	7,999.00	20,252.08	-12,253.08	-60.5%
Total Other Current Assets	41,228.56	24,783.18	16,445.38	66.4%
Total Current Assets	152,918.45	63,870.06	89,048.39	139.4%

2 Scroll the report window to see more of the report.

Notice that the buttonbar at the top of the report is the same buttonbar you saw in the QuickReport window.

3 Keep the report displayed on your screen. You'll use it in the next exercise.

Refer to Handout 26, "Seeing more of an onscreen report."

Filtering reports

You can customize preset reports the same way you customize QuickReports. In this exercise you'll customize the balance sheet comparison report and *filter* it to include only the transactions you specify.

Report filters let you set custom criteria for the transactions you want included in a report. When you filter a report, QuickBooks includes only those transactions that match the rules you create.

To filter a preset report:

1 With the balance sheet comparison report displayed, click Modify Report on the report buttonbar, and then click the Filters tab.

QuickBooks displays the Filters tab of the Modify Report window.

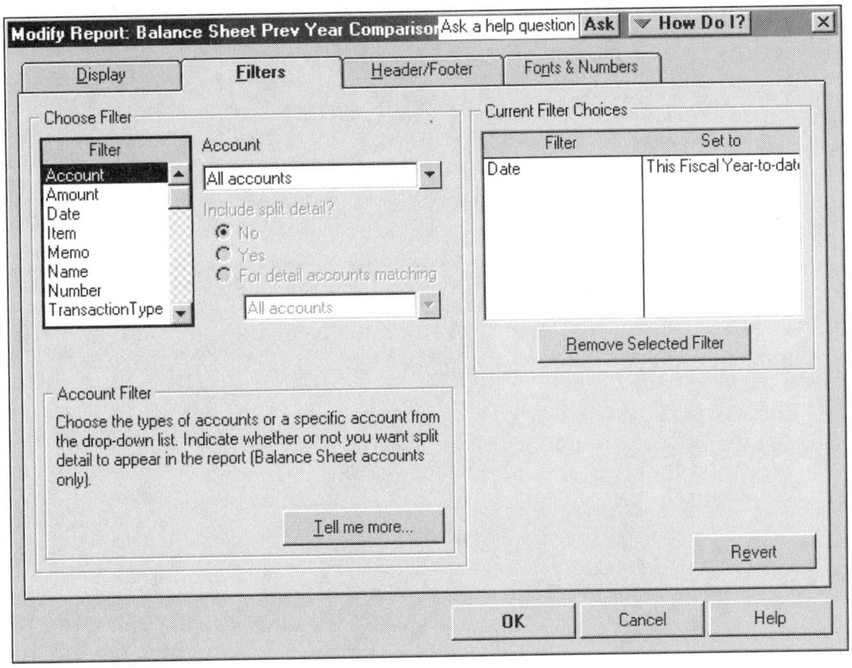

Suppose you want to see only the asset accounts on the comparison balance sheet. You can filter the report by account.

2 In the Filter scroll box, make sure Account is selected.

Notice that QuickBooks provides a description of the selected filter below the list of filters. If you need more information about how applying a particular filter will affect the report, click Tell me more.

3 In the Account field, choose All assets from the drop-down list.

4 Click OK.

QuickBooks displays the customized balance sheet comparison report.

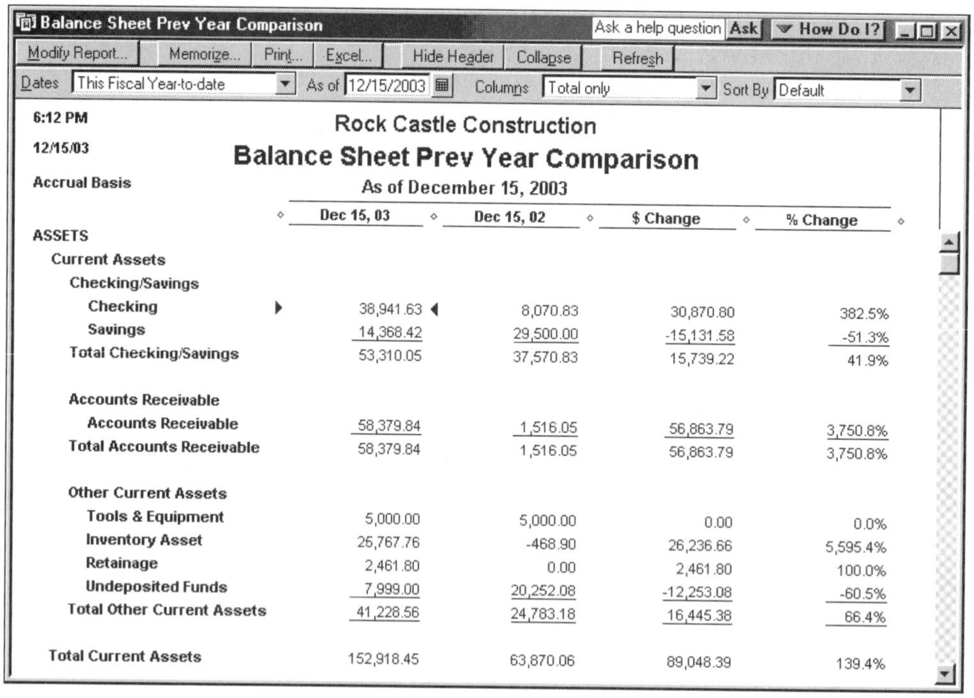

6:12 PM
12/15/03
Accrual Basis

Rock Castle Construction
Balance Sheet Prev Year Comparison
As of December 15, 2003

	Dec 15, 03	Dec 15, 02	$ Change	% Change
ASSETS				
Current Assets				
Checking/Savings				
Checking	38,941.63	8,070.83	30,870.80	382.5%
Savings	14,368.42	29,500.00	-15,131.58	-51.3%
Total Checking/Savings	53,310.05	37,570.83	15,739.22	41.9%
Accounts Receivable				
Accounts Receivable	58,379.84	1,516.05	56,863.79	3,750.8%
Total Accounts Receivable	58,379.84	1,516.05	56,863.79	3,750.8%
Other Current Assets				
Tools & Equipment	5,000.00	5,000.00	0.00	0.0%
Inventory Asset	25,767.76	-468.90	26,236.66	5,595.4%
Retainage	2,461.80	0.00	2,461.80	100.0%
Undeposited Funds	7,999.00	20,252.08	-12,253.08	-60.5%
Total Other Current Assets	41,228.56	24,783.18	16,445.38	66.4%
Total Current Assets	152,918.45	63,870.06	89,048.39	139.4%

If you scroll to the bottom of the report, you'll see that QuickBooks removed the liability and other accounts from the report.

5 Close the report window.

6 Click No when QuickBooks asks if you want to add this report to the Memorized Report list.

Creating and customizing a sales report

In this exercise, you'll create a QuickBooks sales report, which you will then customize by changing the date range it covers.

To create a sales report:

1 From the Reports menu, choose Sales, and then choose Sales By Customer Summary from the submenu.

QuickBooks displays the sales by customer summary report.

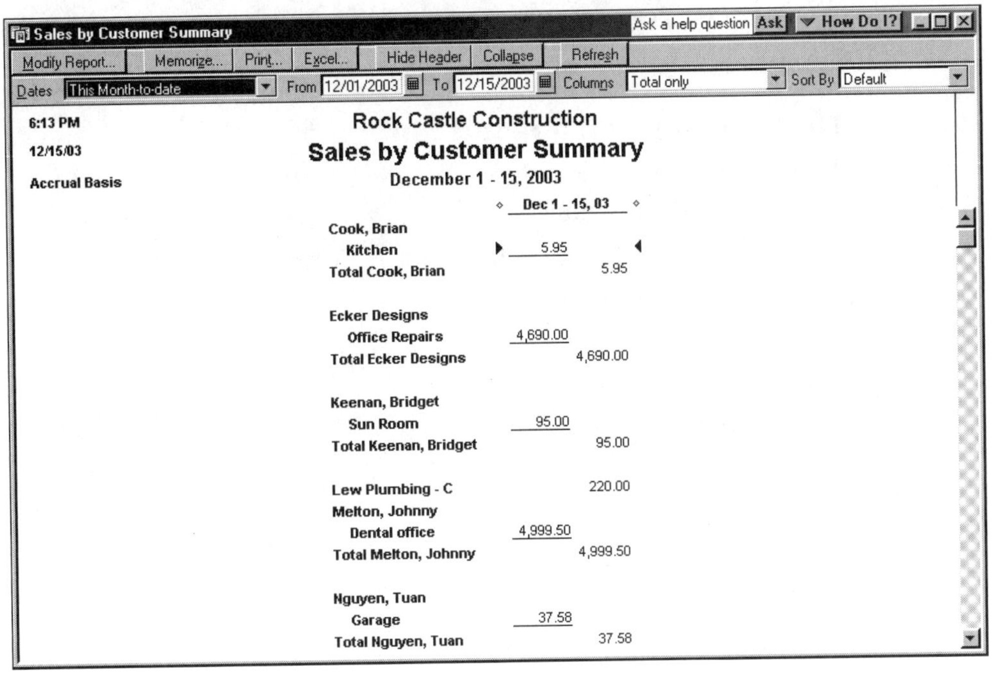

The Dates field in the report buttonbar shows that the report covers "This Month-to-date." Customize the report so you can see sales figures from January 2003.

To customize a report:

1 In the Dates field, select All from the drop-down list.

QuickBooks updates the report and displays the new data.

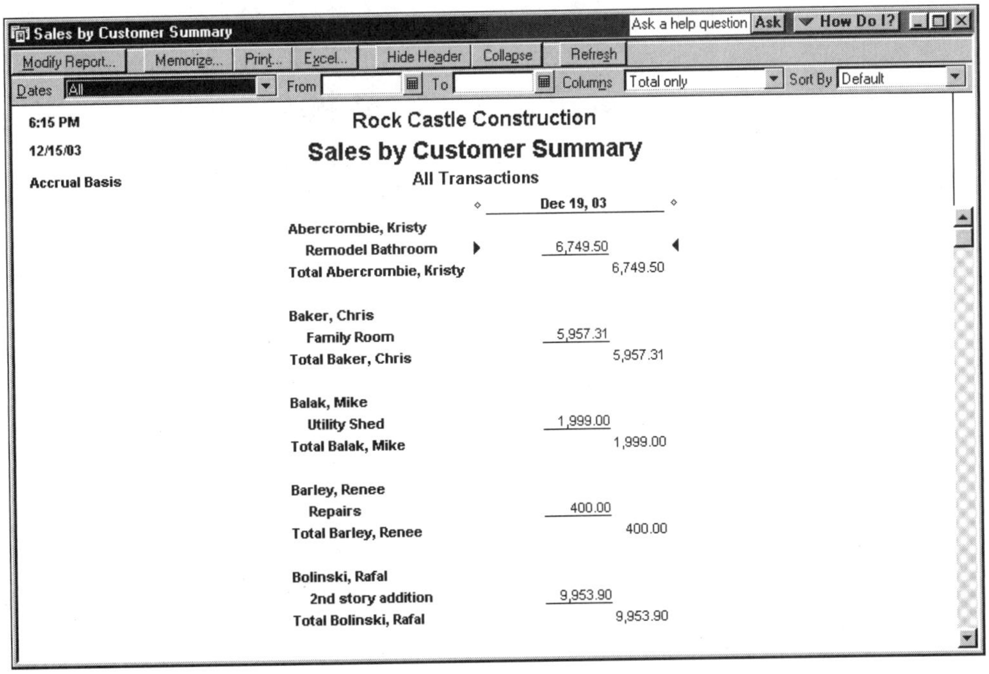

Using QuickZoom in a preset report

As with all QuickBooks reports, you can QuickZoom any item in the report to see more detail.

To QuickZoom on a report item:

1 Position the mouse pointer over the $11,105.00—the amount for Anton Teschner's sun room.

The arrow pointer turns into a magnifying glass with a Z in it.

2 Double-click $11,105.00.

QuickBooks displays a QuickZoom report showing sales by customer detail.

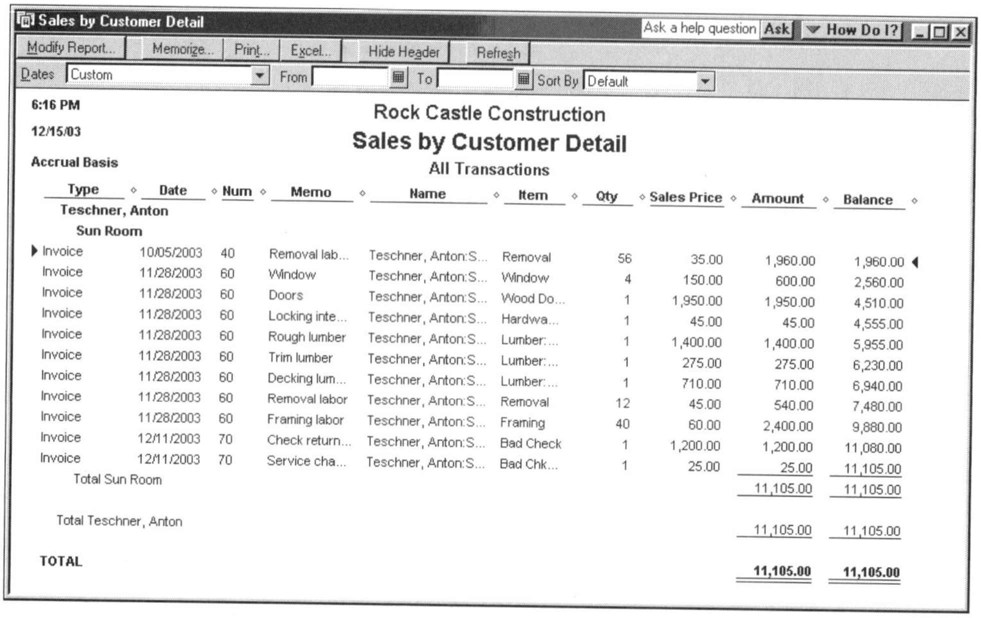

6:16 PM
12/15/03
Accrual Basis

Rock Castle Construction
Sales by Customer Detail
All Transactions

Type	Date	Num	Memo	Name	Item	Qty	Sales Price	Amount	Balance
Teschner, Anton									
Sun Room									
Invoice	10/05/2003	40	Removal lab...	Teschner, Anton:S...	Removal	56	35.00	1,960.00	1,960.00
Invoice	11/28/2003	60	Window	Teschner, Anton:S...	Window	4	150.00	600.00	2,560.00
Invoice	11/28/2003	60	Doors	Teschner, Anton:S...	Wood Do...	1	1,950.00	1,950.00	4,510.00
Invoice	11/28/2003	60	Locking inte...	Teschner, Anton:S...	Hardwa...	1	45.00	45.00	4,555.00
Invoice	11/28/2003	60	Rough lumber	Teschner, Anton:S...	Lumber:...	1	1,400.00	1,400.00	5,955.00
Invoice	11/28/2003	60	Trim lumber	Teschner, Anton:S...	Lumber:...	1	275.00	275.00	6,230.00
Invoice	11/28/2003	60	Decking lum...	Teschner, Anton:S...	Lumber:...	1	710.00	710.00	6,940.00
Invoice	11/28/2003	60	Removal labor	Teschner, Anton:S...	Removal	12	45.00	540.00	7,480.00
Invoice	11/28/2003	60	Framing labor	Teschner, Anton:S...	Framing	40	60.00	2,400.00	9,880.00
Invoice	12/11/2003	70	Check return...	Teschner, Anton:S...	Bad Check	1	1,200.00	1,200.00	11,080.00
Invoice	12/11/2003	70	Service cha...	Teschner, Anton:S...	Bad Chk...	1	25.00	25.00	11,105.00
Total Sun Room								11,105.00	11,105.00
Total Teschner, Anton								11,105.00	11,105.00
TOTAL								**11,105.00**	**11,105.00**

To QuickZoom further to display the original invoice for a transaction:

1 Position the mouse pointer over the first item on the report (invoice #40 dated 10/05/2003 for Removal labor).

2 Double-click anywhere in the first line.

QuickBooks displays Invoice #40 for Anton Teschner's sun room.

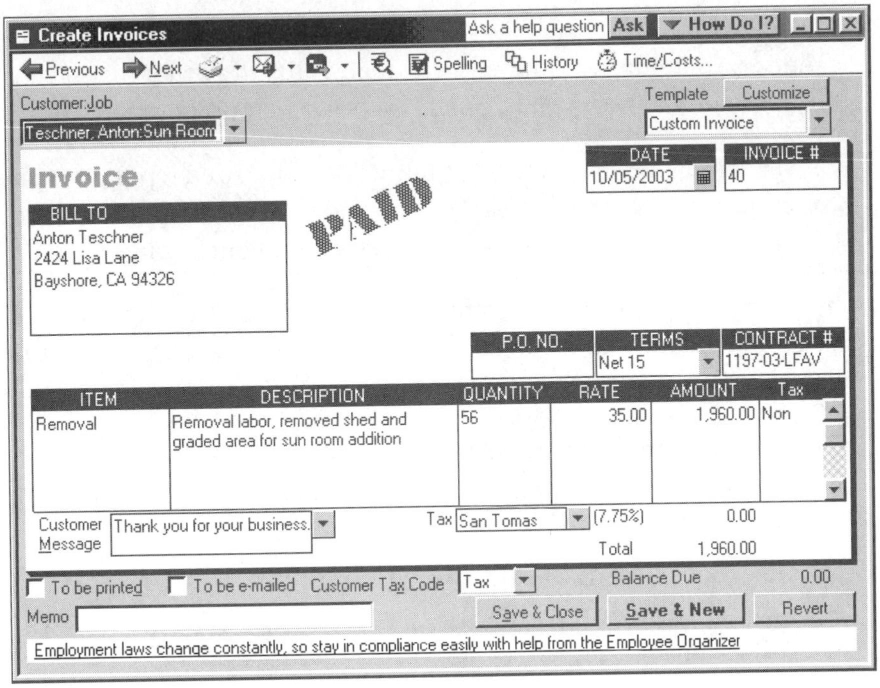

Notice that QuickBooks puts a paid stamp on invoices for which payment has been received in full.

3 From the Window menu, choose Close All.

4 Click No when QuickBooks asks if you want to memorize the report.

What you see when you QuickZoom in a report depends on the type of report displayed:

- If the report shows summary figures (like the sales by customer summary report we just displayed) and you QuickZoom an amount, QuickBooks displays a transaction report that includes the transactions which contribute to that amount.
- If the report shows transactions and you QuickZoom a transaction, QuickBooks displays the invoice, bill, or other form for the requested transaction.

Saving report settings

After you have customized a report to provide the information you need, you can have QuickBooks *memorize* the settings so you can quickly produce the same report in the future. (QuickBooks memorizes a report's settings, not the actual data.)

If you use one of the QuickBooks Premier products, you can export the settings for memorized reports as report templates. A report template lets you specify all of a report's settings in advance—for example, report date, format, and filters. Report templates can be imported into other QuickBooks data files and then accessed from the Memorized Report list.

Creating memorized report groups

In addition to saving report settings, you can create memorized report groups that you can use to organize your memorized reports in a way that makes sense for your business and to allow you to quickly process a group of reports at once.

QuickBooks comes preset with a number of memorized report groups each containing common reports for each area. You can add your own reports to these groups, modify the groups to meet your needs, and even create your own groups.

In this exercise, you'll create a memorized group called "Year End" to which you will add some memorized reports. Later, you learn how you can batch process memorized reports.

To create a memorize report group:

1 Choose Memorized Reports from the Reports menu, and then choose Memorized Report List.

QuickBooks opens the Memorized Report list.

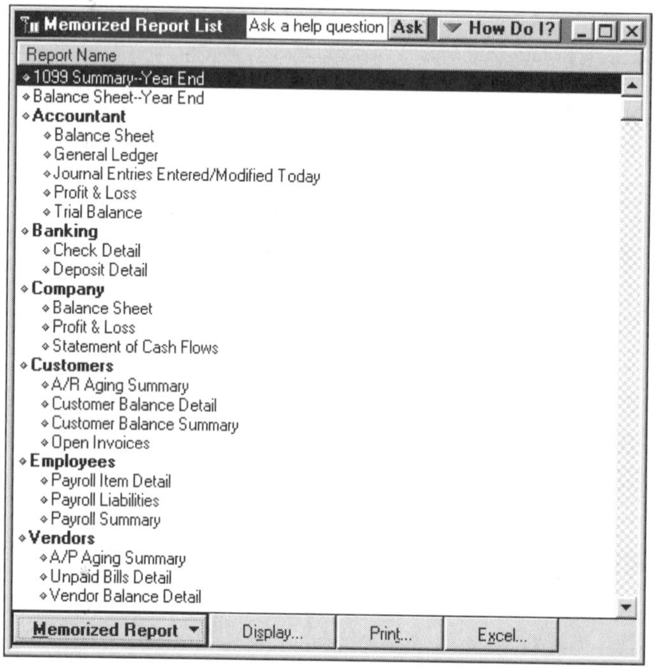

2 In the Memorized Report list, click the Memorized Report menu button, and choose New Group.

3 In the Name field of the New Memorized Report Group window, type ***Year End***.

Your window should look like this.

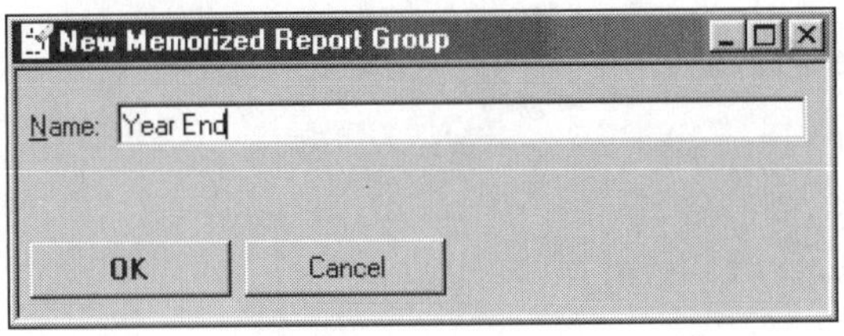

4 Click OK.

QuickBooks adds the new group to the Memorized Report list.

Memorizing preset reports

Now, you'll memorize a report and it to the memorized report group you just created.

To memorize a report:

1 From the Reports menu, choose Accountant & Taxes, and then choose Income Tax Summary.

2 On the report buttonbar, click Memorize.

QuickBooks displays the Memorize Report window.

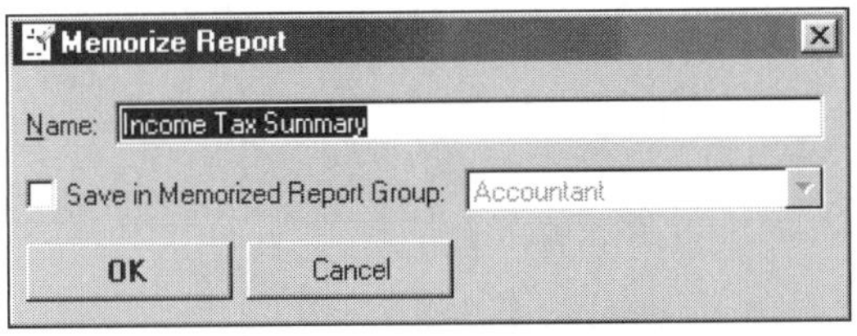

3 Leave the name of the report as is.

4 Click the "Save in Memorized Report Group" checkbox to select it, and then choose Year End from the drop-down list.

Your window should look like this.

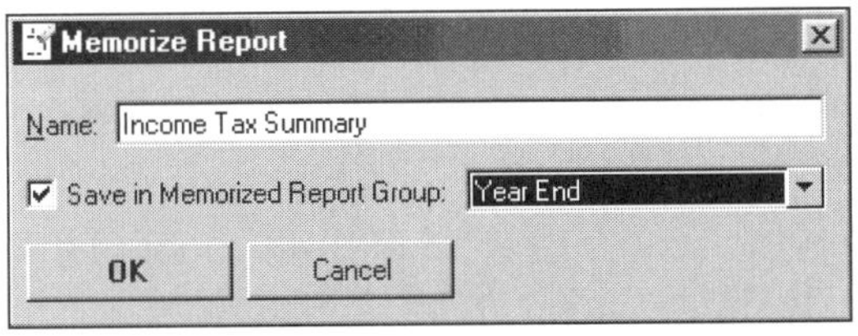

5 Click OK to memorize the report and add it to the Year End memorized report group.

6 Close the income tax summary report.

Adding reports to memorized report groups

Now, you'll add two previously memorized reports to the Year End group.

To add memorized reports to a memorized report group:

1. In the Memorized Report List window, select the report called "1099 Summary--Year End."
2. Click the Memorized Report menu button, and then choose Edit.

   QuickBooks opens the Edit Memorized Report window.
3. Leave the report name as is.
4. Click the "Save in Memorized Report Group" checkbox to select it, and then choose Year End from the drop-down list.
5. Click OK.

   QuickBooks moves the 1099 Summary report to the Year End memorized report group.

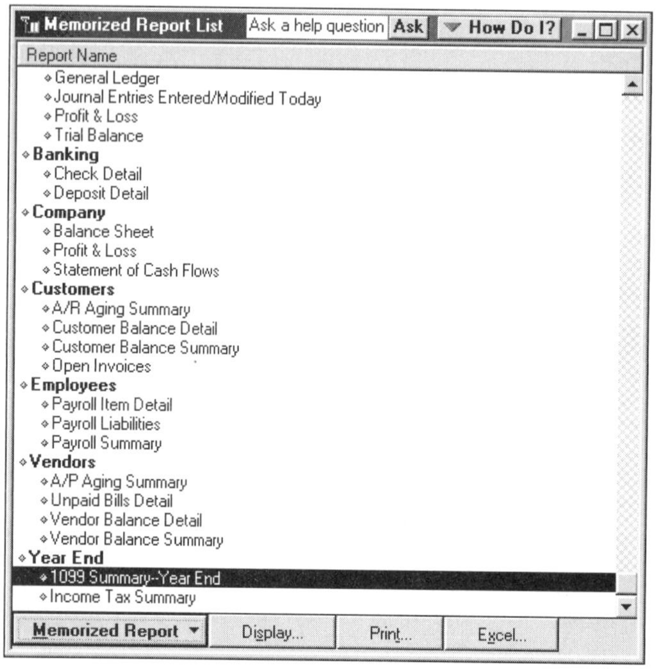

6. In the Memorized Report List window, select the report called "Balance Sheet--Year End."
7. Click the Memorized Report menu button, and then choose Edit.
8. Leave the report name as is.
9. Click the "Save in Memorized Report Group" checkbox to select it, and then choose Year End from the drop-down list.
10. Click OK.

Once a report is memorized, you can easily display it from the QuickBooks Memorized Report list.

To display a memorized report:

1 In the Memorized Report list, select "Balance Sheet--Year End."

2 Click Display.

QuickBooks displays the report.

3 Leave the report open.

Printing reports

Any time you have a report displayed in the report window, you can print it by clicking the Print button in the report buttonbar.

To print a report:

1 With the balance sheet summary report displayed, click Print.

QuickBooks displays the Print Reports window.

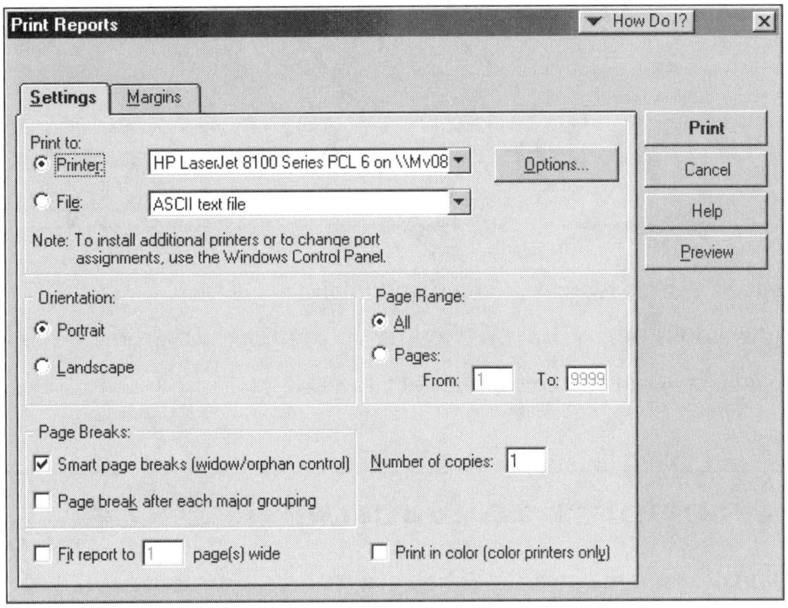

In the Print Reports window you can select the print orientation and tell QuickBooks where you would like the pages to break in multi-page reports.

2 Click Preview to see how the report will look when you print it.

QuickBooks displays a preview of your report onscreen.

3 Click Close to close the Print Preview window.

4 Close the Print Reports window, and then close the report.

Processing reports in groups

Organizing your memorized reports in groups makes it fast and easy to process several reports at once. Now, you'll process the reports you added to the Year End report group you created in the previous exercise.

To batch process reports:

1. In the Memorized Report list, select Year End.
2. Click Display.

   QuickBooks opens the Process Multiple Reports window. You can use this window to display or print the selected reports. You can also change the date range for reports in this window before you display or print them by clicking in the From or To columns.

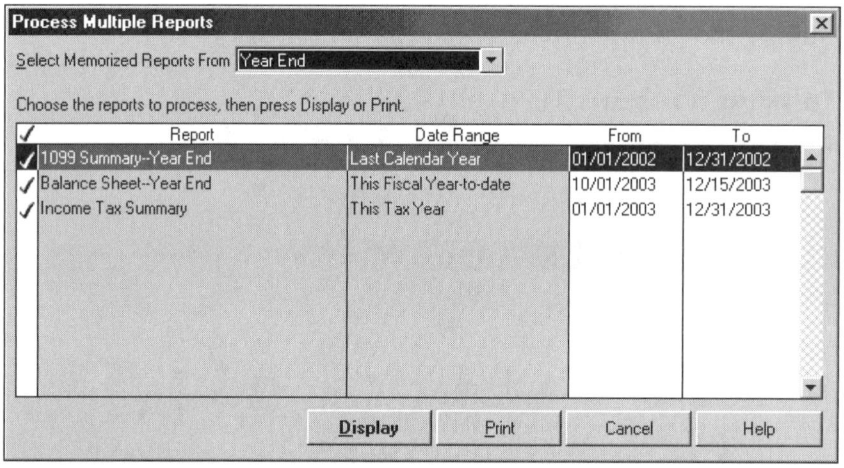

3. Leave all three reports selected and click Display.

   QuickBooks opens the three reports in the Year End group.
4. From the Window menu, choose Close All.

Exporting reports to Microsoft Excel

Occasionally, you may want to change a report's appearance or contents in ways that aren't available in QuickBooks, filter report data in ways that you can't in QuickBooks, or run what-if scenarios on your QuickBooks data.

You can send QuickBooks Pro or Premier reports to Microsoft Excel. Since the changes you make in Excel don't affect your QuickBooks data, you're free to customize reports as needed, and even change data to run what-if scenarios.

Note: **To proceed with this exercise, you need QuickBooks Pro or Premier and Microsoft Excel 97, 2000, or 2002.** If you don't have Excel, proceed to "Creating QuickInsight graphs" on page 200.

Sending a report to Microsoft Excel

When exporting a report to Microsoft Excel, you indicate whether or not you want to preserve the formatting from your QuickBooks report. You also have the option of turning on or off several Excel features from within QuickBooks.

By default, QuickBooks preserves the look of your report when exporting to Microsoft Excel, and turns on the following Excel features:

- **AutoFit** sets column widths in Excel wide enough to display your data without cutting off words or numbers.
- **Freeze panes** allows you to scroll through data while keeping the row and column headers in view.
- **Show Gridlines** turns on gridlines in Excel.

In this exercise, you learn how to select which QuickBooks report formatting options you want to preserve in Excel, and how to turn on and off certain Excel features from within QuickBooks.

To send a report to Microsoft Excel:

1. From the Reports menu, choose Company & Financial, and then choose Balance Sheet Standard.
2. On the Report buttonbar, click Modify Report.

   QuickBooks displays the Modify report window.

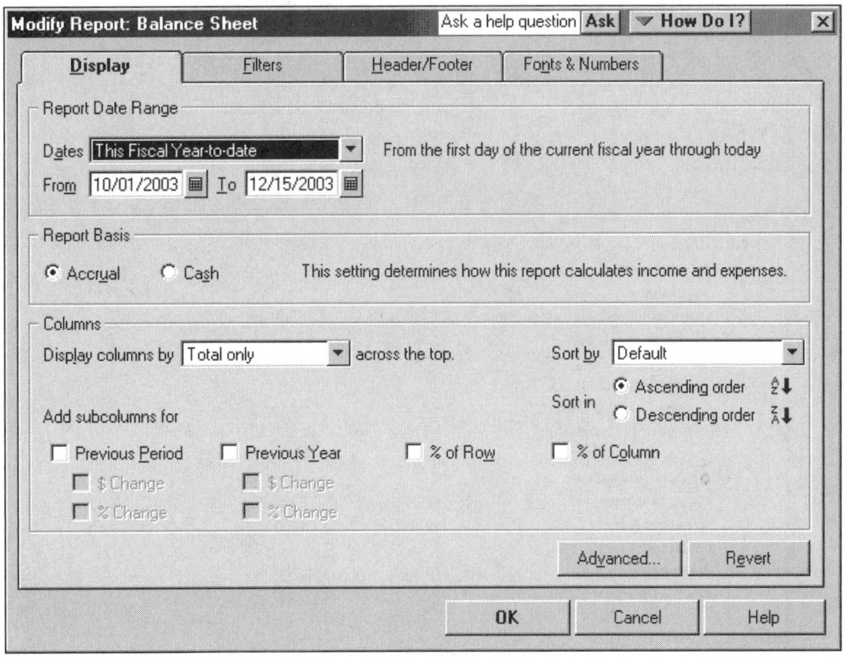

3. In the "Add subcolumns for" area, click the Previous Period checkbox, and then click the $ Change and % Change checkboxes.

Your screen should resemble the following.

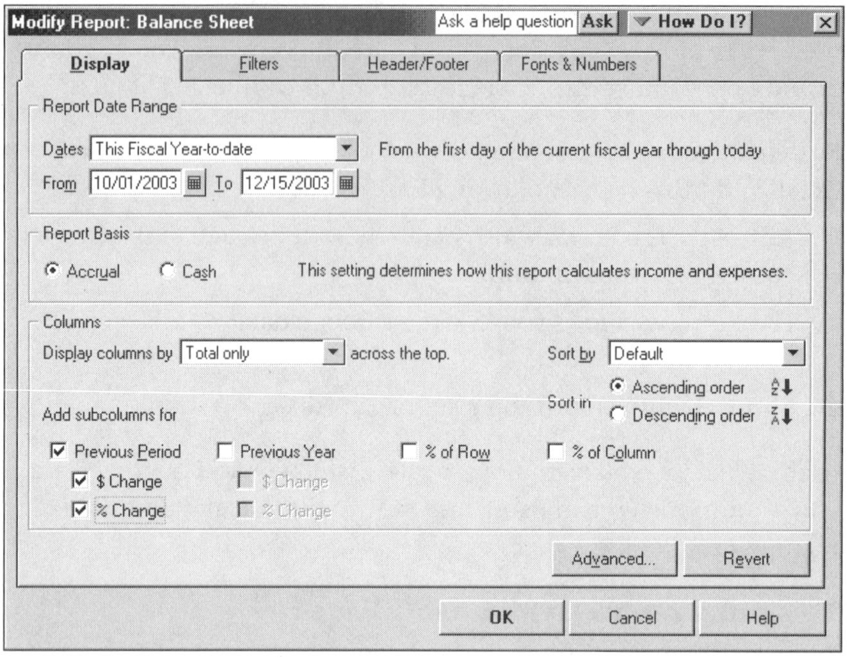

4 Click OK.

Your balance sheet should now look like this.

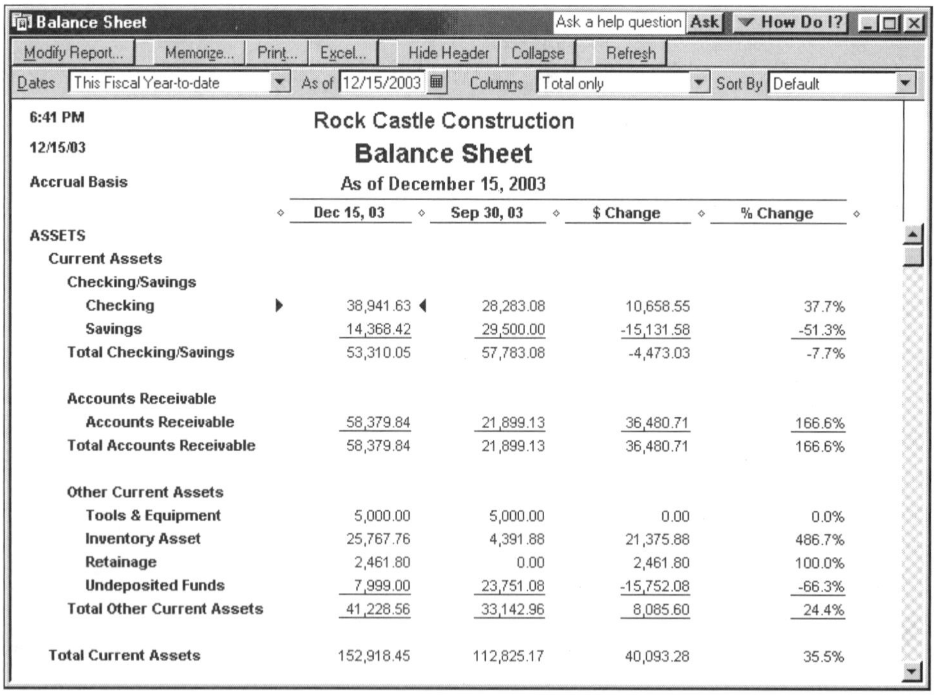

5 On the Report buttonbar, click Excel.

QuickBooks displays the Export Report to Excel window.

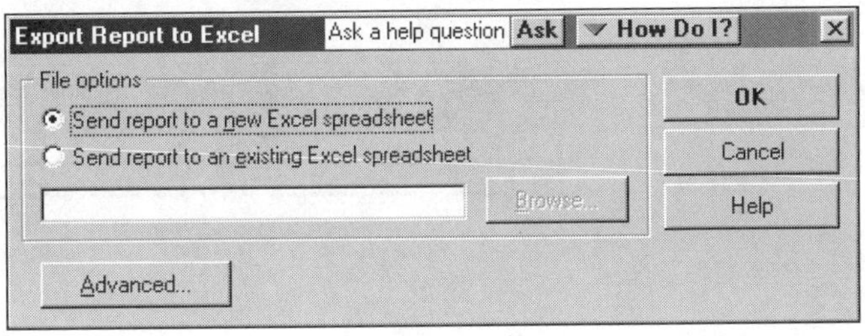

6 Make sure that "Send report to a new Excel spreadsheet" is selected.

7 Click Advanced.

QuickBooks displays the Export Report to Excel - Advanced options window.

8 Under Formatting options, click the Colors checkbox to clear it.

The title font will remain blue in QuickBooks, but display in black in Excel.

9 Under Excel features, select the Auto Filtering checkbox.

Your screen should now resemble the following.

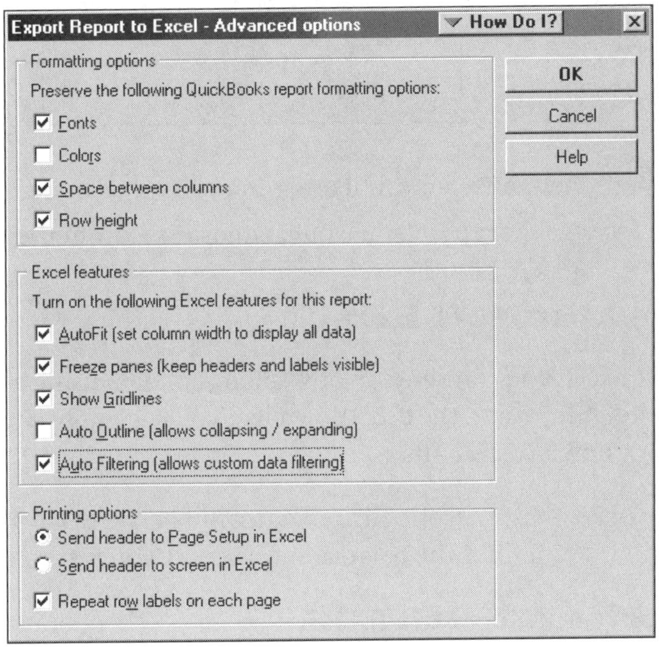

10 Click OK to close the Advanced options window.

11 Click OK.

QuickBooks starts Excel (if it's not running already) and sends the report to a new spreadsheet.

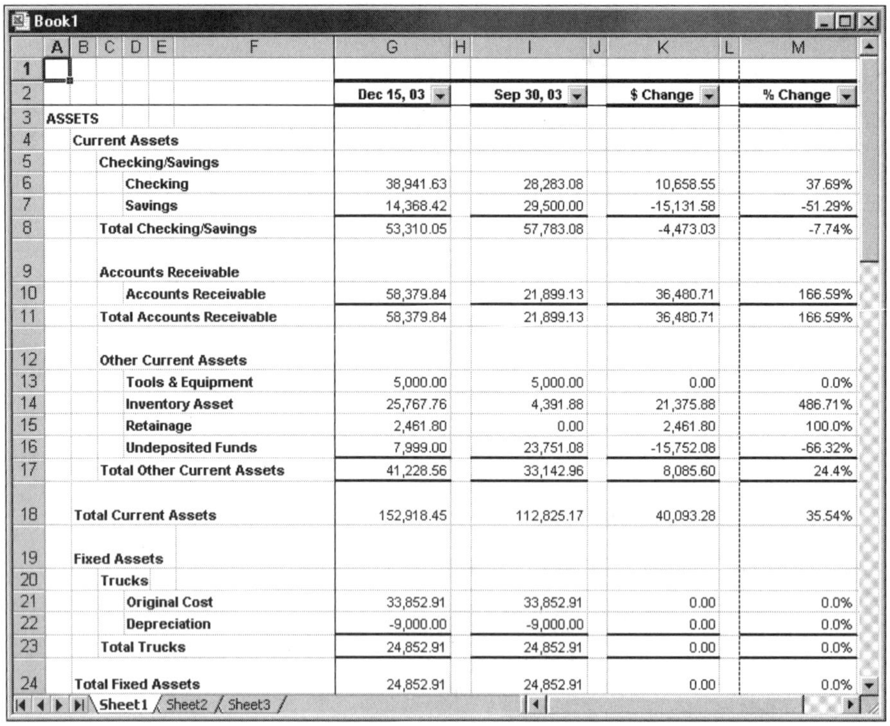

		Dec 15, 03	Sep 30, 03	$ Change	% Change
3	ASSETS				
4	Current Assets				
5	Checking/Savings				
6	Checking	38,941.63	28,283.08	10,658.55	37.69%
7	Savings	14,368.42	29,500.00	-15,131.58	-51.29%
8	Total Checking/Savings	53,310.05	57,783.08	-4,473.03	-7.74%
9	Accounts Receivable				
10	Accounts Receivable	58,379.84	21,899.13	36,480.71	166.59%
11	Total Accounts Receivable	58,379.84	21,899.13	36,480.71	166.59%
12	Other Current Assets				
13	Tools & Equipment	5,000.00	5,000.00	0.00	0.0%
14	Inventory Asset	25,767.76	4,391.88	21,375.88	486.71%
15	Retainage	2,461.80	0.00	2,461.80	100.0%
16	Undeposited Funds	7,999.00	23,751.08	-15,752.08	-66.32%
17	Total Other Current Assets	41,228.56	33,142.96	8,085.60	24.4%
18	Total Current Assets	152,918.45	112,825.17	40,093.28	35.54%
19	Fixed Assets				
20	Trucks				
21	Original Cost	33,852.91	33,852.91	0.00	0.0%
22	Depreciation	-9,000.00	-9,000.00	0.00	0.0%
23	Total Trucks	24,852.91	24,852.91	0.00	0.0%
24	Total Fixed Assets	24,852.91	24,852.91	0.00	0.0%

12 Leave the report open in Excel; you'll use it in the next exercise.

If you wanted to save the report, you would choose Save from the Excel File menu.

Filtering a report in Microsoft Excel

Within Microsoft Excel, you can filter on any column of data using a drop-down list at the top of the column. Using the drop-down list, you can apply a number of preset filters or create your own custom filter.

To find out if any of Rock Castle Construction's account balances have decreased since the previous period, you'll filter the balance sheet report you just created.

To filter a report in Microsoft Excel:

1 In the Excel window, click the down arrow in the $ Change column of the balance sheet report, and choose (Custom...) from the drop-down list.

Excel displays the following window.

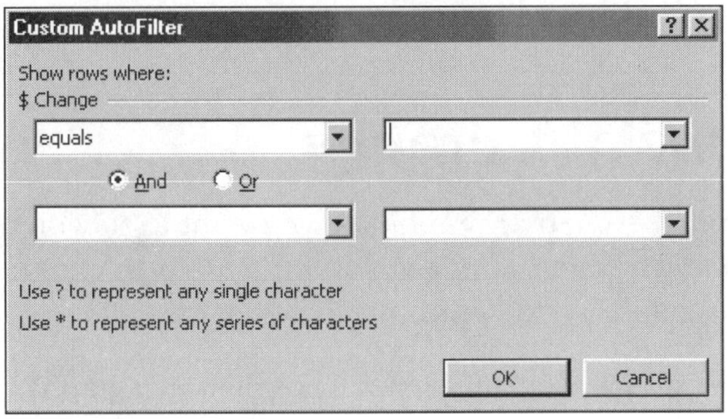

2 In the $ Change field, choose "is less than" from the drop-down list.

3 In the field to the right, type ***0***.

Your screen should resemble the following.

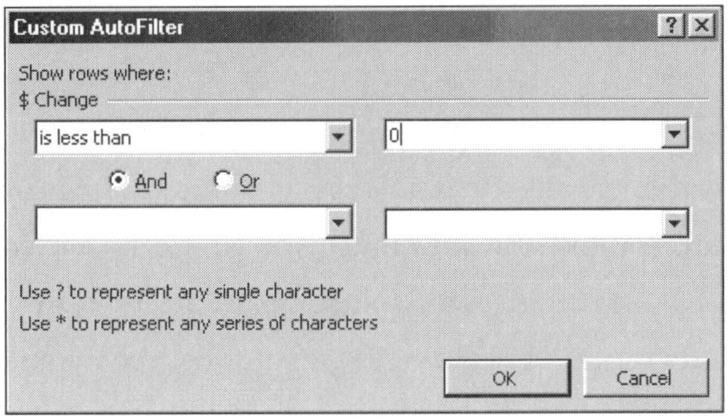

4 Click OK.

Excel filters the $ Change column for negative amounts and displays the results.

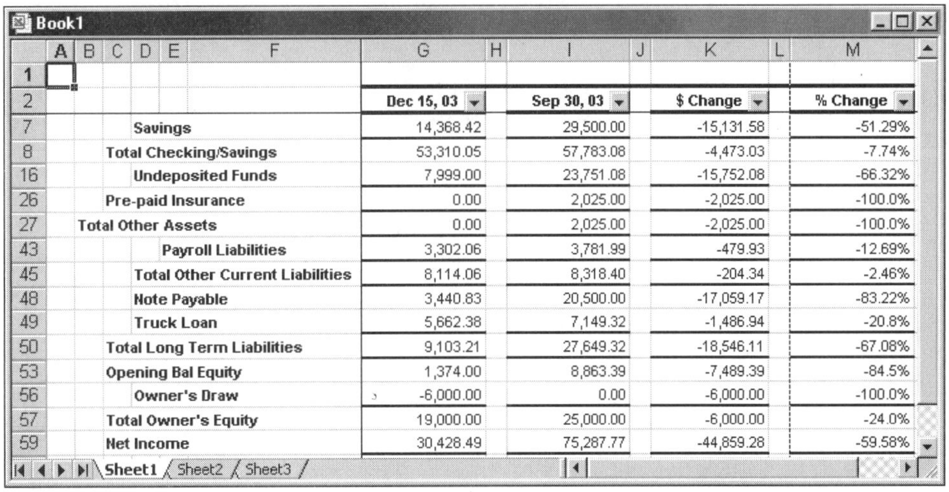

Row		Dec 15, 03	Sep 30, 03	$ Change	% Change
7	Savings	14,368.42	29,500.00	-15,131.58	-51.29%
8	Total Checking/Savings	53,310.05	57,783.08	-4,473.03	-7.74%
16	Undeposited Funds	7,999.00	23,751.08	-15,752.08	-66.32%
26	Pre-paid Insurance	0.00	2,025.00	-2,025.00	-100.0%
27	Total Other Assets	0.00	2,025.00	-2,025.00	-100.0%
43	Payroll Liabilities	3,302.06	3,781.99	-479.93	-12.69%
45	Total Other Current Liabilities	8,114.06	8,318.40	-204.34	-2.46%
48	Note Payable	3,440.83	20,500.00	-17,059.17	-83.22%
49	Truck Loan	5,662.38	7,149.32	-1,486.94	-20.8%
50	Total Long Term Liabilities	9,103.21	27,649.32	-18,546.11	-67.08%
53	Opening Bal Equity	1,374.00	8,863.39	-7,489.39	-84.5%
56	Owner's Draw	-6,000.00	0.00	-6,000.00	-100.0%
57	Total Owner's Equity	19,000.00	25,000.00	-6,000.00	-24.0%
59	Net Income	30,428.49	75,287.77	-44,859.28	-59.58%

5 Close Excel without saving the report.

6 Close the balance sheet report in QuickBooks.

7 Choose No when QuickBooks displays a message asking if you want to memorize the report.

Creating QuickInsight graphs

A report gives you numbers that are essential if you want to stay on top of your business finances. But when you want a visual picture to plan current or future business decisions, a graph is another invaluable tool.

A QuickInsight graph shows your data pictured as either a bar graph or a pie chart. The bar graphs and pie charts are simply different views of the same company financial information.

Refer to Handout 27, "QuickInsight graph types."

QuickBooks has six types of graphs, providing up to 15 different views of your data:

- **Income and Expenses graphs** show your income and expenses for the period you specify.
- **Sales graphs** show your company's sales income for the period you specify.
- **Accounts Receivable graphs** show how much your customers owe.
- **Accounts Payable graphs** show how much you currently owe your vendors.
- **Net Worth graphs** show changes in your company's net worth.
- **Budget vs. Actual graphs** let you see the variance between your budgeted amounts and the actual amount you earned or spent.

To create a QuickInsight graph, select the type of graph you want from a report submenu.

Creating an Income and Expense graph

If you want your business to be profitable, you need to keep an eye on your expenses. The income and expense graph shows you exactly what you're spending and where.

You should be especially concerned with the proportion you're spending relative to the income you receive. As a simplistic example, if you're earning only $20,000 in income, you don't want to spend $30,000 in expenses.

To create an income and expense graph:

1 From the Reports menu, choose Company & Financial, and then choose Income & Expense Graph.

QuickBooks displays a graph depicting your income and expenses.

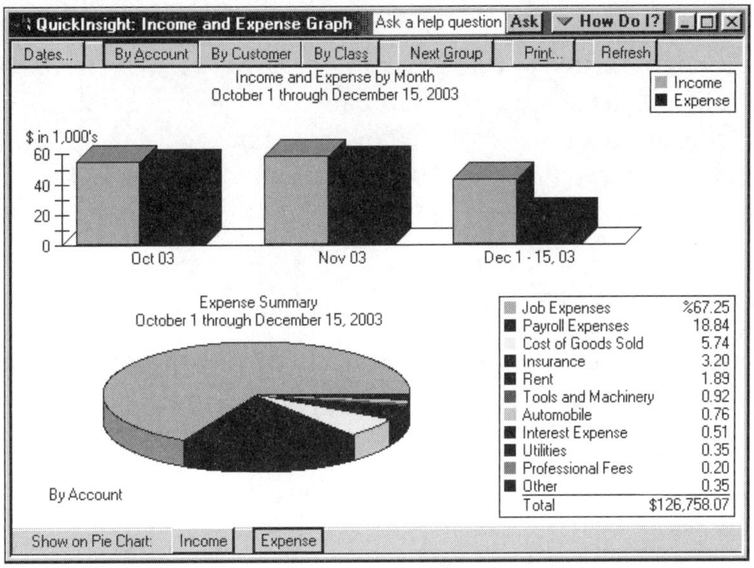

In the top portion of the graph window, QuickBooks displays a bar graph and legend showing total income and expenses. In the lower portion of the window, QuickBooks displays a pie chart and legend showing expense percentages by account.

2 QuickBooks can display only 10 accounts at a time. To display more accounts, click the Next Group button at the top of the graph window.

Features of QuickInsight graphs

These features are common to all QuickInsight graphs:

- Every graph window, except for the Net Worth and the Budget vs Actual graphs, shows a bar graph in the top part of the window and a pie chart in the bottom half.

  The bar graph usually shows totals. For example, the Income and Expense graph shows the total for income and the total for expenses in each month of the period.

  The pie chart shows a breakdown of the information shown in the bar graph; each pie slice in the Income and Expense graph represents a type of income or expense. The legend to the right of the pie chart shows you which income or expense account corresponds to the color shown in the pie chart; it also shows you what percentage of the pie each slice represents.

- Every graph window has a buttonbar with buttons you can click to customize the graph. For example, you can change the time period shown in the graph by clicking the Dates button. If you want the pie chart to show a breakdown by customer or class rather than a breakdown by account, just click By Customer or By Class.

- Just as you can use QuickZoom in a report to get more detail on the numbers, you can use QuickZoom in a graph to see the numbers behind the picture. When you position the mouse pointer over a bar or pie slice, QuickBooks shows you the numbers represented by that graphic image. For example, the pie chart legend tells which income/expense accounts are represented by each pie slice, and tells you what percentage of the whole is represented by each slice. When you zoom in on a pie slice, you can find out exactly how much you received or spent (in dollars) for each account.

Customizing graph data

To display income accounts instead of expense accounts:

1 Click Income at the bottom of the graph window.

2 Click By Customer.

QuickBooks changes the pie chart to display income by customers.

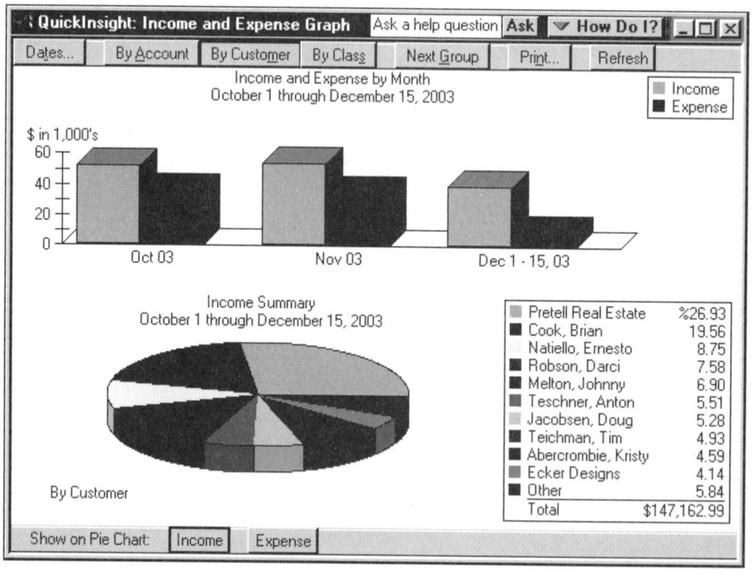

Using QuickZoom with graphs

To help you better understand the information shown in the graphs, QuickBooks lets you trace graphical data using QuickZoom graphs.

To display the sales for Anton Teschner:

1 Position the mouse pointer over the Teschner, Anton slice of the pie chart.

(Use the Key on the right side of the window.)

The pointer changes to a magnifying glass with the letter Z inside.

2 Double-click the Teschner, Anton slice.

Note: If a slice is too small to click, click on its legend representation instead.

QuickBooks displays a QuickZoom graph depicting sales for Anton Teschner by month.

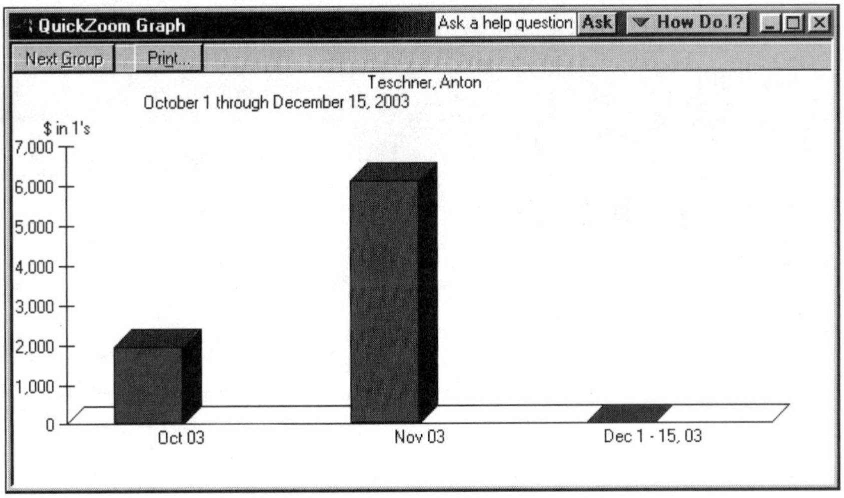

To display a report describing the transactions for a given month:

1 Position the mouse pointer over the bar representing November 2003.

The pointer turns into the QuickZoom symbol.

2 Double-click the bar.

QuickBooks displays the custom transaction detail report for the month of November 2003.

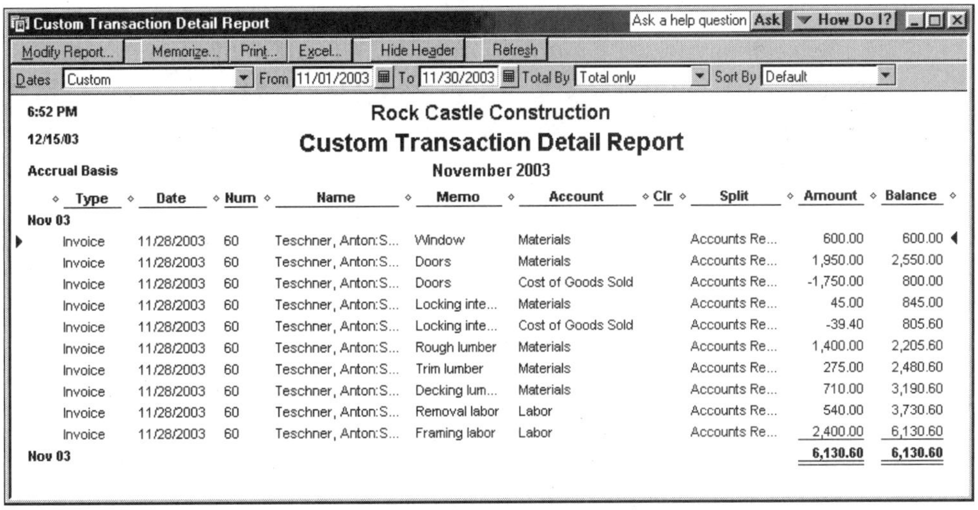

6:52 PM
12/15/03
Accrual Basis

Rock Castle Construction
Custom Transaction Detail Report
November 2003

Type	Date	Num	Name	Memo	Account	Clr	Split	Amount	Balance
Nov 03									
Invoice	11/28/2003	60	Teschner, Anton:S...	Window	Materials		Accounts Re...	600.00	600.00
Invoice	11/28/2003	60	Teschner, Anton:S...	Doors	Materials		Accounts Re...	1,950.00	2,550.00
Invoice	11/28/2003	60	Teschner, Anton:S...	Doors	Cost of Goods Sold		Accounts Re...	-1,750.00	800.00
Invoice	11/28/2003	60	Teschner, Anton:S...	Locking inte...	Materials		Accounts Re...	45.00	845.00
Invoice	11/28/2003	60	Teschner, Anton:S...	Locking inte...	Cost of Goods Sold		Accounts Re...	-39.40	805.60
Invoice	11/28/2003	60	Teschner, Anton:S...	Rough lumber	Materials		Accounts Re...	1,400.00	2,205.60
Invoice	11/28/2003	60	Teschner, Anton:S...	Trim lumber	Materials		Accounts Re...	275.00	2,480.60
Invoice	11/28/2003	60	Teschner, Anton:S...	Decking lum...	Materials		Accounts Re...	710.00	3,190.60
Invoice	11/28/2003	60	Teschner, Anton:S...	Removal labor	Labor		Accounts Re...	540.00	3,730.60
Invoice	11/28/2003	60	Teschner, Anton:S...	Framing labor	Labor		Accounts Re...	2,400.00	6,130.60
Nov 03								**6,130.60**	**6,130.60**

You may need to scroll to the right to see the entire report.

To display the first transaction in the report:

1 Double-click any of the lines in the report for Invoice #60.

QuickBooks displays the invoice.

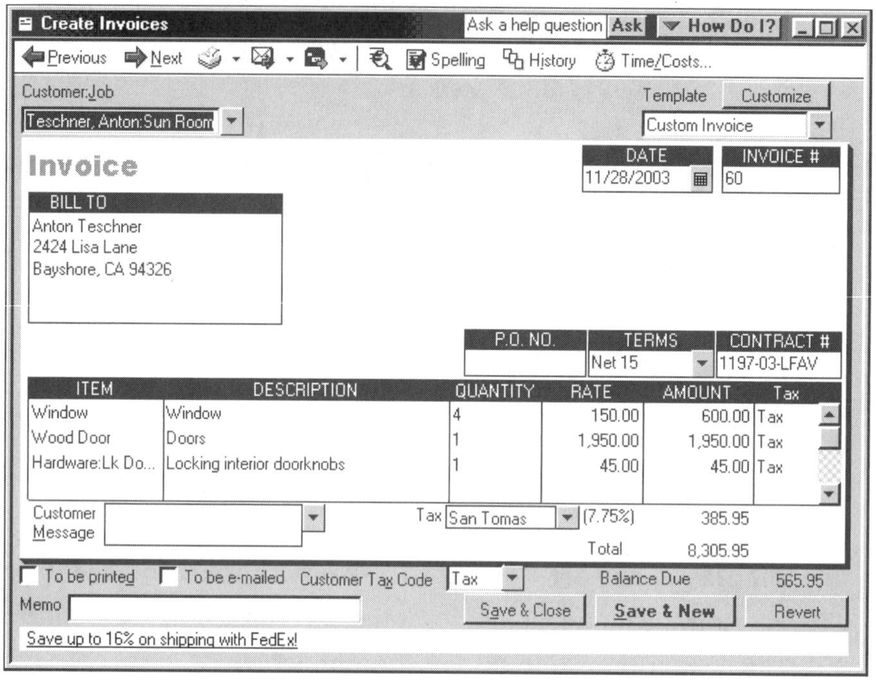

2 From the Window menu, choose Close All.

Customizing how graphs display

You can customize graphs to control what data they include and how the data is displayed. In this exercise, you'll change the display from three-dimensional (3D) to two-dimensional (2D) graphs.

To change from 3D to 2D:

1 From the Edit menu, choose Preferences.

QuickBooks displays the Preferences window.

2 In the left scroll box, click Reports & Graphs.

QuickBooks displays the Preferences window for Reports and Graphs.

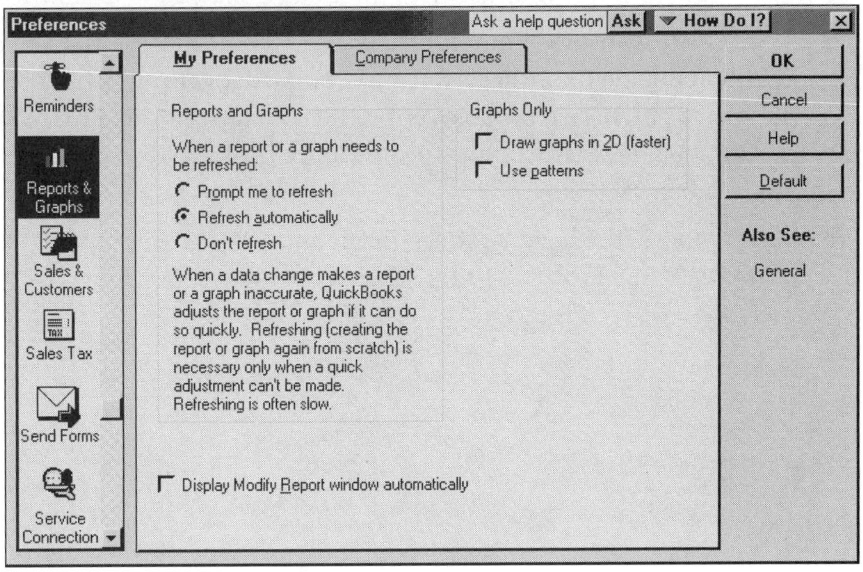

3 Click "Draw graphs in 2D (faster)."

A checkmark appears in the checkbox to indicate that Draw graphs in 2D (faster) is selected.

4 Click OK.

5 From the Reports menu, choose Sales. Then choose Sales Graph.

QuickBooks displays the sales graph in 2D.

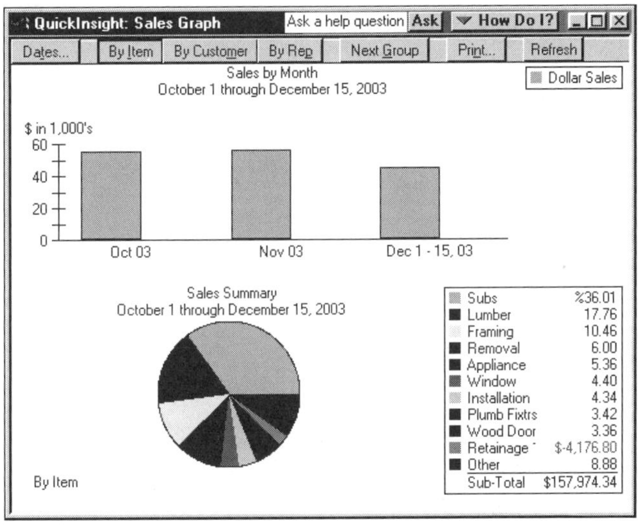

Displaying graphs in 2D often allows your computer to draw them on your screen faster than displaying them in 3D.

6 Close the graph.

Student test and review

1. Create a QuickReport on an item in one of Rock Castle Construction's lists.
2. Rock Castle Construction wants to create a report that shows how much they have spent on lumber for projects during the month of November, 2003. Create an item summary purchase report, covering the date range from 11/01/2003 to 11/30/2003. Filter the report to show only Rock Castle Construction's purchases for Lumber.
3. Batch process the balance sheet, profit and loss statement, and statement of cash flows using the Process Multiple Reports window.

LESSON 10 Setting up inventory

Lesson objectives

- To get an overview of inventory in QuickBooks
- To practice filling out a purchase order for inventory items
- To track the receipt of the inventory items in QuickBooks
- To adjust inventory manually, to enter a stock loss or increase
- To create and build inventory assemblies (finished goods)

Handout materials

- Handout 28: Inventory in QuickBooks
- Handout 29: Paying for inventory items

Instructor preparation

- Review the lesson, including the examples, to make sure you're familiar with the material.
- Ensure that all students have a copy of qblesson.qbb on their computer's hard disk.
- Have Handouts 28 and 29 ready for distribution.

To start this lesson

Before you perform the following steps, make sure you have installed the exercise file (qblesson.qbb) on your hard disk. See "Installing the exercise file" in the Introduction to this guide if you haven't installed it.

The steps that follow will restore the exercise file to its original state so that the data in the file matches what you see on the screen as you proceed through each lesson.

To restore the exercise file (qblesson.qbb):

1. From the File menu in QuickBooks, choose Restore.

   QuickBooks displays the Restore Company Backup window.

2. In the "Get Company Backup From" section of the window, click Browse and select your c:\QBtrain directory.
3. Select the qblesson.qbb file, and then click Open.

4 In the "Restore Company Backup To" section of the window, click Browse and select your c:\QBtrain directory.

5 In the File name field of the Restore To window, type ***lesson 10*** and then click Save.

6 Click Restore.

Turning on the inventory feature

The QuickBooks inventory feature is turned on in your exercise file, but you'll review how to turn on this feature so you become familiar with QuickBooks preferences. If you need to track inventory for your company, you can turn the feature on while completing the EasyStep Interview. If you want to turn on the inventory feature after you've completed the EasyStep Interview, follow this procedure.

To turn on the inventory feature:

1 From the Edit menu, choose Preferences.

2 Select Purchases & Vendors from the scroll box.

3 Click the Company Preferences tab.

Note: Only the QuickBooks Administrator can change company preferences.

4 Click the "Inventory and purchase orders are active" checkbox to select it.

A checkmark shows that the inventory feature is turned on.

5 Click OK.

Entering products into inventory

Many small businesses that stock inventory don't know the number of units they have on hand or on order at any given time, and have no way of getting that information quickly. Using QuickBooks to manage your inventory, you'll be able to track the number of items in stock and the value of your inventory after every purchase and sale. As you order inventory items, receive the items, and later sell the items from inventory, QuickBooks tracks each inventory-related transaction. You will know the status of your inventory and will have a more accurate picture of your business's assets.

To track inventory, you must enter each product into the Item list as an inventory part. Once you enter a product, QuickBooks tracks it as you sell or reorder the product.

To enter a product into inventory:

1 From the Vendors menu, choose Item List.

QuickBooks displays the Item list.

2 Click the Item menu button, and then choose New.

QuickBooks displays the New Item window.

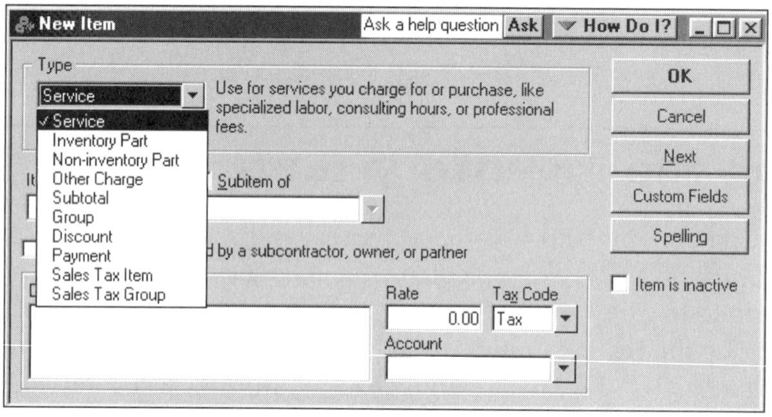

You'll enter one new item into your inventory.

3 In the Type field, choose Inventory Part from the drop-down list.

QuickBooks changes the New Item window to accept information for an inventory part.

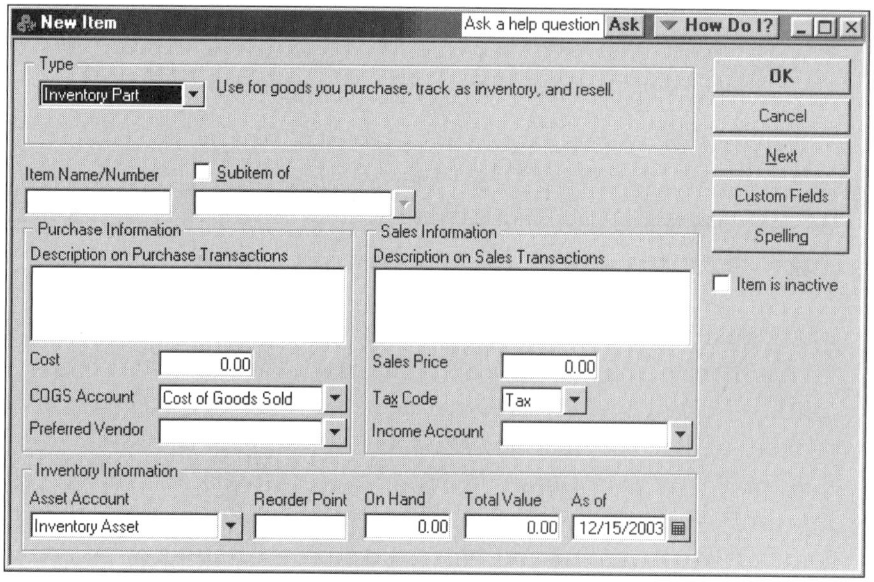

4 In the Item Name/Number field, type ***Cab 2015*** (2015 is the style number).

5 Select the "Subitem of" checkbox, and then choose Cabinets from the drop-down list.

6 In the Description on Purchase Transactions field, type ***Kitchen Cabinet #2015***, and then press Tab to move to the Cost field.

Notice that QuickBooks fills in the Description on Sales Transactions field with the same description you entered for the purchase side. You can leave the sales description the same or change it later.

7 In the Cost field, type ***169***.

8 In the Preferred Vendor field, choose Thomas Kitchen and Bath from the drop-down list.

Or, type the first few letters of your selection and QuickBooks fills in the rest.

9 In the Sales Price field, type ***225***.

10 Leave the Tax Code setting as is.

If you wanted to assign a different tax code, you could select a different code from the drop-down list when setting up the item.

11 In the Income Account field, choose Construction:Materials.

12 Press Tab to move to the Asset Account field.

Inventory Asset was filled in when you selected Inventory Part as the type of item. Leave this default setting.

13 In the Reorder Point field, type ***15***.

14 In the Qty-on-Hand field, type ***20***, and then press Tab to move to the Total Value field.

Notice that QuickBooks has calculated the value of your item by multiplying the number in the On Hand field by the number in the Cost field.

Your New Item window should resemble the following figure.

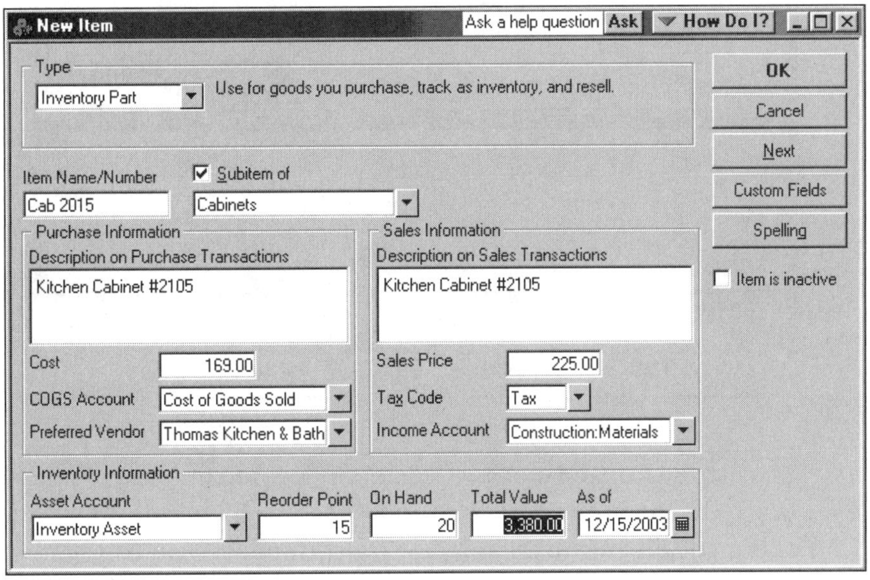

15 Click OK to close the New Item window.

QuickBooks adds the new item to the Item list.

16 Close the Item list.

Ordering products

Once you enter your current products and vendors into the Item and Vendor lists, you'll need to order products to keep your inventory stocked.

Creating purchase orders

In Lesson 6, you created a sales order for door frames. Now, create the purchase order to order the items from the vendor.

To order a product using a purchase order:

1 From the Vendors menu, choose Create Purchase Orders.

QuickBooks displays the Create Purchase Orders window.

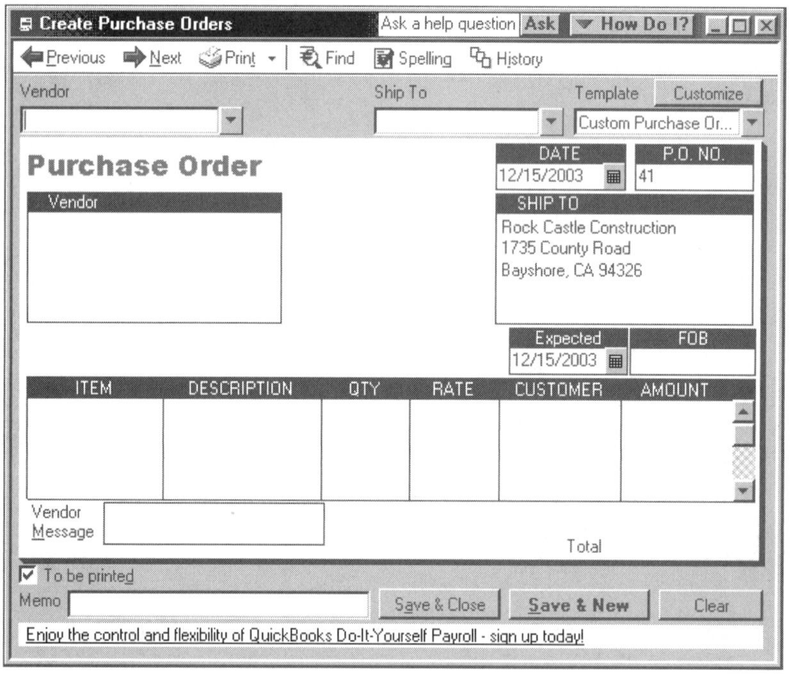

You use the Create Purchase Orders window to enter the products you wish to order, the quantities, and the vendor. As you fill in this information, QuickBooks automatically calculates purchase order number, item cost, and total cost.

Notice that QuickBooks has already entered today's date and a sequential purchase order number.

2 In the Vendor field, choose Perry Windows & Doors from the drop-down list.

Notice that QuickBooks displays all of the information about Perry Windows & Doors in the appropriate places on the purchase order form.

3 In the Item column, select Frame from the drop-down list.

4 In the QTY field, type ***10***.

5 In the Vendor Message field of the purchase order, type ***Please rush ship this order.***
Your Purchase Order should resemble the following figure.

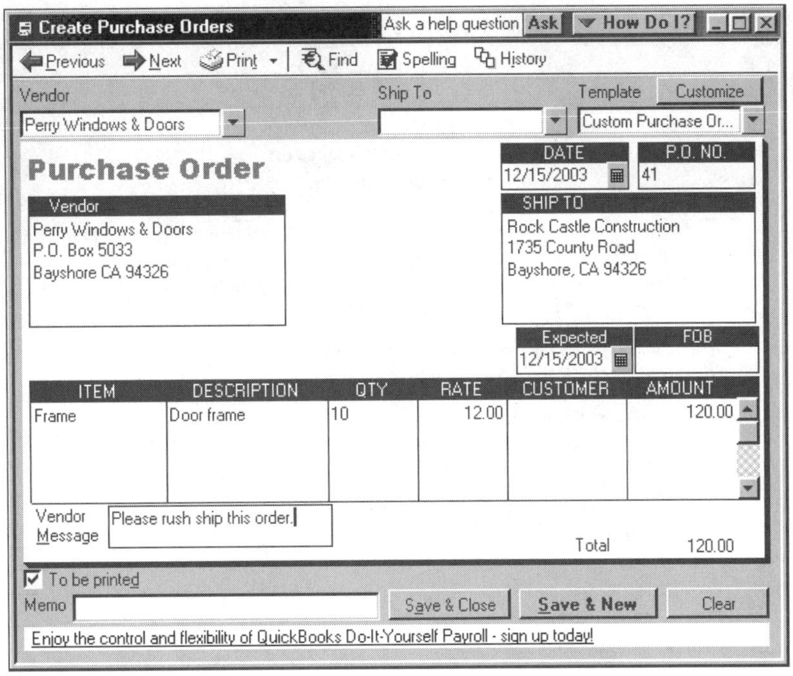

6 Click Save & Close to record the purchase order.

After you have created a purchase order, QuickBooks adds an account to the chart of accounts called Purchase Orders. This is a non-posting account and does not affect your balance sheet or income statement. The Purchase Orders account is used to produce a QuickReport showing current purchase orders so you always know what is on order.

Getting a report of purchase orders

To get a chronologically ordered report of all the purchase orders you have written:

1 From the Lists menu, choose Chart of Accounts.

2 In the chart of accounts, click Purchase Orders once to select it.

3 Click the Reports menu button and choose QuickReport:Purchase Orders. QuickBooks displays a report of all purchase orders.

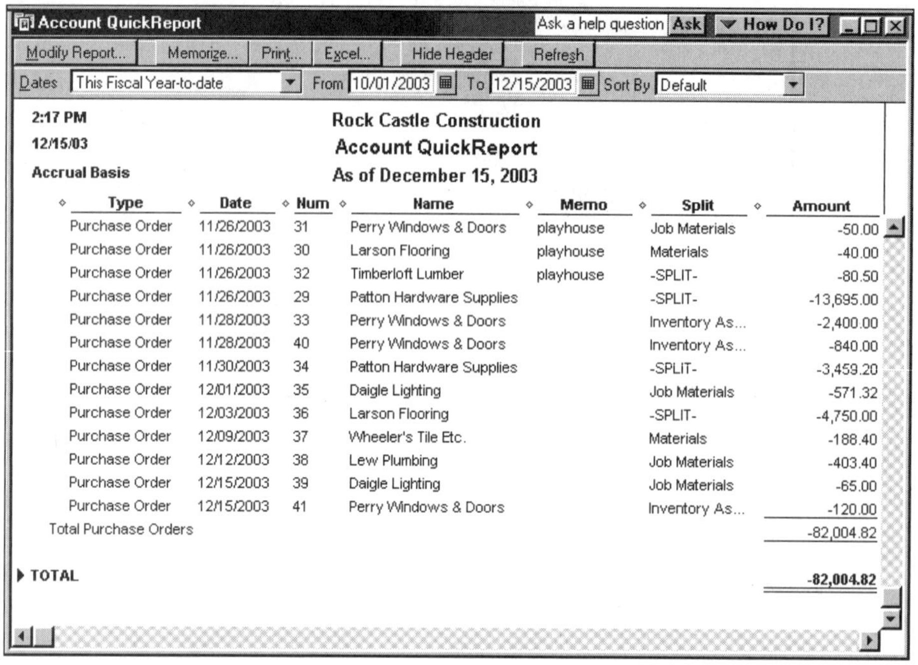

Type	Date	Num	Name	Memo	Split	Amount
Purchase Order	11/26/2003	31	Perry Windows & Doors	playhouse	Job Materials	-50.00
Purchase Order	11/26/2003	30	Larson Flooring	playhouse	Materials	-40.00
Purchase Order	11/26/2003	32	Timberloft Lumber	playhouse	-SPLIT-	-80.50
Purchase Order	11/26/2003	29	Patton Hardware Supplies		-SPLIT-	-13,695.00
Purchase Order	11/28/2003	33	Perry Windows & Doors		Inventory As...	-2,400.00
Purchase Order	11/28/2003	40	Perry Windows & Doors		Inventory As...	-840.00
Purchase Order	11/30/2003	34	Patton Hardware Supplies		-SPLIT-	-3,459.20
Purchase Order	12/01/2003	35	Daigle Lighting		Job Materials	-571.32
Purchase Order	12/03/2003	36	Larson Flooring		-SPLIT-	-4,750.00
Purchase Order	12/09/2003	37	Wheeler's Tile Etc.		Materials	-188.40
Purchase Order	12/12/2003	38	Lew Plumbing		Job Materials	-403.40
Purchase Order	12/15/2003	39	Daigle Lighting		Job Materials	-65.00
Purchase Order	12/15/2003	41	Perry Windows & Doors		Inventory As...	-120.00
Total Purchase Orders						-82,004.82
TOTAL						**-82,004.82**

Notice the purchase order you have just created is at the bottom of the report.

4 Close the QuickReport.

5 Close the chart of accounts.

Receiving inventory

When you receive the items you have ordered with your purchase order, you have to enter the items into inventory. You can receive items with a bill or without a bill.

This exercise shows you how to enter into QuickBooks inventory items you've received when the bill for those items will follow later.

To receive inventory without a bill attached:

1 From the Vendors menu, choose Receive Items.

QuickBooks displays the Create Item Receipts window.

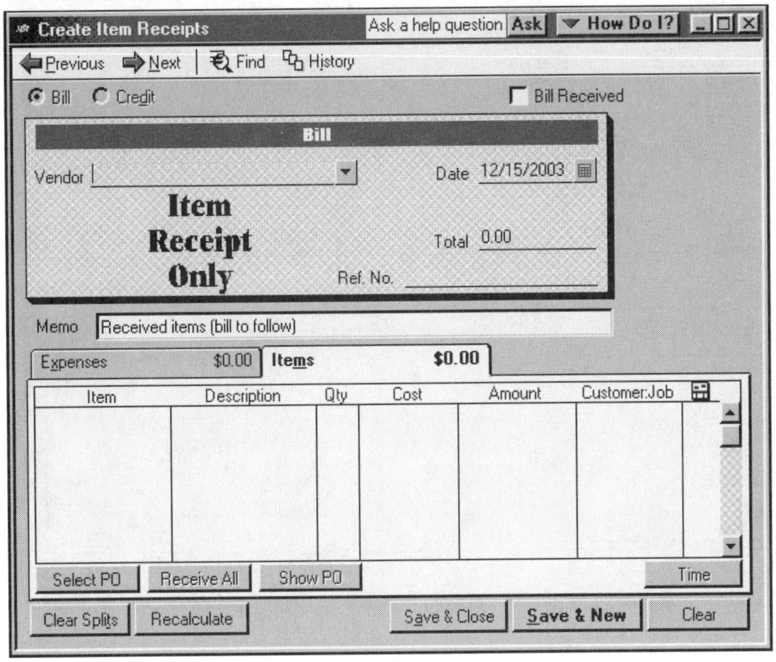

The Create Item Receipts window lets you enter information for inventory parts you've received.

2 In the Vendor field, choose Perry Windows & Doors from the drop-down list and press Tab.

QuickBooks tells you that there are open purchase orders for this vendor and asks if you wish to receive against one of these orders.

3 Click Yes.

QuickBooks displays the Open Purchase Orders for Perry Windows & Doors.

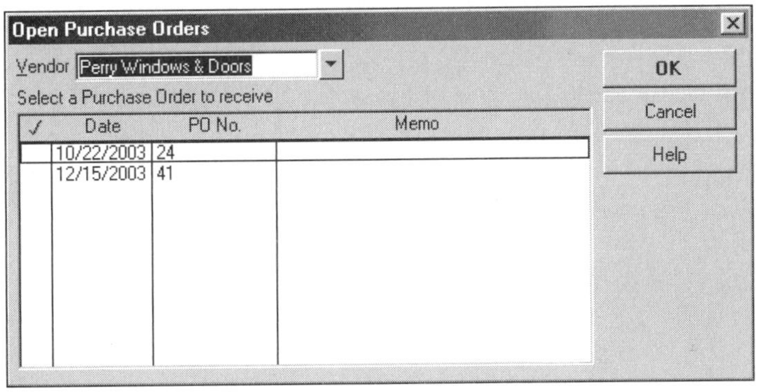

4 Click the second purchase order (#41, dated 12/15/2003) to select it.

QuickBooks places a checkmark in the left-most column for the item selected.

5 Click OK to move the information to the item receipt.

The Create Item Receipts window should resemble the following figure.

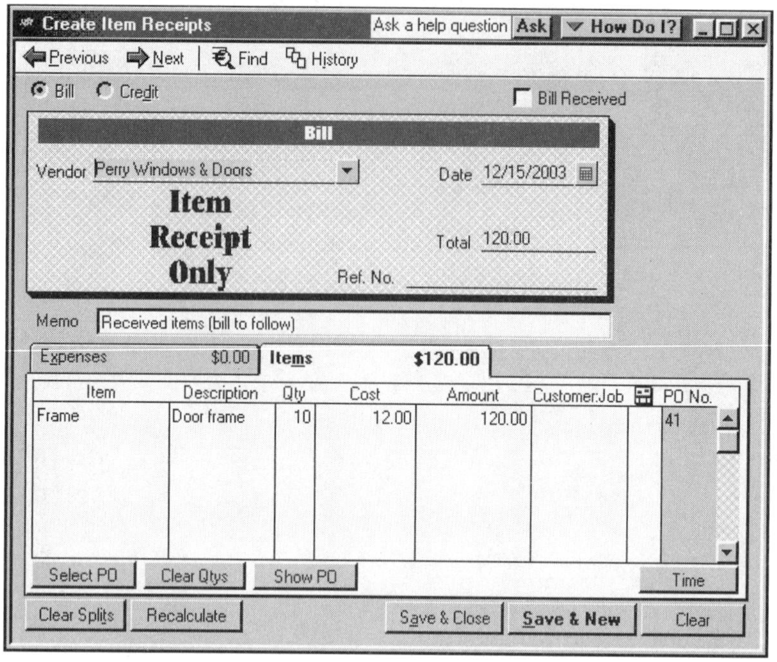

6 Click Save & Close to process the receipt.

QuickBooks processes the items and adds them to your inventory. If you display the Item list, you'll see that you now have 10 additional door frames on hand.

Entering a bill for inventory

If you've entered an item receipt for inventory, but the bill hasn't arrived yet, you can still record the bill amount in QuickBooks. Entering the bill as shown in this exercise records the amount in your accounts payable account so you can track how much you owe.

When the bill comes, you pay the bill just like you would pay any other bill in QuickBooks (from the Pay Bills window).

To enter the bill:

1 From the Vendors menu, choose Enter Bill for Received Items.

QuickBooks displays the Select Item Receipt window, where you can select the vendor and the item for which you have a bill.

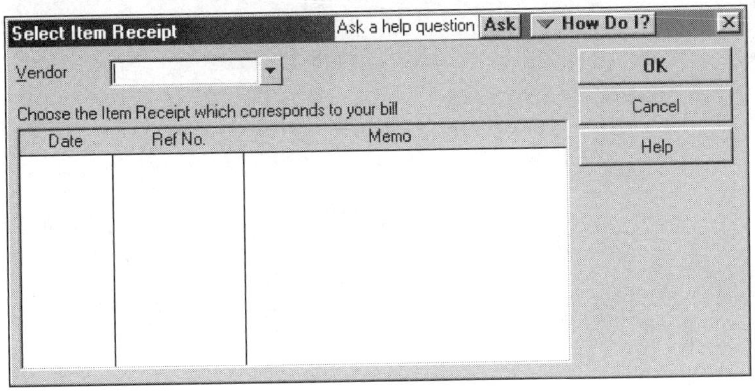

2 In the Vendor field, select Perry Windows & Doors in the drop-down list and press Tab.

QuickBooks fills in the Date and Memo fields with information that corresponds to your bill.

3 Select "Received items (bill to follow)," dated 12/15/2003.

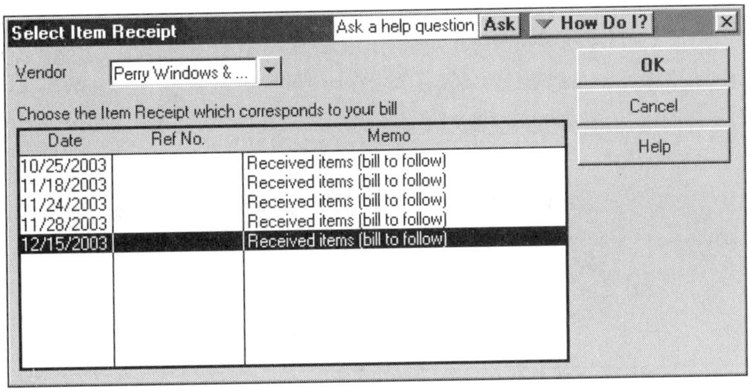

4 Click OK.

QuickBooks displays the Enter Bills window.

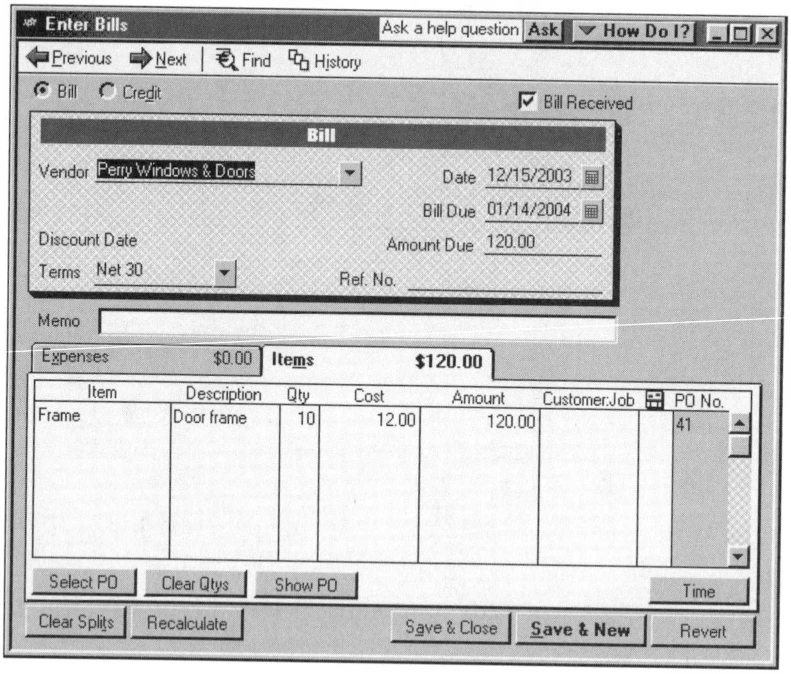

5 Click Save & Close.

QuickBooks changes the item receipt to a bill in the Accounts Payable account and lists the bill in the Pay Bills window. If you look at the Accounts Payable, you'll see that the balance increased by $120.00, based on the bill entered for Perry Windows & Doors.

Because you must have inventory on hand before you can enter a sale for inventory parts, we recommend that you enter you item receipts before entering sales.

Manually adjusting inventory

When you have spoilage or send out samples of your products, you can adjust your inventory manually.

To adjust the inventory manually:

1 From the Vendors menu, choose Inventory Activities, and then choose Adjust Quantity/Value on Hand.

QuickBooks displays the Adjust Quantity/Value on Hand window.

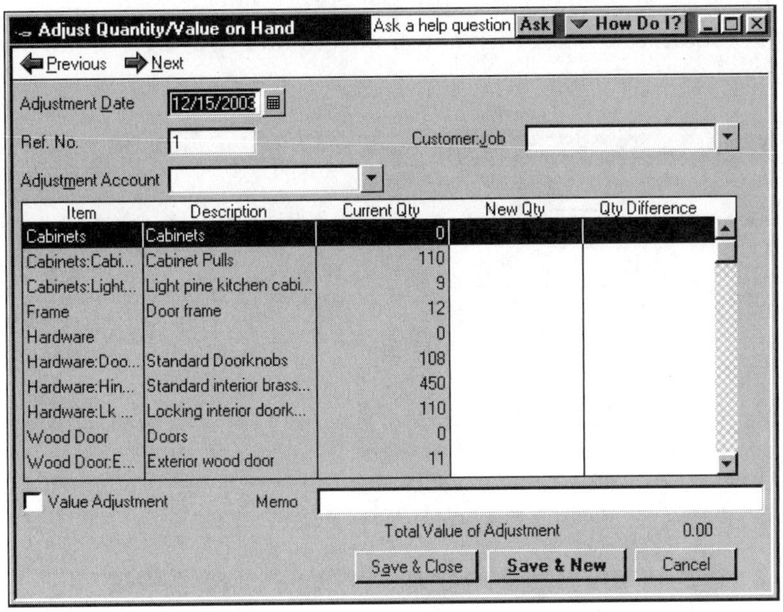

The Adjust Quantity/Value on Hand window lets you enter the adjustment account, and either the New Qty or the Qty Difference.

Since two wood interior doors were damaged, you'll adjust the inventory account to remove two doors.

2 In the Adjustment Account field, type ***Inventory Adjustment*** and press Tab.

3 Click Set Up in the window telling you that Inventory Adjustment is not in the account list.

QuickBooks opens the New Account window.

4 In the Type field, choose Expense from the drop-down list, if it is not selected already.

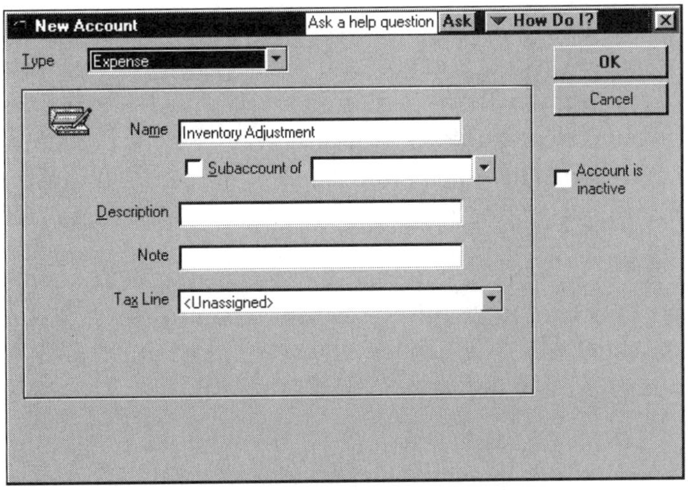

5 Click OK to close the New Account window.

6 In the Qty Difference column for Wood Door:Interior wood door, type ***–2*** (the number of damaged doors), and then press Tab.

QuickBooks calculates the value adjustment and decreases the inventory by two items.

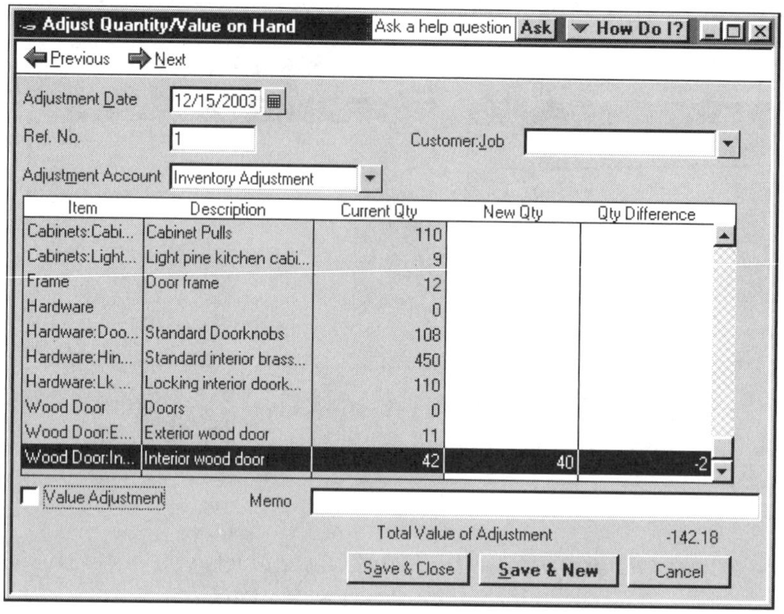

7 Click Save & Close.

Tracking finished goods

QuickBooks Premier products let you track the building and sale of finished goods using assembly items. When you define assembly items, you tell QuickBooks how many of each inventory item is needed to create the finished product.

Inventory assembly items allow you to create an item that contains assembled material units (finished goods) you buy or produce, track as inventory, and resell. You can keep track of how many items remain in stock after a sale, how many items you have on order, your cost of goods sold, and the value of your inventory. Note that inventory assembly items in QuickBooks are appropriate for indicating "light" assembled items on sales forms and in reports. QuickBooks does not track inventory throughout a manufacturing process.

You must have a QuickBooks Premier Edition product to create and build inventory assembly items. Afterwards, you can use any version of QuickBooks to view, sell, and report on existing assembly items.

Deciding whether to use group items or create inventory assemblies

Both group items and inventory assembly items record a group of items as a single entry on purchase or sales forms in QuickBooks.

Using group items

Group items are useful for quickly entering a group of individual items that you've already set up as single items on your list and often sell together.

Group items let you track the items you sell in greater detail. For example, a construction firm that remodels houses could set up a group item that lists the significant components of a remodeling job: lumber, carpentry hours, markup, etc. Sales reports for the company would then show income broken down by each component instead of a single lump sum for all remodeling jobs.

If you need to track a lot of detail about your items but you also want to give your customers simple, uncluttered invoices, you can use group items to do both. You can set up a group item so that the printed version of an invoice reduces a group item to a single line item and one amount. Yet when you view the invoice on your screen, you see a separate line entry and amount for each item in the group.

Group items also give you a way to enter a great amount of line item detail quickly. On a sales or purchase form, all you have to do is enter the name of the group item—QuickBooks fills in all the details about the items in the group for you.

Using inventory assemblies

When you build an assembly, an assembled unit is automatically added to quantity on hand and its component parts (inventory items or other assembly items) are automatically deducted from quantity on hand. By using assembly items, you always know how many assembled and component items you actually have in stock.

You can specify a price for an assembly that's different than the sum of component items.

You can easily access the date items were assembled, quantity and cost of assembled items, and a detailed list of component items.

You can set a build point and QuickBooks will automatically remind you to build finished goods when stock is running low. At build time, QuickBooks will notify you if you don't have enough component items in stock to build the specified number of assembly items.

Note: **The ability to create inventory assemblies is available only in QuickBooks Premier products.** To proceed through this exercise, you must be using QuickBooks Premier.

Creating inventory assembly items

Creating assembly items in QuickBooks is a two-part process: first you define an assembly item, and then you build the assembly. Assembly item units are not added to inventory and assembly components (inventory parts or other assemblies) are not deducted from inventory until you build the assembly.

Inventory assembly items can include inventory part and other assembly items only. If you want to include a different type of item (a service item to charge for labor, for example), then you must include the assembly item and service item in a group item.

All items included in an inventory assembly item must be defined in the Item list. You can define them before you create the inventory assembly item, or as you create the assembly item. Note, however, that you cannot edit the items included in the assembly item once it's been used in transactions, or saved with a quantity on hand.

In addition to selling individual items, Rock Castle sells pre-assembled interior door kits. In this exercise, you define the assembly item for the interior door kits. All of the component items are already defined in the Item list.

To create an inventory assembly item:

1. From the Lists menu, choose Item List.
2. Click the Item menu button and select New.

   QuickBooks displays the New Item window.
3. In the Type field, select Inventory Assembly.
4. In the Item Name/Number field, type ***Interior Door Kit***.

5 In the Description field, type ***Complete interior door kit***.

The New Item window should resemble the following graphic.

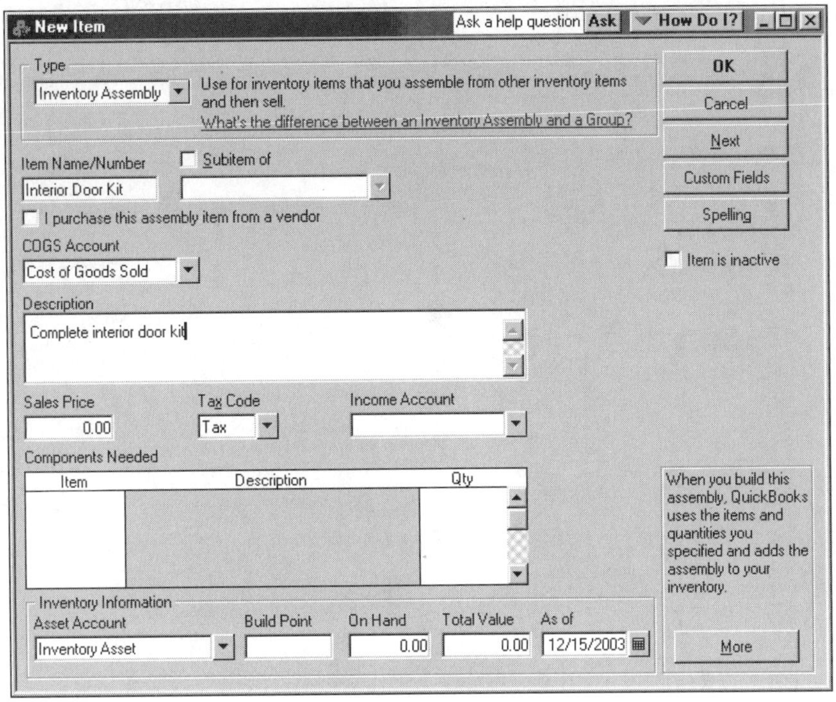

6 In the Sales Price field, type ***200***, and then press Tab twice.

QuickBooks allows you to set any price for assembled items; the price is independent of the sales price of the component items.

In this case, the assembly item uses the same sales tax code as the component parts, but you can use different sales tax codes for the assemblies, if necessary.

7 In the Income Account field, select Construction:Materials from the drop-down list.

8 In the Components Needed section, click in the Item column.

9 In the Item drop-down list, select Frame, and then press Tab.

10 In the Qty field, type ***1***, and then press Tab.

11 In the Item drop-down list, select Hardware:Doorknobs Std, and then press Tab.

12 In the Qty field, type ***1***, and then press Tab.

13 In the Item drop-down list, select Hardware:Hinges, and then press Tab.

14 In the Qty field, type ***3***, and then press Tab.

15 In the Item drop-down list, select Wood Door:Interior, and then press Tab.

16 In the Qty field, type ***1***.

The New Item window should resemble the following graphic.

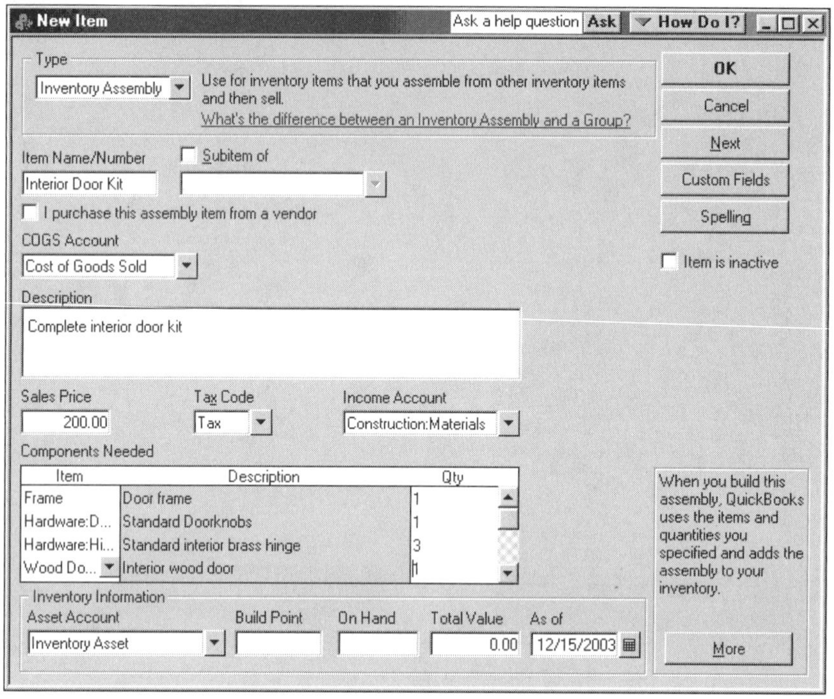

Assembly definition details, such as the list and quantity of components, can be edited until the assembly is used in a transaction. After an assembly has been used in a transaction, you can't edit the assembly's component list. However, you can still modify most other aspects of an assembly definition.

Because you cannot change components in an assembly, if a part changes, for example, you'll have to create a whole new assembly.

17 In the Build Point field, type ***5***.

18 Leave the On Hand and Total Value fields blank.

The New Item window should now resemble the following graphic.

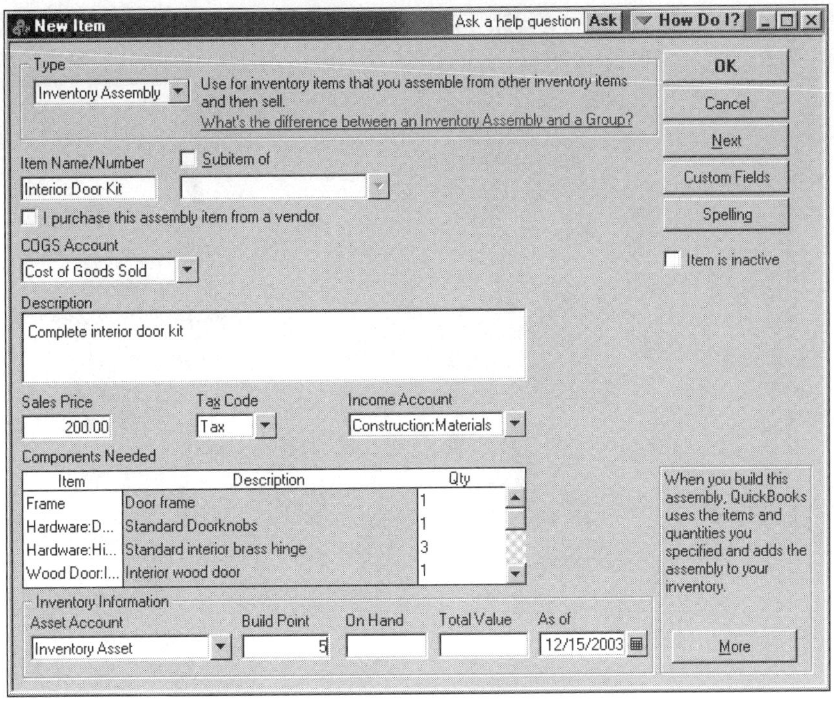

19 Click OK.

20 Close the Item list.

Building finished goods

Once you've defined assembly items that define the pieces you build, you are ready to enter the builds into QuickBooks. In this exercise, you build five interior door kits for Rock Castle.

To build an inventory assembly:

1 From the Vendors menu, choose Inventory Activities, and then choose Build Assemblies from the submenu.

QuickBooks displays the Build Assemblies window.

2 In the Assembly Item field, select Interior Door Kit from the drop-down list.

The Build Assemblies window should resemble the following graphic.

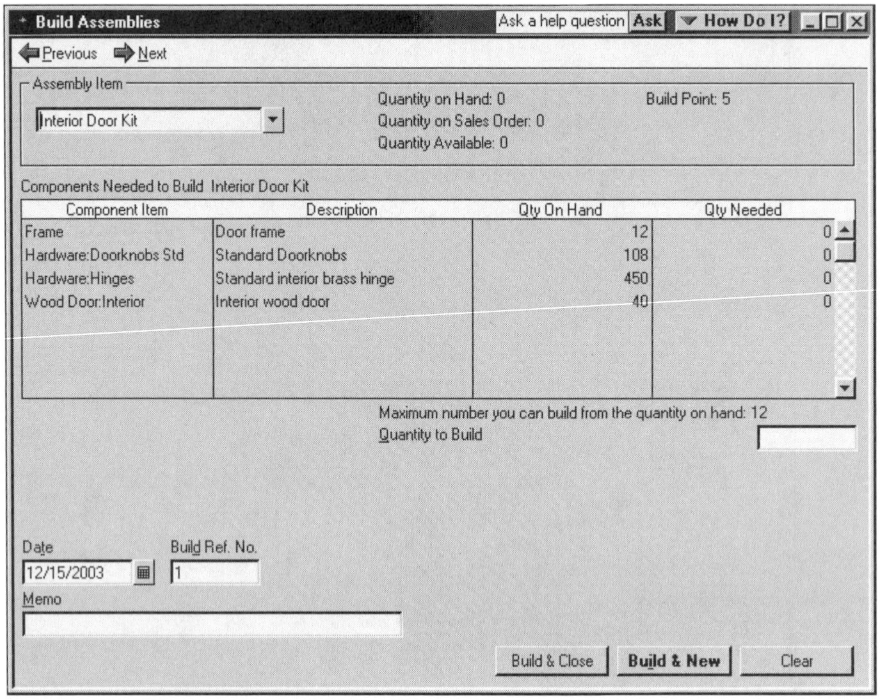

3 In the Quantity to Build field, type ***5***.

QuickBooks warns you when you do not have sufficient inventory items on hand to complete a build.

If you choose to build an assembly and do not have enough components in inventory to build the number of assemblies you have specified, you can postpone the build by marking it pending. If you don't mark the build as pending, you have to reduce the number of assemblies or you won't be able to save the build.

4 Click Build & Close.

Understanding the effect of builds on inventory

When you build an assembly item, QuickBooks decrements the appropriate number of individual inventory items from inventory and increments the number of inventory assembly items. It takes the inventory asset value of the component items and transfers the value to the assembly item. The parts and the values are combined into the quantity and value of the assembly item.

The following graphic shows the number of component and built items before the build.

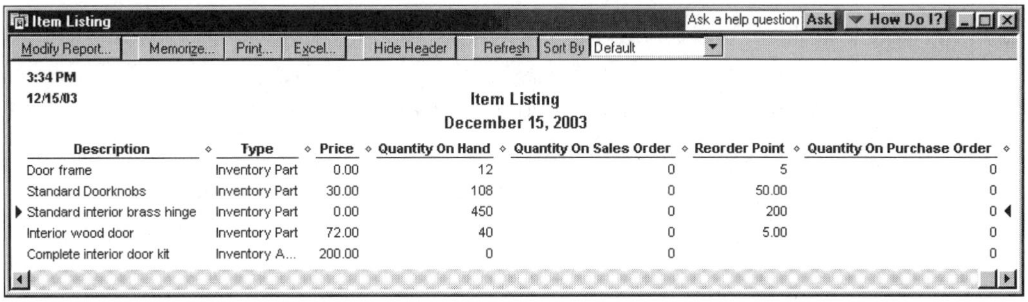

3:34 PM
12/15/03

Item Listing
December 15, 2003

Description	Type	Price	Quantity On Hand	Quantity On Sales Order	Reorder Point	Quantity On Purchase Order
Door frame	Inventory Part	0.00	12	0	5	0
Standard Doorknobs	Inventory Part	30.00	108	0	50.00	0
Standard interior brass hinge	Inventory Part	0.00	450	0	200	0
Interior wood door	Inventory Part	72.00	40	0	5.00	0
Complete interior door kit	Inventory A...	200.00	0	0		0

The following graphic shows the number of component and built items after the build.

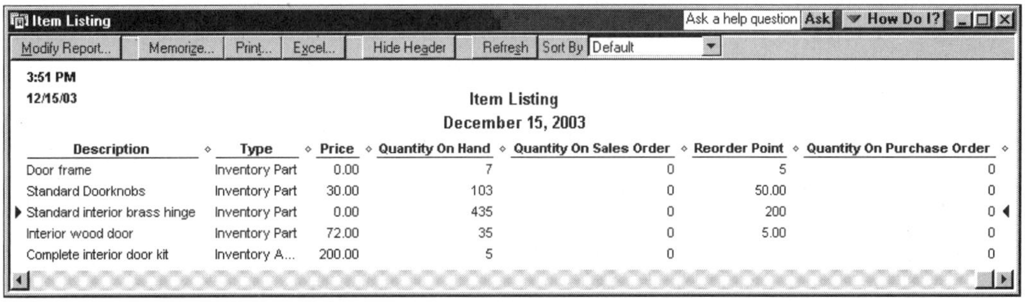

3:51 PM
12/15/03

Item Listing
December 15, 2003

Description	Type	Price	Quantity On Hand	Quantity On Sales Order	Reorder Point	Quantity On Purchase Order
Door frame	Inventory Part	0.00	7	0	5	0
Standard Doorknobs	Inventory Part	30.00	103	0	50.00	0
Standard interior brass hinge	Inventory Part	0.00	435	0	200	0
Interior wood door	Inventory Part	72.00	35	0	5.00	0
Complete interior door kit	Inventory A...	200.00	5	0		0

Managing pending builds

A pending build is an inventory assembly build transaction that could not be finalized because there were not enough component parts in inventory to build the specified number of assemblies at build time. When a build is pending, "Pending" appears in the Build Assemblies window to remind you that these assemblies haven't been built.

If you modify or delete a previous build transaction, or change inventory quantities or the dates of purchase orders, invoices, or sales receipts, assembly builds that were finalized could change to pending. Finalized builds change to pending when the quantity of at least one component drops below the quantity needed to build the specified number of assemblies on the build transaction date. You can use the pending builds report to see a list of all builds that are currently pending.

In addition, you can choose to manually mark a build as pending even if you currently have enough components in stock to build the specified quantity. This allows you to set up build information but postpone building the assembly until later.

Disassembling inventory assemblies

There are several ways to disassemble inventory assemblies and return component items to inventory. You can do any of the following:

- Use the Adjust Quantity/Value on Hand window to adjust the quantity on hand for each assembly component and the assembly item.
- Reduce quantity to build in the Build Assemblies window and then click Build & Close. The quantity of assembly units in inventory are decreased and the quantity of component inventory parts are increased accordingly.
- Delete a build transaction completely. The quantity of assembly units in inventory are decreased and the quantity of component inventory parts are increased accordingly, but this method completely removes the build transaction from QuickBooks and should not be used if you want to maintain a record of the transaction.

Selling finished goods

When assembly items appear on any form (for example a sales receipt or in a report), their component items are hidden. Only the assembly name, description, and price appear.

If you attempt to sell more assembly units than you have available in inventory, QuickBooks warns you that quantities are insufficient to fulfill the order. If you decide to go ahead with this transaction, the quantity on hand for the specified assembly changes to a negative value. You can set a build point in the Build Assemblies window to remind you when assembly stock is getting low and you need to build more units. If you turn on reminders, a list of assemblies that need to be built appear in the Reminders window.

Student test and review

1 Enter a new inventory item using the following information.
   - Item Name/Number: Kitchen counter
   - Purchase Description: Kitchen counter
   - Cost: 280.00
   - COGS Account: Cost of Goods Sold
   - Preferred Vendor: Patton Hardware Supplies
   - Sales Description: Same as Purchase Description
   - Sales Price: 340.00
   - Income Account: Construction:materials
   - Asset Account: Inventory Asset
   - Reorder Point: 5
   - Qty on Hand: 6

2 Create a purchase order for 20 Standard doorknobs.

3 Receive the 20 Standard doorknobs into inventory and record the bill for the doorknobs.

4 Process the bill and pay for the 20 Standard doorknobs.

LESSON 11 Tracking and paying sales tax

Lesson objectives

- To get an overview of sales tax in QuickBooks (the steps involved in tracking, collecting, and paying it)
- To see how to set up QuickBooks to track sales tax
- To see how to apply sales tax to a sale
- To learn how to determine a business's sales tax liability
- To write a QuickBooks check to the appropriate tax agency for sales tax liability

Handout materials

- Handout 30: Sales tax in QuickBooks
- Handout 31: When to use a sales tax group
- Handout 32: Viewing your sales tax liability

Instructor preparation

- Review the lesson, including the examples, to make sure you're familiar with the material.
- Ensure that all students have a copy of qblesson.qbb on their computer's hard disk.
- Have Handouts 30 through 32 ready for distribution.

To start this lesson

Before you perform the following steps, make sure you have installed the exercise file (qblesson.qbb) on your hard disk. See "Installing the exercise file" in the Introduction to this guide if you haven't installed it.

The steps that follow will restore the exercise file to its original state so that the data in the file matches what you see on the screen as you proceed through each lesson.

To restore the exercise file (qblesson.qbb):

1. From the File menu in QuickBooks, choose Restore.

   QuickBooks displays the Restore Company Backup window.
2. In the "Get Company Backup From" section of the window, click Browse and select your c:\QBtrain directory.
3. Select the qblesson.qbb file, and then click Open.

4 In the "Restore Company Backup To" section of the window, click Browse and select your c:\QBtrain directory.

5 In the File name field of the Restore To window, type ***lesson 11*** and then click Save.

6 Click Restore.

Overview of sales tax in QuickBooks

If you have a business where you need to collect sales tax, you already know how complicated the process can be. These are some of the issues you may have to deal with:

- You may have to collect and pay more than one tax (for example, one rate for local taxes and one rate for state taxes).
- You may have some items that are taxable and some that aren't.
- You may tax some customers while others are non-taxable.

QuickBooks reduces some of the complication, because it lets you automatically apply sales tax on particular sales and keep track of how much you collect and from whom. Then, when you're ready to pay your taxes, QuickBooks can write a check for the correct amount.

Refer to Handout 30, "Sales tax in QuickBooks," for the following discussion.

To use QuickBooks to track and pay your sales tax:

1 **Set up your tax rates and agencies.**

In the QuickBooks Item list, set up the separate tax rates you need to charge. In the Vendor list, set up the agencies to whom you submit the taxes you've collected.

You can also set up sales tax codes, which can help you classify why a transaction (or part of one) is either taxable or non-taxable.

2 **Indicate who and what gets taxed.**

Not all of the items you sell are taxable, and not all of your customers pay tax. In your Item and Customer:Job lists, you can indicate which items or customers are taxable.

3 **Apply tax to each sale.**

When you fill out an invoice or sales receipt form, and choose a taxable item from your Item list, QuickBooks applies the appropriate sales tax.

4 **Find out what you owe.**

As you record taxable sales, QuickBooks keeps track of the tax you've collected in your Sales Tax Payable account. When you're ready to pay your sales tax agency, you can open the Sales Tax Payable register to see how much you owe, or you can create a sales tax liability report.

5 **Pay your tax agencies.**

When you go to the Pay Sales Tax window, QuickBooks shows the amount you owe and writes a check to the tax agency for that amount.

This lesson walks you through each of these steps.

Setting up your tax rates and agencies

The first step is to enter your sales tax rates, and then provide information about the tax agencies to which you pay the taxes.

Creating a tax item for each single tax you apply

Some businesses need to apply more than one sales tax to their sales; for example, they may collect a state sales tax as well as several county sales taxes. You need to create a separate sales tax item for each tax whose amount you must report (not necessarily for each tax you collect—some states want you to report state sales tax and county sales tax as separate items, while others let you report them as one item).

Even if you're paying more than one type of tax, you usually want your customers to see one overall tax amount, not separate taxes for the state and county. You'll learn how to do that in this lesson.

On the Item list, you already have sales tax for San Tomas and San Domingo County. Because Rock Castle Construction now does business in the city of Bayshore, you need to add sales tax items for that city.

To add a sales tax item:

1 From the Lists menu, choose Item List.

QuickBooks displays the Item list.

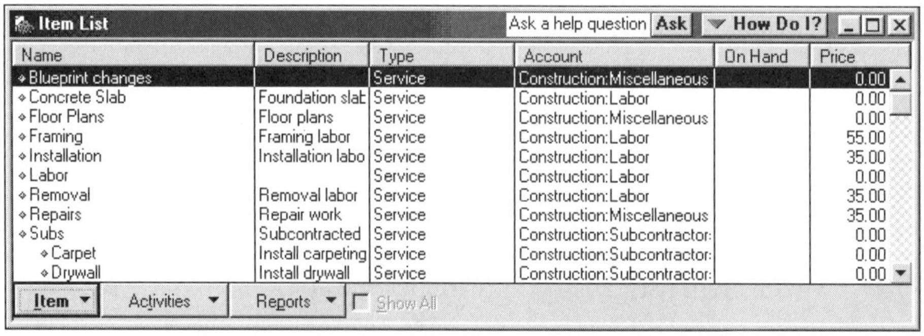

2 Click the Item menu button, and then choose New.

QuickBooks displays the New Item window.

3 In the Type field, choose Sales Tax Item from the drop-down list.

4 In the Tax Name field, type ***Bayshore***.

5 In the Description field, type ***Bayshore City.***

6 In the Tax Rate (%) field, type ***1.***

7 In the Tax Agency field, type ***Bayshore Tax Agency.***

Your New Item window should now resemble the following figure.

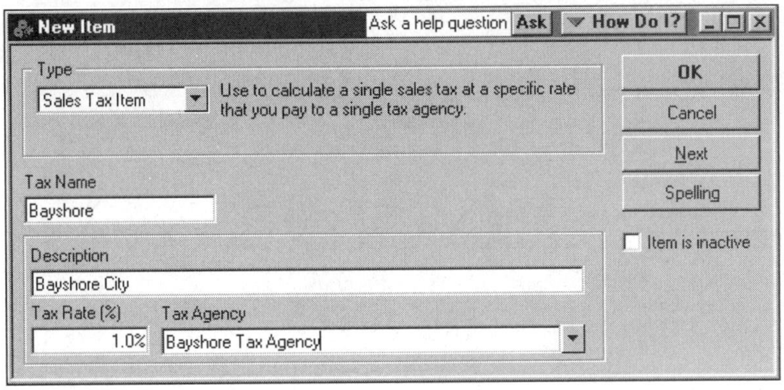

8 Click OK.

QuickBooks displays a message telling you that Bayshore Tax Agency is not on your Vendor list.

9 Click Quick Add.

QuickBooks adds Bayshore Tax Agency to the Vendor list.

10 Click OK.

Your Item list should resemble the following figure.

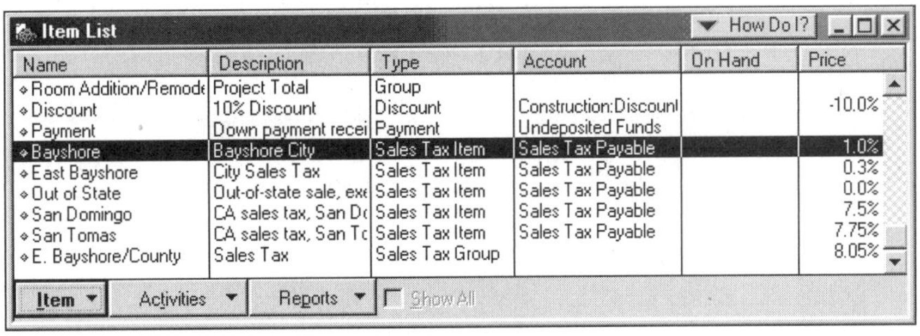

Grouping single taxes together

Refer to Handout 31, "When to use a sales tax group," for this discussion.

Even if you collect a combination of sales taxes (for example, city tax and county tax) that you report separately, you probably don't want to confuse customers by showing separate taxes on your invoices or sales forms. QuickBooks lets you group some or all of your tax items so that customers see a single tax amount on your invoices and sales receipts. Instead of a sales tax item, you'll be creating a sales tax group.

To create a sales tax group:

1 With the Item list displayed, click the Item menu button, and then choose New.

2 In the Type field, choose Sales Tax Group.

The New Item window on your screen should resemble the figure below.

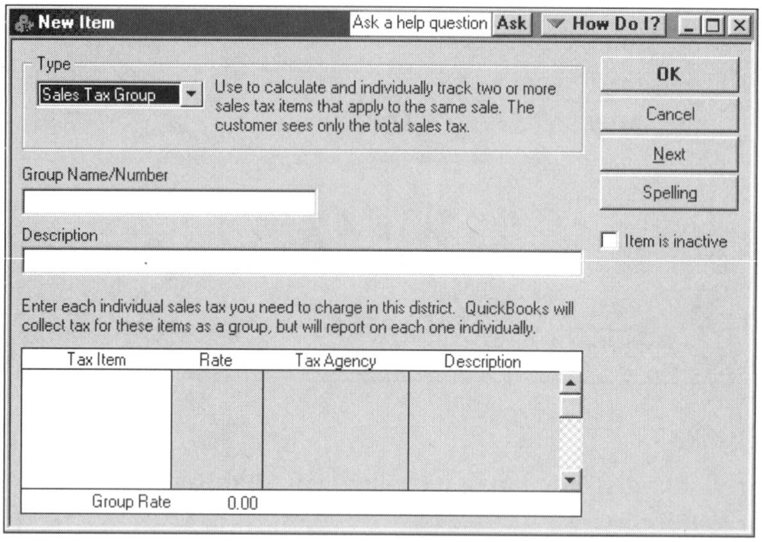

3 In the Group Name/Number field, type ***Bayshore Grp***.

4 In the Description field, type ***Sales Tax, Bayshore***.

5 Click in the Tax Item column, and then choose Bayshore from the drop-down list.

6 Click on the second line in the Tax Item column, and then choose San Tomas.

Your New Item window should resemble the following figure.

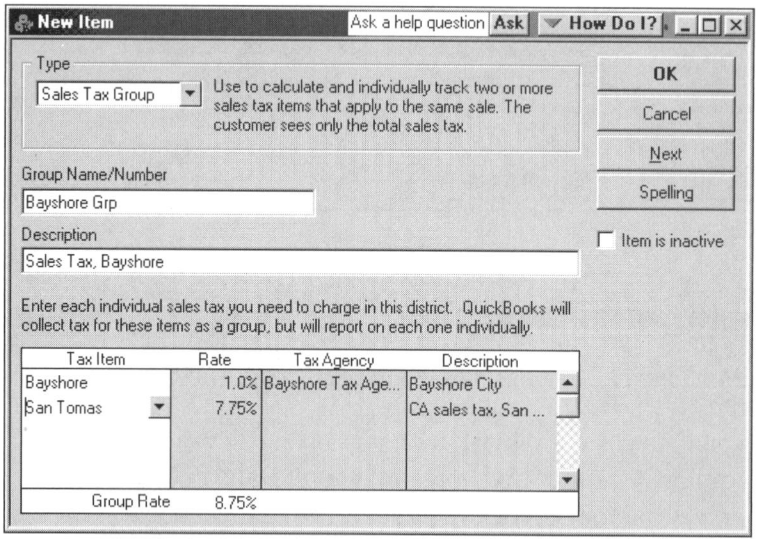

Notice that the total group rate is 8.75%.

7 Click OK.

QuickBooks adds the Bayshore Group to the Item list.

Identifying your most common tax

If you want QuickBooks to apply sales tax to your invoices and sales receipts, you have to tell it which sales tax item or group is the one you use most often. Once you do that, QuickBooks applies that sales tax when you fill out an invoice or a sales receipt. (You can choose a different sales tax from the sales form if you don't want the default tax.)

Assume Rock Castle Construction uses the San Tomas sales tax most often, and it wants to set that up as the default sales tax.

To set up a default sales tax:

1 From the Edit menu, choose Preferences.

QuickBooks displays the Preferences window.

2 In the Preferences window, click the Sales Tax icon in the left scroll box, and then click the Company Preferences tab.

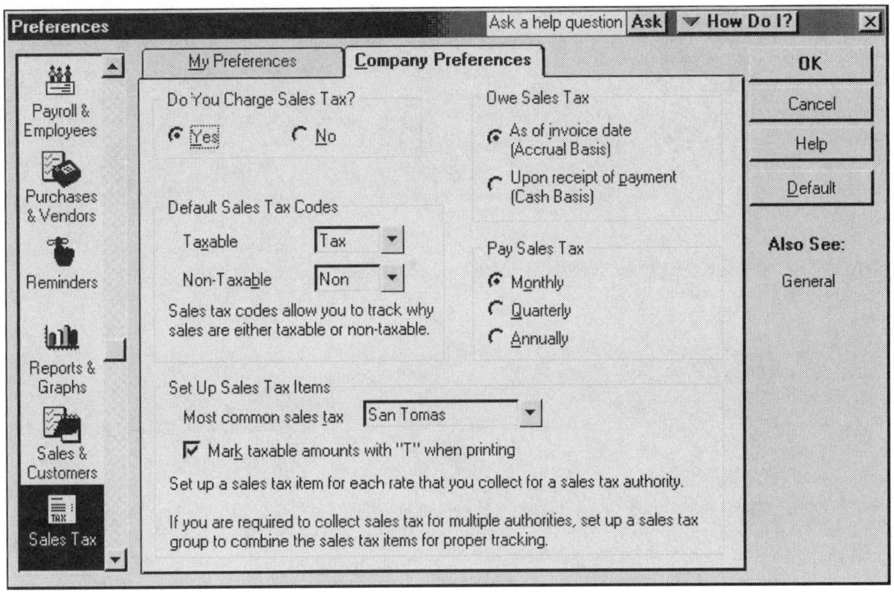

3 In the "Most common sales tax" field, make sure San Tomas is selected.

4 Click OK.

If you're using sales tax codes, you can use the Preferences window to tell QuickBooks which sales tax codes to use as the default taxable and non-taxable codes. You can use the codes that come preset with QuickBooks, or define your own. You can also manage sales tax codes using the Sales Tax Code list, which is available on the Lists menu when the sales tax feature is turned on in a company data file.

Indicating who and what gets taxed

The next step in setting up sales tax is to indicate who and what gets taxed. You have to tell QuickBooks whether or not a customer is taxable and assign a default tax item or tax group to that customer.

You must also distinguish between taxable and non-taxable items on the Item list. When you add an item to the Item list, there's a place in the window where you can indicate whether you charge tax for the item. QuickBooks remembers this information, and shows whether or not an item is taxable when you enter the item on a sales form.

In the next exercise, you'll take a look at an item on Rock Castle's Item list to see how to indicate that an item is taxable.

To indicate a taxable item:

1 In the Item list, select Doorknobs Std (under Hardware).

2 Click the Item menu button, and then choose Edit.

QuickBooks displays the Edit Item window.

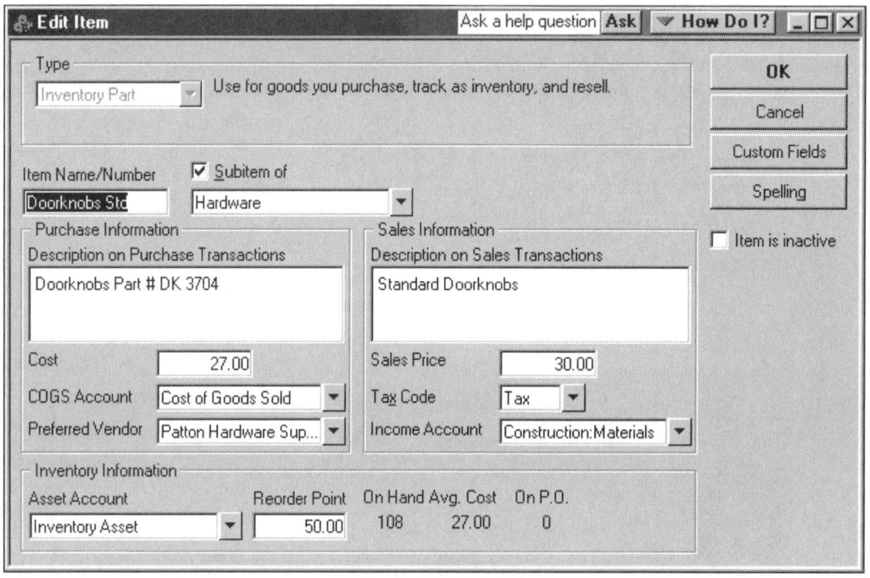

The code in the Tax Code field is a taxable code, which tells you that this item is taxable. When you choose the item to be included on a sales form, QuickBooks knows that the item is taxable and automatically applies the default sales tax (San Tomas sales tax with a rate of 7.75%).

To indicate that an item is non-taxable, select a non-taxable code from the drop-down list.

3 Click OK to close the Edit Item window.

4 Close the Item list.

In the same way that you can specify that an item in the Item list is taxable, you can indicate whether or not a particular customer is taxable or non-taxable in that customer's record.

To see an existing customer record:

1. From the Lists menu, choose Customer:Job List.

   QuickBooks displays the Customer:Job list.

2. Select Jimenez, Cristina.
3. Click the Customer:Job menu button, and then choose Edit.

   QuickBooks displays the Edit Customer window.

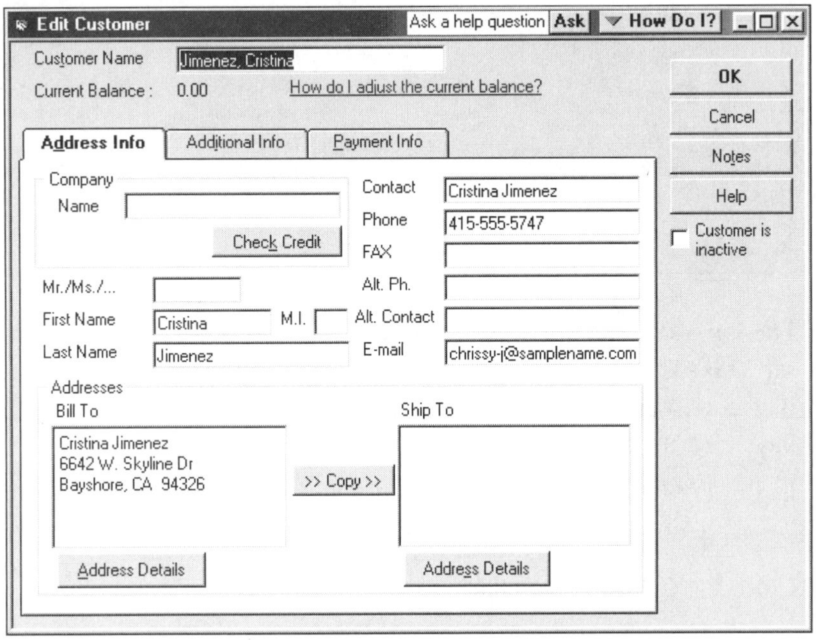

4 Click the Additional Info tab.

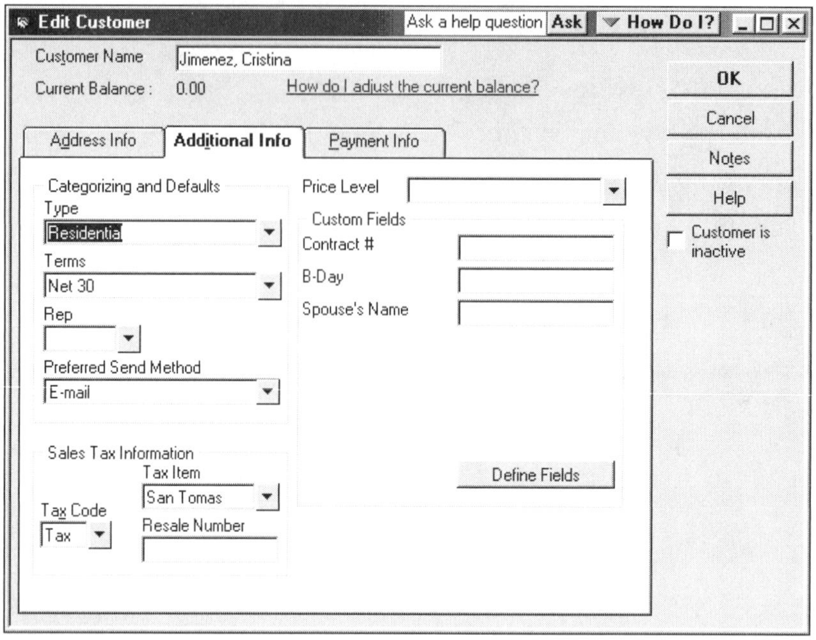

The tax code selected indicates that transactions with this customer are subject to sales tax. The San Tomas tax item is assigned, however, this customer is located in Bayshore, which has just instituted its city sales tax, so change the tax item to Bayshore Group.

5 In the Tax Item field, choose Bayshore Grp from the drop-down list.

6 Click OK.

7 Close the Customer:Job list.

Applying tax to each sale

If you've set up a default sales tax, assigned taxes to your customers, and marked taxable items you sell as taxable, QuickBooks automatically calculates and applies the tax when you make a sale.

To apply tax to a sale:

1 From the Customers menu, choose Create Invoices.

QuickBooks displays the Create Invoices window.

2 In the Customer:Job field, choose Jimenez, Cristina:Utility Shed from the drop-down list. (Select both the customer and the job.)

3 Click in the Item column and select Doorknobs Std from the drop-down list.

The Create Invoices window should resemble the figure below.

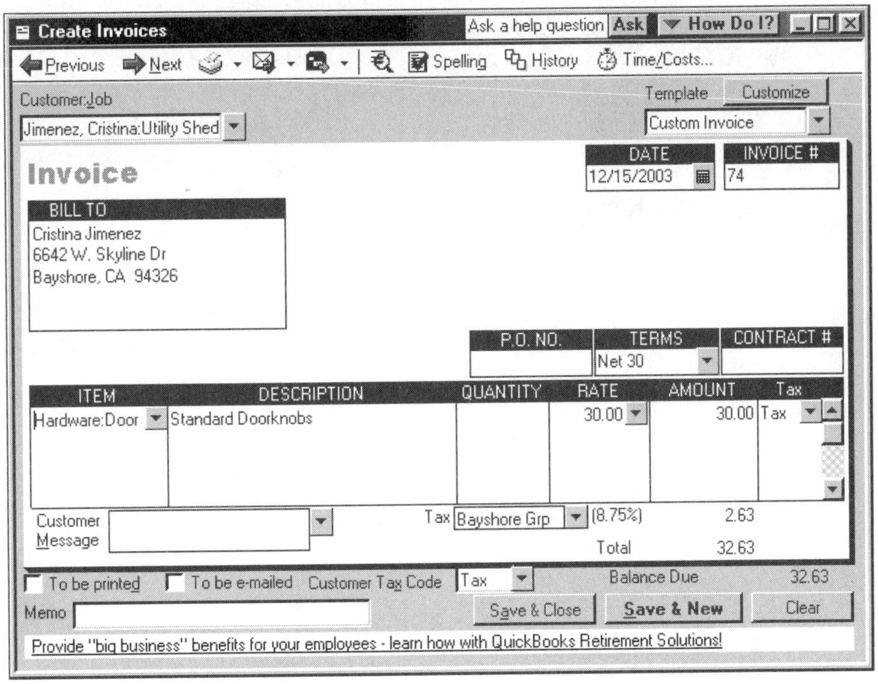

When you enter a taxable item, QuickBooks displays the tax code associated with that item in the Tax column (which appears to the right of the Amount column). If the customer is taxable, QuickBooks includes all items associated with a taxable tax code in its tax calculation.

Tip: **You can select a different tax code from the list to turn taxable status on and off for unique situations.** You can also change the customer's taxable status by selecting a non-taxable code from the Customer Tax Code drop-down list.

Notice that QuickBooks applies to the Bayshore Group tax automatically because this is the sales tax you assigned to this customer.

4 In the Quantity column, type ***4***, and then press Tab.

The Create Invoices window should resemble the following figure.

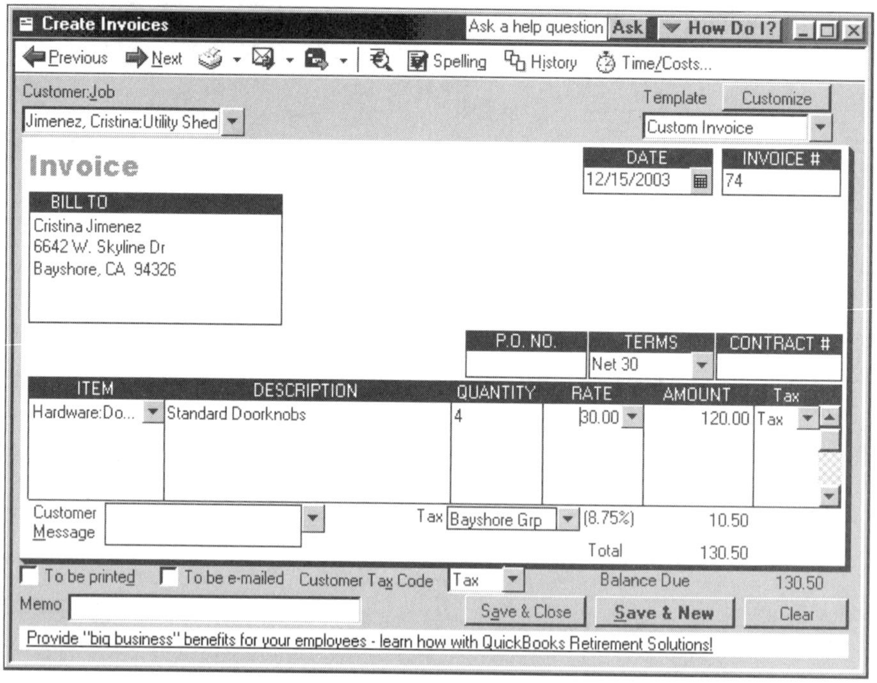

5 Click Save & Close.

Determining what you owe

If you're required to collect sales tax from customers, you also have to make periodic payments of the sales tax you've collected. QuickBooks gives you three ways to determine the amount of your sales tax liability: the sales tax liability report, the Sales Tax Payable register, and the Pay Sales Tax window.

Refer to Handout 32, "Viewing your sales tax liability."

Creating a sales tax liability report

The sales tax liability report provides complete information about the sales tax your company owes for a particular period of time.

To create the sales tax liability report:

1. From the Reports menu, choose Vendors & Payables, and then choose Sales Tax Liability.

   Your report should resemble the following figure.

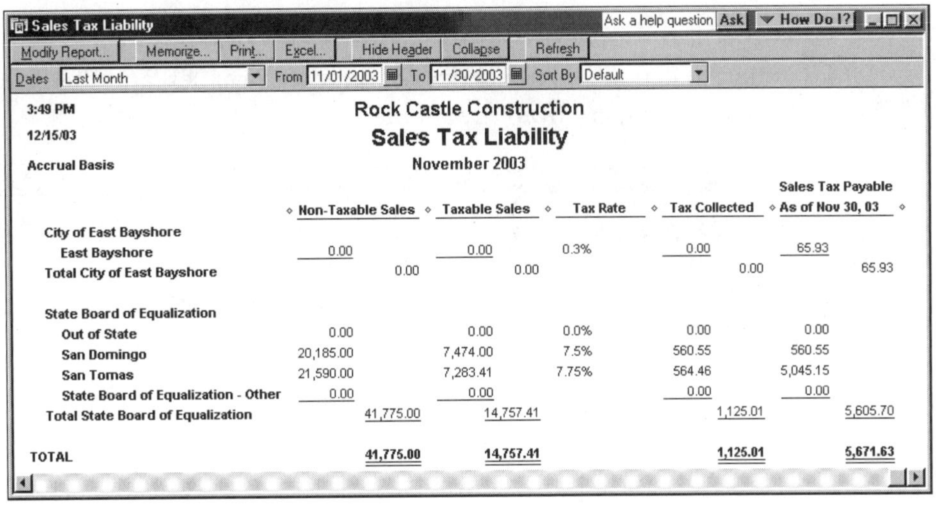

3:49 PM
12/15/03
Accrual Basis

Rock Castle Construction
Sales Tax Liability
November 2003

	Non-Taxable Sales		Taxable Sales		Tax Rate	Tax Collected		Sales Tax Payable As of Nov 30, 03	
City of East Bayshore									
East Bayshore	0.00		0.00		0.3%	0.00		65.93	
Total City of East Bayshore		0.00		0.00			0.00		65.93
State Board of Equalization									
Out of State	0.00		0.00		0.0%	0.00		0.00	
San Domingo	20,185.00		7,474.00		7.5%	560.55		560.55	
San Tomas	21,590.00		7,283.41		7.75%	564.46		5,045.15	
State Board of Equalization - Other	0.00		0.00			0.00		0.00	
Total State Board of Equalization		41,775.00		14,757.41			1,125.01		5,605.70
TOTAL		41,775.00		14,757.41			1,125.01		5,671.63

2. In the Dates field, choose This Month-to-date from the drop-down list.

   Your report should resemble the following figure.

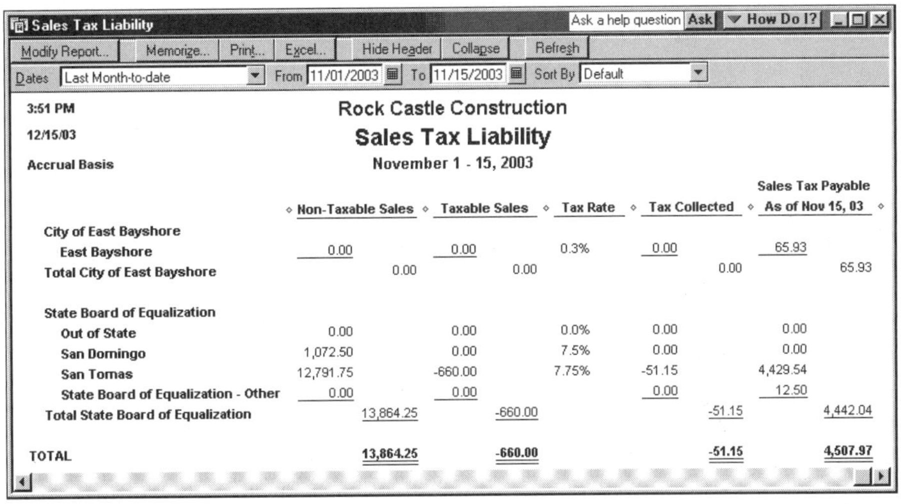

3:51 PM
12/15/03
Accrual Basis

Rock Castle Construction
Sales Tax Liability
November 1 - 15, 2003

	Non-Taxable Sales		Taxable Sales		Tax Rate	Tax Collected		Sales Tax Payable As of Nov 15, 03	
City of East Bayshore									
East Bayshore	0.00		0.00		0.3%	0.00		65.93	
Total City of East Bayshore		0.00		0.00			0.00		65.93
State Board of Equalization									
Out of State	0.00		0.00		0.0%	0.00		0.00	
San Domingo	1,072.50		0.00		7.5%	0.00		0.00	
San Tomas	12,791.75		-660.00		7.75%	-51.15		4,429.54	
State Board of Equalization - Other	0.00		0.00			0.00		12.50	
Total State Board of Equalization		13,864.25		-660.00			-51.15		4,442.04
TOTAL		13,864.25		-660.00			-51.15		4,507.97

The sales tax liability report shows the total taxable sales as of a date you choose, total non-taxable sales, and the amount of sales tax you owe each tax agency.

QuickBooks displays the sales tax liability report on an accrual basis (unless you changed the default setting in the Sales Tax Preferences window). The report shows exactly how much sales tax you collected.

3. Close the sales tax liability report.
4. If QuickBooks asks if you want to memorize the report, click No.

Determining the source of sales tax revenue

If you'd like to see where your sales tax revenue is coming from, you can run the sales tax revenue summary report, which shows you the sources of all taxable and non-taxable sales transactions, broken down by individual sales tax codes.

To run the sales tax revenue summary report:

1 From the Reports menu, choose Vendors & Payables, and then choose Sales Tax Revenue Summary from the submenu.

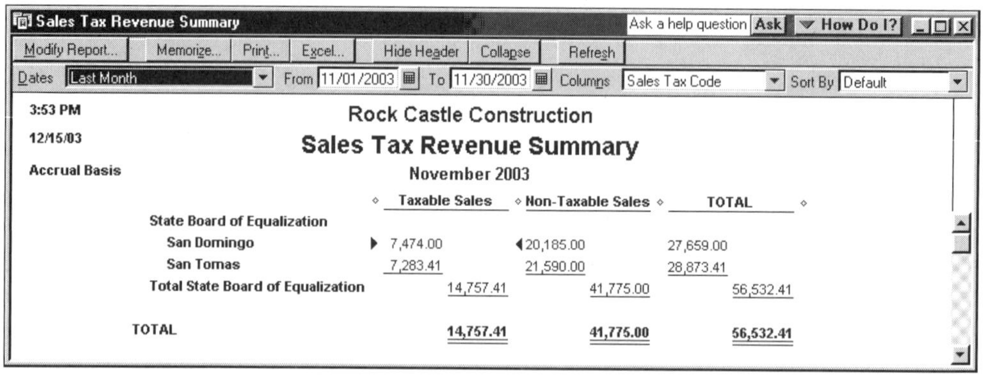

You can QuickZoom on the numbers in the report to get more information about specific sales transactions.

2 Close the report.

Using the sales tax payable register

Each time you write an invoice or sales receipt that includes sales tax, QuickBooks enters the information in the sales tax payable register. QuickBooks keeps track of transactions for all tax vendors in the same Sales Tax Payable account.

To see the sales tax payable register:

1 From the Company menu, choose Chart of Accounts.

QuickBooks displays the chart of accounts.

2 Click Sales Tax Payable once to select it.

3 Click the Activities menu button and select Use Register.

QuickBooks displays the Sales Tax Payable register.

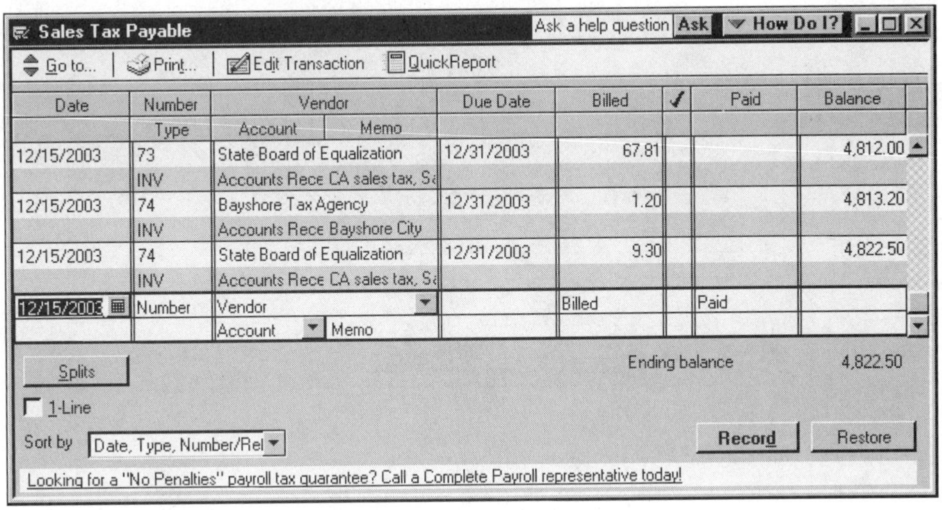

Each entry in the register is a single tax transaction. Taxes you record on invoices and sales receipts appear as increases, and payments you make to tax agencies appear as decreases. The ending balance of the register is your current tax liability.

Notice how some transactions have the same invoice number. When you record two tax rates on the same invoice or cash sale, the register shows a separate transaction for each tax agency. (This is because you have to make separate payments to individual tax agencies.)

4 Close the register.

5 Close the chart of accounts.

Paying your tax agencies

When it's time to pay sales tax, you use the Pay Sales Tax window to write a check to your tax agency or agencies. Suppose Rock Castle Construction is ready to make a sales tax payment.

To make a sales tax payment:

1 From the Vendors menu, choose Sales Tax, then choose Pay Sales Tax from the submenu.

QuickBooks displays the Pay Sales Tax window.

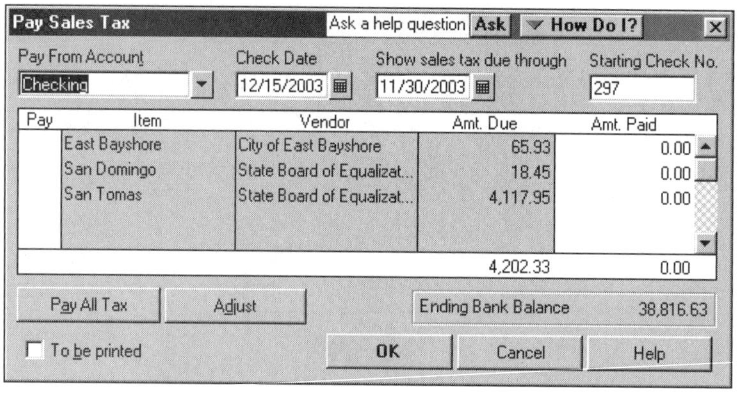

2 Select the "To be printed" checkbox.

3 In the "Show sales tax due through" field, type ***12/15/03***, and then press Tab.

QuickBooks displays tax agencies and the amounts you owe. To mark them for payment, click the Pay All Tax button.

The Pay Sales Tax window should resemble the figure below.

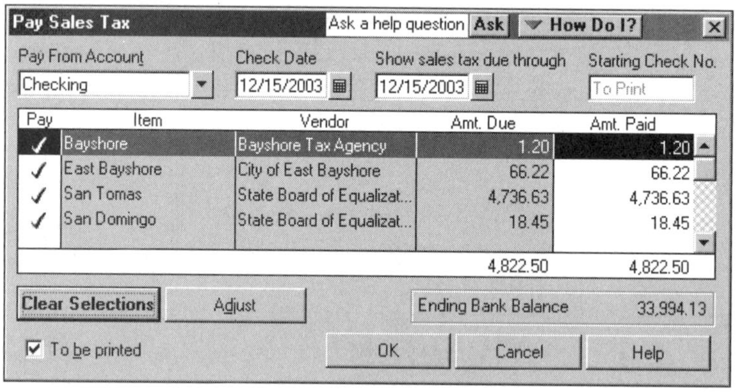

4 Click OK.

QuickBooks writes and records checks to the tax agencies you indicated. All you need to do is print the checks. QuickBooks updates your the tax report and sales tax payable register to show that you've paid the tax agencies.

Student test and review

1 Create an invoice for Pretell Real Estate's 155 Wilks Blvd. job, for 10 interior wood doors and 2 exterior wood doors.

2 After you record the invoice, open the sales tax payable register to see how QuickBooks has recorded the tax due from the invoice.

LESSON 12 Doing payroll with QuickBooks

Lesson objectives

- To gain an overview of payroll in QuickBooks
- To learn more about payroll setup
- To set up employee payroll information
- To practice writing and printing a payroll check
- To learn how QuickBooks tracks your tax liabilities
- To practice paying payroll taxes

Handout materials

- Handout 33: Overview of payroll tracking
- Handout 34: Items on the Payroll Item list
- Handout 35: Tracking payroll expenses and payroll liabilities

Instructor preparation

- Review the lesson, including the examples, to make sure you're familiar with the material.
- Ensure that all students have a copy of qblesson.qbb on their computer's hard disk.
- Have Handouts 33 through 35 ready for distribution.

To start this lesson

Before you perform the following steps, make sure you have installed the exercise file (qblesson.qbb) on your hard disk. See "Installing the exercise file" in the Introduction to this guide if you haven't installed it.

The steps that follow will restore the exercise file to its original state so that the data in the file matches what you see on the screen as you proceed through each lesson.

To restore the exercise file (qblesson.qbb):

1. From the File menu in QuickBooks, choose Restore.

   QuickBooks displays the Restore Company Backup window.
2. In the "Get Company Backup From" section of the window, click Browse and select your c:\QBtrain directory.
3. Select the qblesson.qbb file, and then click Open.

4 In the "Restore Company Backup To" section of the window, click Browse and select your c:\QBtrain directory.

5 In the File name field of the Restore To window, type ***lesson 12*** and then click Save.

6 Click Restore.

Overview of payroll tracking

Refer to Handout 33, "Overview of payroll tracking," for the following discussion.

This lesson is designed to demonstrate some of the QuickBooks payroll features. The way you process payroll for your company may differ from this lesson depending on which (if any) payroll service you subscribe to.

Because payroll information is already set up in the exercise file, you will not go through the payroll setup process in this lesson. For information about setting up payroll for your company in QuickBooks, see "Setting up payroll" in Chapter 21 of the QuickBooks *User's Guide.*

To calculate payroll, QuickBooks uses tax tables. The exercise file includes the tax table data needed to complete this lesson. To get the tax tables to use with your own QuickBooks company data file, you need to subscribe to one of the Intuit Payroll Services—either Do-It-Yourself Payroll or Assisted Payroll. Intuit also offers a full service payroll option. To learn about these options or subscribe to one of them, from the Employees menu, choose Payroll Services, and then choose Learn About Payroll Options from the submenu. Or see "About Intuit Payroll Services" in Chapter 21 of the User's Guide to get an overview of these services and to find contact information.

QuickBooks calculates each employee's gross pay, and then calculates taxes and deductions to arrive at the net pay. With QuickBooks, you can write the paycheck, record the transaction in your QuickBooks checking account, keep track of your tax liabilities, and pay them.

You, as the employer, must subtract taxes and other deductions before issuing an employee's paycheck. Some typical paycheck deductions are federal and state withholding (income) taxes, social security taxes (FICA), Medicare taxes, and state unemployment insurance. You may also deduct for benefits such as a 401(k) plan, or contributions to your company's medical/dental plan.

When you withhold social security, Medicare, and federal withholding taxes from employees' paychecks, you must submit regular deposits of the withheld tax money (semiweekly or monthly, depending on the size of your payroll), and file quarterly forms that list the total amounts you withheld from each employee's paycheck.

Calculating payroll with QuickBooks

To do its payroll calculations, QuickBooks needs four kinds of information:

- **Information about your company**

  Besides the company name and address, this includes information about your federal and state tax ID numbers. You enter this information in the EasyStep Interview when you set up your QuickBooks company data file. (You can view most company information by choosing Company Information from the Company menu.)

- **Information about your employees**

  The QuickBooks Employee list stores general information about each of your employees, and specific information related to payroll (such as the employee's salary or hourly rate, filing status, number of exemptions, and miscellaneous additions, deductions, and company contributions). You can store payroll information that most employees have in common in employee defaults. Whenever you have a new employee to add, simply enter information that's specific to that employee (name, address, and so on).

- **Information about your payroll items**

  QuickBooks maintains a list of items that affect the amount on a payroll check, including company expenses related to payroll. When you specify you want to use payroll, QuickBooks creates a number of payroll items for you. You add others as you need them.

- **Tax tables for federal, state, and local withholdings**

  QuickBooks uses tax tables to calculate payroll. You get the current tax tables and keep them current when you subscribe to one of the Intuit Payroll Services mentioned on page 249. If you choose not to subscribe to one of these two payroll services, you need to calculate and enter your payroll tax deductions manually for each paycheck.

  Once you've set up your company, employee data, and payroll items, to run payroll you enter the number of hours worked during the pay period for each employee. QuickBooks calculates the gross wages for the employee, and then refers to its tax tables (if you've subscribed to one of the Intuit Payroll Services—Do-It-Yourself Payroll or Assisted Payroll) and the company and employee information you've entered to calculate all withholdings and deductions and to arrive at the net pay figure. QuickBooks also calculates your company payroll expenses (for example, your contributions to social security and Medicare).

Setting up for payroll

By default, the QuickBooks payroll feature is turned on.

To turn payroll off in a company data file:

1 From the Edit menu, choose Preferences, and click the Payroll & Employees icon.

2 Click the Company Preferences tab and select "No payroll."

Note: You can also turn off the payroll feature during the EasyStep Interview.

3 Click OK.

Understanding payroll items

Refer to Handout 34, "Items on the Payroll Item list," for this discussion.

QuickBooks maintains a list for everything that affects the amount on a payroll check and for every company expense related to payroll. This list is called the Payroll Item list. There are payroll items for compensation, taxes, other additions and deductions, and employer-paid expenses. QuickBooks uses payroll items to track individual amounts on a paycheck and accumulated year-to-date wage and tax amounts for each employee.

QuickBooks adds some items to the list for you, and you can add others as you need them. For common payroll items, such as compensation and benefits, QuickBooks provides extra assistance so you can set them up quickly and accurately.

You work directly with payroll items as you do payroll tasks. Behind the scenes, QuickBooks tracks your payroll liabilities in the Payroll Liabilities account (an Other Current Liability account) and your payroll expenses in the Payroll Expenses account.

To view the Payroll Item list:

1 From the Employees menu, choose Payroll Item List. (You must have payroll turned on to see this choice.)

QuickBooks displays the Payroll Item list.

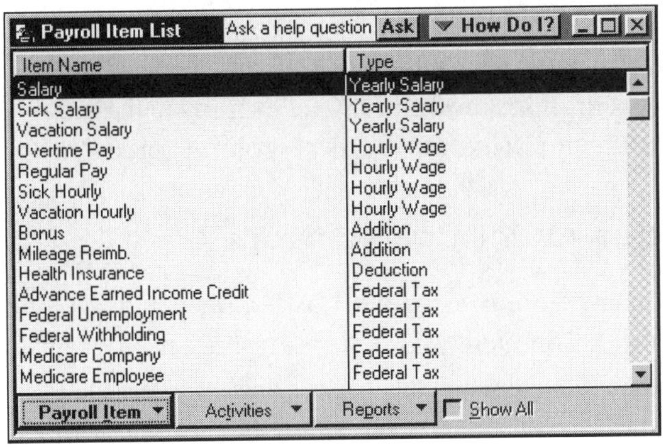

You've already used the QuickBooks Item list, so this list should look familiar. Just like the regular Item list, each payroll item has a Name and a Type.

The names of the payroll items are what you'll see on paychecks and in payroll reports.

2 Close the Payroll Item list.

You won't add a new payroll item in this lesson, but if you need to add an item after you've set up payroll in QuickBooks, you can use the following procedure.

To add a payroll item:

1 From the Employees menu, choose Payroll Item list.

2 Click the Payroll Item menu button, and then choose New.

3 QuickBooks displays the Add new payroll item window, which steps you through the payroll item setup process.

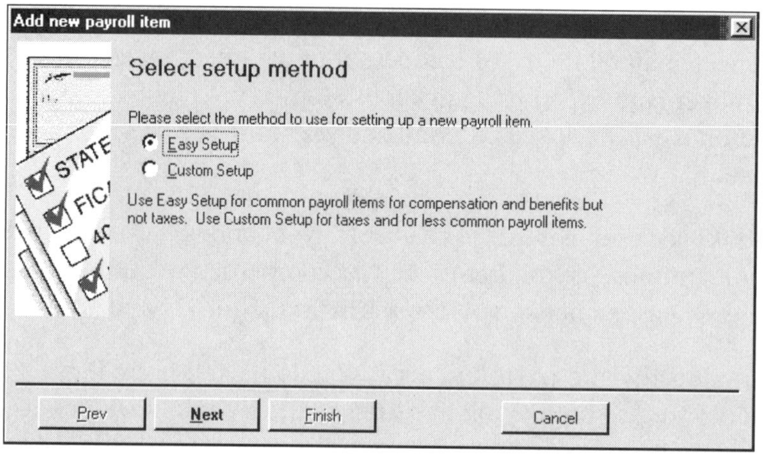

Select Easy Setup for common payroll items or compensation and benefits. Use Custom Setup for taxes and less common payroll items.

Setting up employee payroll information

QuickBooks calculates payroll for each employee on the basis of that employee's pay rate, marital status, exemptions, and so on. The Employee list stores general information about each employee, as well as payroll information.

What information does QuickBooks store?

You're going to add a new employee to Rock Castle Construction payroll in a moment. First, look at the information QuickBooks stores in the Employee list.

To view information stored in the Employee list:

1 From the Employees menu, choose Employee List.

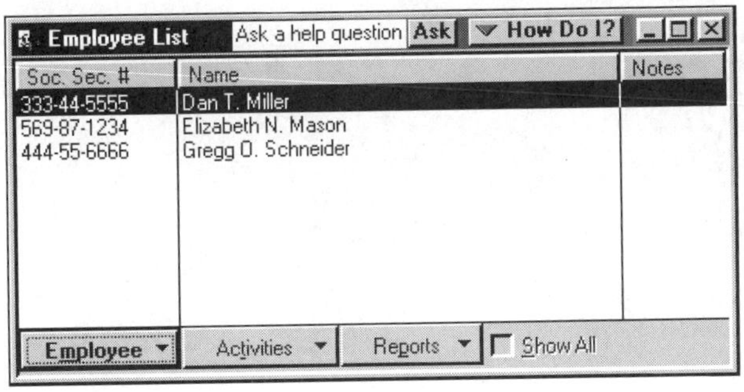

2 Select Dan T. Miller in the list, and then choose Edit from the Employee menu button.

QuickBooks displays the Edit Employee window for Dan T. Miller.

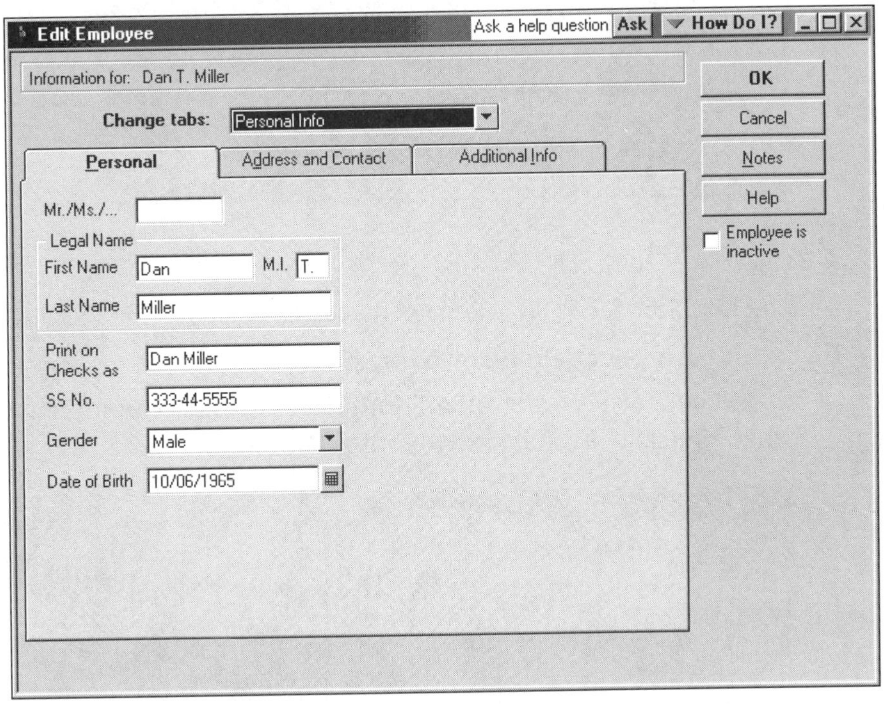

The Personal tab contains general information about Dan Miller, such as his name, social security number, and date of birth.

3 Click the Address and Contact tab.

This is where QuickBooks stores employees' addresses, telephone numbers, and other contact information.

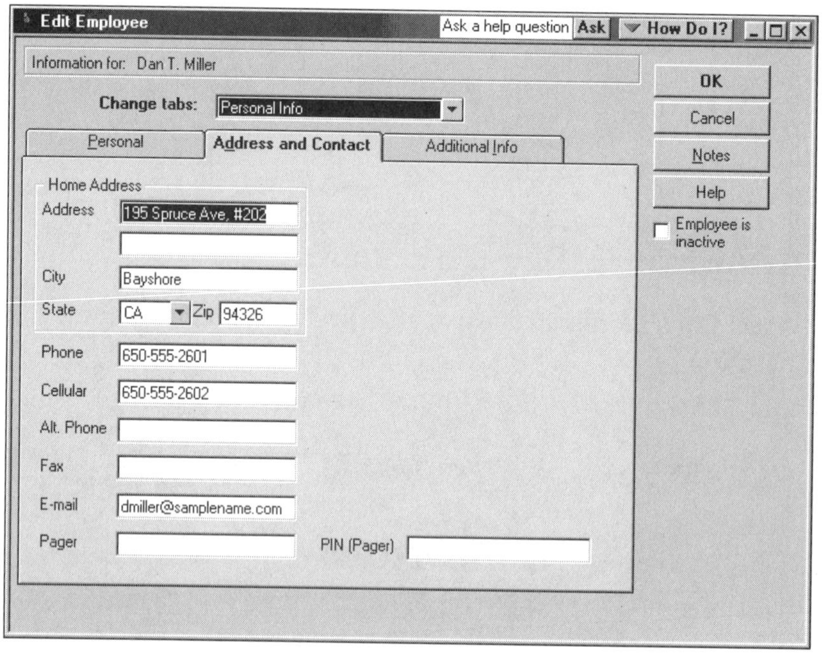

4 Click the Additional Info tab.

The Additional Info tab lets you add custom fields to the Employee list.

5 In the Change tabs drop-down list, select Payroll and Compensation Info.

QuickBooks displays the Payroll Info tab of the Edit Employee window. This is where QuickBooks stores payroll information.

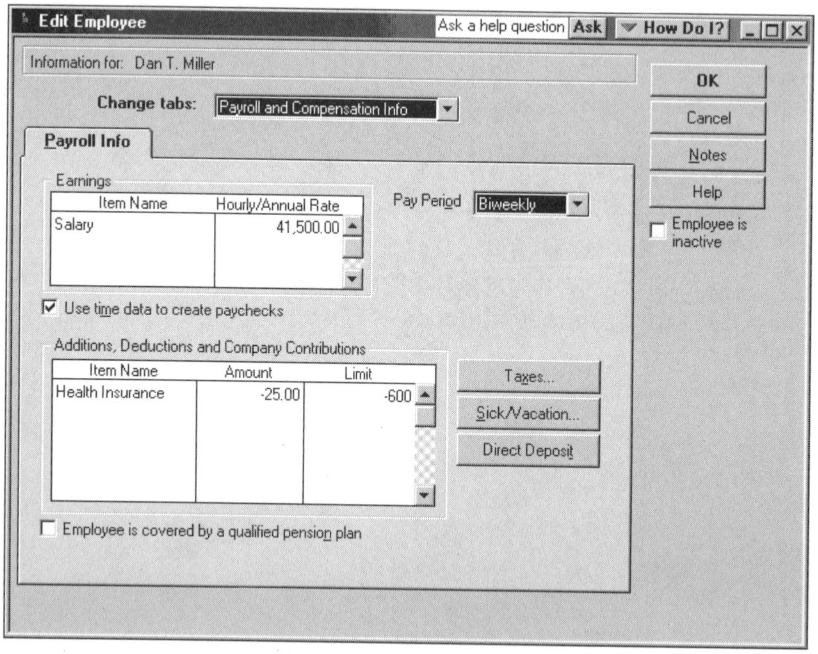

The Payroll Info tab contains an employee's specific salary or hourly rate, and any additions, deductions, or company contributions. You can see tax information for this employee (the type of information you get from a W-4) by clicking the Taxes button.

6 Click Taxes.

QuickBooks displays the Federal tab of the Taxes for Dan T. Miller window.

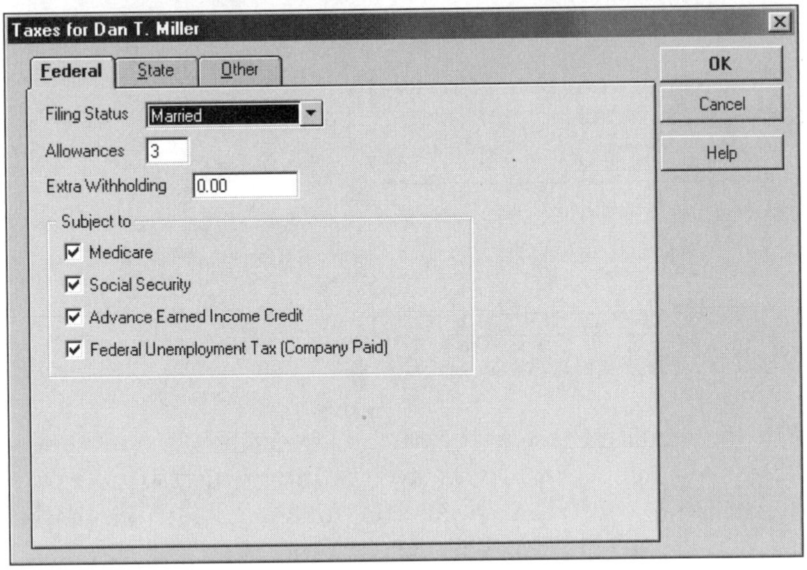

The checkboxes indicate the types of taxes the employee should have deducted from each paycheck. A checkmark in the Federal Unemployment checkbox indicates that this employee's pay is subject to the employer-paid federal unemployment tax.

7 Click the State tab to check the state withholdings.

This window stores information about state withholding taxes, state unemployment, and state disability.

8 Click OK to return to the Edit Employee window.

9 Click OK again to return to the Employee list.

Using the employee defaults to store common information

QuickBooks stores a wealth of information about each employee, but it doesn't require you to enter the same information over and over. When you have information that applies to most of your employees, you can enter it into your employee defaults. Then, when you add an employee, QuickBooks automatically fills in the information stored with the defaults. You just need to add or change any information that is different for a particular employee.

To view employee defaults:

1 With the Employee list displayed, choose Employee Defaults from the Employee menu button.

QuickBooks displays the Employee Defaults window.

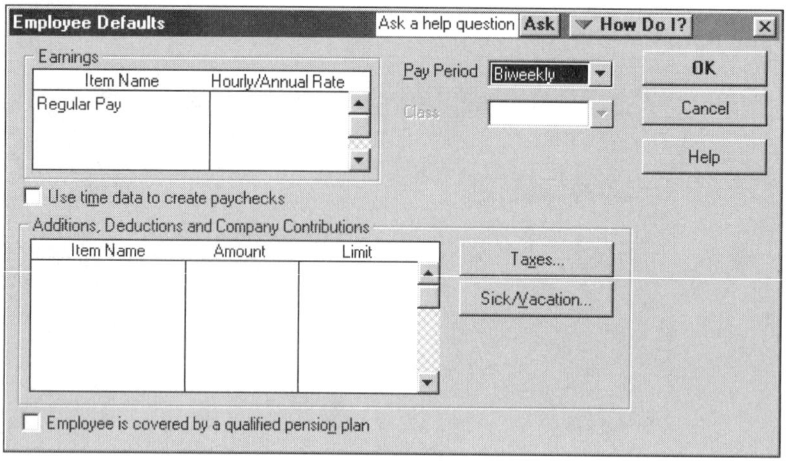

Use this window to set up the payroll information that most of your employees have in common. QuickBooks saves the information so you won't have to re-enter it when you set up the payroll record for an individual employee.

All Rock Castle Construction employees have the same biweekly pay period, so that is entered in the employee defaults.

In addition, all employees are subject to a deduction for health insurance, limited to a maximum of $1,200. This information isn't reflected in the defaults, so you can add it now.

2 Select the "Use time data to create paychecks" checkbox to include pay for time entered using the time tracking feature (available in QuickBooks Pro and Premier products only).

3 In the Additions, Deductions and Company Contributions area, click in the Item Name column, and then choose Health Insurance from the drop-down list.

4 In the Amount column, type ***50*** and press Tab.

Your screen should look like the following.

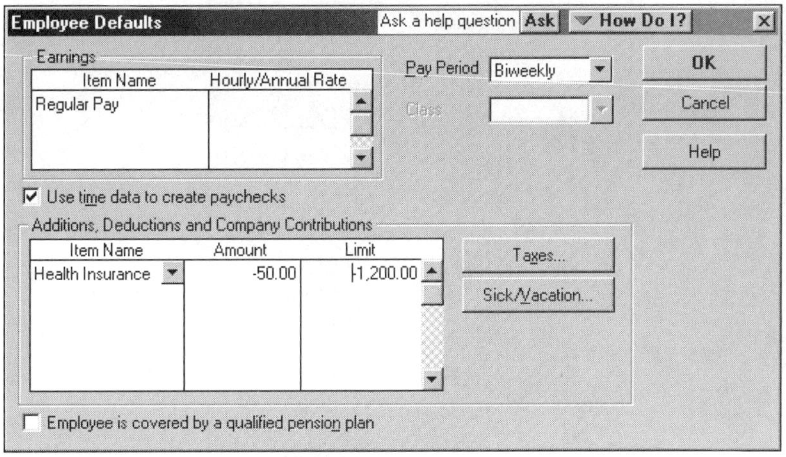

5 Click Taxes.

QuickBooks displays the Federal tab of the Taxes Defaults window.

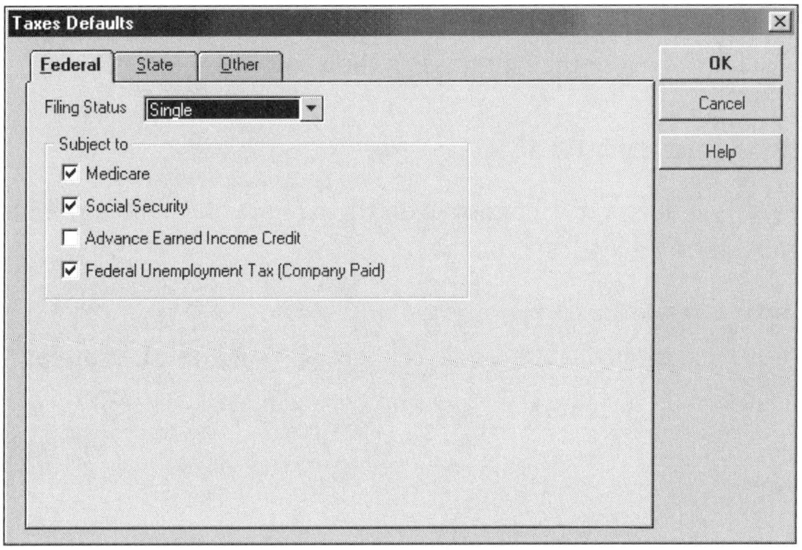

The withholding taxes that should be deducted from each employee paycheck are entered in this window.

6 Click Cancel to close the Taxes Defaults window.

7 Click Sick/Vacation.

QuickBooks displays the Sick & Vacation Defaults window.

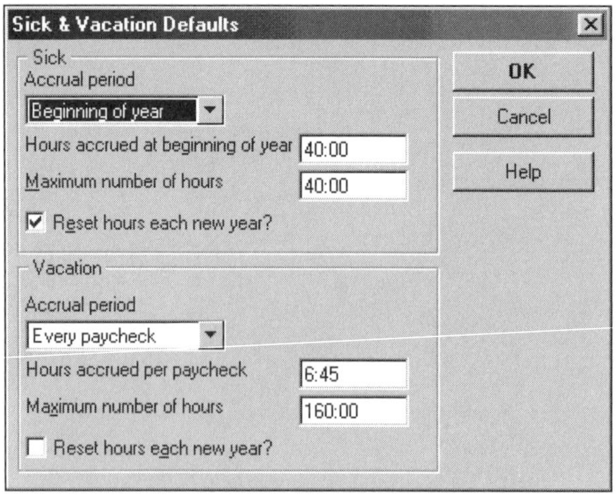

Information regarding earned sick days and vacation days is entered in this window. QuickBooks keeps track of the earned time each pay period.

8 Click Cancel to close the Sick & Vacation Defaults window.

9 Click OK to close the Employee Defaults window.

Adding a new employee

Suppose you have a new employee on the payroll, and want to add him to your records.

To add a new employee:

1 With the Employee list displayed, choose New from the Employee menu button.

QuickBooks displays the New Employee window.

2 On the Personal tab, enter the employee data as shown below.

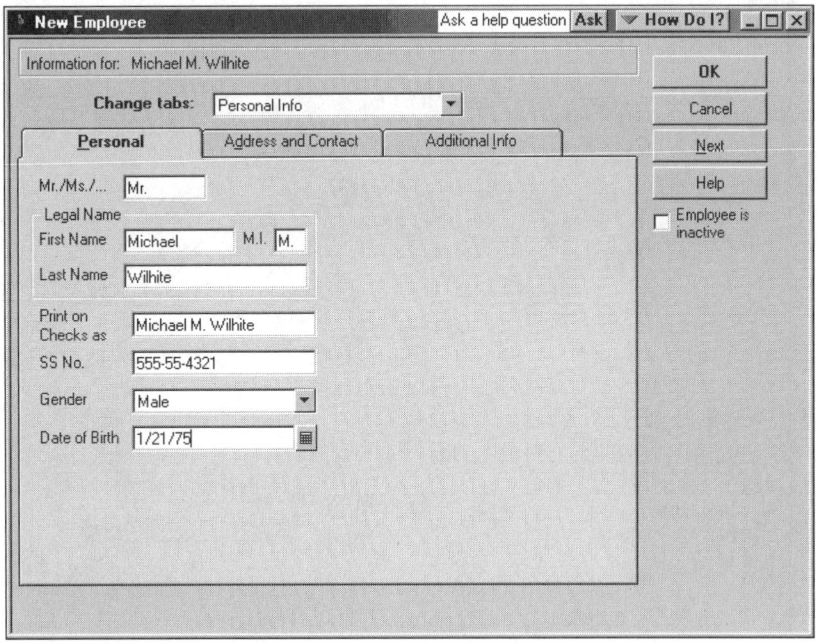

3 On the Address and Contact tab, enter the employee data as follows.

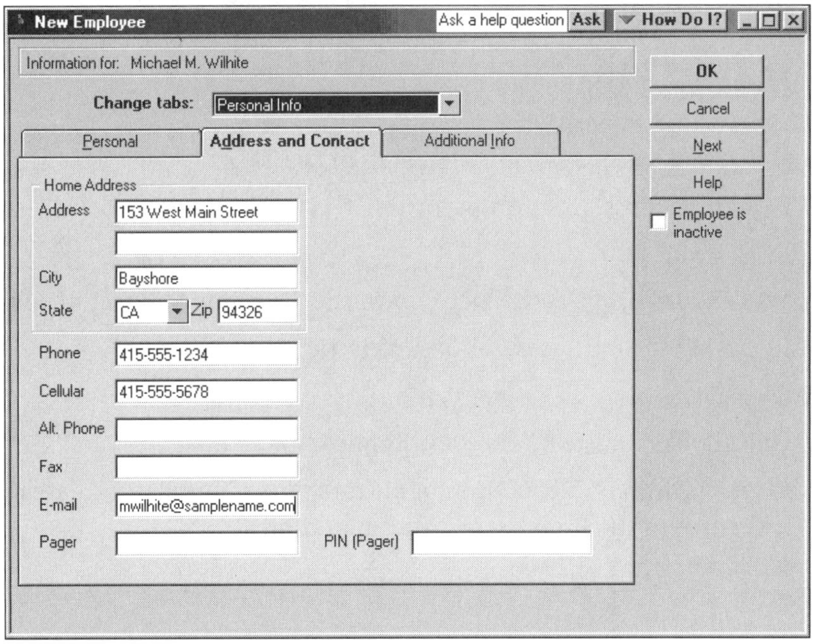

4 In the Change tabs drop-down list, select Employment Info.

5 In the Hire Date field, enter 11/28/2003.

6 In the Change tabs drop-down list, select Payroll and Compensation Info.

7 In the Earnings section of the window, click the Item Name column and press Tab. (Notice that the Regular Pay item is displayed already.)

8 In the Hour/Annual Rate column for the Regular Pay payroll item, type ***15***. Then press Tab.

The Payroll Info tab should look like the following.

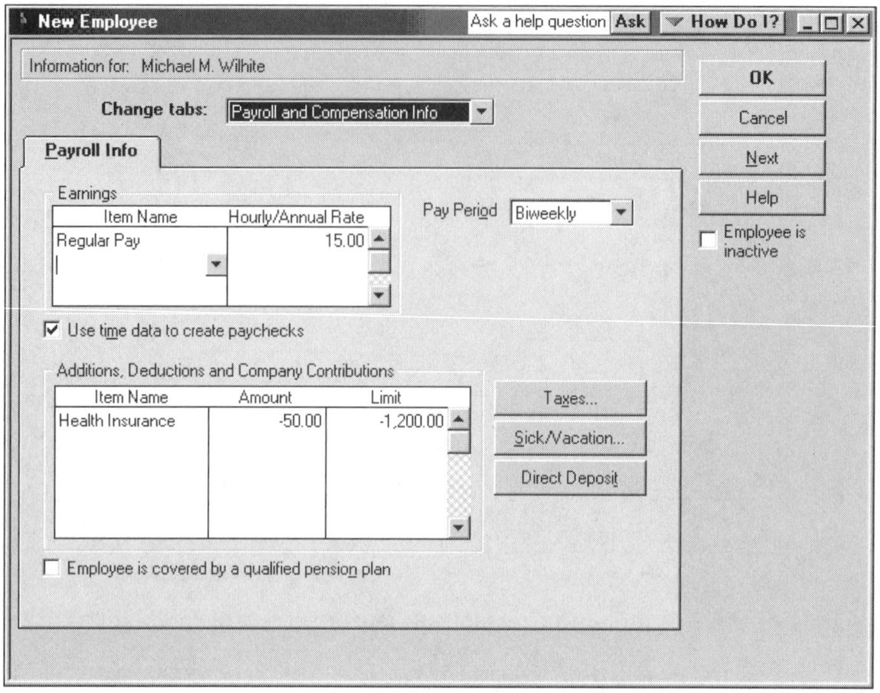

9 Click Taxes.

QuickBooks displays the Federal tab of the Taxes for Michael M. Wilhite window.

10 From the Filing Status drop-down list, choose Married.

11 Click State.

QuickBooks displays the State tab of the Taxes for Michael M. Wilhite window.

12 In the Filing Status field, choose "Married (two incomes)."

13 Click OK.

QuickBooks returns to the New Employee window.

14 In the Additions, Deductions, and Company Contributions area, select Health Insurance in the Item Name column and press Tab.

15 In the Amount column, type ***15*** and press Tab.

QuickBooks enters –15.00 in the Amount column. Your New Employee window should now look like this.

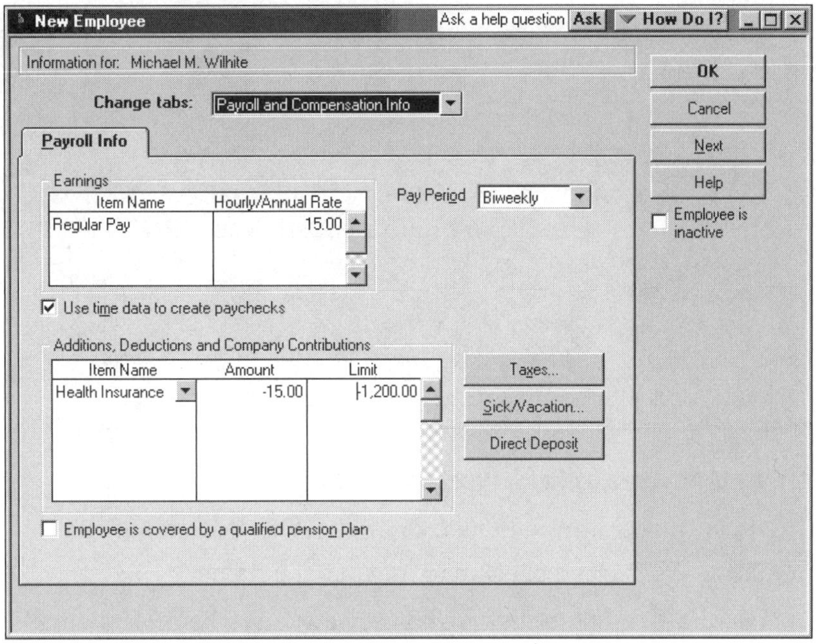

16 Click OK.

17 When QuickBooks asks whether you want to set up additional payroll information, click Leave As Is.

QuickBooks returns to the Employee list, where the new employee's name is now displayed.

18 Close the Employee list.

Writing a paycheck

QuickBooks lets you print payroll checks in a batch or one at a time. You may want to process the paychecks of salaried employees in a batch, and do payroll for the hourly employees one at a time.

To run a paycheck:

1 From the Employees menu, choose Pay Employees.

QuickBooks displays the Select Employees To Pay window.

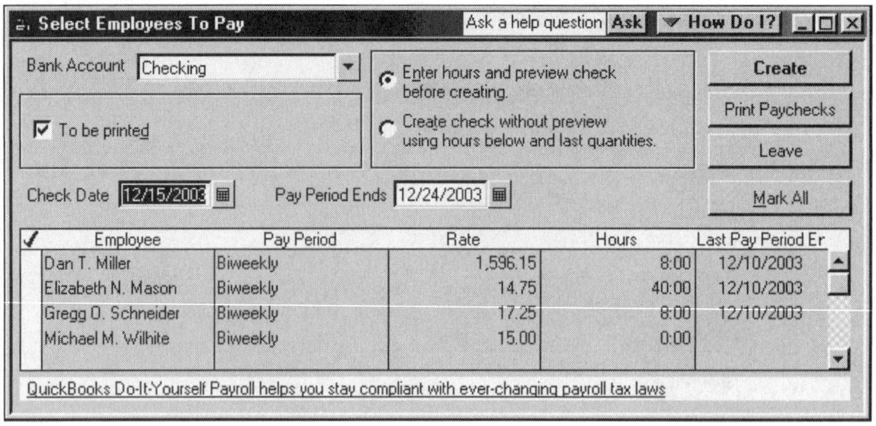

2 In the Period Ends field, type ***12/15/2003***.

3 Click in the column to the left of Michael M. Wilhite's name.

QuickBooks places a checkmark next to the name.

4 Make sure that "Enter hours and preview check before creating" is selected.

5 Click Create.

6 If QuickBooks indicates that there is no time data for this employee, click OK.

QuickBooks displays the Preview Paycheck window. Now you can enter the time Michael worked.

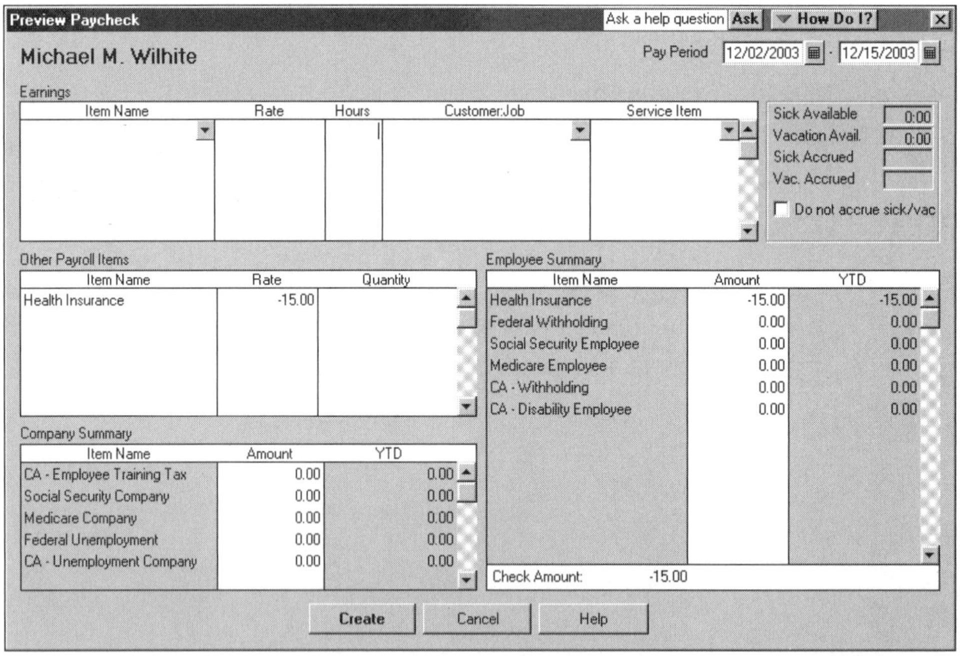

7 In the Earnings section, click in the Item Name column, and then select Regular Pay from the drop-down list.

8 Tab to the Rate column and type ***15***.

9 In the Hours column, type ***80*** and press Tab.

QuickBooks fills in the Employee Summary area of the Preview Paycheck window, showing the gross regular pay and all of the deductions from Michael's paycheck. The net amount of the check appears at the bottom.

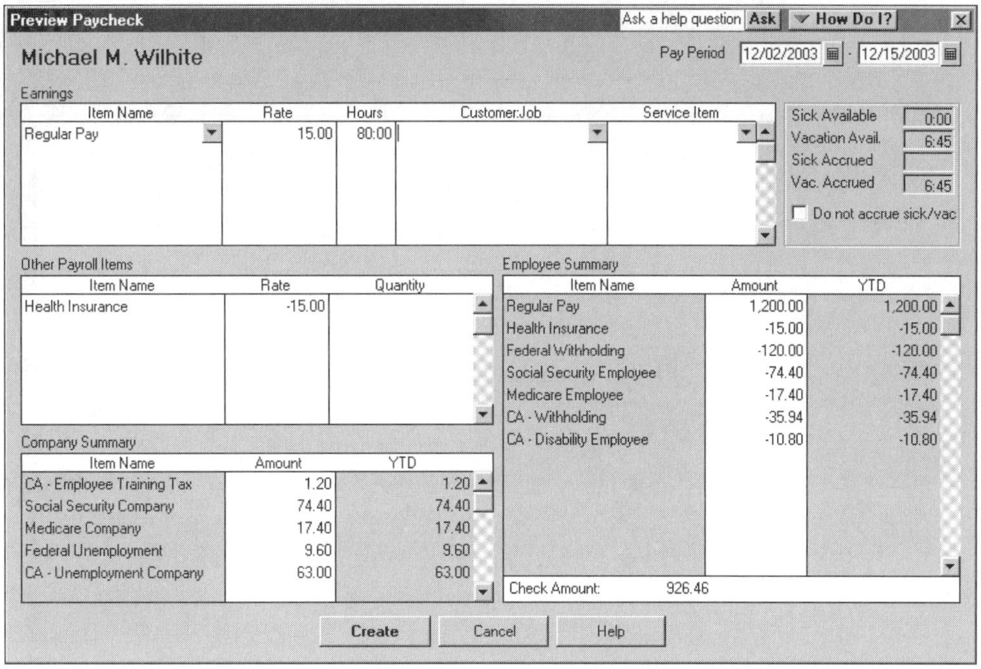

Because payroll tax rates change regularly, your numbers may vary from this illustration.

The Company Summary area of the window shows company-paid taxes and contributions that don't affect the amount of the paycheck (company-paid benefits).

10 Click Create.

QuickBooks writes a payroll check for the correct net amount, showing the deductions in the voucher area.

QuickBooks displays the Select Employees To Pay window.

11 Click Leave.

Viewing the paycheck

QuickBooks records payroll checks in your QuickBooks checking account register. You can see the check by going to the register.

To view the paycheck from the register:

1 From the Lists menu, choose Chart of Accounts.

2 Double-click "Checking."

QuickBooks displays the Checking account register.

3 Select the paycheck transaction for Michael M. Wilhite, and click Edit Transaction.

QuickBooks displays the Paycheck – Checking window for Michael. Notice that the Paycheck Summary shows a summary of the check's deductions. If you want to see the deductions that make up this total, you can click the Paycheck Detail button.

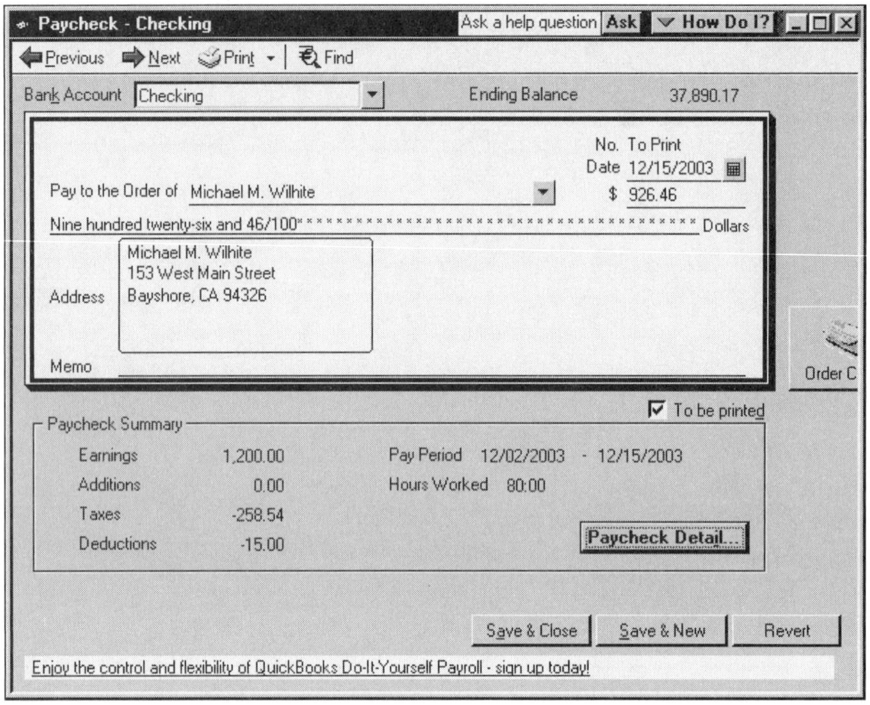

4 Click Save & Close to close the Paycheck – Checking window.

5 Close the checking account register, but leave the chart of accounts open.

Printing paycheck stubs

You can print paychecks as you would any QuickBooks check. If you use voucher checks, QuickBooks prints the payroll item detail in the voucher area. If you don't use voucher checks, you can print a paystub to give to your employees.

To print a paycheck:

1 From the File menu, choose Print Forms, and then choose Paychecks.

QuickBooks displays the Select Paychecks to Print window.

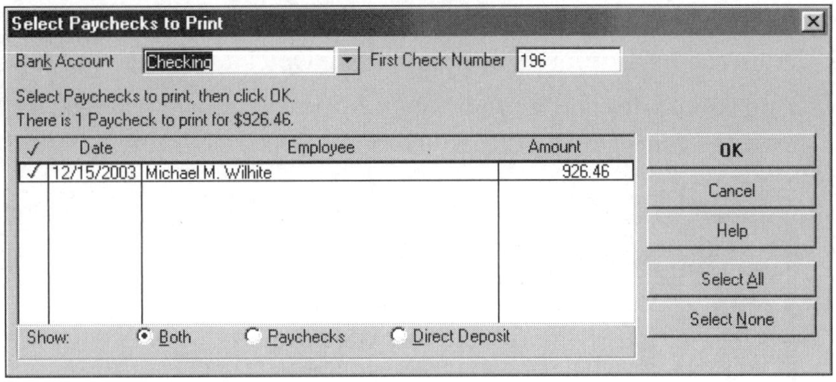

2 In the First Check Number field, type ***296***.

3 Make sure there's a checkmark next to Michael Wilhite's name, and then click OK.

4 Click Print.

Tracking your tax liabilities

Refer to Handout 35, "Tracking payroll expenses and payroll liabilities."

As an employer, you need to track both payroll expenses and payroll liabilities. These are the company payroll expenses you need to track:

- Employees' gross pay
- Employer payroll taxes, such as contributions to social security (FICA), Medicare, federal and state unemployment insurance, and state disability insurance

QuickBooks uses an expense account called Payroll Expenses to track these actual costs to your company. (The funds you deduct from employee paychecks aren't considered an actual cost because they're monies you're holding for the government; they don't come directly from your company assets.) Whenever you run your payroll, QuickBooks keeps track of your company's expenses for each employee. You can then see totals for these expenses on the payroll summary by employee report and on the profit and loss statement.

QuickBooks uses the Payroll Liabilities account (an Other Current Liability account) to track what you owe to the government. When you do your payroll, QuickBooks calculates how much you owe for each tax, deduction, or company contribution payroll item and records that information as a transaction in the liability account. This produces a record of how much tax you owe at any time, so you can plan to have the cash available for payment. When you pay your payroll taxes or other payroll liabilities, QuickBooks decreases the balance of the liability account.

Look at the payroll expense and liability accounts, so you can see how QuickBooks recorded expenses and liabilities related to Michael Wilhite's paycheck.

To display the payroll expenses QuickReport:

1. In the Chart of Accounts window, select the Payroll Expenses account.
2. From the Reports menu button, choose QuickReport: Payroll Expenses.

   QuickBooks displays the QuickReport. You can scroll through the report to see the expense items paid by the company for Michael Wilhite's paycheck.

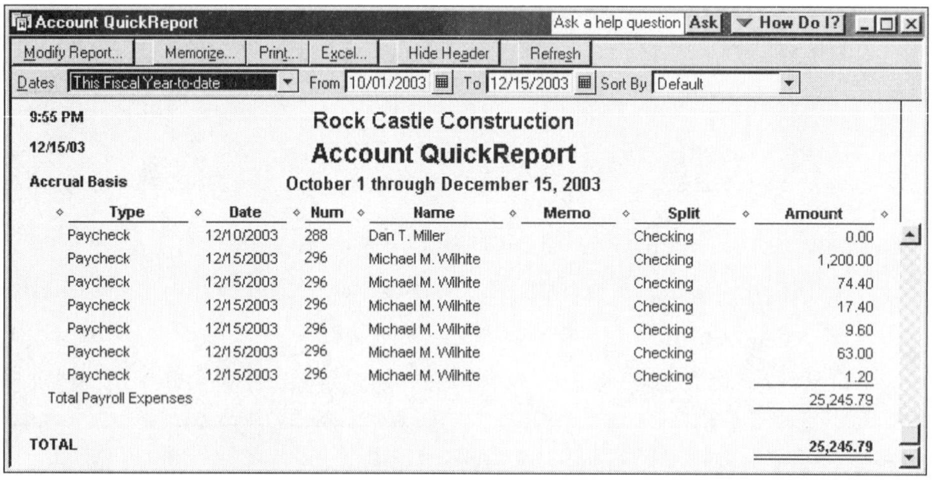

9:55 PM
12/15/03
Accrual Basis

Rock Castle Construction
Account QuickReport
October 1 through December 15, 2003

Type	Date	Num	Name	Memo	Split	Amount
Paycheck	12/10/2003	288	Dan T. Miller		Checking	0.00
Paycheck	12/15/2003	296	Michael M. Wilhite		Checking	1,200.00
Paycheck	12/15/2003	296	Michael M. Wilhite		Checking	74.40
Paycheck	12/15/2003	296	Michael M. Wilhite		Checking	17.40
Paycheck	12/15/2003	296	Michael M. Wilhite		Checking	9.60
Paycheck	12/15/2003	296	Michael M. Wilhite		Checking	63.00
Paycheck	12/15/2003	296	Michael M. Wilhite		Checking	1.20
Total Payroll Expenses						25,245.79
TOTAL						25,245.79

3. Close the QuickReport.

4 In the chart of accounts, double-click the Payroll Liabilities account.

QuickBooks displays the register for the account. The register shows a separate transaction for each item from Michael's paycheck. The running balance shows an increase for every liability.

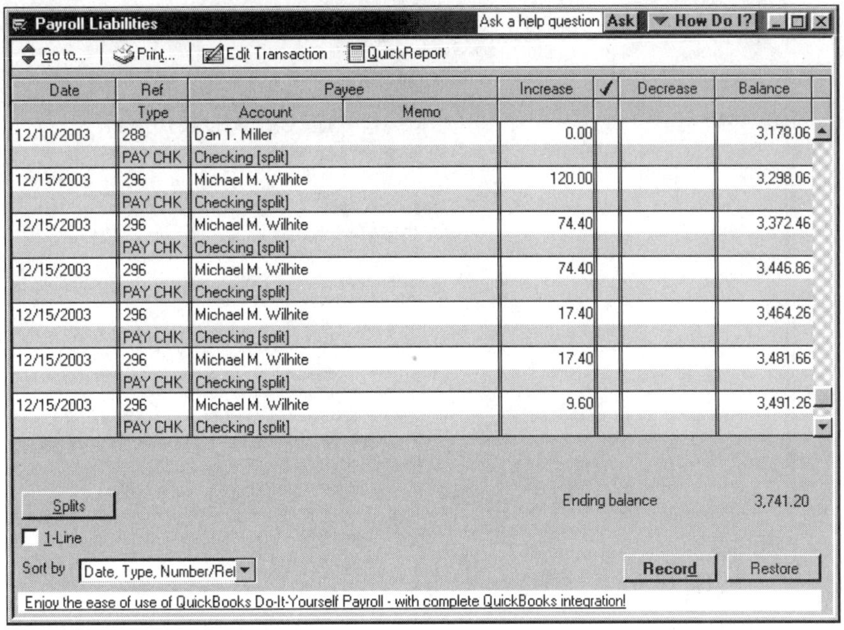

5 Close the register.

6 Close the chart of accounts.

Paying payroll taxes

As long as you have a valid subscription to one of the Intuit Payroll Services, QuickBooks uses current tax tables to keep track of your tax liabilities as they accrue, so you know how much you owe at any time.

Figuring out what you owe

If you're about to pay taxes or other liabilities, the payroll liabilities report shows you how much to pay. Suppose you are ready to make a tax payment, and you want to see how much you owe.

To create a payroll liabilities report:

1 From the Reports menu, choose Employees & Payroll, and then choose Payroll Liability Balances.

2 Click Modify Report, select "Display columns by **Year** across the top," and then click OK.

QuickBooks displays a report that shows what you owe for each payroll item.

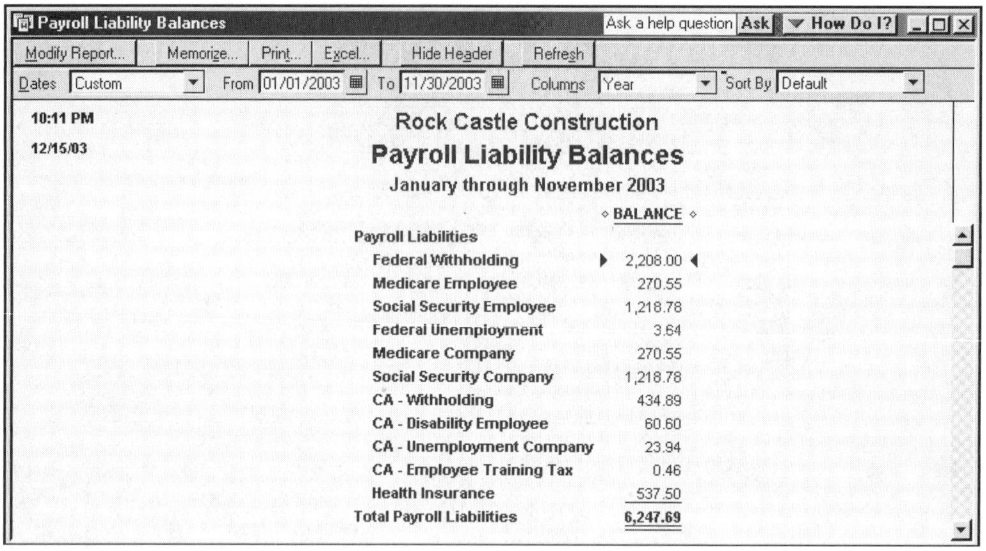

3 Close the report.

4 Click No at the message asking if you'd like to memorize the report.

Writing a check for payroll taxes

When it's time to deposit payroll taxes with your deposit institution, use the Liability Check window to fill out a QuickBooks check.

Note: **Don't just open the Write Checks window and write a check from there.** QuickBooks can't properly adjust your Payroll Liabilities account unless you use the Pay Liabilities feature.

To pay payroll liabilities:

1 From the Employees menu, choose Process Payroll Liabilities, and then choose Pay Payroll Liabilities from the submenu.

QuickBooks displays the Select Date Range For Liabilities window.

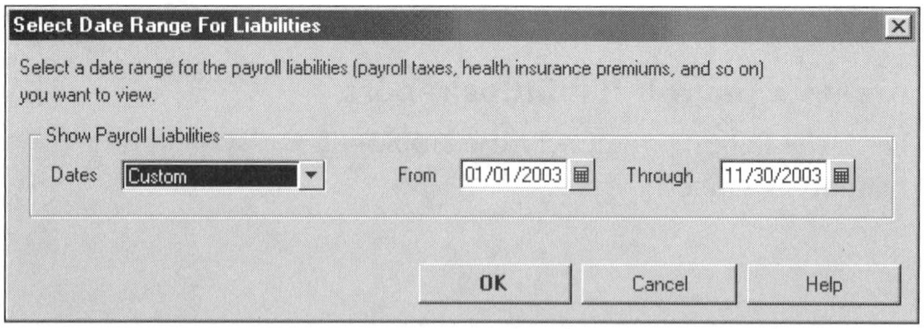

2 In the "From" field type ***11/30/2003***, and then type ***12/15/2003*** in the "Through" field.

3 Click OK.

QuickBooks displays the Pay Liabilities window.

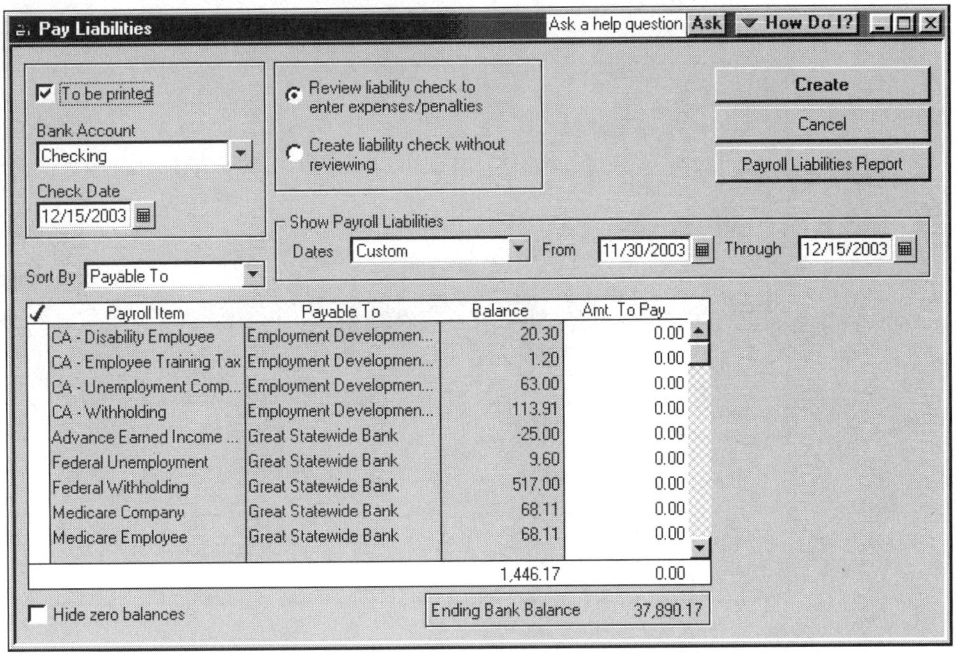

4 Click in the column to the left of the Federal Withholding payroll item.

QuickBooks places a checkmark in the column to show that the item will be paid. It also places a checkmark next to the Advanced Earned Income Credit item.

5 Click in the column to the left of the Medicare Company payroll item.

QuickBooks places checkmarks in the column for both Medicare Company and Medicare Employee.

6 Click in the column to the left of the Social Security Company payroll item.

QuickBooks places checkmarks in the column for both Social Security Company and Social Security Employee.

Now your Pay Liabilities window should look like the following.

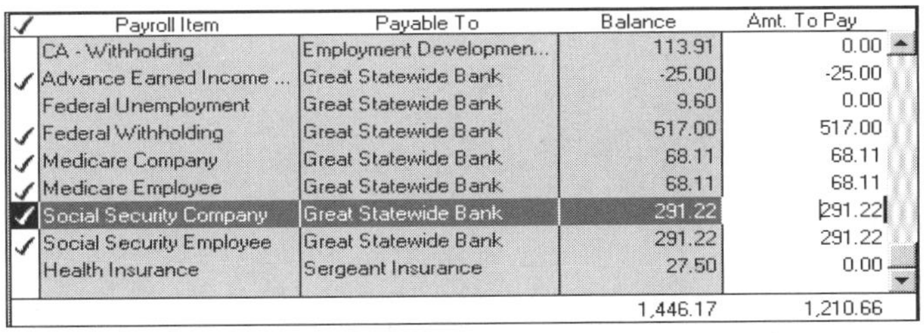

7 Make sure "Review liability check to enter expenses/penalties" is selected and then click Create.

QuickBooks displays the Liability Check window, with your check displayed.

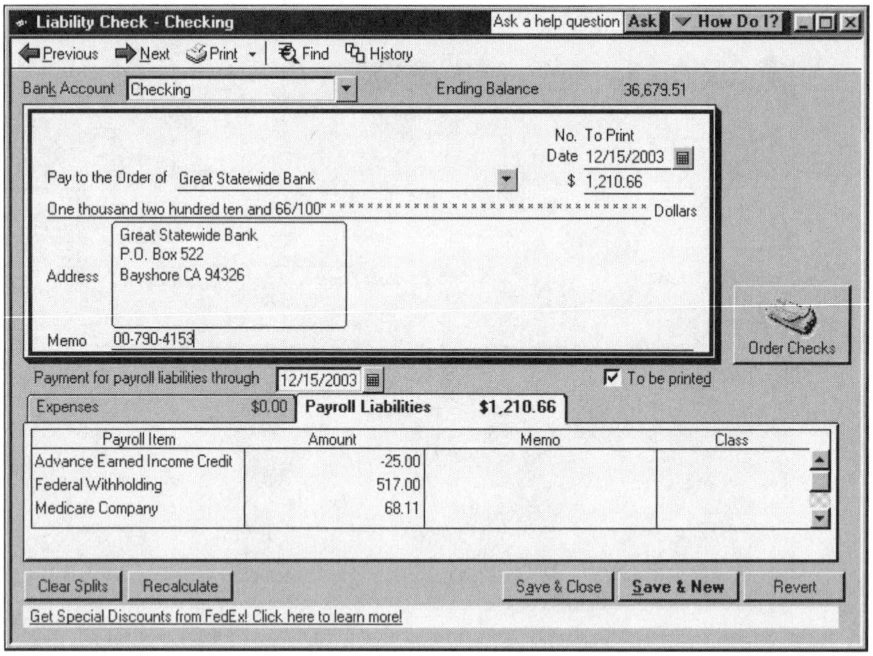

You should use a separate check for each type of deposit coupon (for example, 941 or 940).

8 In the Memo field, type ***EIN 96-4820567, Form 941***.

The Liability Check window should now look like the following.

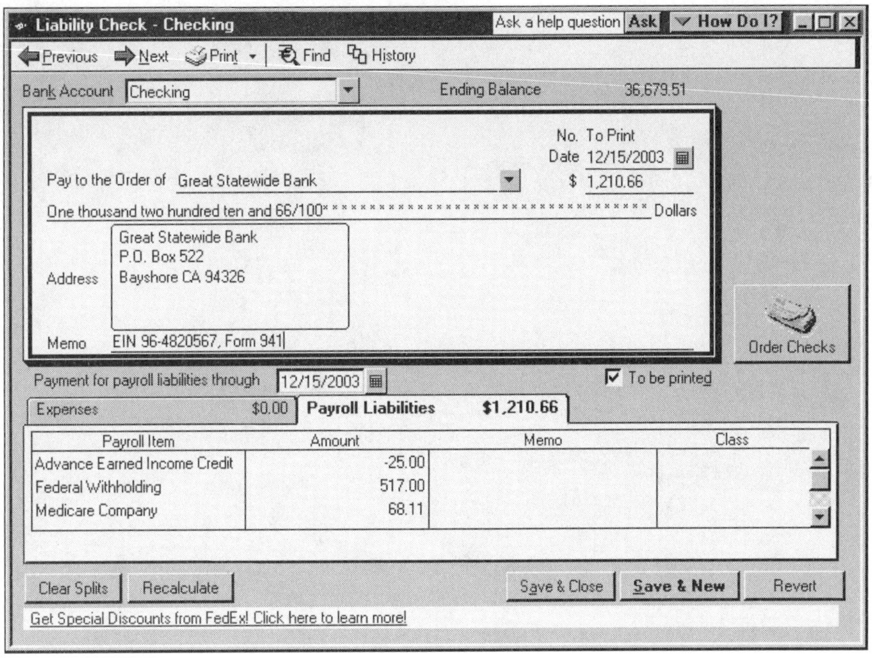

9 Click Save & Close to record the check.

10 Click Yes if QuickBooks asks if you wish to save changes made to this transaction.

Whenever you make a payment and record your check this way, QuickBooks decreases the balance of the Payroll Liabilities account.

Student test and review

1 Add a salaried employee to the employee list. Enter the employee's personal information, federal and state tax information, and at least one additional paycheck deduction.

2 Process a paycheck for the new employee. Then, view the check in QuickBooks. Open at least one payroll liability account register to see how the paycheck changes the account's balance.

3 Select one of the payroll expense accounts from the chart of accounts. Create a QuickReport for that expense account.

LESSON 13 Estimating and progress invoicing

Lesson objectives

- To learn how to create job estimates
- To find an estimate in a data file
- To learn to duplicate an existing estimate
- To create an invoice from an estimate
- To display project reports for estimates
- To update a job's status
- To make an estimate inactive

Handout materials

- Handout 36: Creating an estimate
- Handout 37: Creating invoices from an estimate

Instructor preparation

- **You must be using QuickBooks Pro or Premier to complete this lesson.**
- Review the lesson, including the examples, to make sure you're familiar with the material.
- Ensure that all students have a copy of qblesson.qbb on their computer's hard disk.
- Have Handouts 36 and 37 ready for distribution.

To start this lesson

Before you perform the following steps, make sure you have installed the exercise file (qblesson.qbb) on your hard disk. See "Installing the exercise file" in the Introduction to this guide if you haven't installed it.

The steps that follow will restore the exercise file to its original state so that the data in the file matches what you see on the screen as you proceed through each lesson.

Note: **To proceed through this lesson, you must be using QuickBooks Pro or Premier. Estimates are not available in QuickBooks Basic.**

To restore the exercise file (qblesson.qbb):

1. From the File menu in QuickBooks, choose Restore.

   QuickBooks displays the Restore Company Backup window.

2 In the "Get Company Backup From" section of the window, click Browse and select your c:\QBtrain directory.

3 Select the qblesson.qbb file, and then click Open.

4 In the "Restore Company Backup To" section of the window, click Browse and select your c:\QBtrain directory.

5 In the File name field of the Restore To window, type ***lesson 13*** and then click Save.

6 Click Restore.

Creating jobs and estimates

Refer to Handout 36, "Creating an estimate," for this discussion.

An estimate is a description of work or products you propose to sell to a current or prospective customer. You can create multiple estimates for each name (customer or customer:job combination). If the customer accepts an estimate, you can turn the estimate into an invoice, modifying it as necessary. When you have actual costs and revenues, you can compare them to your estimated costs and revenues to see if you were over or under the estimate.

Estimates are "non-posting" transactions—they do not affect any financial reports or income and expense balances. QuickBooks allows you to create invoices from estimates either by transferring the entire estimate to an invoice or by allowing you to choose a percentage or selected items to invoice from the estimate. The ability to bill for only a percentage of the estimate or selected items on an estimate is called *progress invoicing.*

When you create a new QuickBooks company using the EasyStep Interview, QuickBooks asks you if you use estimates and/or progress invoicing. If you respond yes, QuickBooks turns on these features for you. If you respond no, you need to turn on these features in order to use them. Rock Castle Construction already has estimates and progress invoicing turned on, but you'll review how to do this so you become familiar with QuickBooks preferences.

Turning on estimates and progress invoicing

To turn on estimates and progress invoicing:

1 From the Edit menu, choose Preferences.

2 Click Jobs & Estimates in the left scroll box.

3 Click the Company Preferences tab to display the job and estimate preferences. QuickBooks displays the Jobs & Estimates section of the Preferences window.

4 Click Yes for "Do You Create Estimates?"

5 Click Yes for "Do You Do Progress Invoicing?"

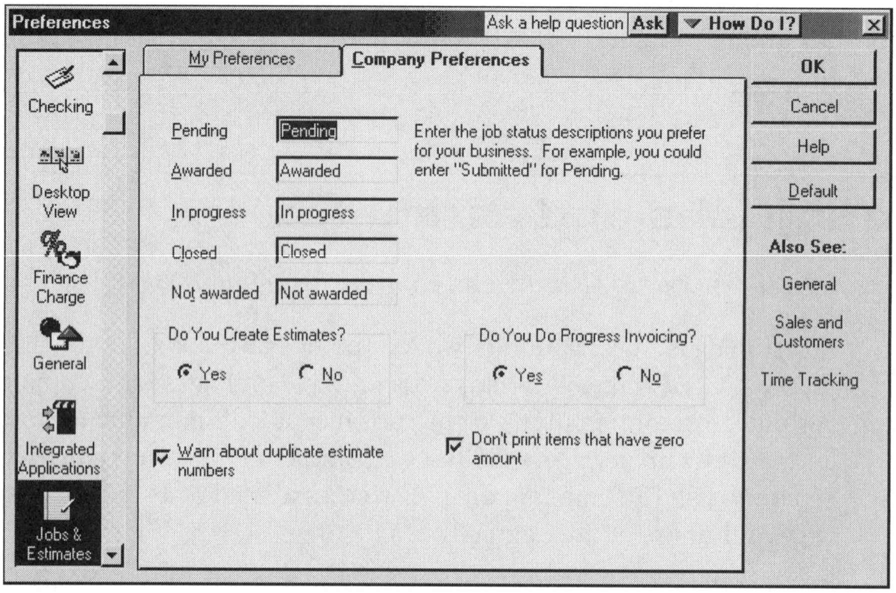

6 Click OK to record your selections and close the Preferences window.

Creating a new job

Now that you've turned on the estimates feature, you can add a new job for a bathroom remodel project for your customer, Ernesto Natiello. Then you'll create an estimate for the job.

To create a new job:

1 From the Customers menu, choose Customer:Job List.

2 In the Customer:Job list, select Natiello, Ernesto.

3 Click the Customer:Job menu button, and then choose Add Job.

QuickBooks displays the New Job window.

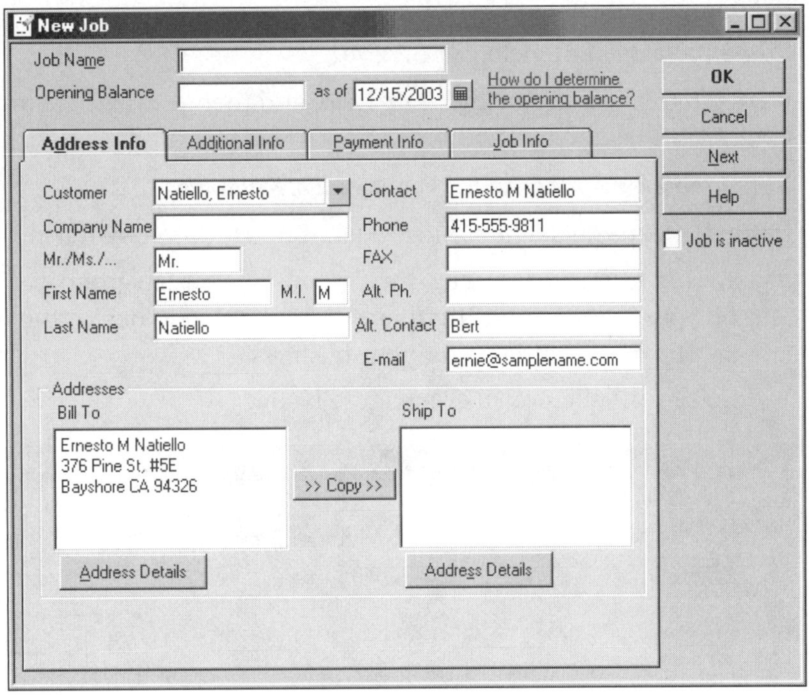

4 In the Job Name field, type ***Bathroom remodel.***

5 Click the Job Info tab.

QuickBooks displays the Job Info portion of the New Job window.

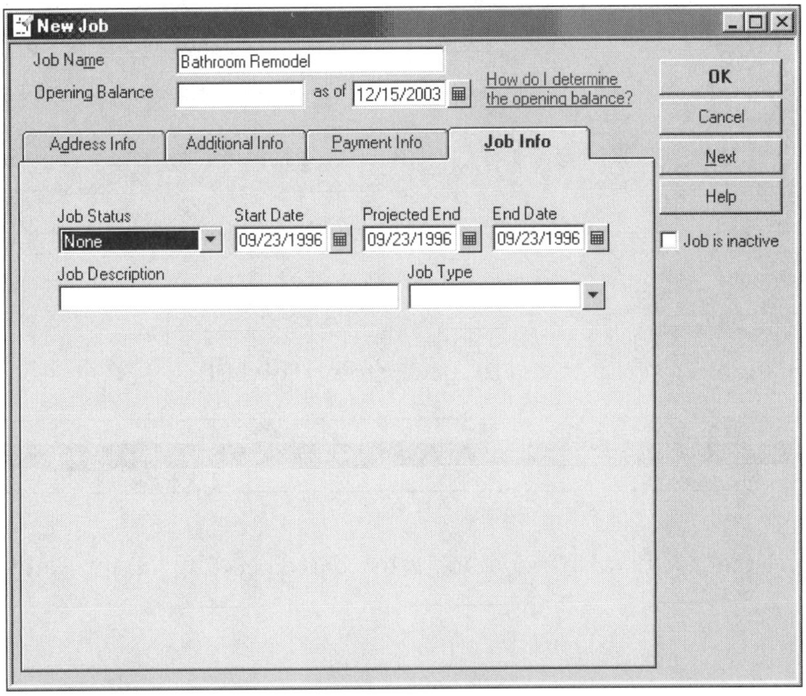

The New Job window is unique to QuickBooks Pro and Premier. Dates appear in the date fields from a previous job done for this customer.

6 In the Job Status field, select Pending from the drop-down list.

7 In the Start Date field, type ***1/4/04***.

8 In the Projected End field, type ***2/28/04***.

9 Press Tab to move to the End Date field, and then press Delete (on the keyboard) to clear this field.

10 In the Job Description field, type ***Remodel bathroom***.

11 In the Job Type field, choose Remodel from the drop-down list.

Job types give you a way to classify your jobs so you can group and subtotal similar jobs on your reports. By using them, you'll be able to determine which kinds of jobs are the most profitable for your business.

Your screen should look like the figure below.

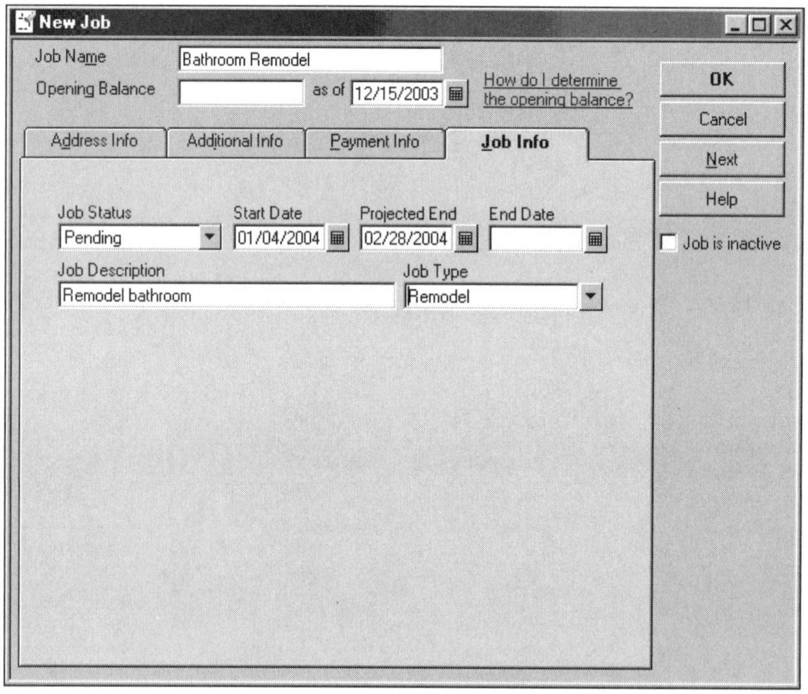

12 Click OK.

QuickBooks returns you to the Customer:Job List.

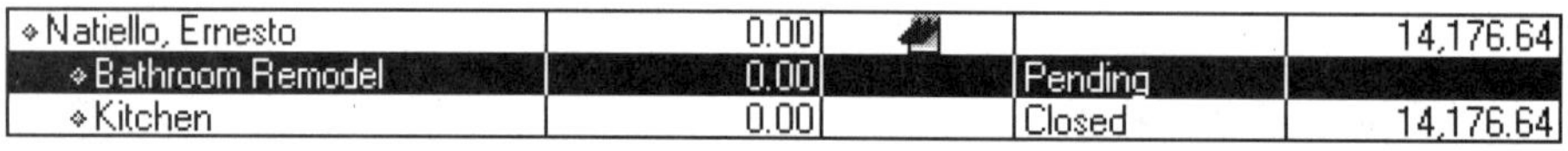

Notice that the new Bathroom job is listed as a pending job for Natiello, Ernesto.

Writing an estimate

Now that you've created a new job for the bathroom remodel, you can create an estimate for it.

To create an estimate:

1. In the Customer:Job list, select Natiello, Ernesto:Bathroom remodel.
2. Click the Activities menu button, and then choose Create Estimates.

   QuickBooks displays the Create Estimates window for this customer and job. You learned in Lesson 6 how to fill out an invoice form, so this form should look familiar.
3. Press Tab to accept Natiello, Ernesto:Bathoom remodel in the Customer:Job field.

   Notice that QuickBooks enters the customer's name and address in the appropriate area of the form.
4. Make sure that Custom Estimate is selected in the Template field.

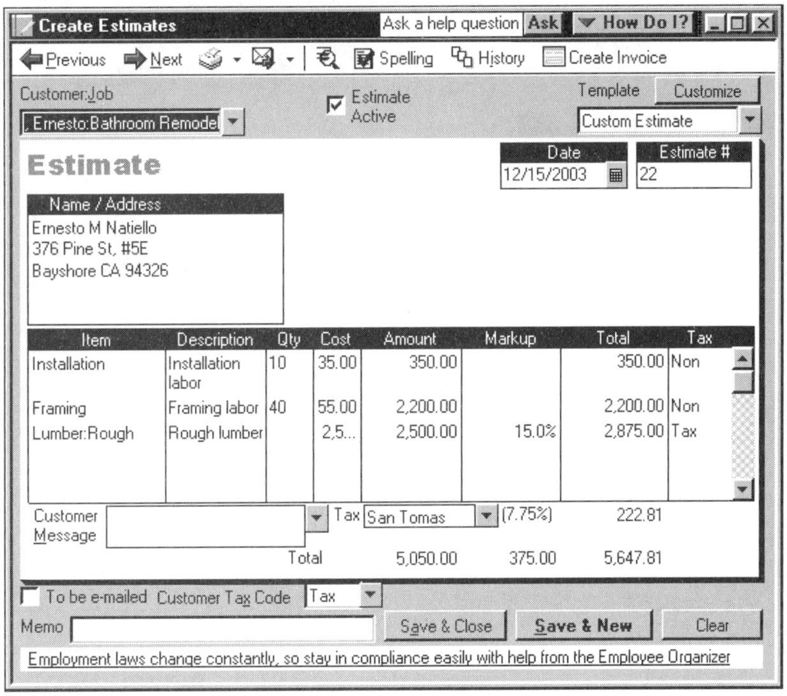

5. Click in the Item column in the middle of the form.

   A Down Arrow appears, indicating that a drop-down list of choices is available.

   The Item list, which contains all the services and goods your business provides, is the same list that is available to you on invoice forms and throughout QuickBooks.
6. Type ***Installation***.

   Before you can finish typing, QuickBooks has filled it in for you, and QuickBooks fills in the default description for this item.

7 Press Tab twice to move to the QTY column.

8 Type ***10*** in the QTY column, and then press Tab.

The total amount is calculated by QuickBooks when you move out of this field.

9 Click the line under "Installation" in the Item column.

10 Type ***Framing***.

11 Press Tab twice to move to the QTY column, and then type ***40***.

12 In the line under Framing in the Item column, type ***Rough***.

QuickBooks completes the field with the item Lumber:Rough.

13 Press Tab three times to move to the Cost column, and then type ***2500***.

14 Press Tab to move to the Markup column.

15 Type ***15%***, and then press Tab twice.

Your estimate should look like the following figure.

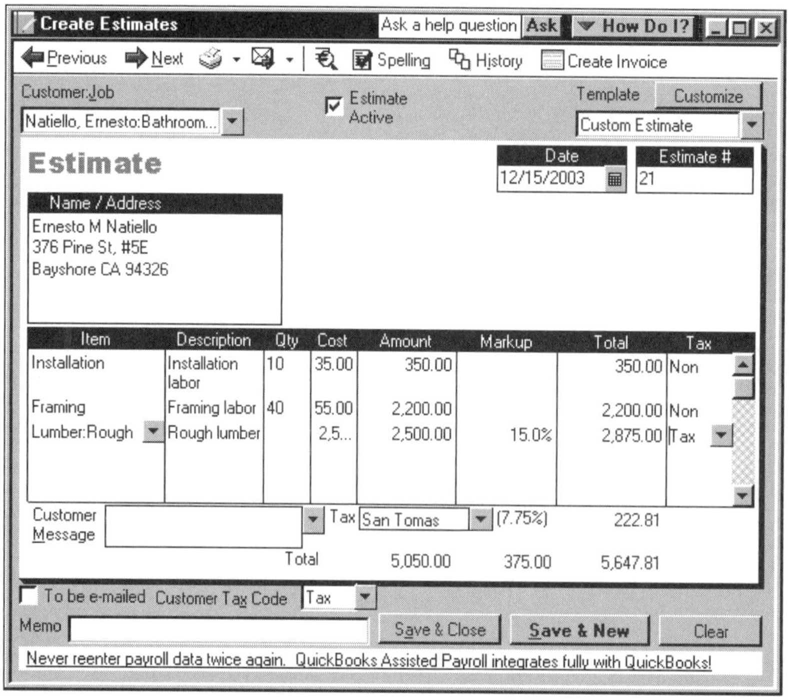

Notice that QuickBooks has filled in most of the information for the estimate based on the items selected.

16 Click Save & Close to save the estimate.

QuickBooks returns you to the Customer:Job list. Notice the Estimate Total column for the Pending Bathroom remodel job for Ernesto Natiello now has a balance of 5,647.81.

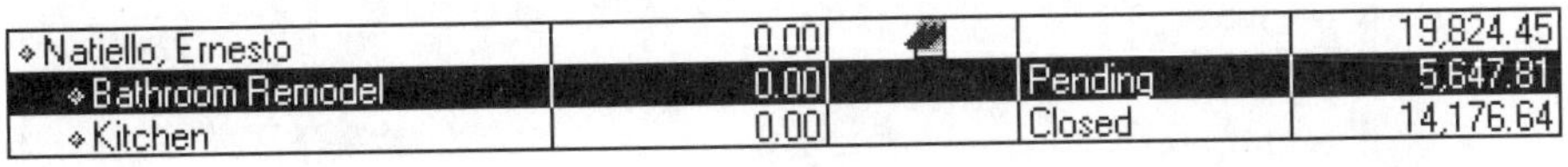

Creating multiple estimates

Just as you've completed the estimate for this customer, he calls and asks you to prepare a second estimate for the same job. He'd like you to price a couple of different options.

Finding estimates

Because you just created the estimate, you can open the Create Estimates window and press Prev and that will take you to the correct estimate. However, when you don't know where an estimate is, there are a couple of methods you can use to locate the estimate you want quickly. You'll use one of them here.

1 From the Customers menu, choose Create Estimates.

2 From the Edit menu, choose Find Estimates.

QuickBooks displays the Find Estimates window.

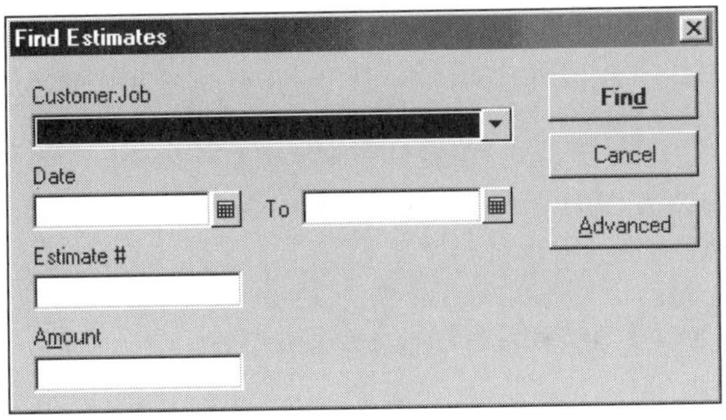

3 In the Customer:Job drop-down list, select Natiello, Ernesto:Bathroom remodel.

4 Click Find.

QuickBooks displays the estimate that you've already created for this job (Estimate # 21).

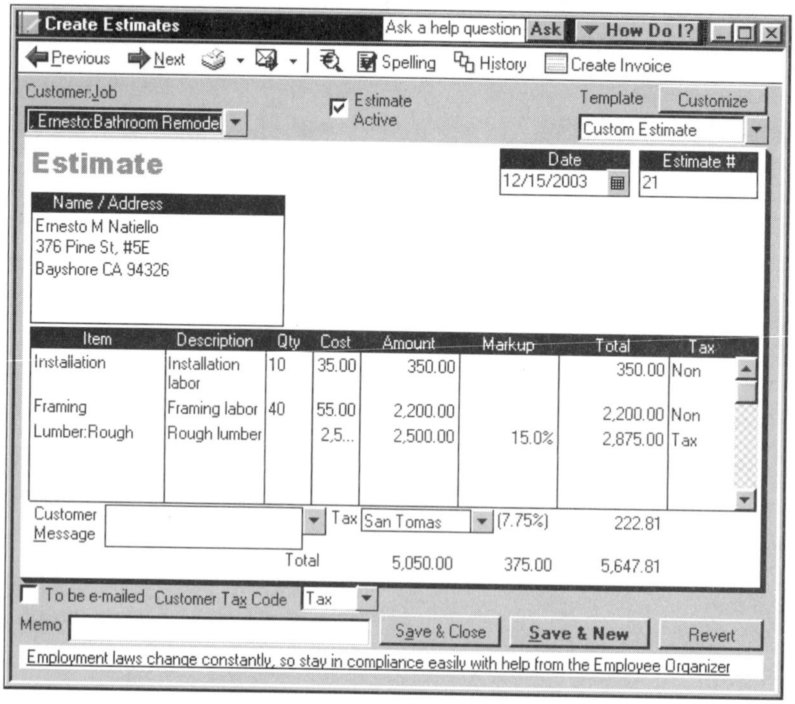

5 Keep the estimate open, you'll use it in the next exercise.

Duplicating estimates

Your customer wants you to prepare a second estimate for the bathroom remodel job because he is considering buying the cabinets from you in addition to having you do the installation work.

First, you'll create a duplicate of the original estimate, and then make the modifications necessary for the second bid.

To create a duplicate of an existing estimate:

1 Right-click in the body of the estimate and choose Duplicate Estimate from the list that displays.

QuickBooks duplicates the estimate and displays the new version on your screen. Notice that QuickBooks assigns the next available estimate number to the new form.

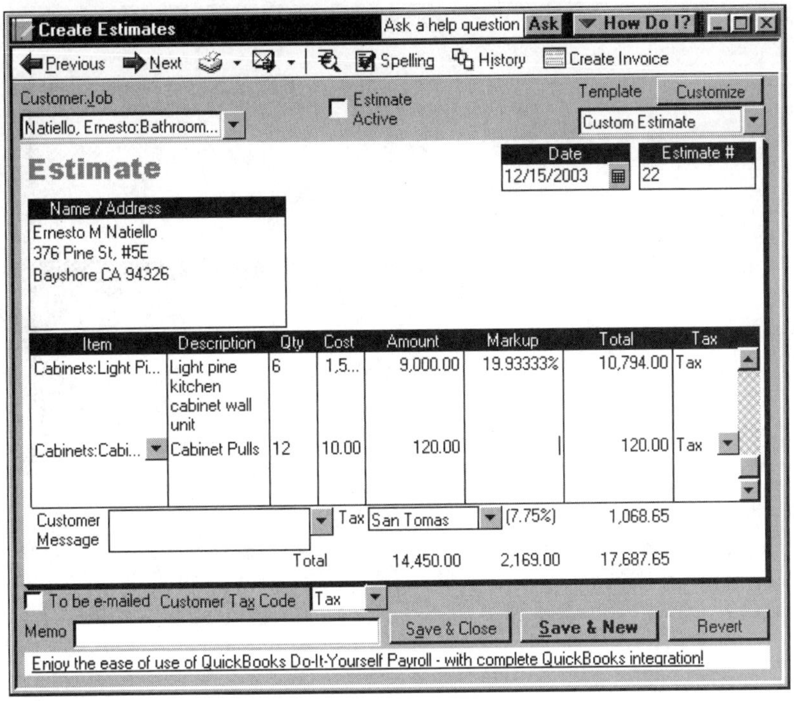

2 Highlight the number in the QTY column on the line for Installation.

3 Type ***18***.

4 Click in the Item column in the line below Lumber:Rough, and select Cabinets:Light Pine from the drop-down list.

5 Press Tab twice and type ***6*** in the QTY column.

6 Click in the Item column in the line below Cabinets:Light Pine and select Cabinets:Cabinet Pulls from the drop-down list.

7 Press Tab twice and type ***12*** in the QTY column.

8 Press Tab and type ***10*** in the Cost field.

9 Press Tab.

Your estimate should look like the following figure.

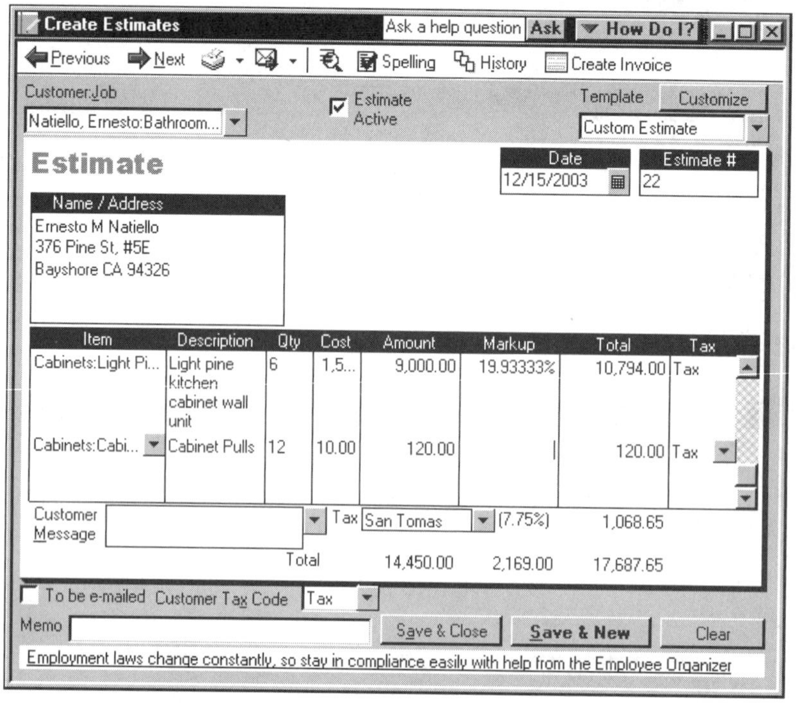

10 Click Save & Close.

Creating an invoice from an estimate

Refer to Handout 37, "Creating invoices from an estimate," for this discussion.

Once you have created an estimate and the customer has approved it, you can use the estimate to invoice the customer. In this exercise, you'll be using the QuickBooks progress invoicing feature.

Progress invoicing (also known as progress billing), lets you invoice for jobs that you work on and complete in phases. When using progress invoicing, you start by creating an estimate for the job (you don't have to give this estimate to the customer). Then, as you complete each phase, you can easily transfer items from the original estimate to an invoice. You can specify which items to include on each invoice and change estimated amounts or percentages. When you use estimates to create progress invoices, you can run reports to help you track your estimated versus actual costs.

To create an invoice from an estimate:

1 In the Customer:Job list, select Natiello, Ernesto:Bathroom remodel.

2 Click the Activities menu button, and then choose Create Invoices.

QuickBooks displays the Create Invoices window.

3 Press Tab to leave the Customer:Job field.

QuickBooks displays a list of estimates created for this job.

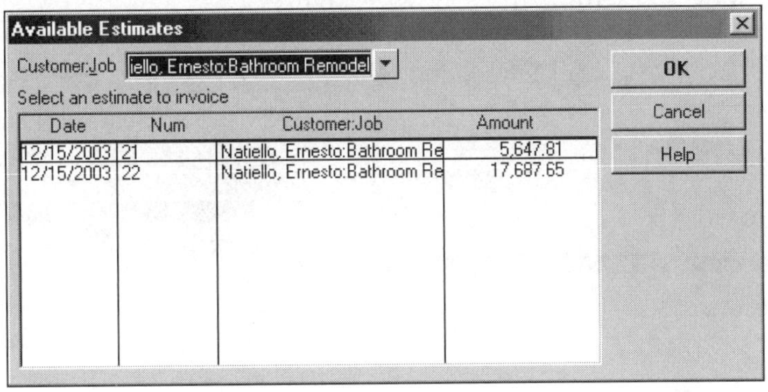

4 The customer accepted the first estimate you created, so select the line containing Estimate #21, and click OK.

QuickBooks displays the Create Progress Invoice Based On Estimate window.

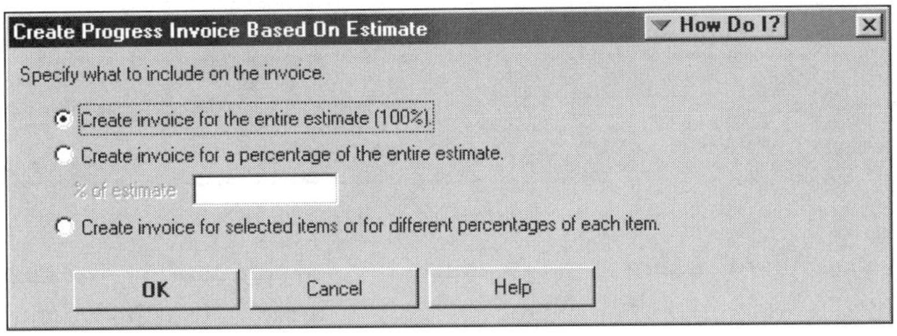

Rock Castle Construction typically bills for one-third of the job before starting work, one-third when the project is one-third complete, and the final one-third when the job is completed.

5 Select "Create invoice for a percentage of the entire estimate."

6 Type ***33.333*** in the "% of estimate" field.

If you need to invoice for only selected items on an estimate or for varying percentages or amounts for different items, select the option "Create invoice for selected items or for different percentages of each item." QuickBooks then displays a table of all items on the estimate and allows you to select which items you want to include and the amounts for each item.

7 Click OK.

8 In the Template drop-down list, select Progress Invoice.

QuickBooks completes the invoice for one-third of each item on the estimate. Your invoice should resemble the following figure.

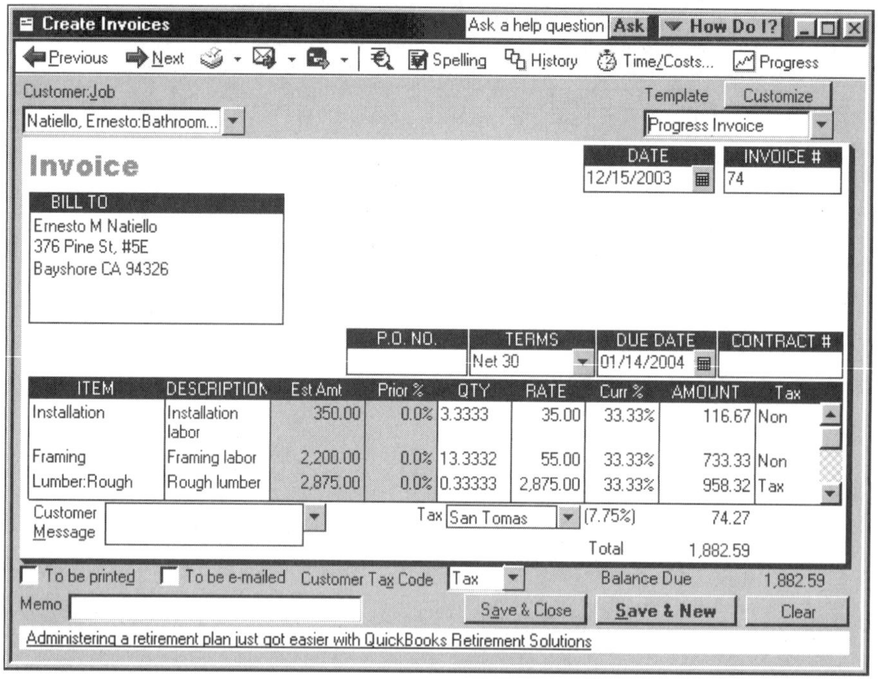

Notice that QuickBooks changed the invoice template to Progress Invoice and added fields for Estimate Amount, Prior %, and Current %. QuickBooks also tracks that one-third of the Natiello bathroom remodel job has been invoiced and that two-thirds has not yet been invoiced.

Note: **If you don't want your customers to see this level of detail on the invoice you send them, you can customize the invoice to remove some of these columns from the printed form.** See Lesson 15, "Customizing forms and writing QuickBooks Letters," for more information.

9 Click Save & Close to record the invoice.

10 Close the Customer:Job list.

Displaying reports for estimates

QuickBooks provides five reports on estimates, as described in the following table. You can create these reports from the Jobs & Time submenu of the Reports menu.

Report	Description
Job Estimates vs. Actuals Summary	Compares estimated cost to actual cost and estimated revenue to actual revenue for all customers and jobs.
Job Estimates vs. Actuals Detail (for one job)	For a particular customer or job, compares estimated costs to actual costs and estimated revenues to actual revenues.
Job Progress Invoices vs. Estimates	Compares each estimate with progress invoices based on the estimate.
Item Estimates vs. Actuals	For each item, compares estimated cost to actual cost and estimated revenue to actual revenue.
Estimates by Job	Lists all estimates by job.

Displaying the job progress invoices vs. estimates report

Because you've just completed a progress invoice, you can see how QuickBooks records this on the job progress invoices vs. estimates report. This report shows job status, estimate total, total invoiced from the estimate on progress invoices, and the percentage of the estimate already invoiced on progress invoices.

To display the job progress invoices vs. estimates report:

1. From the Reports menu, choose Jobs & Time.

   QuickBooks displays a submenu of project reports that deal with customer jobs and estimates.

2 Choose Job Progress Invoices vs. Estimates.

QuickBooks displays the job progress invoices vs. estimates report.

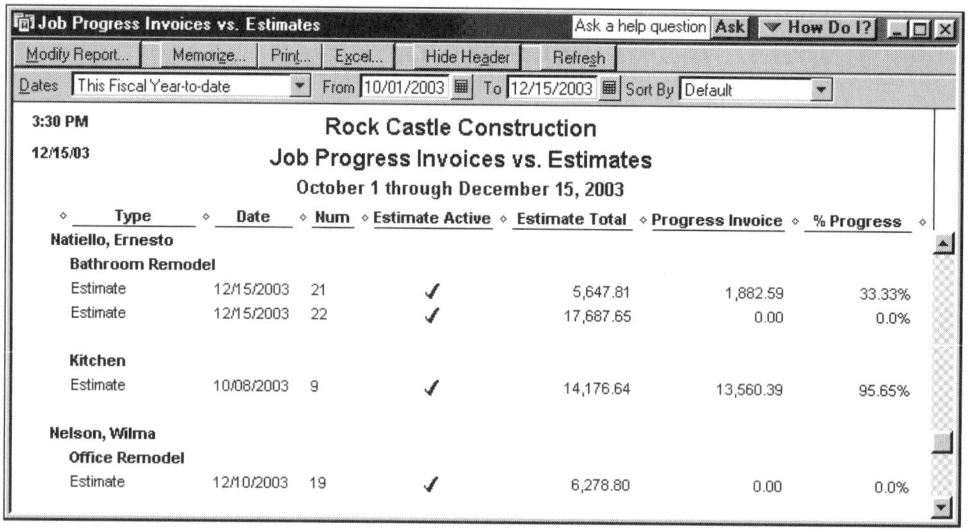

Type	Date	Num	Estimate Active	Estimate Total	Progress Invoice	% Progress
Natiello, Ernesto						
Bathroom Remodel						
Estimate	12/15/2003	21	✓	5,647.81	1,882.59	33.33%
Estimate	12/15/2003	22	✓	17,687.65	0.00	0.0%
Kitchen						
Estimate	10/08/2003	9	✓	14,176.64	13,560.39	95.65%
Nelson, Wilma						
Office Remodel						
Estimate	12/10/2003	19	✓	6,278.80	0.00	0.0%

Notice that the progress invoice you completed for Ernesto Natiello is listed in the Prog. Invoice column. The % Progress column shows how much of the total estimate you've invoiced for so far.

3 Close the report window.

Updating job status

Every time you change the status of a job, you should update its job status in the Customer:Job list. For example, the estimate for the bathroom remodel is no longer pending: Ernesto Natiello awarded you the job and you have started work.

To update the status of a job:

1 From the Customers menu, choose Customer:Job List.

QuickBooks displays the Customer:Job list.

2 In the list, select Natiello, Ernesto:Bathroom remodel.

3 Click the Customer:Job menu button, and then choose Edit.

QuickBooks displays the Edit Job window.

4 Click the Job Info tab.

QuickBooks displays the Job Info portion of the Edit Job window.

5 In the Job Status field, select "In progress."

Your screen should look like this.

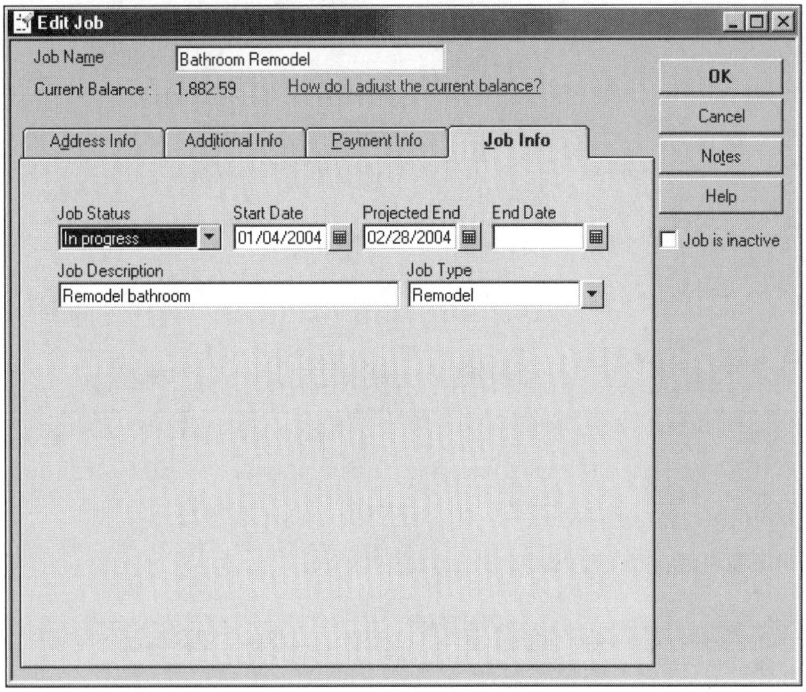

6 Click OK.

QuickBooks returns you to the Customer:Job list. The Customer:Job list now shows this project as being in progress.

7 Close the Customer:Job list.

Making estimates inactive

Now that the customer has accepted one of the estimates for the bathroom remodel job and you have started work, you might want to make the unaccepted estimate inactive. When you make an estimate inactive QuickBooks keeps a record of it, but does not use the numbers in reports.

To mark an estimate inactive:

1 From the Reports menu, choose Jobs & Time.

2 Choose Estimates by Job from the submenu.

QuickBooks displays the estimates by job report.

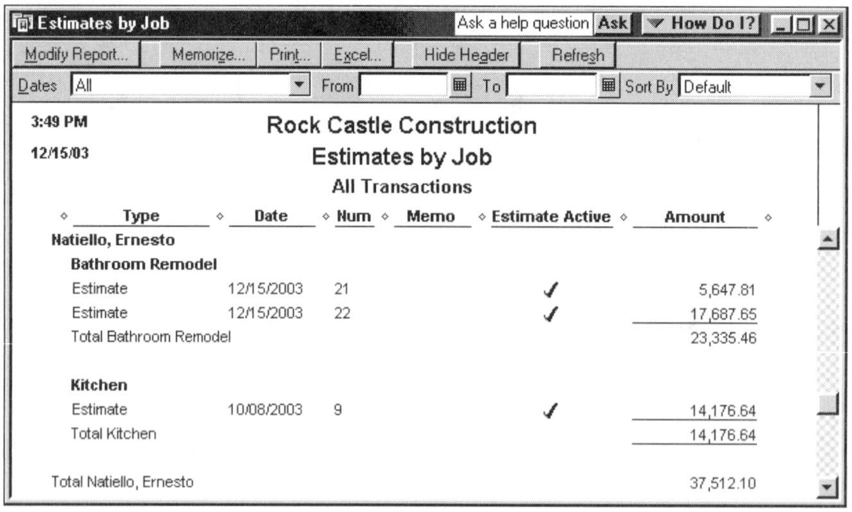

3 Scroll to the section of the report that displays the estimates for Ernesto Natiello.

4 Double-click anywhere on the line for Estimate #22.

QuickBooks displays the estimate.

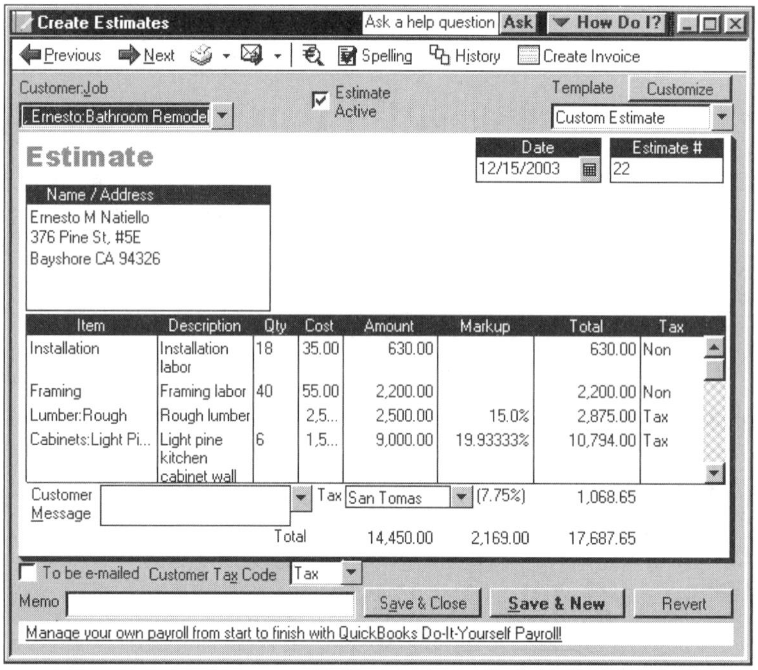

5 Click to clear the checkmark in the Estimate Active checkbox.

6 Click Save & Close.

7 Answer Yes to the message asking if you want to save the changes you made to the transaction.

8 Close the report.

Student test and review

1 Create an estimate for the 75 Sunset Rd. job for Pretell Real Estate. The estimate is for 6 hours of installation labor, 18.5 hours of plumbing work, and 4 hours of drywall work.

2 Create a progress invoice for 50% of the estimate just created for the 75 Sunset Rd. job for Pretell Real Estate.

LESSON 14 Tracking time

Lesson objectives

- To learn how to track time worked on a project
- To learn how to invoice a customer for time worked on a project
- To create project reports for time tracking and learn about other project reports
- To learn how to set up items used to track time worked by owners or partners
- To learn how to pay nonemployees for time worked

Handout materials

- Handout 38: Invoicing customers for time worked

Instructor preparation

- **You must be using QuickBooks Pro or Premier to complete this lesson.**
- Review the lesson, including the examples, to make sure you're familiar with the material.
- Ensure that all students have a copy of qblesson.qbb on their computer's hard disk.
- Have Handout 38 ready for distribution.

To start this lesson

Before you perform the following steps, make sure you have installed the exercise file (qblesson.qbb) on your hard disk. See "Installing the exercise file" in the Introduction to this guide if you haven't installed it.

The steps that follow will restore the exercise file to its original state so that the data in the file matches what you see on the screen as you proceed through each lesson.

Note: **To proceed through this lesson, you must be using QuickBooks Pro or Premier. Time tracking is not available in QuickBooks Basic.**

To restore the exercise file (qblesson.qbb):

1. From the File menu in QuickBooks, choose Restore.

   QuickBooks displays the Restore Company Backup window.
2. In the "Get Company Backup From" section of the window, click Browse and select your c:\QBtrain directory.
3. Select the qblesson.qbb file, and then click Open.

4 In the "Restore Company Backup To" section of the window, click Browse and select your c:\QBtrain directory.

5 In the File name field of the Restore To window, type ***lesson 14*** and then click Save.

6 Click Restore.

Tracking time

QuickBooks provides time tracking for any job. Time tracking lets you keep track of the time a person spends on each job (including sick and vacation time and time spent for general overhead). The person whose time you track can be an employee, an owner or partner, or a subcontractor.

You can use time data to do the following:

- Invoice the customer for the time spent doing a job.
- Provide hours worked on an employee's paycheck, or a check to a nonemployee (vendor, owner, or partner).
- Track the cost of employees' gross pay by job.
- Report on the number of hours worked—by person, by job, or by item.

Turning on time tracking

To turn on time tracking:

1 From the Edit menu, choose Preferences.

2 Click Time Tracking in the left scroll box. Then click the Company Preferences tab. QuickBooks displays the Time Tracking Preferences window.

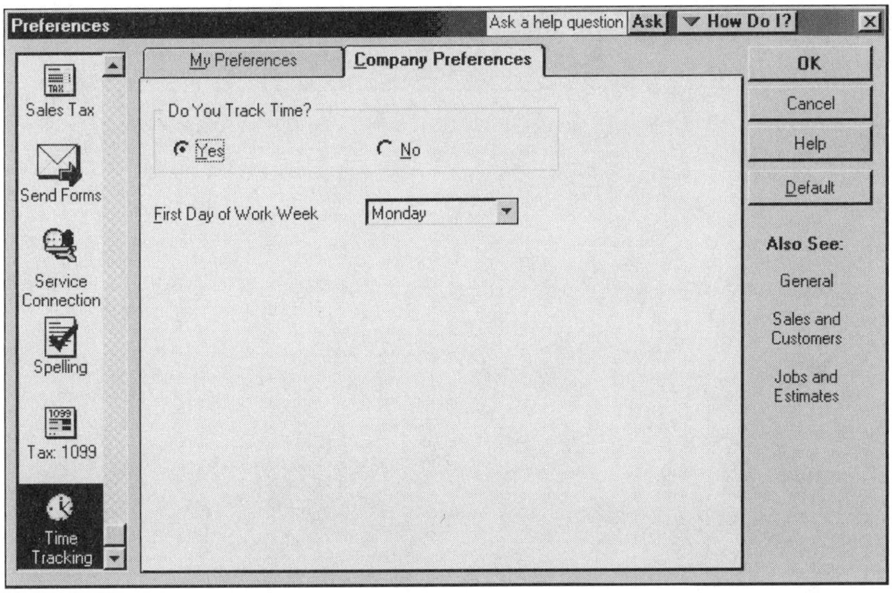

3 Make sure Yes is selected as the answer to the question "Do You Track Time?"

4 Click OK to save the preference setting.

Entering time data

There are three ways to get time data into a company file:

- Enter time directly onto a weekly timesheet or single activity form in QuickBooks.
- Use the Stopwatch to time an activity while you are performing it.
- Use the QuickBooks Timer program to track time and then import the time directly into QuickBooks. (The Timer is available in QuickBooks Pro and Premier only.)

When you track time with QuickBooks, you have a choice of two forms to enter time: Weekly Timesheet or Time/Enter Single Activity window. If you want to enter time for multiple jobs or multiple days, then the Weekly Timesheet is the best choice.

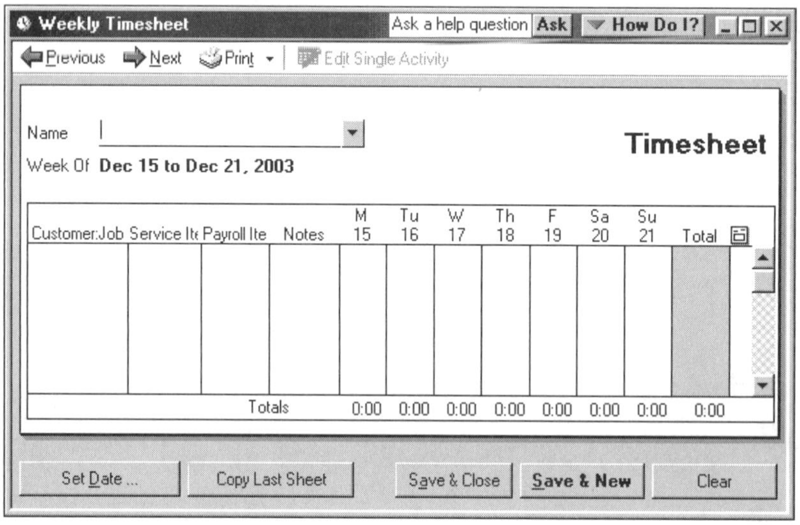

If you tend to enter a lot of detailed notes about your activities, or you prefer to enter time data as you complete an activity, use the Time/Enter Single Activity window instead.

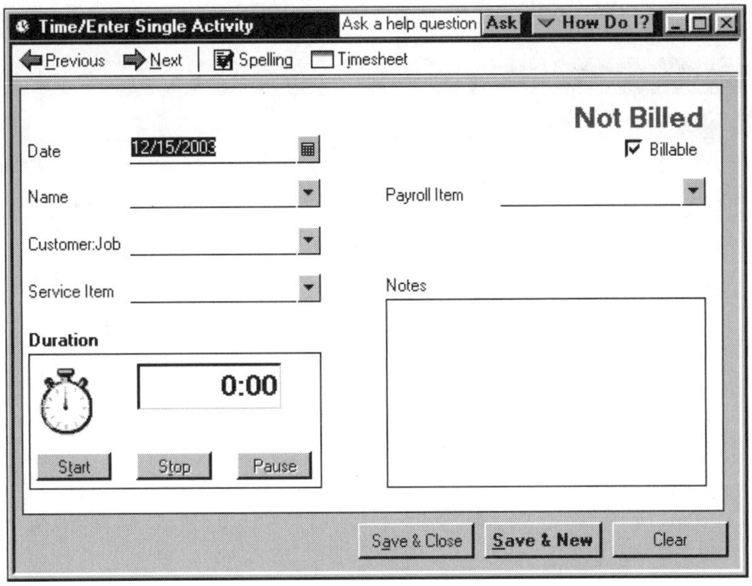

Information you enter in the Time/Enter Single Activity window displays in the Weekly Timesheet, and vice versa. They're different views of the same information.

The Timer program is useful when you have employees or subcontractors who need to track their time but don't need or want to run QuickBooks. When time is imported into QuickBooks from the Timer application, you view the imported time data on the same timesheets you would use if you did the data entry directly into QuickBooks.

If you have employees who don't have access to a computer, you can print blank copies of the weekly timesheet for your employees to fill out by hand.

To print a blank timesheet:

1. From the Employees menu, choose Time Tracking and then choose Use Weekly Timesheet.
2. From the Print drop-down menu, choose Print Blank timesheet.
3. In the Print Timesheets window, click Print.

Recording employee time on a weekly timesheet

In this exercise, you'll complete a weekly timesheet for Gregg Schneider. In a later exercise, you'll learn how to invoice a customer for the time Gregg spent working on a job for that customer.

To enter information on a weekly timesheet:

1 From the Employees menu, choose Time Tracking, and then choose Use Weekly Timesheet from the submenu.

QuickBooks displays the Weekly Timesheet window.

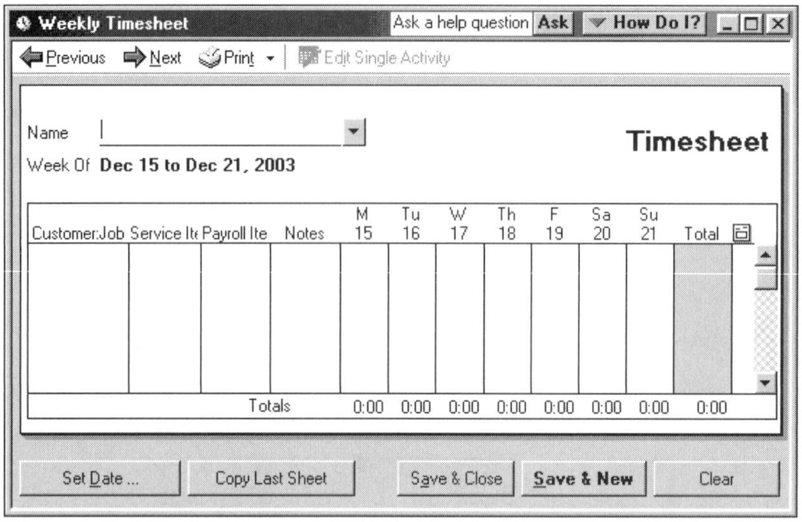

2 In the Name field, select Gregg O. Schneider from the drop-down list.

QuickBooks will track the time you enter for this employee and display it when you are ready to pay employees.

3 Click in the Customer:Job column, and then choose Melton, Johnny:Dental office from the drop-down list.

QuickBooks will associate the time that you enter in this window with the office repairs being completed for Johnny Melton.

4 In the Service Item column, type ***Installation***.

After you type a few characters, QuickBooks fills in the rest of the item for you. The Item list, which contains all the services and goods your business provides, is the same list that is available to you on invoice forms and throughout QuickBooks.

5 Notice that QuickBooks fills in the information in the Payroll Item column for you.

Gregg Schneider is paid by the hour. QuickBooks has his hourly rate stored in the Employee list, on the Payroll Info tab.

Tip: **If you try to select a payroll item that is not associated with this employee, QuickBooks displays a warning message.** For example, if you try to select Salary as the payroll item for Gregg Schneider, QuickBooks tells you that you do not have that type of payroll item set up for the employee. (It still lets you make the selection, but it warns you that the Salary is set up with a $0.00 rate.)

6 Click in the M 15 column.

M stands for Monday and 15 for the date, Monday, the 15th of December, 2003. Note that you can change the first day of your workweek in the QuickBooks time tracking preferences. (From the Edit menu, choose Preferences, and then click Time Tracking.)

7 Type ***8*** to enter the number of hours worked on Monday.

8 In the Tu field, type ***8***.

9 In the W field, type ***8***.

As you enter hours for each day, the Total column displays the total hours for the week.

10 In the Th field, type ***8***.

11 In the F field, type ***8***.

Your screen should resemble the figure below.

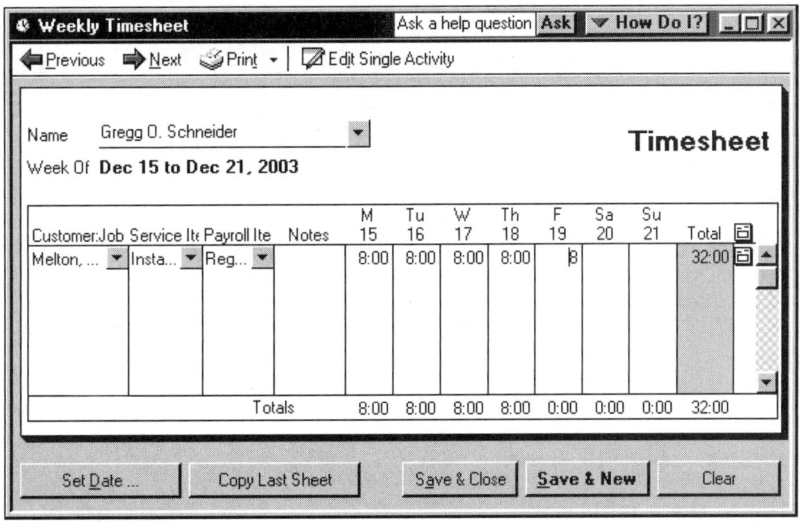

The invoice icon to the right of the Total column tells QuickBooks if the time will be transferred onto an invoice. In its current setting, you're telling QuickBooks that you *do* want to invoice the customer for time worked.

If you do not plan on invoicing the customer for time worked, you can click the invoice icon and QuickBooks displays a red "X" over it.

12 Click Save & Close to record the Weekly Timesheet.

QuickBooks records the time for Gregg Schneider and for Johnny Melton's dental office job.

This time can now be transferred onto an invoice for Johnny Melton's dental office job or used to create a paycheck for Gregg Schneider.

Invoicing a customer based on time

Refer to Handout 38, "Invoicing customers for time worked."

Now you can invoice Johnny Melton for the time Rock Castle Construction's employee, Gregg Schneider, spent on the dental office job.

1. From the Customers menu, choose Create Invoices.
2. Select Melton, Johnny:Dental office as the customer:job.
3. If you're using QuickBooks Pro or Premier, QuickBooks displays the Available Estimates window. Click Cancel.
4. In the Date field, type ***12/22/2003***.
5. Click Time/Costs, and then click the Time tab.

   QuickBooks displays the Choose Billable Time and Costs window.

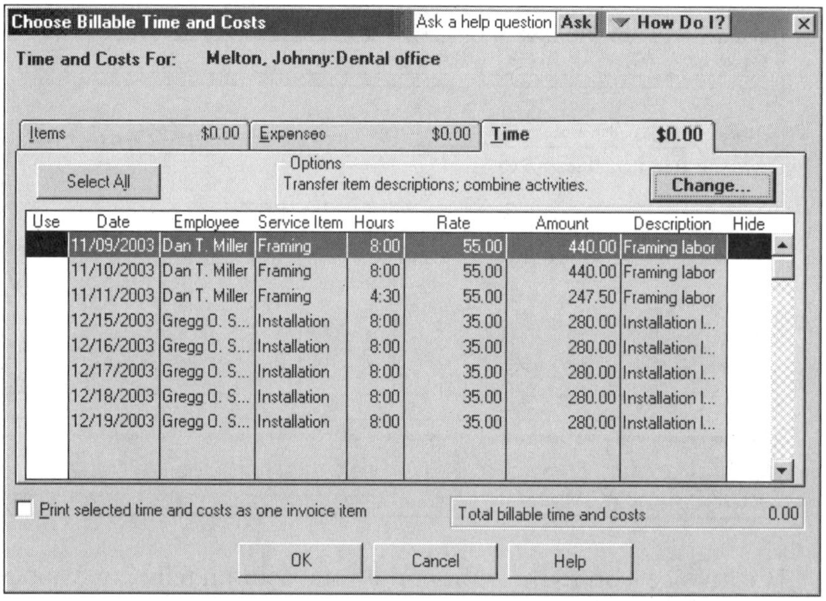

   QuickBooks displays the Time information entered on the timesheet for Gregg Schneider for the Johnny Melton dental office job. (It also displays time that Dan Miller worked on this job in November.)

   Note: By default, QuickBooks combines time for activities that have the same service item, and lists them as one line item on the invoice. If you prefer to have each individual line from the timesheet displayed as a line item on the invoice, click the Change button and select "Do not combine activities."

6. Click in the Use column to select each of the lines that represents time worked by Gregg Schneider. (Don't select the lines for Dan Miller.)

   QuickBooks places a checkmark in the Use column to the left of each entry to indicate it is selected.

7 Click OK.

The top part of your invoice should resemble the figure below.

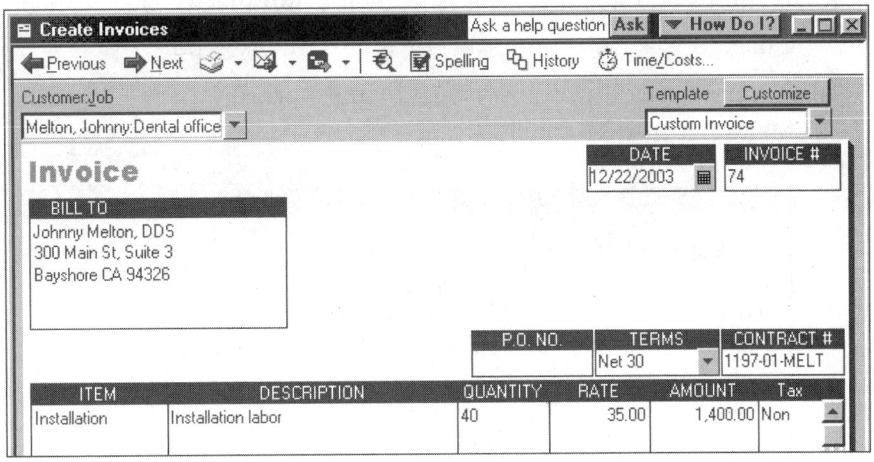

8 Click Save & Close to record the invoice.

Displaying project reports for time tracking

QuickBooks provides four reports on time, as described in the following table. You can create these reports by choosing Jobs & Time from the Reports menu.

Project report	Description
Time by Job Summary	Shows hours worked subtotaled first by customer or job and then by service item.
Time by Job Detail	Lists each time activity (that is, work done by one person for a particular customer or job on a specific date), and shows whether the work is billed, unbilled, or not billable. The report groups and subtotals the activities first by customer and job and then by service item.
Time by Name	Shows hours worked (or tracked as sick or vacation time), subtotaled first by the name of the person who performed the work and then by the customer or job the person performed the work for.
Time by Item	Shows the hours worked, subtotaled first by service item and then by customer or job.

Displaying the time by job report

The time by job summary report summarizes the total hours for each job, and the time by job detail report breaks down those summary figures into hours for each service item and hours for each customer:job.

To create a time by job report:

1. From the Reports menu, choose Jobs & Time.
2. From the submenu, choose Time by Job Summary.

   QuickBooks displays the time by job summary report.
3. Scroll the report until you see the time worked for the Melton, Johnny:Dental office job.

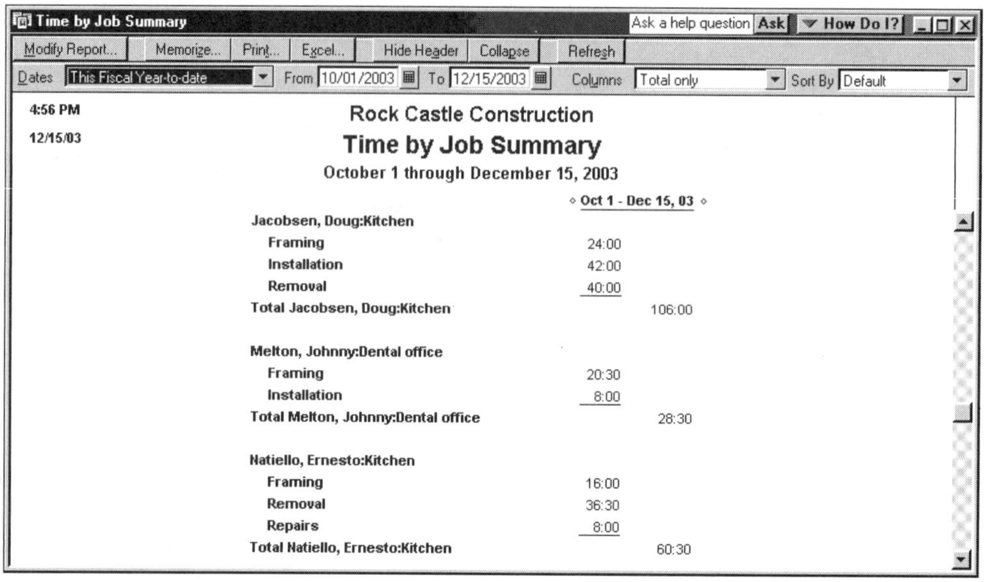

Notice that the report only shows 8 hours for Installation, but we entered 40 hours for this item on Gregg Schneider's timesheet. The reason for this is because the QuickBooks sample data comes set with today's date as December 15, 2003. As you'll remember the hours you entered for Schneider were from December 15 through 19.

Viewing time data in more detail

Like all QuickBooks reports, you can QuickZoom any of the numbers in a report to see more detail. Suppose you want to see who worked the eight hours on installation for Johnny Melton. You can point to that number in the report and double-click to get more information.

1. Position your mouse pointer over the 8 hours for Installation on the Melton, Johnny:Dental office job, and then double-click.

When you position your mouse pointer over the number, the pointer changes into a magnifying glass with a Z in it. After you double-click, QuickBooks displays a time by job detail report for the time data you selected. (This functionality is called QuickZoom.)

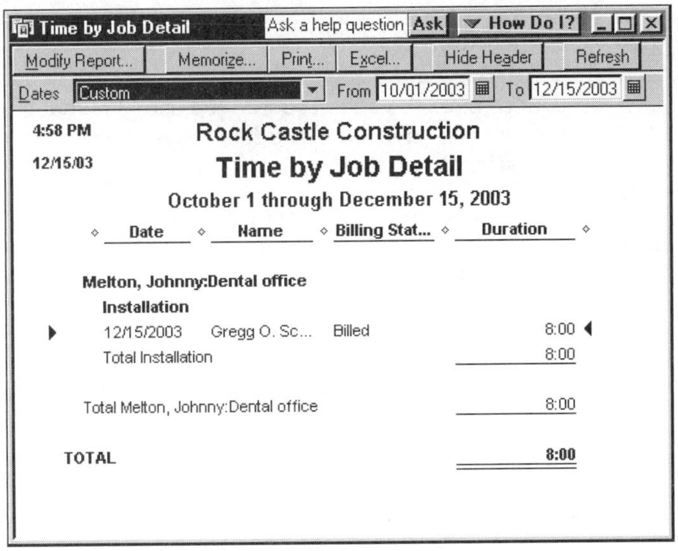

You can see that Gregg Schneider did the work and the time has already been billed to the customer.

Because the report ending date is December 15, it only displays the first eight hours that you entered on Gregg's timesheet. If you want to see all Gregg's hours displayed on this report, you can change the date range it covers. In the To field (on the Report buttonbar), type ***12/31/03*** and press Tab. QuickBooks redisplays the report to cover the new date range.

2 Close the time by job detail and the time by job summary reports.

When QuickBooks asks if you want to memorize the report, click No.

3 Close the time by job summary report.

Displaying other project reports

In addition to the estimate and time reports, QuickBooks provides several project reports to track job profitability, as described in the following table.

Project report	Description
Job Profitability Summary	Compares the actual cost to the actual revenue for all customers and jobs. The report subtotals the data first by customer and then by job.
Job Profitability Detail (for one customer:job)	For a particular customer or job, compares actual costs to actual revenues and shows the difference between the two amounts. The report subtotals the data first by item type and then by item.
Item Profitability	For each item, compares the actual cost to actual revenue and shows the difference between the two amounts. The report subtotals the data first by item type and then by item.

Paying nonemployees for time worked

When the company file has time data for a person who is not on your payroll, you can write checks based on the time worked. QuickBooks can transfer time data for a specified date range to a check. QuickBooks prefills the Items tab of a check with information from the time data, including hours worked and rate.

You can pay a subcontractor, owner, or partner for time worked. The person must be on one of the following lists:

- Vendor (appropriate for subcontractors, especially if you must report payments to them on Form 1099-MISC)
- Other Names (appropriate for owners and partners)
- Employees set up as type "Owner."

  To set an owner up on the Employee list, choose Employee List from the Lists menu. On the Address Info tab, choose Owner from the Type drop-down list. Employees set up as "Owner" do not use payroll.

  Note: To pay an ordinary employee for time worked, use the payroll feature to write a paycheck.

Creating service items for subcontractors, owners, or partners

When you use service items for subcontractors, QuickBooks records expenses and income for the work in separate accounts. You can use such items on both purchase forms and sales forms.

In this section, you learn how to do the following:

- Set up a service item to use to track work performed by an owner or partner
- Enter time worked for an owner or partner
- Prepare a check to pay an owner or partner for time worked

To set up a service item for owners or partners:

1 From the Lists menu, choose Item List.

2 Click the Item menu button, and choose New.

3 In the Type field of the New Item window, choose Service from the drop-down list.

4 In the Item Name/Number field, type ***Planning***.

5 Select the "This service is performed by a subcontractor, owner, or partner" checkbox.

QuickBooks changes the window to display fields for sales and purchase information.

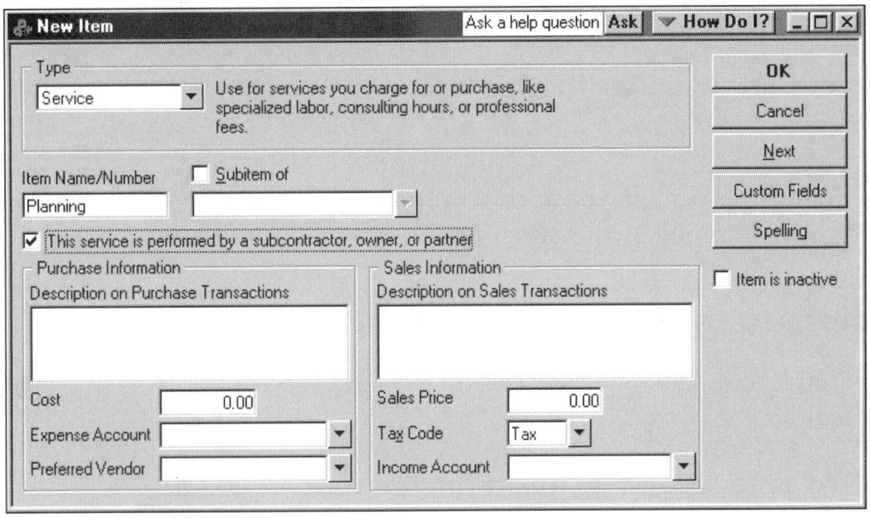

6 In the Description on Purchase Transactions field, type ***Job Planning*** and press Tab.

QuickBooks copies the text into the Description on Sales Transactions field.

7 In the cost field, type ***50*** and press Tab.

8 From the drop-down list in the Expense Account field, choose the equity subaccount called *Owner's Draw.*

If you pay owners (or partners) for time worked, you need a service item that records the cost of the work as a draw against equity, rather than an expense.

9 In the Sales Price field, type ***90***.

10 In the Tax Code drop-down list, select Non.

11 In the Income Account field, type ***Planning*** and press Tab.

12 When QuickBooks tells you that Planning is not on the Account list, click Set Up.

13 In the New Account window, make sure Income is selected in the Type drop-down list and click OK.

Your screen should now look like this.

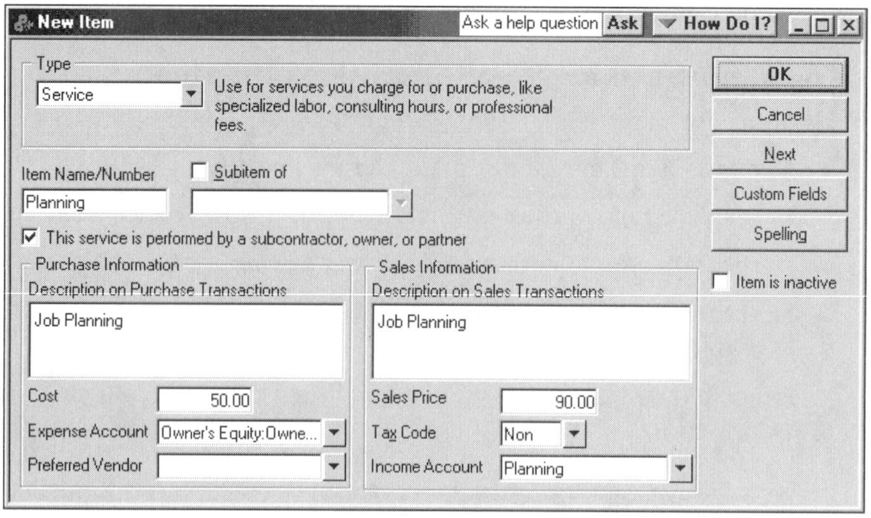

14 Click OK to close the New Item window.

15 Press Esc to close the Item list.

In the next section, you learn how to use the Planning item you've just created to track time performed by the owner of Rock Castle Construction.

Recording nonemployee time worked

You record data for time worked by nonemployees the same way you enter it for employees.

To enter time for nonemployee time worked:

1 From the Employees menu, choose Time Tracking. Then choose Time/Enter Single Activity.

QuickBooks displays the Time/Enter Single Activities window.

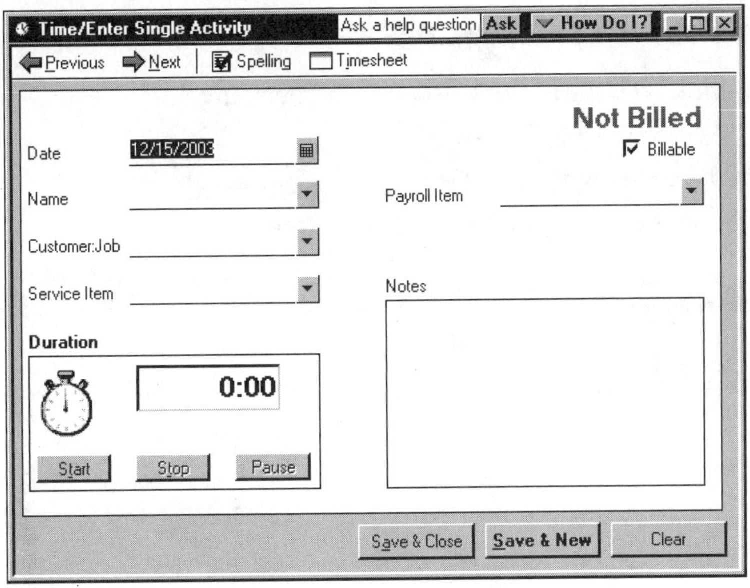

2 In the Name field, choose Tom Ferguson from the drop-down list.

Note: When you selected the owner's name, QuickBooks removed the Payroll Item field from the window. (When class tracking is on, this field is replaced with the class field.) Owners and partners should be set up on the Other Names list, or on the Employee List with the Type set to "Owner" because they are not paid with payroll checks.

3 In the Customer:Job field, choose Abercrombie, Kristy:Family Room.

4 In the Service Item field, select Planning from the drop-down list and press Tab.

5 Type ***8*** in the Duration field and press Tab.

Your screen should resemble the following.

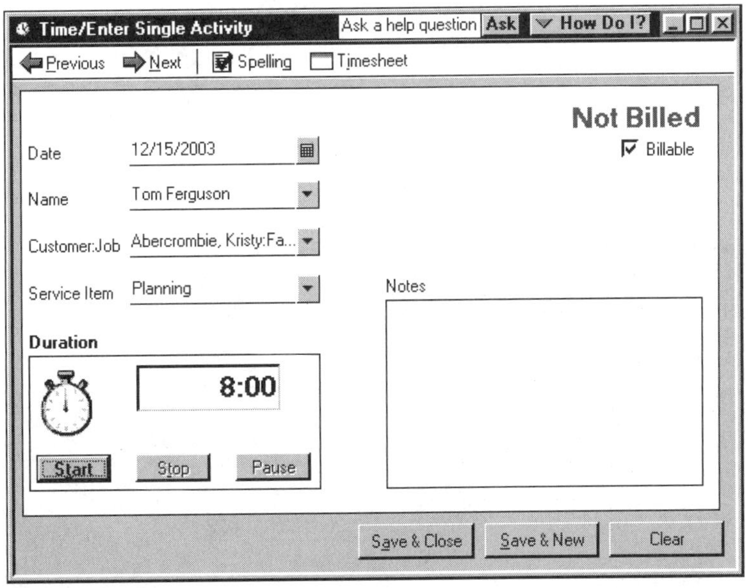

6 Click Save & Close.

Preparing a check to pay for nonemployee time worked

In this section, you'll learn how to create a check to reimburse an owner for time worked on a specific job.

1 From the Banking menu, choose Write Checks.

QuickBooks displays the Write Checks window.

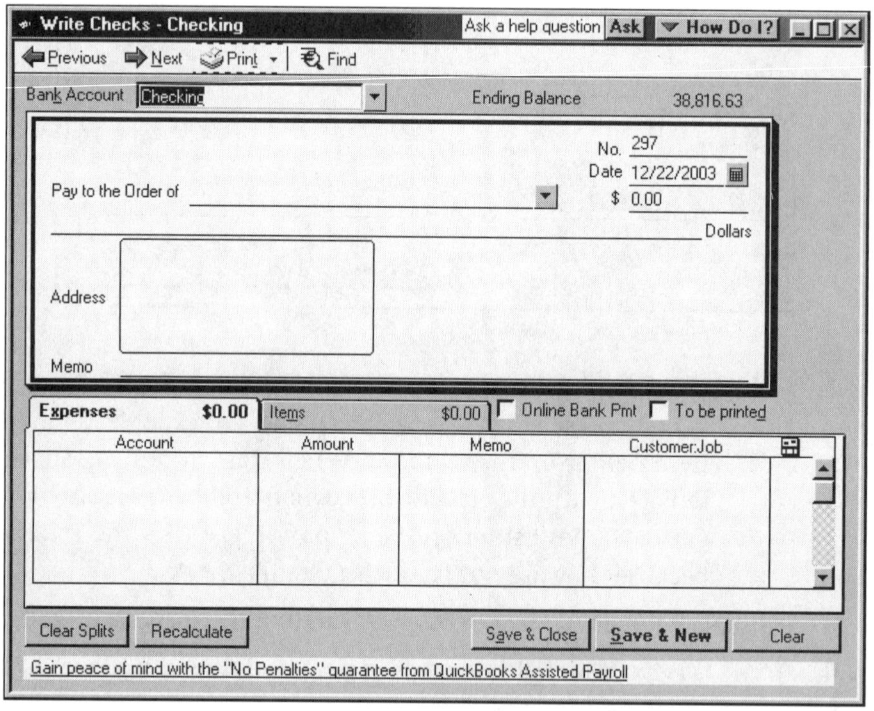

2 Make sure that Checking is selected in the Bank Account field.

3 Click to put a checkmark in the To be printed checkbox.

4 In the Pay to the Order of field, choose Tom Ferguson from the drop-down list.

5 Click Yes at the message QuickBooks displays asking if you want this check to pay for time worked.

QuickBooks displays the Select time period window.

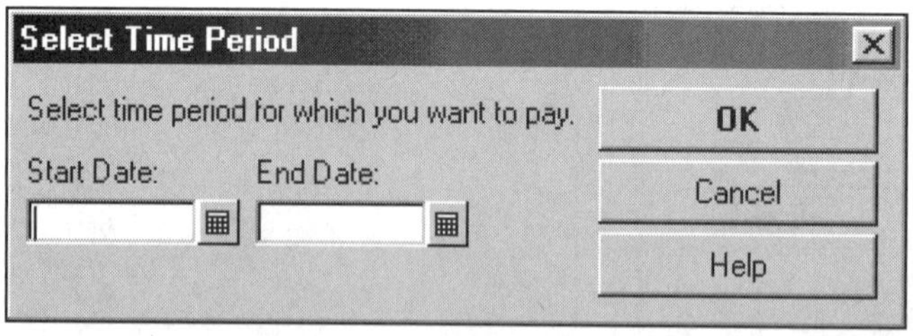

6 Type ***12/15/03*** in the Start Date field and press Tab.

7 Type ***12/19/03*** in the End Date field and click OK.

QuickBooks prefills the Items tab of the check with information from the time data, including hours worked and rate.

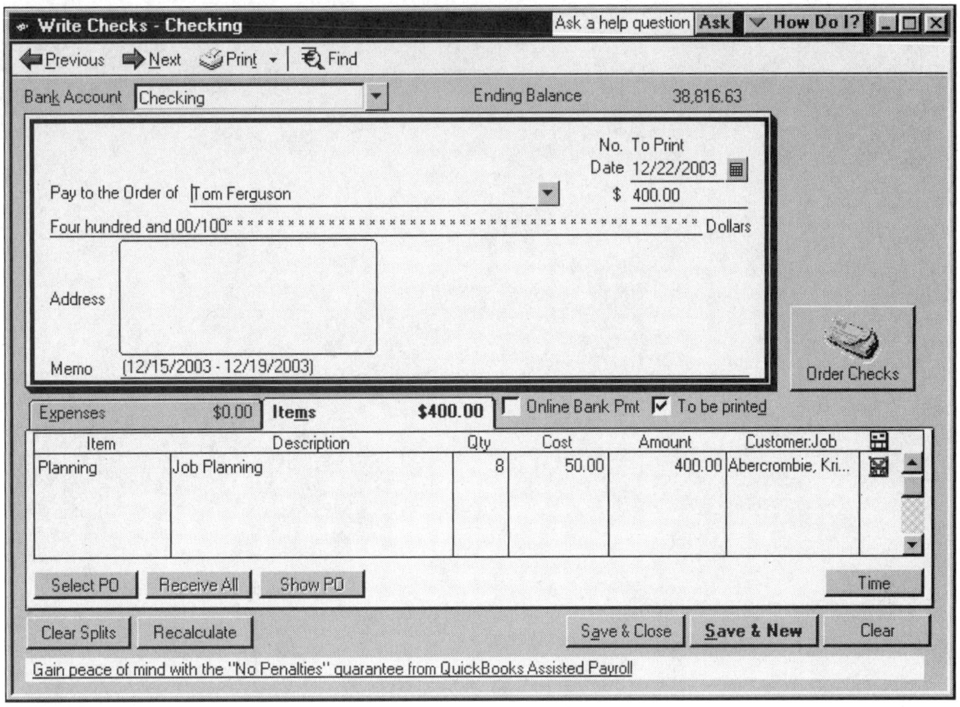

8 Click Save & Close in the Write Checks window.

Notice that time activity is marked unbillable so that it is not billed twice—as a time activity and an item.

Student test and review

1 Create a single activity timesheet for Gregg Schneider, for eight hours worked on the Anton Teschner Sun Room job.

2 Transfer the time you just entered for Gregg Schneider onto an invoice for the Teschner Sun Room job.

On the invoice, click the Time/Costs button and then click the Time tab to display the hours recorded for this job. Select the time by clicking in the Use column and then clicking OK.

3 Display a time by name job report to see how many hours Gregg Schneider has worked for each job.

LESSON 15 Customizing forms and writing QuickBooks Letters

Lesson objectives

- To learn how to modify a preset invoice form
- To design a custom invoice form
- To see how to print invoices
- To learn how to prepare a collection letter for overdue customers
- To learn how to edit a prewritten letter in QuickBooks

Handout materials

- Handout 39: Types of QuickBooks forms you can customize
- Handout 40: QuickBooks Layout Designer

Instructor preparation

- Review the lesson, including the examples, to make sure you're familiar with the material.
- Ensure that all students have a copy of qblesson.qbb on their computer's hard disk.
- Have Handouts 39 and 40 ready for distribution.

To start this lesson

Before you perform the following steps, make sure you have installed the exercise file (qblesson.qbb) on your hard disk. See "Installing the exercise file" in the Introduction to this guide if you haven't installed it.

The steps that follow will restore the exercise file to its original state so that the data in the file matches what you see on the screen as you proceed through each lesson.

To restore the exercise file (qblesson.qbb):

1. From the File menu in QuickBooks, choose Restore.

   QuickBooks displays the Restore Company Backup window.
2. In the "Get Company Backup From" section of the window, click Browse and select your c:\QBtrain directory.
3. Select the qblesson.qbb file, and then click Open.
4. In the "Restore Company Backup To" section of the window, click Browse and select your c:\QBtrain directory.
5. In the File name field of the Restore To window, type ***lesson 15*** and then click Save.

6 Click Restore.

About QuickBooks forms

Refer to Handout 39, "Types of QuickBooks forms you can customize."

Each form you use in QuickBooks has its own layout—that is, its own arrangement of fields and columns for entering information. If the layout of a particular form doesn't meet your needs, you can create your own custom layout and use your version instead of the QuickBooks version.

In Lesson 6, you learned about the three preset formats for invoices: professional, service, and product. If these formats don't precisely meet your needs, you can create your own invoice templates. You can also create templates for other sales and purchase forms.

For each form, you can decide which fields and columns to include, what they are called, and where to place them. Once you have created your forms, you can save the new layouts as *templates*—to use whenever you wish, and to modify whenever you want. The forms you can customize in QuickBooks are the invoice, sales receipt, credit memo, statement, purchase order, estimate (QuickBooks Pro and Premier only), and sales order (QuickBooks Premier editions only).

Note: **You can create custom forms in all QuickBooks products, but some of the customization and layout options described in this lesson are available only in QuickBooks Pro and Premier products.** For example, adding colored backgrounds, using rounded borders on fields, and using fields on forms multiple times are available only in QuickBooks Pro and Premier products.

Customizing invoices

QuickBooks lets you customize an invoice form to suit the needs of your business, but there may be times when you want to design a completely different invoice form. QuickBooks lets you do that, too. You can use the Layout Designer to create a new form design for your business. In the Layout Designer, you can move, resize, or change the width of columns, turn on or off borders around fields, and control font type and size for each field.

In the following exercises, you'll use both the customize forms and Layout Designer features in QuickBooks to create a custom invoice.

Note that these features affect only the printed forms; you cannot customize the onscreen version of QuickBooks forms.

Creating new templates

To create a new invoice template:

1 From the Lists menu, choose Templates.

QuickBooks displays the Templates list.

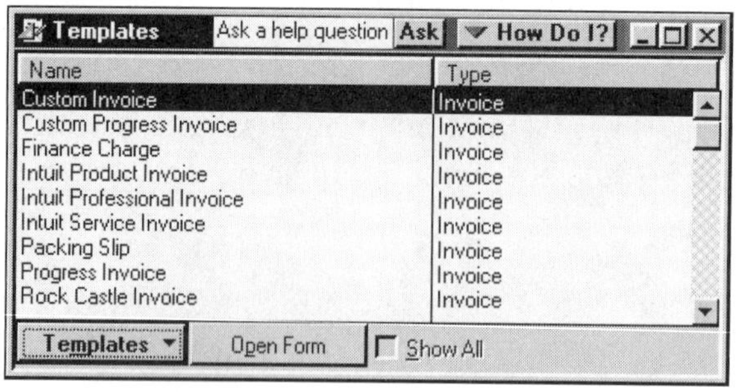

2 Click the Templates menu button, and then choose New.

QuickBooks displays the Select Template Type window.

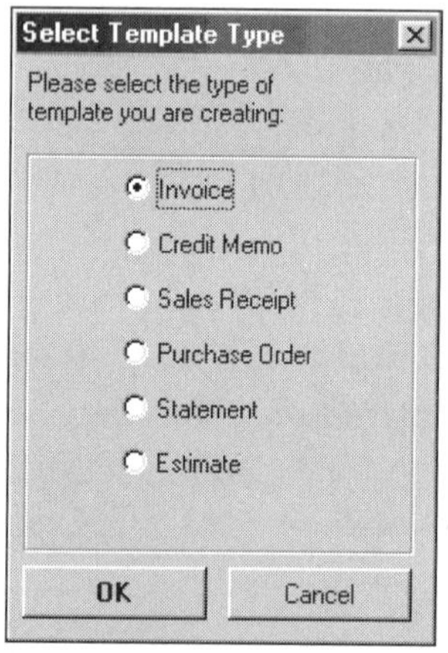

3 Click OK to select the invoice form.

QuickBooks displays the Customize Invoice window, which uses multiple tabs to display several sets of formatting options. Each area of the form is represented by a tab. To display the available formatting options, click the tab for the area of the form you want to change.

4 In the Template Name field, type ***My Invoice***.

This is the name you'll use for the new template. Your window should look like this.

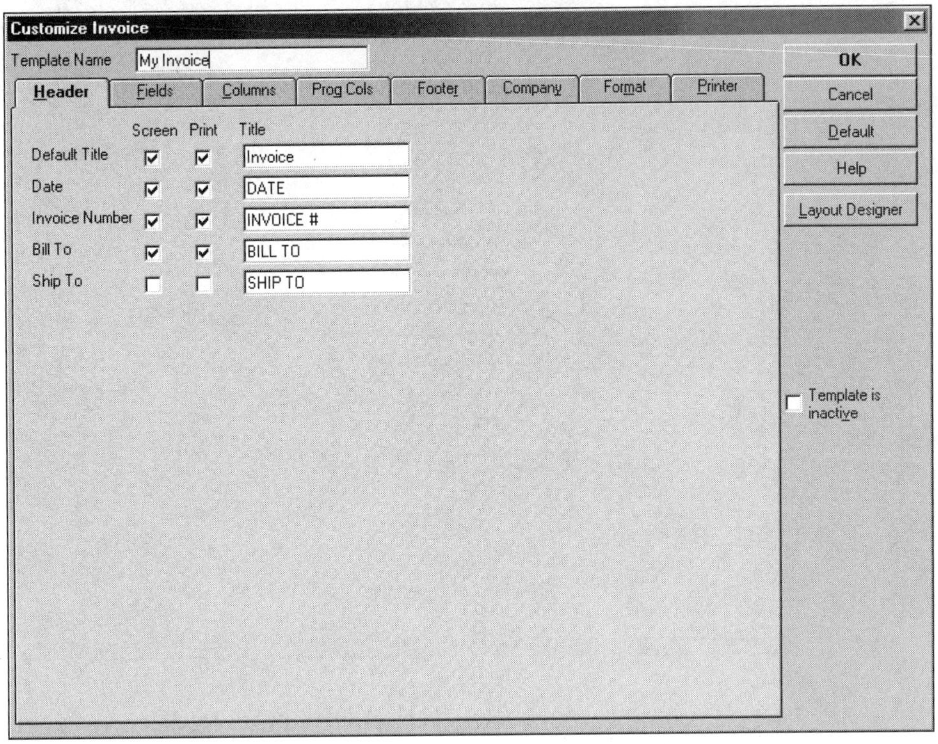

Notice that the Header tab is currently selected. The Header tab displays the formatting options you have for the top part of the invoice form. For each field, you can specify the title you want and whether you want the field displayed onscreen, on paper, both, or neither. You can enter a new title by highlighting the current title text and typing your new one.

If you want to track information about a particular invoice, but don't want your customer to see this information, select the Screen checkbox and clear the Print checkbox.

5 Click the Fields tab.

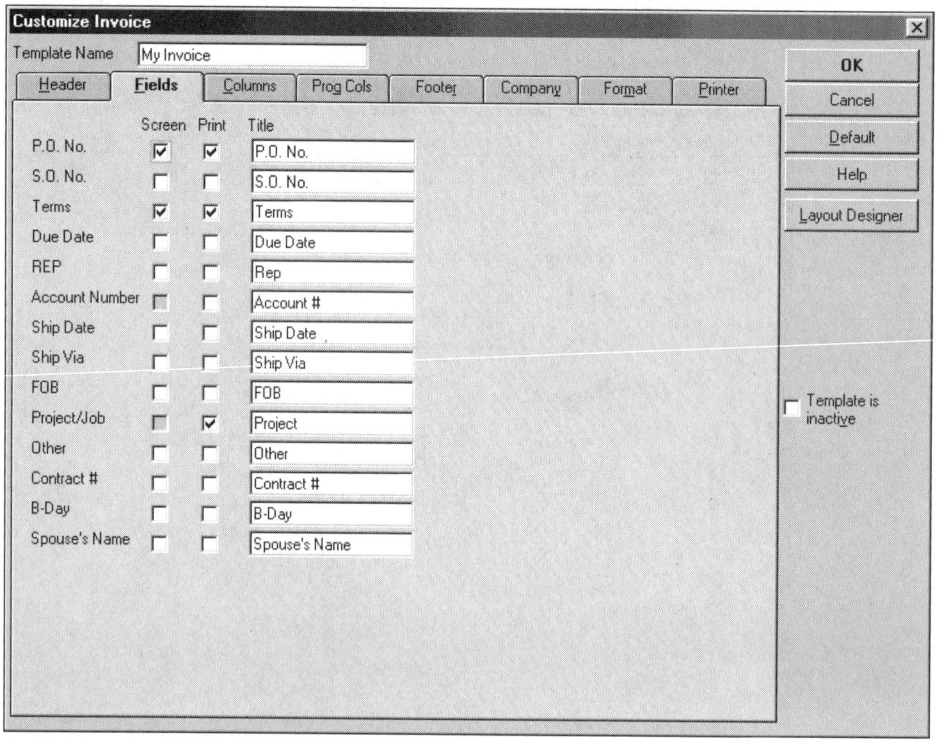

The Fields tab is where you select which fields you want to appear on screen and on paper. You can specify your own title (label) for each field.

Suppose you want to remind customers of payment due dates at the time you send the invoice. You can customize the invoice form to display the Due Date field.

6 To have the Due Date field display both on screen and on the printed form, click the Screen and Print columns for Due Date to select both checkboxes.

Checkmarks appear in both checkboxes.

7 Clear the Screen and Print checkboxes for the P.O. field to remove the field from the form.

Changing field order on forms

The lower half of the standard QuickBooks invoice form is where you enter details about the items or services purchased by the customer. You can change the order of these fields as they appear on your invoices.

The Order column shows you how fields display from left to right on the invoice form. Currently, Item is the first column and Amount is the last column. Suppose you want the Qty field to appear after the Item field, and before the Description field.

To change the order of fields on a form:

1 Click the Columns tab.

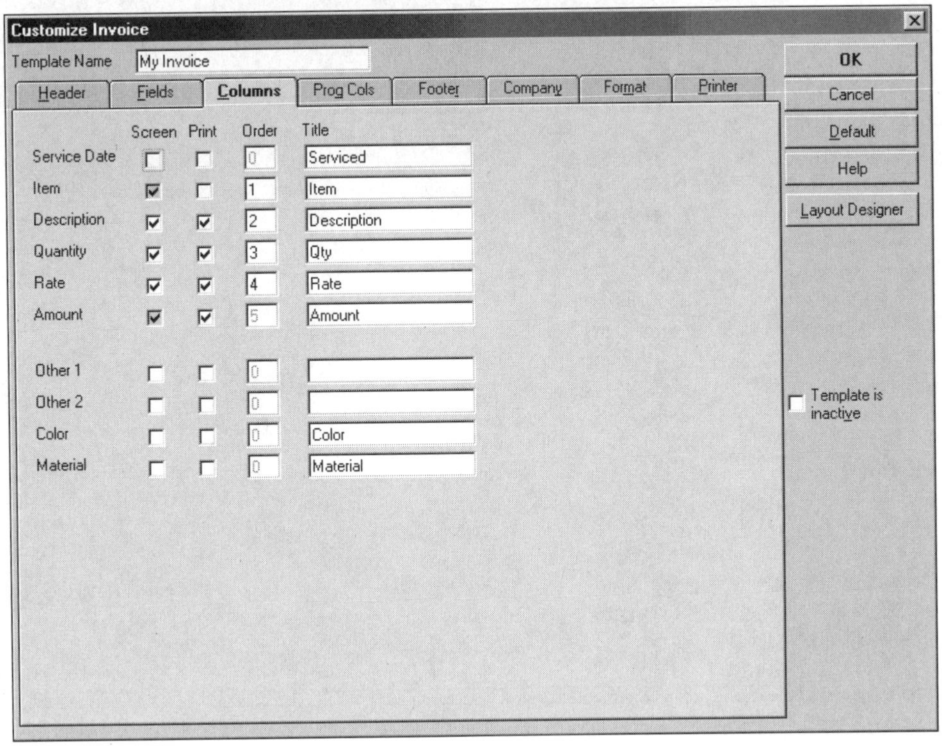

2 Double-click the Order column in the Quantity row to select the number.

3 Type ***2***.

4 Double-click the Order column in the Description row to select it.

5 Type ***3***.

Your screen should look like the following figure.

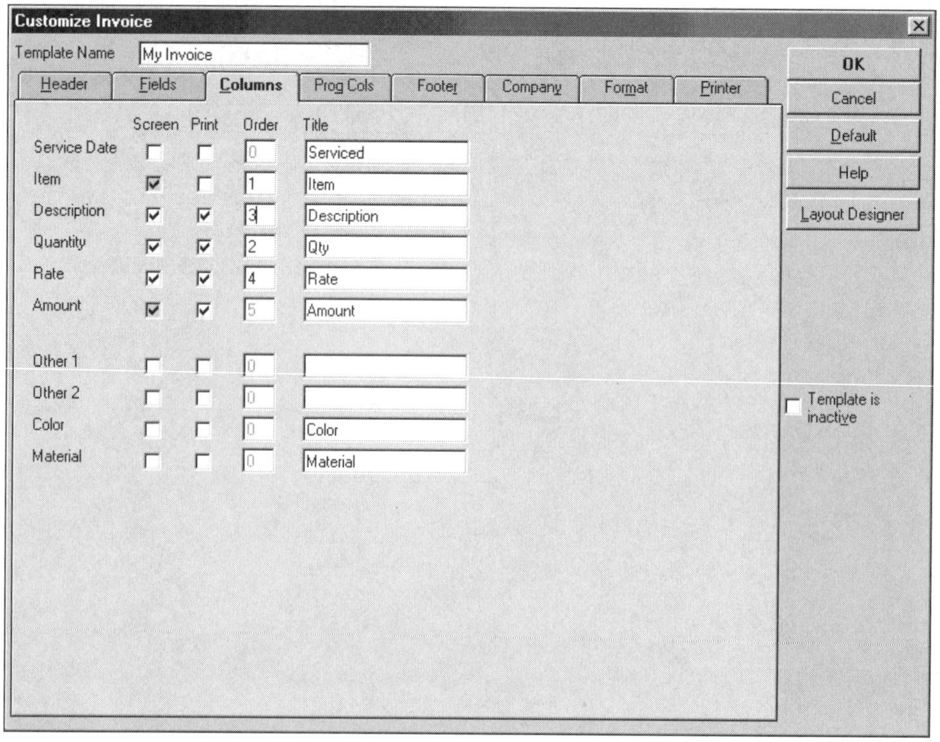

If you use progress invoices or sales orders, use the Prog Cols tab to customize the columns on those forms.

6 Click the Footer tab.

The Footer tab contains information that you usually find at the bottom of the form. It also provides a place for you to enter free-form text, such as a disclaimer, on your form. In the next exercise, you'll learn how to move fields on forms.

7 Click the Company tab.

Use the Company tab to specify which pieces of company information to include on your sales and purchase forms.

8 Select the Print Phone Number checkbox.

Your window should look like the following graphic.

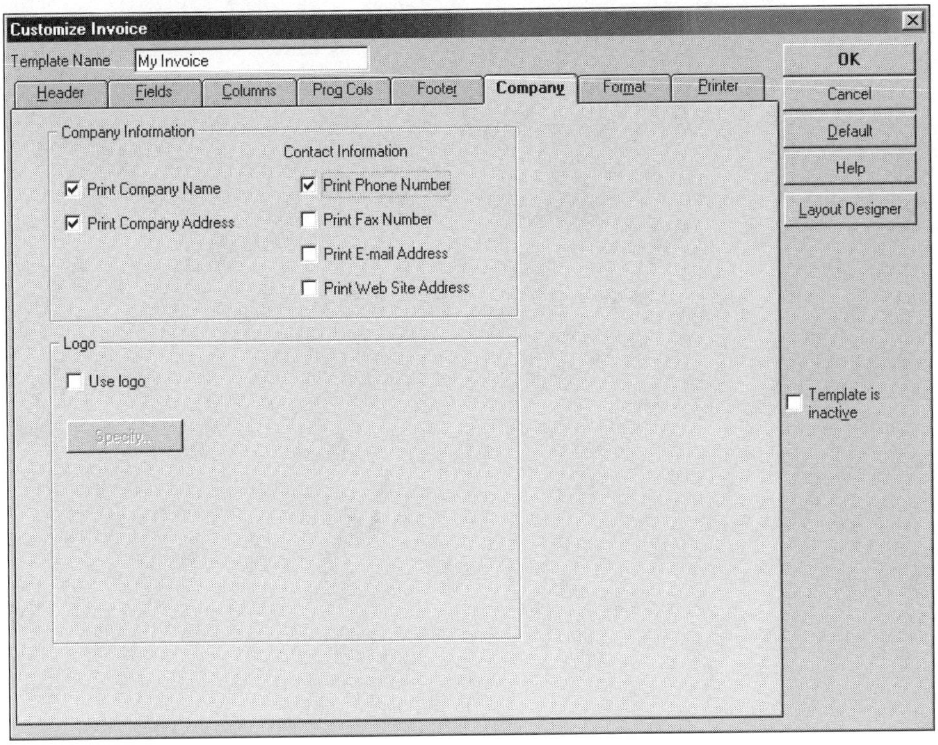

If you wanted to add your company logo to the form, you would select the Use Logo checkbox and tell QuickBooks which file to use. QuickBooks supports BMP, JPEG, TIFF, and GIF graphic formats.

9 Click the Format tab.

Use the Format tab to change the fonts for various textual elements on the form. If your forms print on multiple pages, use the checkbox on this tab to indicate whether or not you want to print page numbers.

If you don't want QuickBooks to print the status stamp (paid, pending, etc.) on forms, clear the Print Status Stamp checkbox on this tab.

10 Click the Printer tab.

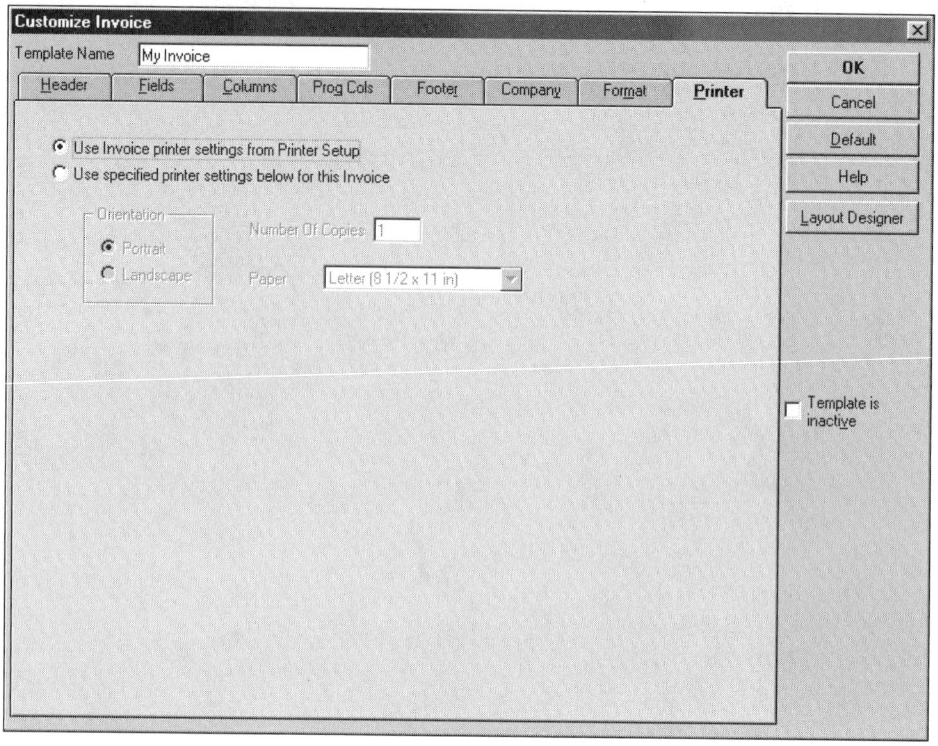

Use the Printer tab to associate print settings with individual form templates. For example, if you print most forms in Portrait mode, but have one form that you print in Landscape, you can associate the Landscape print setting with that form's template. When you send the form to the printer, QuickBooks knows to print it in Landscape.

11 Click OK to record the changes.

12 Close the Templates window.

Displaying your customized form

Now display the customized form to see the changes you made in the previous exercise.

To display the custom form:

1 From the Customers menu, choose Create Invoices.

QuickBooks displays the Create Invoices window with the Custom Invoice template displayed.

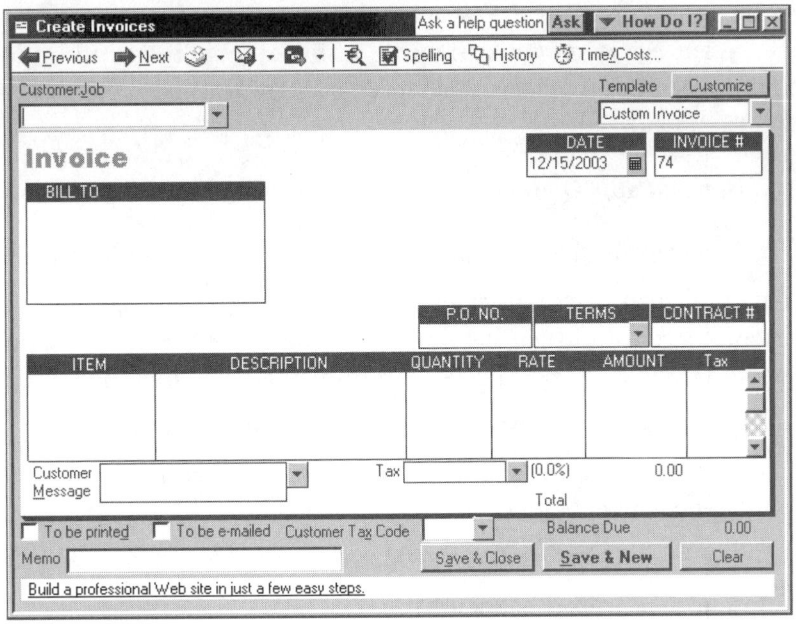

2 In the Form Template field, choose My Invoice from the drop-down list.

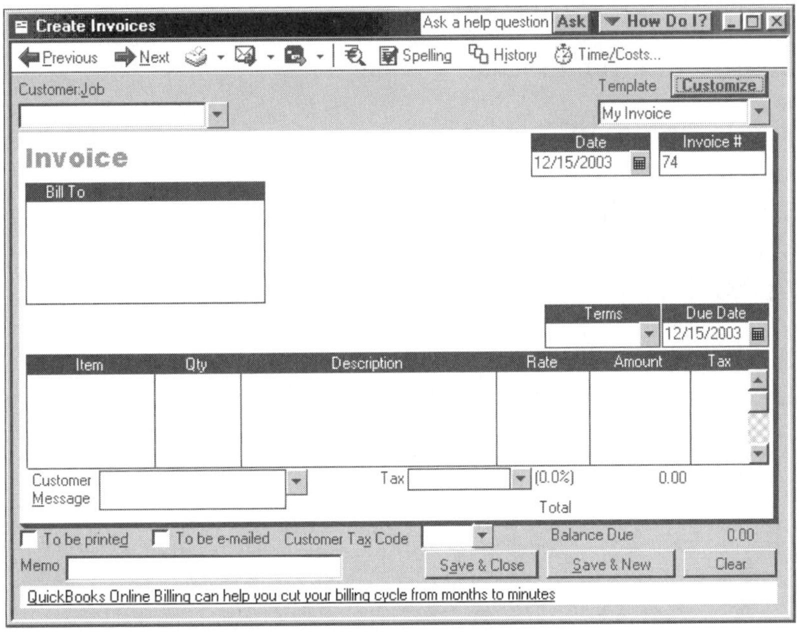

Notice how this form reflects the changes you made in the Customize Invoice window. The Due Date field now displays onscreen and the Qty column appears in its new order before the Description field.

The phone number field that you added to the form only shows on the printed form, so you do not see it onscreen.

3 Leave the Create Invoices window open; you'll use it in the next exercise.

Designing custom layouts for forms

With the QuickBooks Layout Designer, you can change the design or layout of a form. In the Layout Designer, you can move, resize, change the width of columns, turn on or off borders around fields, add colored backgrounds, and control the font type and size for each field.

Refer to Handout 40, "QuickBooks Layout Designer," for this discussion.

Here are a few examples of what you can do with a custom layout:

- Give your company name, address, and logo special treatment on the form. For example, you could center your logo at the top of the form and put your company name and address in a special font immediately below the logo.
- Enlarge a custom field so that it can display more information.
- Position the customer's billing address so that it coincides with the address window in the envelopes you use.
- Change the borders on fields, add background colors, and add extra text fields.
- Add multiple graphics to a form.

Changing the position of fields on forms

Next, you'll use the Layout Designer to move the Phone # and Bill To fields, and to decrease the width of the Quantity column.

To move fields on forms:

1 In the Create Invoices window, click Customize.

QuickBooks displays the Customize Template window.

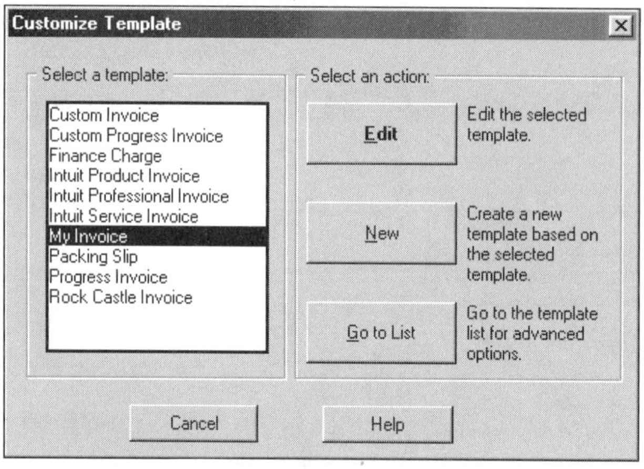

2 Make sure that My Invoice is selected and click Edit.

QuickBooks displays the Customize Invoice window that you used to customize the form.

Now, you'll use the Layout Designer to change the design of the form.

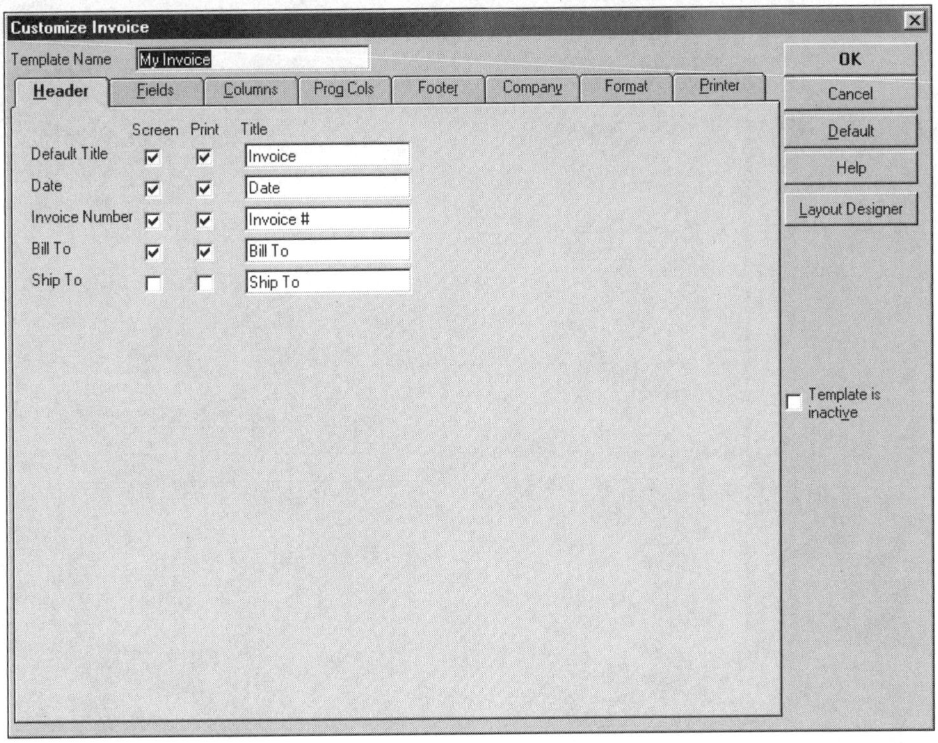

3 Click Layout Designer.

QuickBooks displays the Layout Designer window.

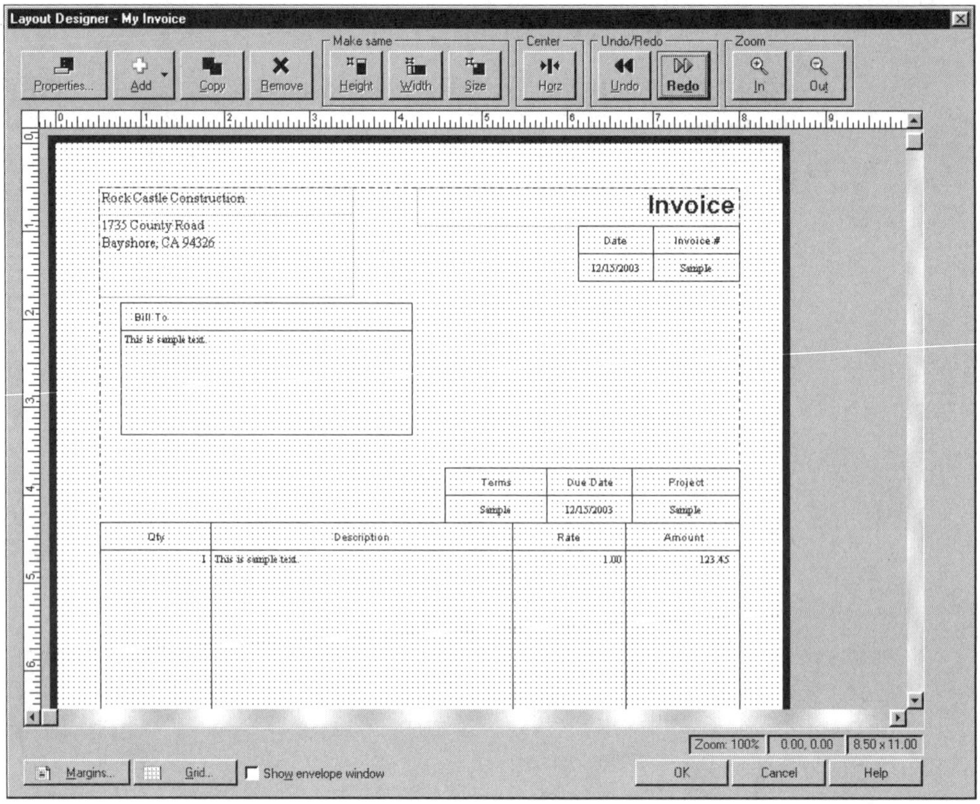

By clicking the Zoom buttons, you can zoom out to see an overall view of the form or zoom in for a closer look at a small section of the form.

4 Click the Bill To field.

5 Press and hold the Shift key.

Holding down the Shift key when clicking on an object allows you to select multiple fields at the same time. Having multiple fields selected lets you move the fields together.

6 Click the field directly below the Bill To field (the field containing the words "This is sample text").

Notice the four-directional arrow that appears when you move the cursor over the selected fields. The selected fields on your screen should look like this.

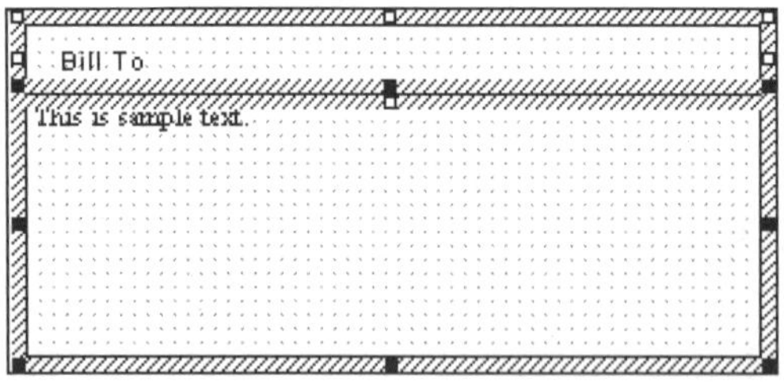

7 Release the Shift key.

8 With the cursor over the selected fields, press and hold the left mouse button.

9 Drag the selected fields down about one inch.

10 Release the mouse button.

Your screen should now look like this.

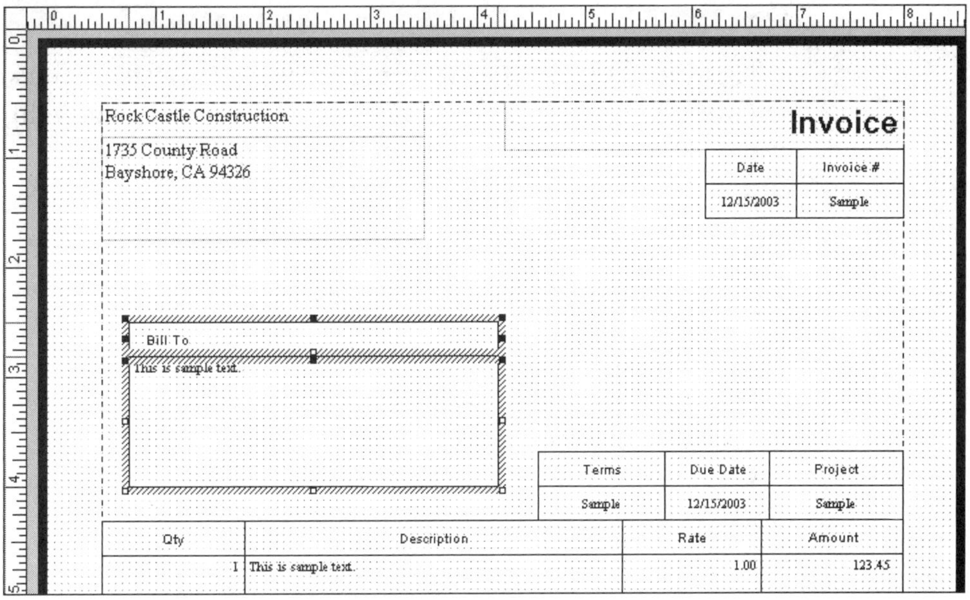

11 Select the field containing Rock Castle's address.

12 Move the mouse over one of the dark squares on the bottom of the field and then hold the mouse button while you drag the bottom of the field up to a point just below the address.

13 Scroll to the bottom of the screen and select the Phone # field.

14 Click Remove.

15 Select the field containing the numbers 555-555-5555.

16 Holding down the mouse button, drag the field so that it sits just below Rock Castle's address.

Changing field widths

In the next exercise, you'll change the font size for Rock Castle's phone number to make it match the address, but first you want to make the field wider so that the phone number isn't cut off.

To change the width of a field:

1 Select the field containing the telephone number and drag the right border further to the right while holding down the mouse button.

The fields should resemble the figure below.

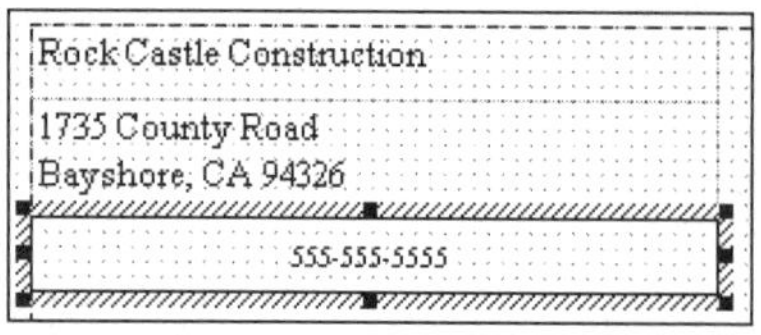

Rock Castle Construction rarely enters a quantity greater than two characters, so you want to make the QTY column smaller. Decreasing the width of the QTY column also increases the width of the Description column.

2 In the Layout Designer window, scroll until the Qty column is visible.

3 Click the Qty column to select it.

Your screen should resemble the figure below.

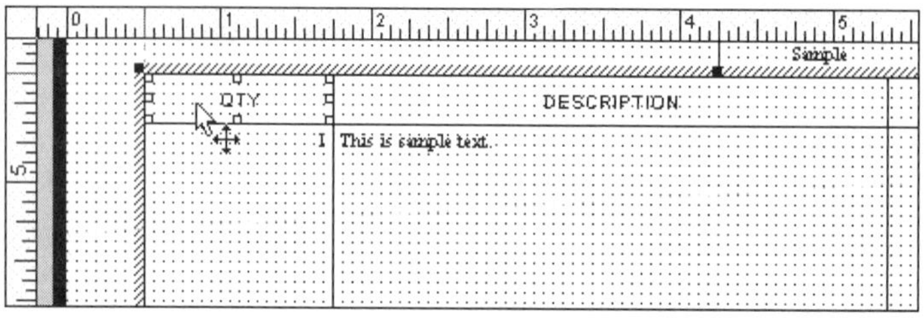

Notice that when the cursor is positioned between the QTY and DESCRIPTION columns, it turns into a two-directional arrow.

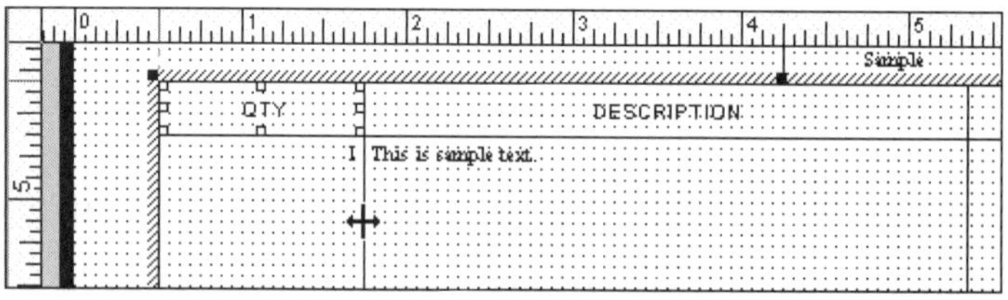

4 Click and hold the left mouse button on the line separating the Qty and Description columns.

5 While holding down the mouse button, drag the column line to the left (to the one-inch mark on the ruler).

6 Release the mouse button.

The forms area on your screen should resemble the figure below.

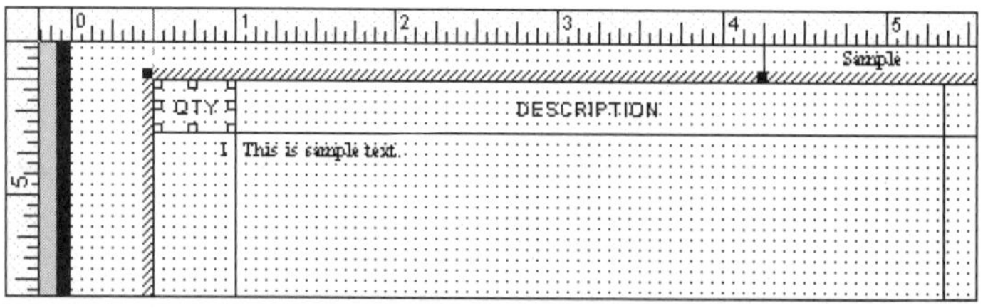

Changing fonts, borders, and colors

Using the Properties window in the Layout Designer, you can change font size and style, text justification. You can also add, remove, or change the borders around fields.

1. With the phone number field selected, click Properties.

   QuickBooks displays the Properties window.
2. On the Text tab, select Left for horizontal justification.

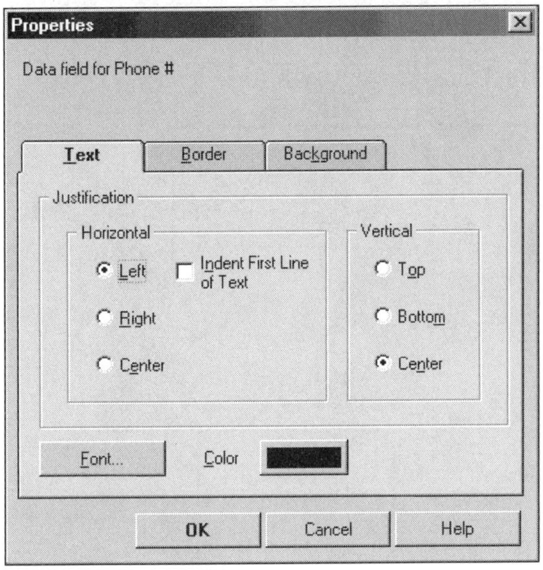

3. Click the Font button.
4. In the Size drop-down list, select 12, and then click OK.
5. Click the Border tab.
6. Click to remove the Top, Bottom, Right, and Left checkboxes.
7. Click OK to save your changes in the Properties window.
8. Click OK to save the changes in the Layout Designer.
9. Click OK to close the Customize Invoice window.

This exercise covers only a portion of the changes you can make with the customization and layout tools. For example, if you wanted to add a background color to the field, you could do so using the Background tab. You could use the Add button to add empty fields into which you can enter your own text—or to add data fields that you forgot to select in the Customize window. If you want a field to appear on a form more than once, select the field and click Copy.

We encourage you to experiment with the tools available to create your own custom forms. For examples of what you can achieve, visit the forms library at http://templategallery.quickbooks.com/forms/.

If you are using QuickBooks Pro or QuickBooks Premier, you can download templates from the forms library to use in your own business.

Previewing new forms

Notice that the invoice form displayed by QuickBooks doesn't show the changes you just made in the Layout Designer. This is because changes made in the Layout Designer only affect the printed invoice and not the invoice QuickBooks displays onscreen for data entry.

To preview the invoice:

1 To see how the printed invoice form will look, click the Print drop-down list on the Create Invoices window toolbar, and then choose Preview.

QuickBooks displays the Print Preview window.

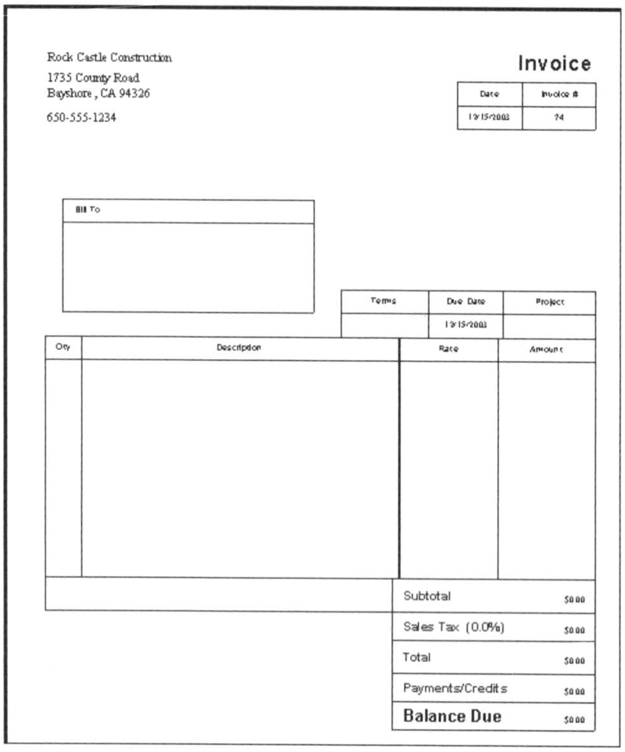

The invoice displayed in the Print Preview window shows exactly how the printed invoice will look. Notice that the changes you made in the Layout Designer are reflected in this preview.

2 When you are finished looking at the preview, click Close.

3 Press Esc to close the Create Invoices window without saving.

Using QuickBooks Letters

From time to time, you may need to send a letter to a customer or vendor (or someone on your employee list or other names list), or to another list of people. With QuickBooks Pro and Premier, you can easily add the pertinent QuickBooks data (such as name, address, and balance information) to a letter without having to re-type it.

QuickBooks provides a number of business letters focusing on collections, news, and announcements. You can edit these letters as needed to suit your business and style of communication.

Note: **To proceed with this lesson, you must be using QuickBooks Pro or Premier and Microsoft Word 97, 2000, or 2002. The QuickBooks Letters feature is not available in QuickBooks Basic.**

Preparing collection letters

In this exercise, you'll learn how to prepare a collection letter to send to customers with overdue payments.

To prepare a collection letter:

1 From the Company menu, choose Write Letters.

2 If QuickBooks prompts you to find letters, click Copy. QuickBooks will copy the QuickBooks letters from your installation directory to your QBtrain folder.

   QuickBooks opens the Write Letters wizard.

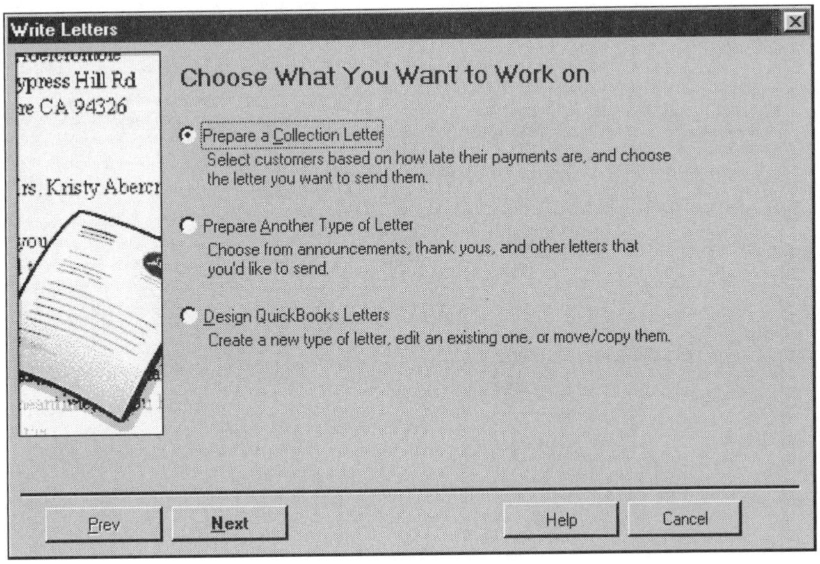

3 Make sure that "Prepare a Collection Letter" is selected and click Next.

4 When QuickBooks prompts you to choose who you want to write to, make the following selections:

   - For number 1, choose Active.
   - For number 2, choose Customer.
   - For number 3, choose 31 days or more.

Your screen should look like this.

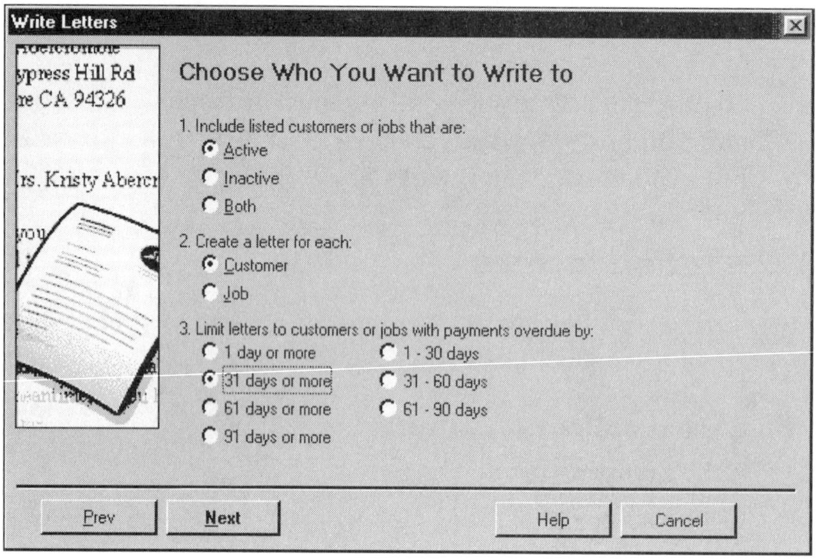

5 Click Next.

QuickBooks displays a list of all active customers with payments 31 days or more past due.

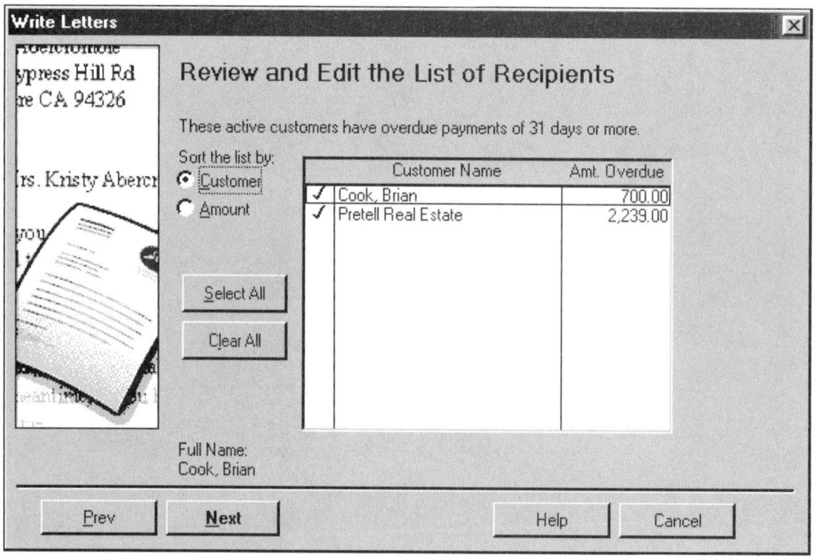

6 Leave both names selected and click Next.

7 When QuickBooks prompts you to choose the letter you want to use, click "Friendly collection" and click Next.

8 In the Name field of the next screen, type ***Tom Ferguson***. In the Title field, type ***President***.

Your screen should look like the following.

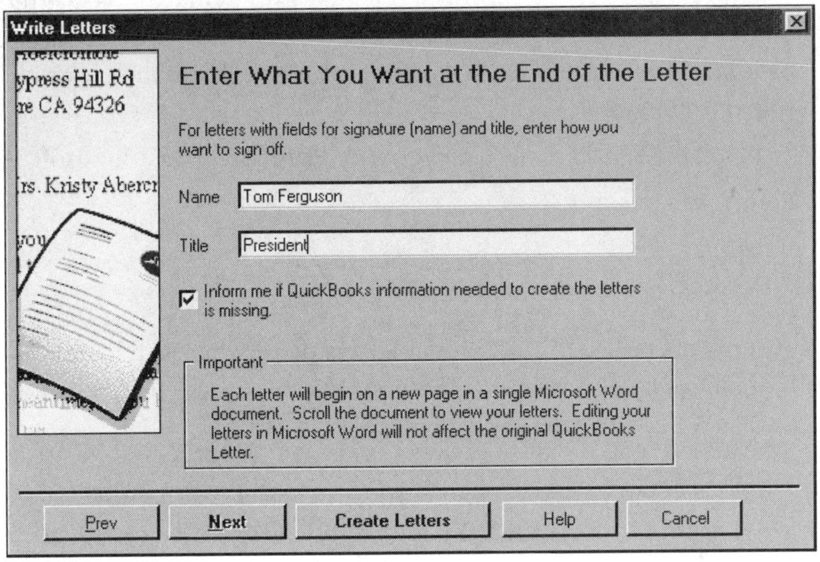

9 Click Create Letters.

10 If QuickBooks displays a message about missing information, click OK.

QuickBooks starts Microsoft Word (if it's not running already) and displays collection letters for the two customers that you selected.

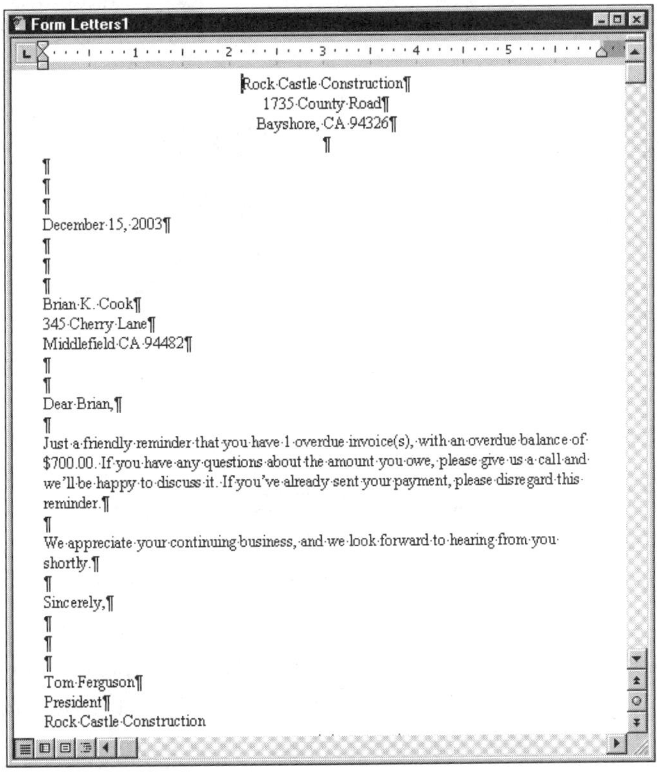

You can scroll through the Microsoft Word document to see both letters. Notice that QuickBooks entered Tom Ferguson's name and title at the end of each letter.

11 Close the Microsoft Word file without saving the letters.

When you do save letters you've created using QuickBooks Letters, don't save them to the QuickBooks Letters folder. The QuickBooks Letters folder should only be used to store the original QuickBooks Letters installed with the QuickBooks software program.

To print the letters, you would choose Print from the Microsoft Word File menu.

12 Return to QuickBooks.

Editing QuickBooks Letters

You can make changes to individual letters using Microsoft Word, or you can make global changes by editing the QuickBooks Letter used to generate a specific letter.

In this exercise, you'll edit the collection letter you prepared in the last exercise (Friendly collection). However, instead of working with completed letters with customer information already filled in, you'll work with the underlying QuickBooks Letter used to create the letters.

To edit a QuickBooks Letter:

1 From the Company menu, choose Write Letters.

2 Click Design QuickBooks Letters, and then click Next.

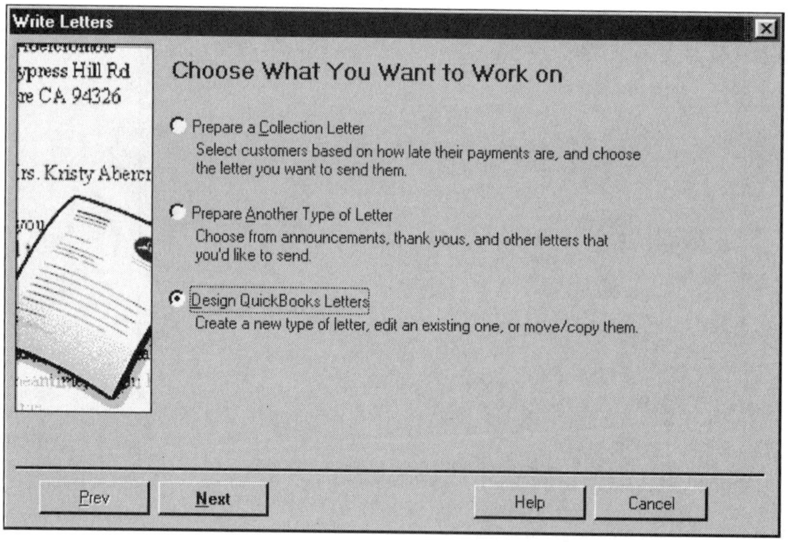

3 In the screen that appears, make sure "View or edit existing letters" is selected and click Next.

4 When QuickBooks prompts you to choose the QuickBooks Letter you want to view or edit, click Overdue customers (collection letters), and then select "Friendly collection" from the list of available letters.

Your screen should look like this.

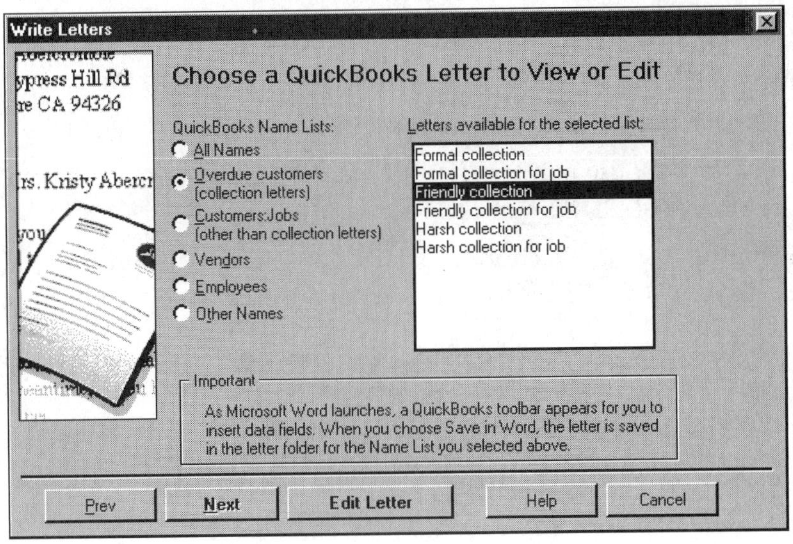

5 Click Edit Letter.

QuickBooks opens Microsoft Word (if it's not running already) and displays the QuickBooks Letter (Friendly collection) and a toolbar (QuickBooks Collection Letter Fields) that you'll use to add information from QuickBooks to the letter in Word.

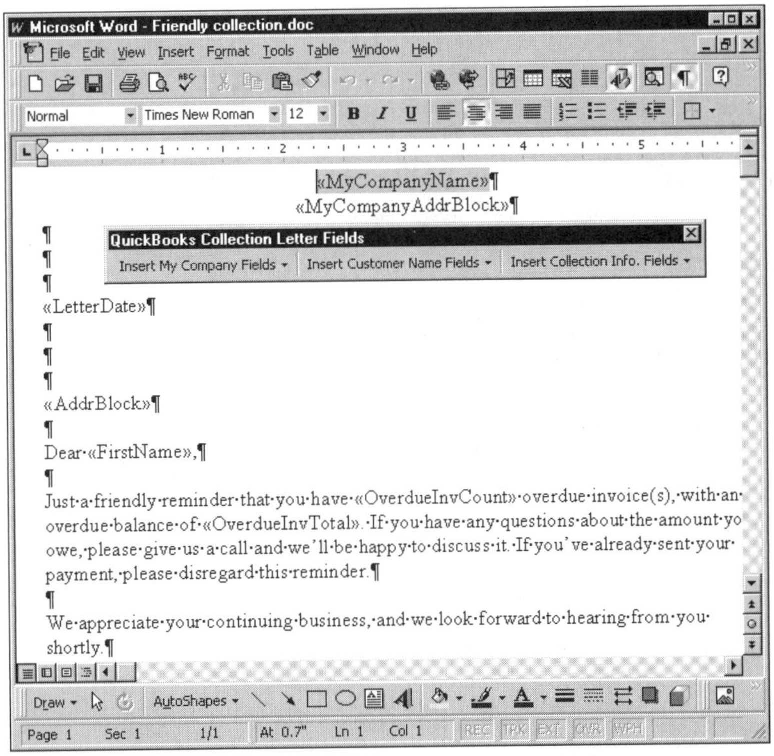

Note that you can move the toolbar by clicking it with your mouse pointer and dragging it to a new location.

Now, you'll enter more text and use the toolbar to insert data from QuickBooks into the "Friendly collection" letter.

6 Click your mouse pointer after the period at the end of the first sentence and the press the Space bar once. (You'll insert a sentence into the paragraph.)

7 Type ***Our records show that your balance is past due.***

8 Click your mouse pointer after the word *is* in the sentence you just typed, and press the Space bar again.

9 From the Insert Collection Info. Fields drop-down list on the QuickBooks Collection Letter Fields toolbar, select Range(days) of Overdue Invoices.

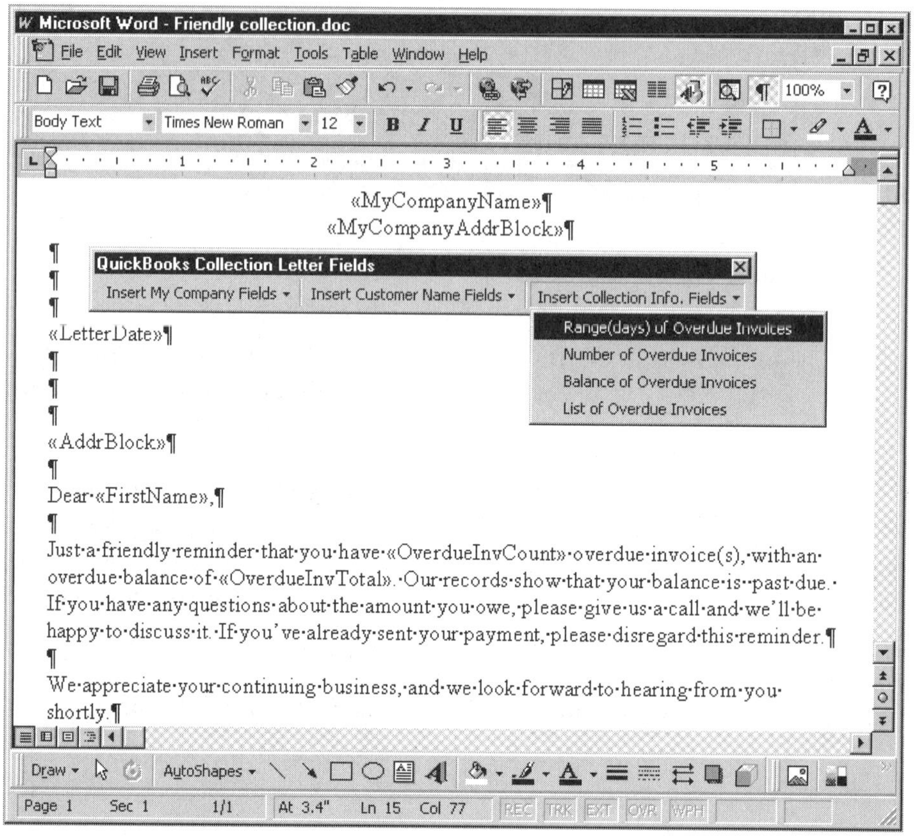

QuickBooks adds the <<OverdueRange>> field to the sentence you just typed.

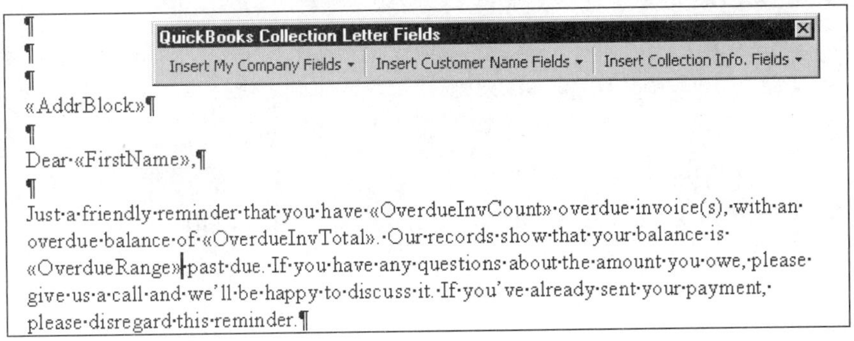

When you create letters using this modified QuickBooks letter, QuickBooks will replace the <<OverdueRange>> field with the number of days each customer you create a letter for is past due.

10 From the Word File menu, choose Save As.

11 Navigate to the Collection Letters folder in your Qbtrain directory and click Save.

If you save the file to your QuickBooks directory (instead of the Qbtrain folder you created to use with this guide) without changing the filename, you will overwrite the original QuickBooks Letter.

12 To see how this change affects the final letter output, close the letter file in Microsoft Word and go through the "Preparing collection letters"exercise again.

When you're done, your letters should resemble the following.

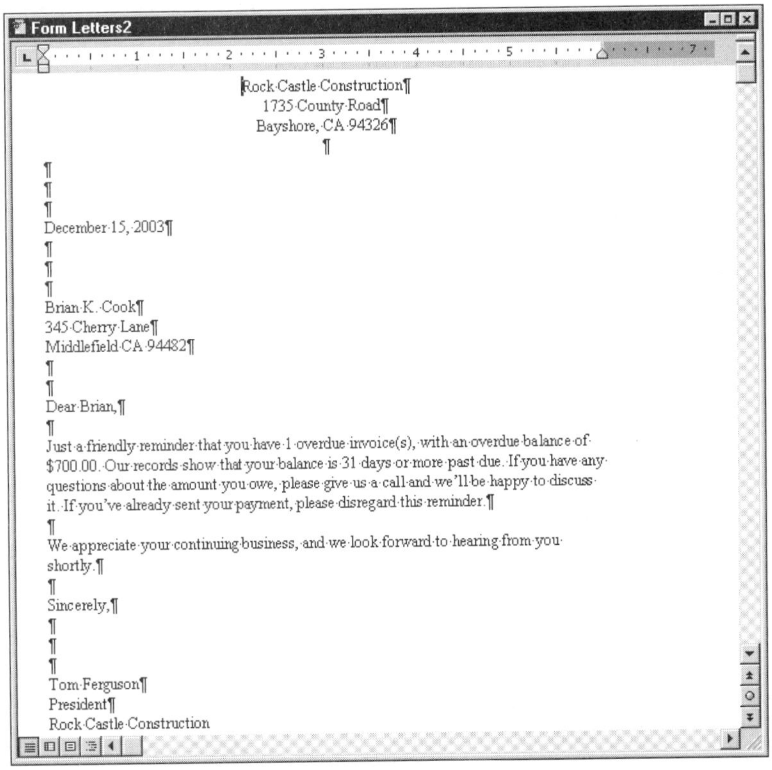

13 Close Microsoft Word.

Student test and review

1 Customize the Sales Receipt form to change the default title on the header from "Sales Receipt" to "Cash Sale."

2 Using the Layout Designer, make the columns for QTY and Rate narrower so the Description field is wider.

3 Customize the P.O. form to include the Terms field.

APPENDIX A Instructor demonstration of QuickBooks

Instructor demo of QuickBooks features

The following demonstration is meant to be presented by the instructor with the class observing. It gives students an introduction to the major QuickBooks features, and lets them see how QuickBooks automates day-to-day bookkeeping.

Restoring the demo data file

Before you start the demonstration, restore the file "qblesson.qbb" in the QBtrain folder you set up using the instructions in the introduction to this guide.

To restore the data file:

1. From the File menu in QuickBooks, choose Restore.

   QuickBooks opens the Restore Company Backup window.
2. In the Get Company Backup section, click Browse, and then select the QBtrain directory you set up following the instructions in the introduction of this guide.
3. Click Open.
4. Select the qblesson.qbb file, and click Open.
5. In the Restore Company Backup To section, click Browse and select your QBtrain directory.
6. Click Open.
7. In the File name field, type ***demo.qbw*** and click Save.
8. When you see the message about the sample file's default date, click OK.
9. If you are not starting the demonstration now, exit QuickBooks.

Explain to students that later they'll be learning how to create their own QuickBooks company. For most of the course, however, we'll be using a sample file for a fictitious construction company called Rock Castle Construction.

Entering sales

One of a business's primary concerns is revenue, so let's begin with that. Suppose your business has made a sale and you need to invoice the customer. To do that in QuickBooks, you fill out an invoice that looks just like a paper form.

Creating an invoice

You can choose any QuickBooks task from the QuickBooks menu bar located on the top of the screen. The menu bar is organized by business areas (for example, customers, vendors, employees).

To create an invoice:

1 From the Customers menu, choose Create Invoices.

The Create Invoices window looks just like a paper invoice form. The upper part of the form is where you enter customer information; the bottom part of the form is where you enter the items or services you've sold.

You can move from field to field by pressing Tab, or you can use the mouse to point to the field you want, and then click the mouse button.

2 Click the drop-down list next to the Customer:Job field.

If you see this arrow next to a field, it means there's a QuickBooks list where you can choose an entry.

3 Choose Kitchen under Jacobsen, Doug from the Customer list.

Notice how QuickBooks automatically fills in other information about the customer.

Point out the address and payment terms.

4 Press Tab three times to move to the Date Field.

QuickBooks automatically displays today's date here (the sample data file is set up with December 15, 2003 as today's date). If you want to change it, all you have to do is press the Plus key (+) or Minus key (-). Now change the date to December 17.

5 Press the Plus key (+) twice to display 12/17/2003.

When you're finished, this is how the top half of the invoice should look.

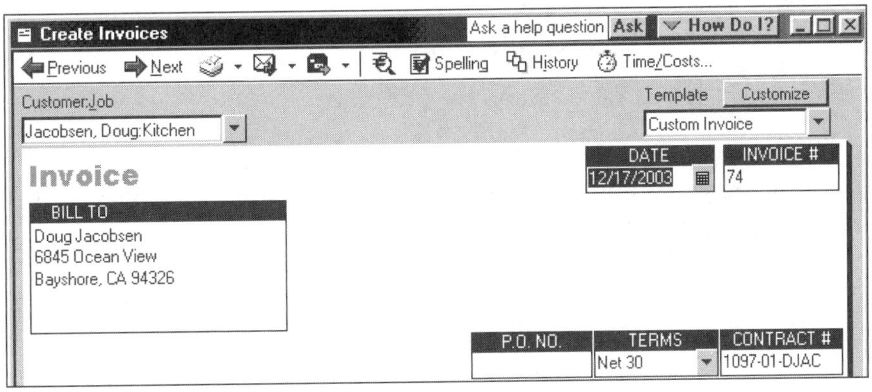

Now you're ready to fill out the bottom half of the invoice form.

Filling in the details

The bottom part of the invoice is where you list the items the customer has purchased. You list each service or product you're selling on its own line of the invoice, along with the amount the customer owes for each item. The lines on this part of the invoice are called line items, because each individual item is on its own line.

All the information about your line items is in the QuickBooks Item list. The Item list stores information about each service you render and each product you sell. It also stores information about other types of line items you'll want to put on invoices, like discounts, sales taxes, and subtotals. You'll be learning more about the Item list later in the course.

To fill in details:

1 Click in the Item column. Then click the arrow next to the field to display the drop-down list.

When you click in the Item column, QuickBooks displays a drop-down list where you can choose the items you want to invoice the customer for.

Suppose you've done nine hours of installation for Doug's kitchen remodelling project.

2 Choose Installation from the drop-down list.

This item is already entered in Rock Castle Construction's Item list, so QuickBooks can automatically fill in the item description and a rate ($35.00). It also knows that this is not a taxable item.

Point out the 0.00 for sales tax below the Amount column.

Now you just need to enter a quantity.

3 Click in the Quantity field, and type ***9***. Then press Tab.

When you enter the quantity, QuickBooks calculates the amount for the nine hours of work.

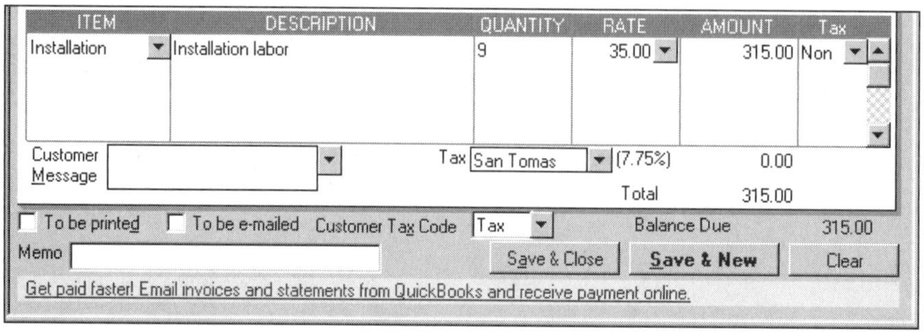

4 Click Save & Close to record the invoice.

Viewing the customer's register

The money owed to your business, by customers or from other sources, is your accounts receivable. When you fill out and save an invoice form, QuickBooks automatically makes an entry for you in your customer's accounts receivable register.

To display the register:

1. From the Customers menu, choose Customer:Job list.
2. Click Jacobsen, Doug once to select it.
3. Click the Activities menu button, and then choose Use Register.

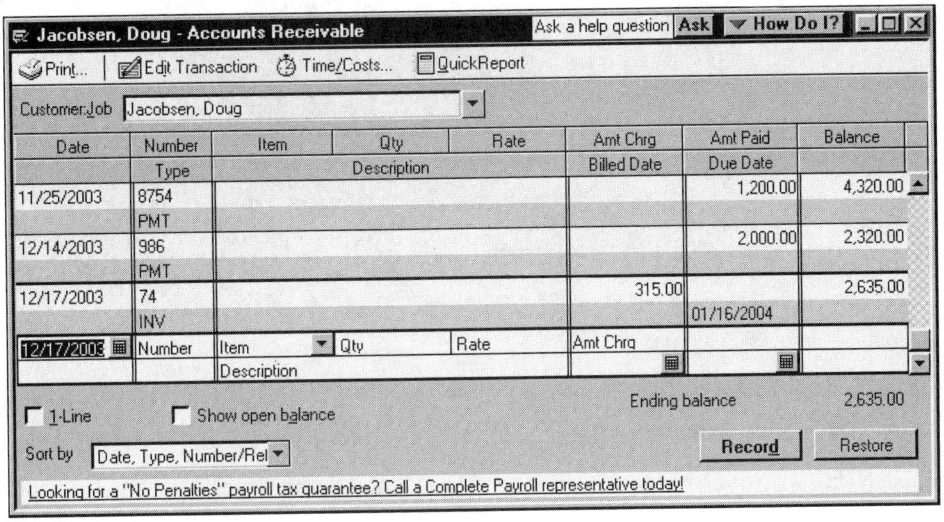

The customer accounts receivable register looks similar to a paper check register. The register shows every transaction for this customer that affects your company's receivables. The invoice you just recorded is in the register in order of its date. The second column shows the invoice number and the type of transaction it is (invoice). When you wrote the invoice, QuickBooks automatically updated the register and account balance.

4. Close the register and then close the Customer:Job List.

Receiving a customer payment

When you receive a payment from a customer for outstanding invoices, you want to record receipt of the payment and indicate which invoices are being paid. Suppose you've received a check in the mail from Pretell Real Estate, a customer that has several outstanding invoices for different jobs. This check is for the job at 155 Wilks Blvd.

To receive a payment:

1. From the Customers menu, choose Receive Payments.
2. From the drop-down list in the Customer:Job field, choose the 155 Wilks Blvd. job under Pretell Real Estate.

QuickBooks lists all the outstanding invoices for the job you entered.

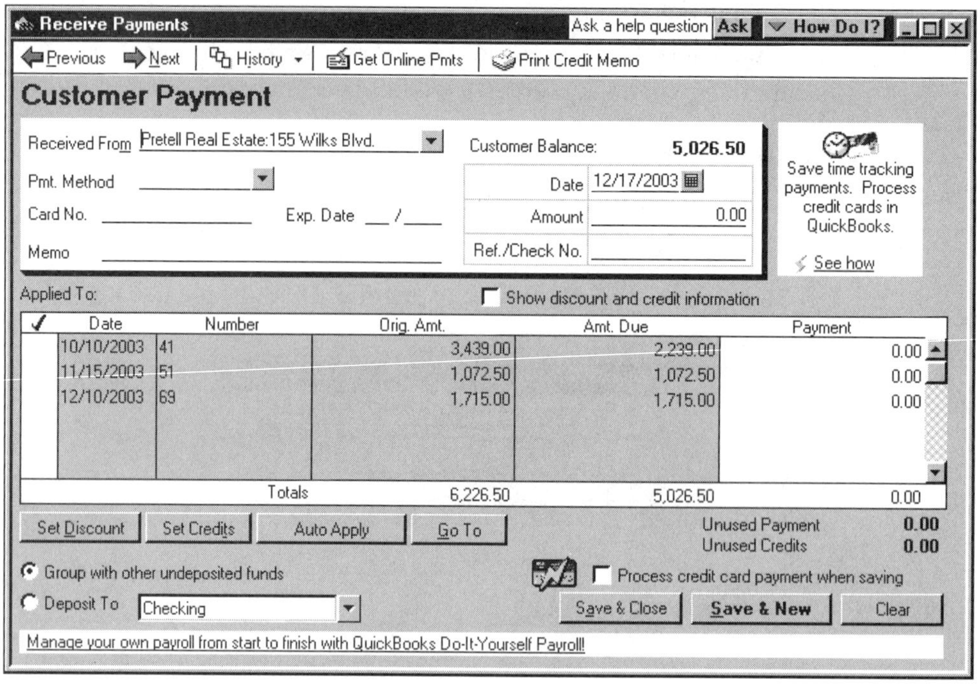

3 In the Amount field, type ***2239*** and press Tab.

4 Type ***659*** in the Ref./Check No. field and press Tab.

5 In the Pmt. Method drop-down list, select Check.

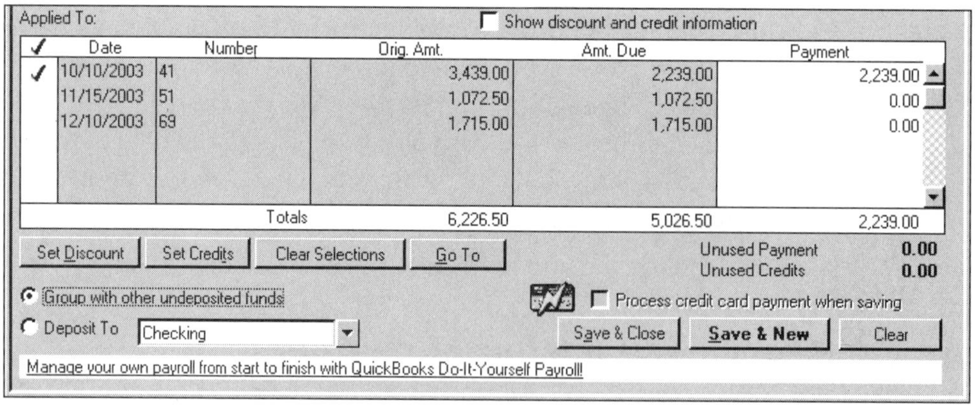

QuickBooks applies the amount to the oldest outstanding invoice, followed by the next oldest invoice. If you want to apply the payment differently, QuickBooks is flexible—you can choose to apply payments to the invoices of your choice. You'll see how to do that later in the course.

6 Make sure "Group with other undeposited funds" is selected.

When you record a customer payment, you have a choice of where to put the payment.

If you want to deposit several payments at once, select "Group with other undeposited funds," and QuickBooks holds the payment in an account called Undeposited Funds until you deposit the payments in a bank account. The Undeposited Funds account is like a cash drawer.

If you are depositing this payment in a bank account by itself, you can click "Deposit to" and choose the bank account. Then QuickBooks records the deposit in the bank account automatically.

7 Click Save & Close.

Making a deposit

If you've selected "Group with other undeposited funds," QuickBooks keeps customer payments in the Undeposited Funds account until you're ready to go to the bank. Then you just tell QuickBooks you're ready to make a deposit.

To record a deposit:

1 From the Banking menu, choose Make Deposits.

The Payments to Deposit window shows all the payments you have in Undeposited Funds waiting to be deposited.

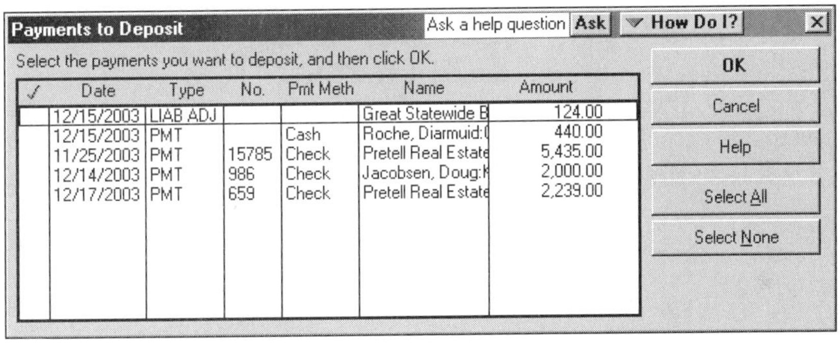

2 Click Select All to place a checkmark next to all the undeposited payments, and click OK.

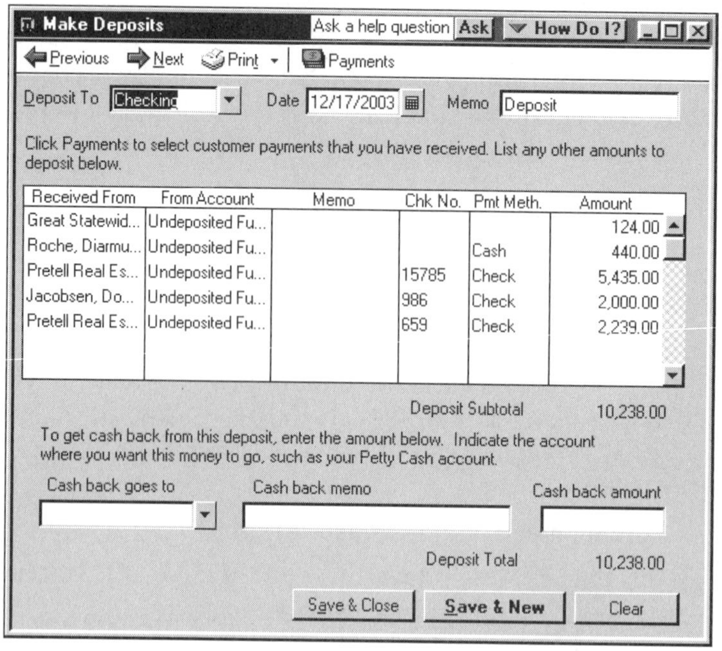

3 In the Make Deposits window, be sure you are set to record the deposit in the checking account, and click Save & Close.

If you click Print in the Make Deposits window before recording the deposit, QuickBooks prints a deposit summary that lists each payment you are depositing.

QuickBooks enters the deposit transaction in your checking account.

You can show students the register if you have time.

Entering and paying bills

Accounts payable is the record of outstanding bills your business owes. By tracking your account payable, you'll know exactly how much you owe and when. This is the only way you can get an accurate picture of your business's finances.

Using accounts payable in QuickBooks is easy: When you're billed for an expense, just enter the bill in QuickBooks when it arrives. This lets QuickBooks track the money you owe vendors in the accounts payable account.

Entering a bill

Suppose you receive a bill from Sergeant Insurance for an insurance premium and want to enter it in QuickBooks but pay it later.

To enter a bill:

1 From the Vendors menu, choose Enter Bills.

2 In the Vendor field, type ***se*** for Sergeant Insurance and press Tab.

QuickBooks fills in the full name, using the feature called QuickFill, since Sergeant Insurance is the only vendor name that begins with "se."

QuickBooks assigns a due date for the bill based on the payment terms you've entered for this vendor. If you don't have specific payment terms assigned, QuickBooks assumes bills are due 10 days from the date of receipt. You can change the due date if you wish.

3 In the Amount Due field, enter ***2000***.

4 Click in the Account column of the Expenses tab, and then click the arrow to display the list of expense accounts.

This part of the form lets you track exactly what you spend your money on. The Expenses tab lets you assign the bill amount to one of your expense accounts; the Items tab is for entering details about service or product items you are purchasing. When you assign a bill to one of your expense accounts, you can later create reports that show how much you've spent in specific areas.

5 Choose Liability Insurance (under Insurance) from the list.

You can also assign expenses to a particular customer or job, in the Customer:Job field. This lets you keep track of your costs for a specific project.

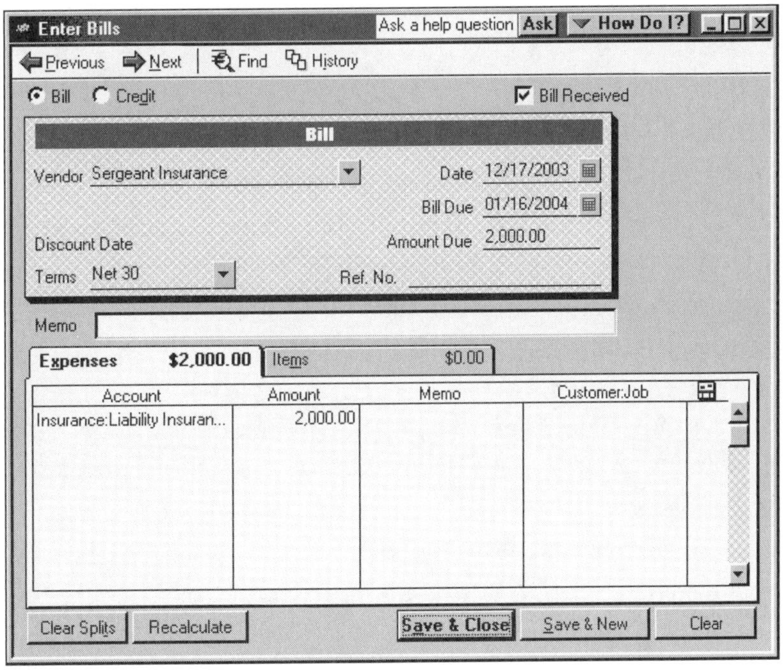

6 Click Save & Close.

When you record a bill, QuickBooks automatically adds the amount due to the vendor's balance.

7 From the Lists menu, choose Vendor List.

QuickBooks displays the Vendor list, which shows outstanding balances for all your vendors.

8 Type "*S*" to go to Sergeant Insurance. Notice the balance is 2000.

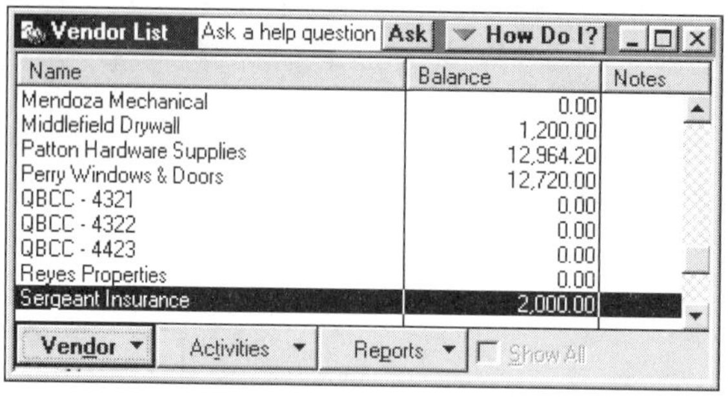

9 Close the Vendor list.

Using QuickBooks to remind you when to pay

QuickBooks has a reminder system that can tell you when you have transactions due. You can set up QuickBooks to display a Reminders window that lists the due dates for each transaction coming due. You can decide whether you want QuickBooks to remind you, and choose exactly which transactions you want to be reminded of.

Any time you want to change the behavior of QuickBooks in a particular area, you go to the Preferences window.

To change preferences:

1 From the Edit menu, choose Preferences.

2 Scroll down through the icons for preferences and click Reminders.

The My Preferences tab for reminders allows you to select whether to display the Reminders window every time you start QuickBooks.

3 Click the Company Preferences tab.

If you share a company file with others, the company preferences are in effect for everyone who uses this file. The Company Preferences tab for reminders lists all the ways QuickBooks can remind you of transactions. For each type of reminder, QuickBooks can give you a detailed list of transactions due, a summary only, or not remind you at all.

4 Click Cancel to close the window.

Any time you want to see the Reminders window, you can choose Reminders from the Company menu.

5 From the Company menu, choose Reminders.

The Reminders window gives you a summary of the transactions coming due. If you want to see a detailed list, you can click the Expand All button.

6 In the Reminders window, click Expand All.

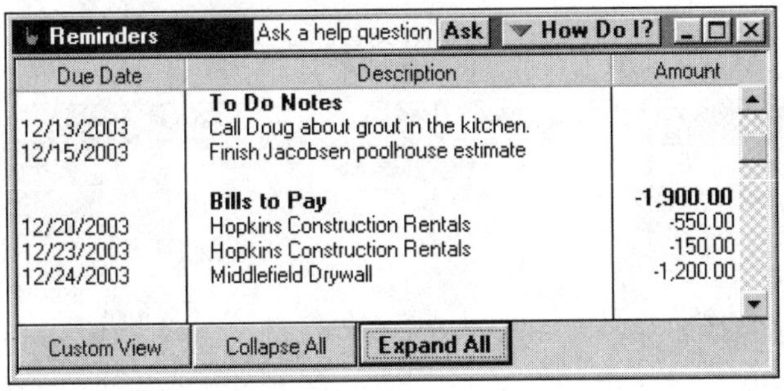

7 Double-click the Bills to Pay transaction for Middlefield Drywall.

QuickBooks displays the original bill form.

8 Close the Enter Bills window; then close the Reminders window.

The Preferences window is where you customize QuickBooks to work the way you want. You'll explore the preferences in more detail as you go through the course.

Paying bills

When QuickBooks reminds you that bill payments are due, you can decide which bills you want to pay and even have QuickBooks print the checks for you.

To record a bill:

1 From the Vendors menu, choose Pay Bills.

QuickBooks displays a list of all bills due on or before 12/27/2003 (which is 10 days after "today"). Just click to select the ones you want to pay, or click Pay All Bills to select all the bills in the window.

Suppose you want to pay by check from your Checking account.

2 Under Payment Method, choose Check and select "To be printed" (that is, be sure there is a checkmark in the box). Be sure that "Checking" is selected as the account under Payment Account.

3 Select the first two bills on the list. To select a bill, click in the left-hand column.

QuickBooks writes the checks for you automatically. It also enters a transaction for them in your checking account. At the same time, it enters a transaction in your accounts payable register, to reduce the total of your amounts payable by the amount of your checks.

If you select "To be printed," you can print the checks from QuickBooks. If you clear the checkbox, QuickBooks enters the checks in your register with numbers. (You can edit the numbers if they are incorrect.)

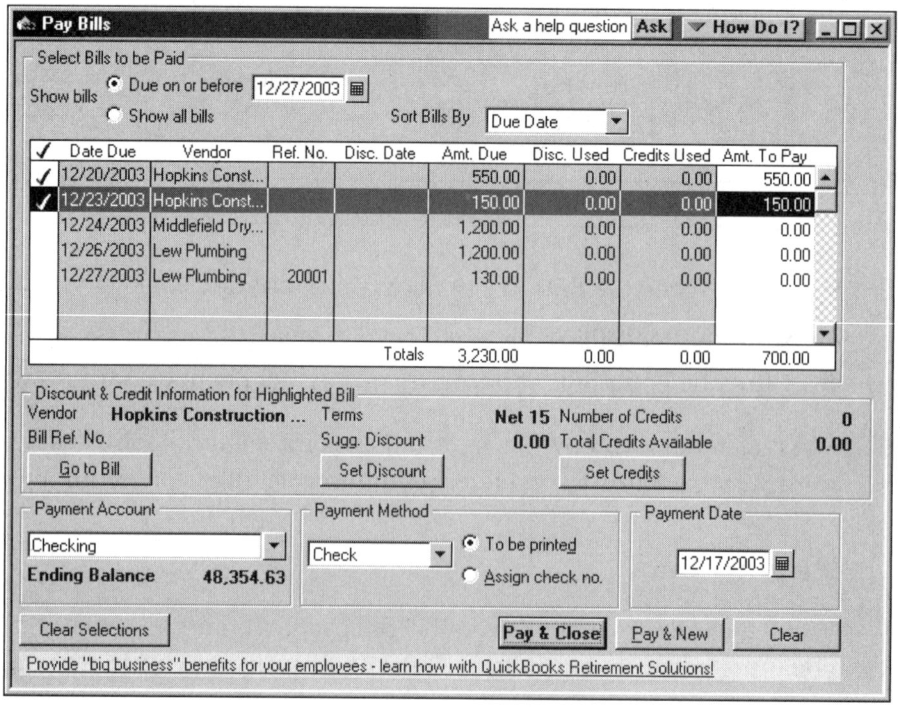

4 Click Pay & Close.

Now look at the checks QuickBooks wrote for you.

5 From the Banking menu, choose Write Checks.

6 At the Write Checks window, be sure the Checking account is in the Bank Account field.

7 Click Previous twice to see the check dated 12/17/2003 that QuickBooks wrote to Hopkins Construction for $700.00. (Notice that QuickBooks wrote one check to cover both bills—one for $550 and $150.)

The window now says Bill Payments (Check) instead of Write Checks to indicate this is a check that QuickBooks wrote to pay a bill.

The lower part of the window lists the bills that this check paid.

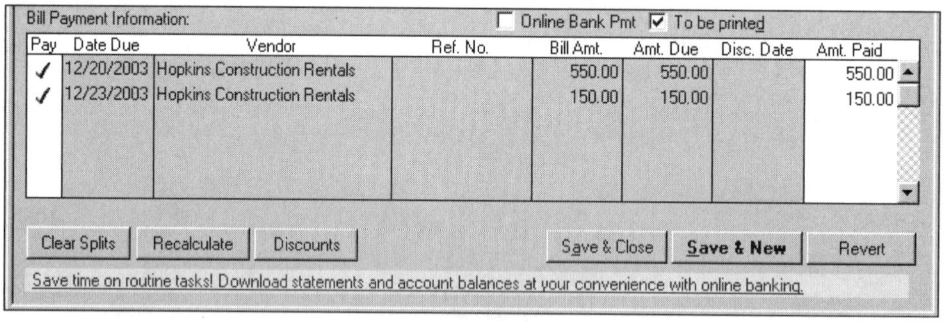

Intuit has checks you can purchase that are made to work with QuickBooks. You can have QuickBooks print all your checks at once, and save yourself from writing checks by hand. You can get Intuit checks for tractor-feed printers or single-sheet printers.

8 Close the Write Checks window.

Now, open the accounts payable register to see how the payments affect your accounts payable. You can open the register of any balance sheet account by starting from the chart of accounts.

To display the accounts payable register:

1 From the Lists menu, choose Chart of Accounts.

You could select the Accounts Payable account, click the Activities menu button at the bottom of the window, and then choose Use Register. But you can use another shortcut: Just double-click any account to open its register.

2 Double-click the Accounts Payable account.

Here's the register with the 12/17/2003 bill payment QuickBooks entered for Hopkins Construction Rentals.

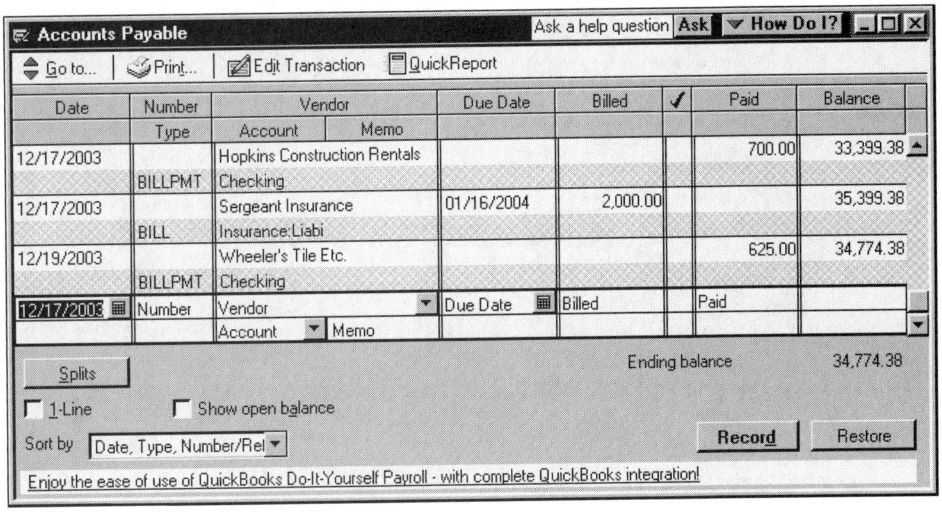

3 Close the Accounts Payable register and the chart of accounts.

Handling purchases you pay for on the spot

When you pay for a purchase on the spot, you don't need to enter a bill first. You can write a check at the Write Checks window for a manually written check or a check you want to print. (You can even set up a QuickBooks "bank" account for petty cash and record "checks" for payments made from petty cash.)

Suppose Kershaw Computer Services sends over a technician to improve the network for your office, and you want to write and print a check.

To record a check:

1. From the Banking menu, choose Write Checks.
2. At the Write Checks window, be sure the Checking account is in the Bank Account field.

   Now, fill out the check the same way you would a paper check.
3. In the "Pay to the Order of" field, select Kershaw Computer Services.
4. Type ***253.45*** as the amount, and press Tab.

   QuickBooks automatically writes the amount for you on the next line.
5. Click in the Account column of the Expenses tab and assign the check to the Office Supplies expense account.
6. To print the check right now, click Print.

   QuickBooks keeps track of two separate check numbers: the number of the last check you printed and the number of the last check you wrote by hand and recorded later. It tells you the number it expects to be the next number for a printed check.

   If you plan to print the check later, click the "To be printed" checkbox to select it.

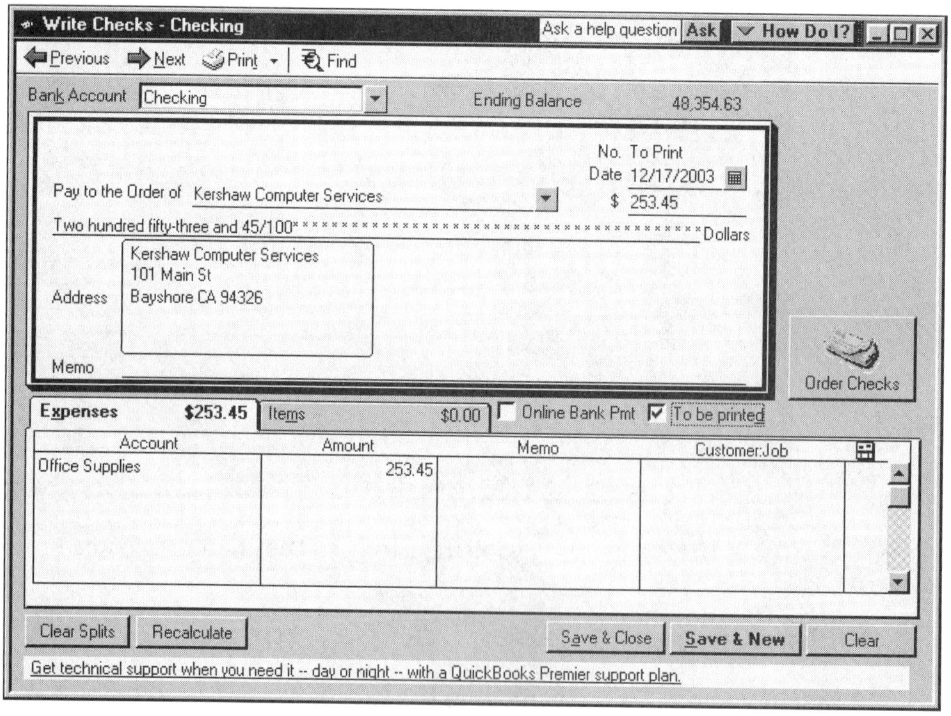

7. Click Save & Close to record the check and close the window.

   Be sure to click Save & Close or Save & New. If you click Clear or close the window, QuickBooks does not record the check.

   QuickBooks enters the check in the register of your checking account.

When you've written a handwritten check (for example, you stop at the office supply store and purchase a box of laser printer paper), just enter the transaction directly in the Write Checks window when you get back to the office.

Managing inventory

If your business has inventory items to resell, you can use QuickBooks to keep track of ordering items, receiving items, paying for items, and selling items.

Ordering inventory

The first step is to order some inventory items. Now, create a purchase order for doors from Perry Windows & Doors.

To create a purchase order:

1 From the Vendors menu, choose Create Purchase Orders.

2 In the Vendor field, start typing ***pe*** and let QuickFill fill in the rest of the vendor name. Press Tab.

3 Click in the Item column and choose Interior under Wood Door from the Item list.

4 In the Qty field, type ***35***. Then press Tab.

QuickBooks multiplies the quantity by the cost to calculate the amount.

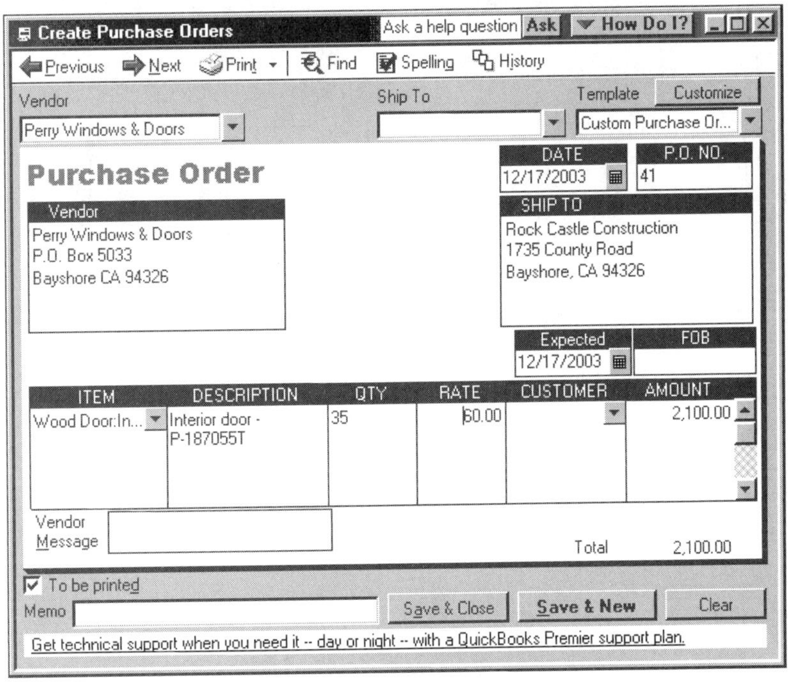

5 Click Save & Close to record the purchase order.

Receiving inventory items

Receiving items is the second step. A few days after you order the doors, they are delivered, and you want to receive the shipment to update your inventory records (the amount of the item you have on hand). Suppose you've received the inventory items, but you haven't received a bill with the items. (This is a very common occurrence.)

To record the receipt of inventory items:

1 From the Vendors menu, choose Receive Items.

2 In the Vendor field, type ***pe***. When QuickFill completes the entry for you, press Tab.

You'll see a message letting you know that open purchase orders exist for Perry, and asking if you want to receive the items against one of the outstanding purchase orders.

3 In the Open PO's Exist window, click Yes.

Now you need to choose the purchase orders filled by the shipment.

QuickBooks lets you receive shipments against multiple purchase orders at one time. That's important, because it's very common for vendors to ship items from different purchase orders in the same shipment.

4 Select both purchase orders.

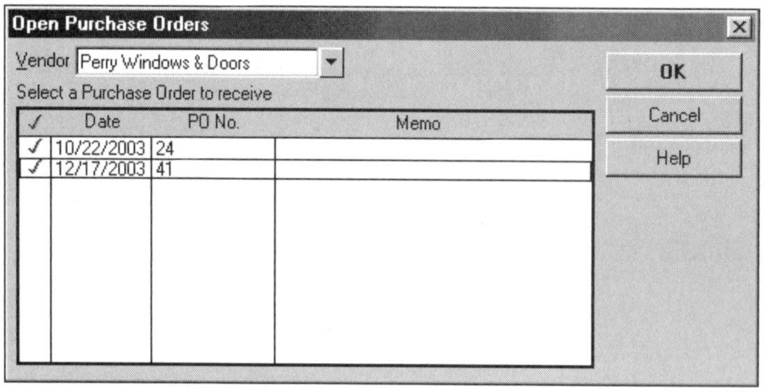

5 Click OK.

QuickBooks looks up the purchase orders you've selected and tells you which items, and how many, you should be receiving. All you have to do is make sure that everything has been shipped in the proper quantities.

Suppose you've received only one of the two windows.

6 Change the 2 in the Qty field for Windows to 1.

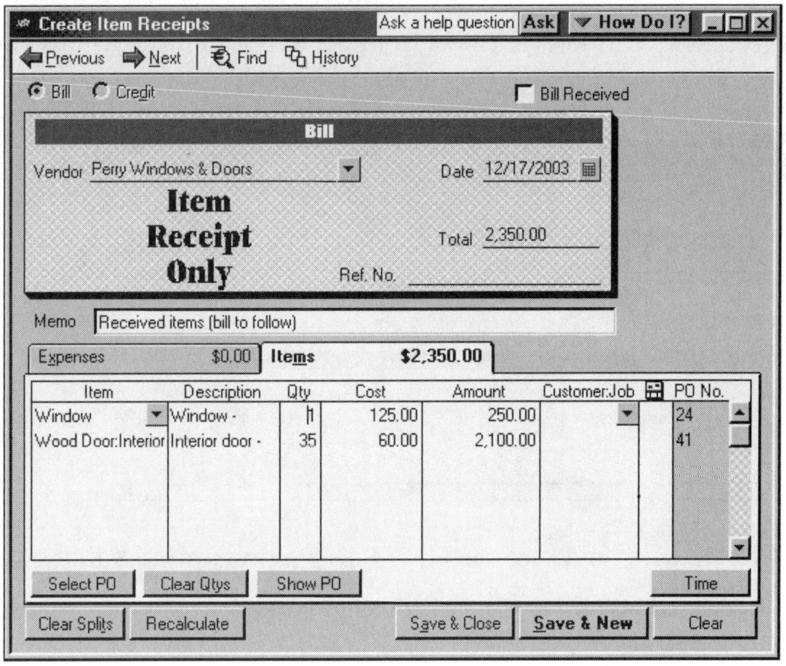

QuickBooks keeps track of the missing two windows, and lets you know they are still due.

7 Click Save & Close to record the item receipt.

Receiving bills after receiving items

The third step is to deal with the final bill for the items you ordered. Perhaps two weeks go by, and you get the bill from Perry. QuickBooks makes it painless to reflect any changes that appear on the final bill. As it turns out, there's one change you need to record when you pay this bill: Perry charged you $32 for shipping.

To record a bill:

1 From the Vendors menu, choose Enter Bill for Received Items.

2 Select Perry Windows & Doors from the Vendor drop-down list, and select the 12/17/2003 item receipt (the one you recorded today).

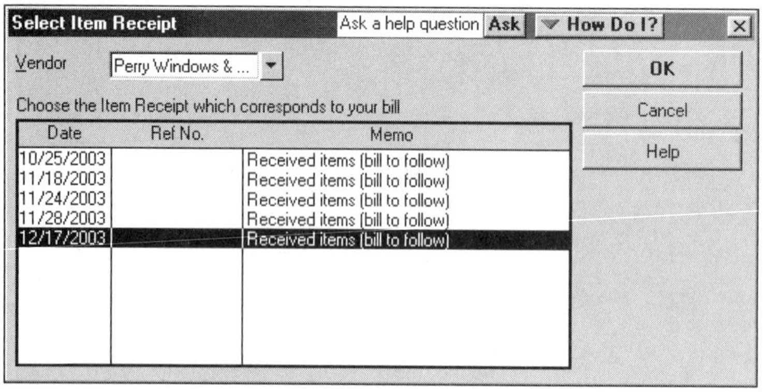

3 Click OK, and you'll see the Enter Bills window with the items already filled in.

4 Click the Expenses tab and type ***Postage and Delivery*** in the Account field and press Tab.

5 At the message telling you that QuickBooks could not find the account, click Set Up.

6 In the New Account window, make sure Expense is listed in the Type field and click OK.

7 Enter the $32 shipping charge in the Amount field to assign it to the Postage and Delivery account.

8 Press Tab.

9 Click Recalculate.

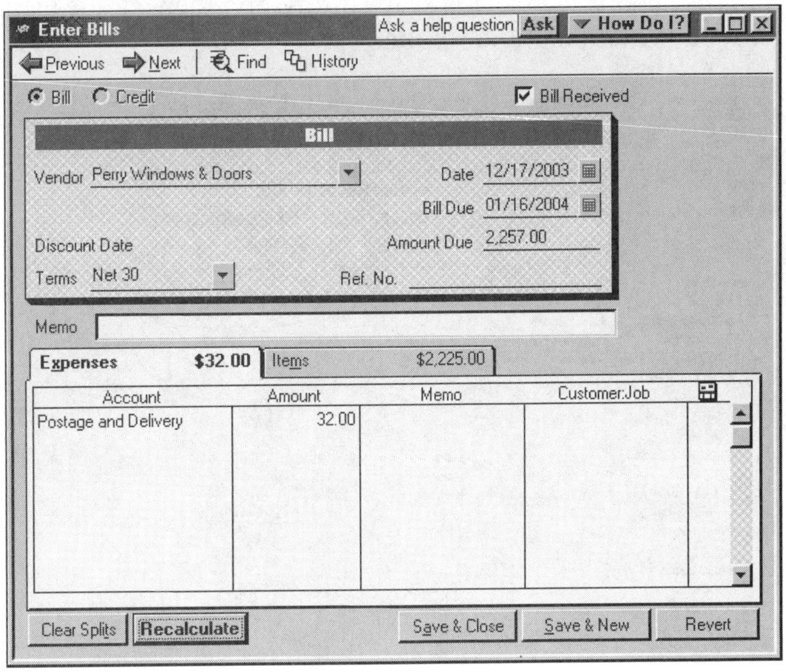

10 Click Save & Close to record the bill.

11 If QuickBooks displays a message asking if you want to change the transaction, click Yes.

Selling items

You can sell inventory items by creating an invoice the same way you did earlier. QuickBooks automatically keeps track of the items sold and updates your financial reports. If you sell three doors, QuickBooks automatically reduces the number of doors on hand by three, and adds both the revenue and the cost of goods sold associated with these doors to your financial reports.

Generating inventory reports

QuickBooks has a variety of inventory reports to tell you everything you might want to know about your inventory. Now that you've entered the bill, you can generate an inventory stock status by item report to make sure that all the items you've received are accounted for.

To generate an inventory report:

1 From the Reports menu, choose Inventory, and then choose Inventory Stock Status by Item from the submenu.

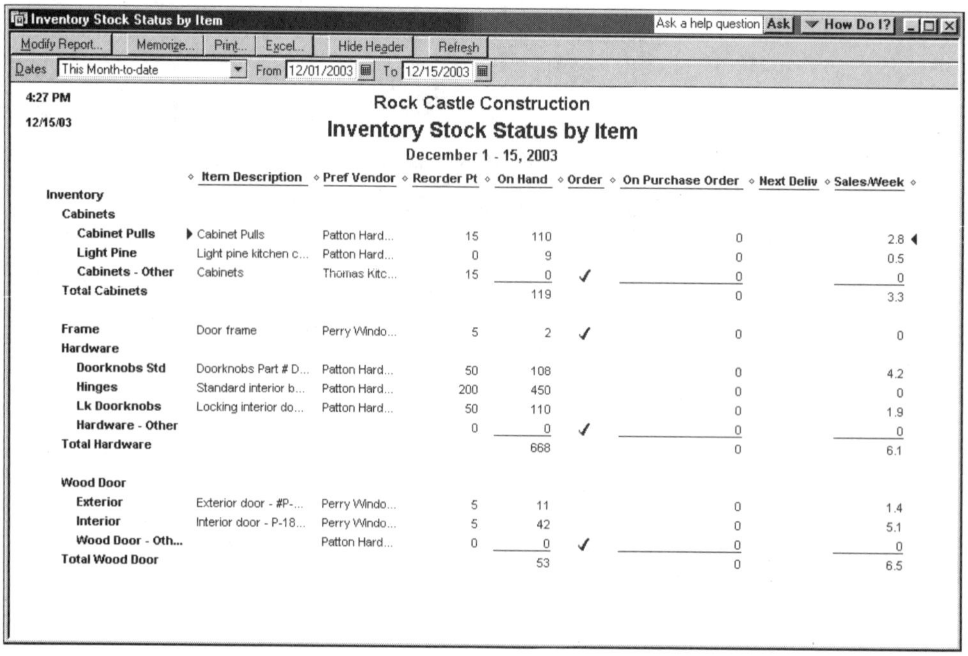

	Item Description	Pref Vendor	Reorder Pt	On Hand	Order	On Purchase Order	Next Deliv	Sales/Week
Inventory								
Cabinets								
Cabinet Pulls	Cabinet Pulls	Patton Hard...	15	110		0		2.8
Light Pine	Light pine kitchen c...	Patton Hard...	0	9		0		0.5
Cabinets - Other	Cabinets	Thomas Kitc...	15	0	✓	0		0
Total Cabinets				119		0		3.3
Frame	Door frame	Perry Windo...	5	2	✓	0		0
Hardware								
Doorknobs Std	Doorknobs Part # D...	Patton Hard...	50	108		0		4.2
Hinges	Standard interior b...	Patton Hard...	200	450		0		0
Lk Doorknobs	Locking interior do...	Patton Hard...	50	110		0		1.9
Hardware - Other			0	0	✓	0		0
Total Hardware				668		0		6.1
Wood Door								
Exterior	Exterior door - #P-...	Perry Windo...	5	11		0		1.4
Interior	Interior door - P-18...	Perry Windo...	5	42		0		5.1
Wood Door - Oth...		Patton Hard...	0	0	✓	0		0
Total Wood Door				53		0		6.5

For each inventory item, this report shows quantity on hand, quantity on order, date of next order receipt, and the average quantity sold per week.

If you want to see the transactions that make up any amount in a report, you can use the QuickZoom feature. Whenever you see the mouse pointer change from an arrow to a magnifying glass with a Z inside, double-click the amount you want to investigate.

2 Double-click the line for Cabinet Pulls on the report.

QuickBooks creates a QuickReport that shows more detail on that specific inventory item. You can also use QuickZoom from here.

3 On the QuickReport, double-click the Item Receipt transaction.

Now you see the Item Receipt recording the receipt of cabinet pulls.

4 From the Window menu, choose Close All to close all the windows you have open.

Creating reports and graphs

The Reports menu has a wide variety of preset reports. You can customize any of the preset reports to show the exact data you need. To create a report, you choose the report you want from the QuickBooks Reports menu.

To generate a report of overdue customers and balances:

1. From the Reports menu, choose Customers & Receivables, and then choose A/R Aging Summary.

   The report lists the jobs with open balances for each customer. The columns show which amounts are current (not yet due) and which are overdue. Notice that Brian Cook is more than 30 days overdue on his kitchen job.

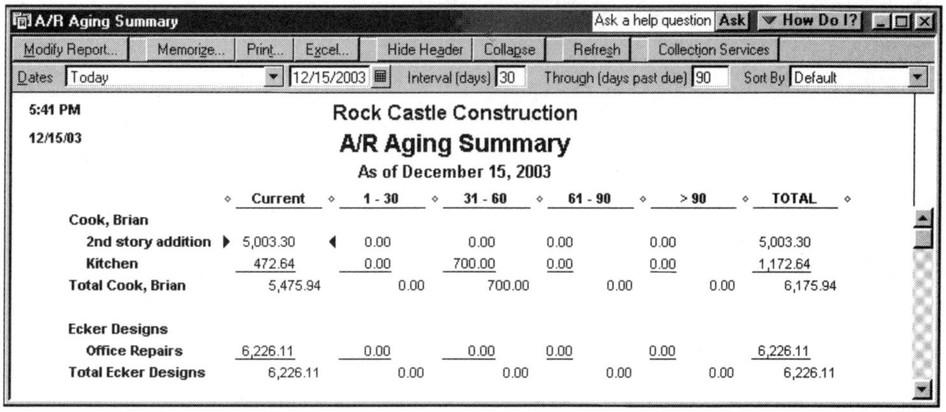

2. To see whether anyone is more than 60 days overdue, change the "Through (days past due)" field at the top of the report from 90 to 60. Press Tab.

   QuickBooks makes a column for >60. Since all the amounts in that column are 0.00, you can see that no one is more than 60 days overdue.

3. Click No at the message asking if you would like to memorize the report.
4. Close the report window.

If you want to see a visual display of how much you're owed by customers, you can create an accounts receivable graph.

To create an accounts receivable graph:

1. From the Reports menu, choose Customers & Receivables and then choose Accounts Receivable Graph.
2. When you finish viewing the graph, close the graph window.

APPENDIX B What's new in QuickBooks 2003

Summary of new features in QuickBooks 2003

QuickBooks Basic, QuickBooks Pro, QuickBooks Premier, and QuickBooks Premier: Accountant Edition 2003 offer new features that give you fast access to information about your company, improve your productivity, and provide new services that can simplify your day-to-day business transactions.

QuickBooks Basic, QuickBooks Pro, and QuickBooks Premier

The features described in this section are available in QuickBooks Basic, QuickBooks Pro, and QuickBooks Premier products.

- Automated and scheduled backups
- Easier budgeting features
- Ability to assign classes to finance charges, service charges, etc. You can also specify classes on a line-by-line basis for items on invoices and other forms. A new P & L report lists accounts that lack class assignments.

QuickBooks Pro and QuickBooks Premier products only

The features described in this section are available in QuickBooks Pro and QuickBooks Premier products only.

- Advanced budgeting features that allow users to create budgets based on last year's data
- More forms customization options. Access to the Forms Template Library with over 100 downloadable forms available (online and via the QuickBooks CD-ROM)
- Sales order tracking
- Integrates with more business applications

QuickBooks Premier and Premier: Accountant Edition only

QuickBooks Premier and QuickBooks Premier: Accountant Edition contain the additional features described in this section.

- Forecasting with two reports to analyze data
- Ability to create inventory assembly items for manufacturing and retail. These items are tracked, reported and sold as single items.

QuickBooks Premier: Accountant Edition only

The following features are found only in QuickBooks Premier: Accountant Edition.

- Customized reports for accountants
- Condensed report with more concise information
- General journal entry: one-click access to the journal from any form, displays a list of entries on the Make Journal Entry window, access to five reports from this window.
- Financial reports that include Debit and Credit columns
- Additional tax line assignments and income tax preparation report enhancements

APPENDIX C Course handouts

Using the course handouts

In this section, you'll find copies of all the handouts referenced in this course. The handout files are included on your QuickBooks exercise CD-ROM, and have been saved in rich text format (RTF). You can open the file containing the handouts (handout.rtf) using your word processor allowing you to print and modify the handouts as desired.

Handout 1

Course Syllabus

Introduction

Lesson 1—Getting started

Course introduction
Introducing QuickBooks
Getting around in QuickBooks
All the accounting you need to know
Exiting QuickBooks
Moving between company files

Lesson 2—Setting up QuickBooks

Creating a QuickBooks company
Entering company info
Setting up QuickBooks preferences
Choosing a start date
Setting up income and expense accounts
Providing details about your income
Entering opening balances
Finishing the Interview
Getting help while using QuickBooks

Lesson 3—Working with lists

Using QuickBooks lists
Editing the chart of accounts
Working with the Customer:Job list
Working with the Employee list
Working with the Vendor list
Adding custom fields
Managing lists

Lesson 4—Working with bank accounts

Writing a QuickBooks check
Using bank account registers
Entering a handwritten check
Transferring money between accounts
Reconciling checking accounts

Lesson 5—Working with other accounts

Using other account types in QuickBooks
Tracking credit card transactions
Working with asset accounts
Working with liability accounts
Understanding equity accounts

Handout 1 (continued)

Lesson 6—Entering sales and invoices

Using sales forms in QuickBooks
Filling in a sales form
Memorizing a sale
Entering a new service item
Using multiple price levels
Using statements to bill customers
Processing sales orders

Lesson 7—Receiving payments and making deposits

Recording customer payments
Making deposits

Lesson 8—Entering and paying bills

Handling bills in QuickBooks
Using QuickBooks for accounts payable
Entering bills
Paying bills

Lesson 9—Analyzing financial data

Reports and graphs help you understand your business
Creating QuickReports
Creating and customizing preset reports
Saving report settings
Printing reports
Exporting reports to Microsoft Excel
Creating QuickInsight graphs

Lesson 10—Setting up inventory

Turning on the inventory feature
Entering products into inventory
Ordering products
Receiving inventory
Entering a bill for inventory
Manually adjusting inventory
Tracking finished goods

Lesson 11—Tracking and paying sales tax

Overview of sales tax in QuickBooks
Setting up your tax rates and agencies
Applying tax to each sale
Determining what you owe
Paying your tax agencies

Handout 1 (continued)

Lesson 12—Doing payroll with QuickBooks

- Overview of payroll tracking
- Setting up for payroll
- Setting up employee payroll information
- Writing a paycheck
- Tracking your tax liabilities
- Paying payroll taxes

Lesson 13—Estimating and progress invoicing

- Creating jobs and estimates
- Writing an estimate
- Creating multiple estimates
- Creating an invoice from an estimate
- Displaying reports for estimates
- Updating job status

Lesson 14—Tracking time

- Tracking time
- Invoicing a customer based on time
- Displaying project reports for time tracking
- Paying nonemployees for time worked

Lesson 15—Customizing forms and writing QuickBooks Letters

- About QuickBooks forms
- Customizing invoices
- Designing custom layouts for forms
- Using QuickBooks Letters

Appendix A—Instructor demonstration of QuickBooks

Appendix B—New features in QuickBooks 2003

Appendix C—Course handouts

Handout 2

Record your daily transactions on QuickBooks forms

Some examples of forms you use in QuickBooks include the following:

- Invoices
- Purchase orders
- Checks

The Write Checks window looks just like a check.

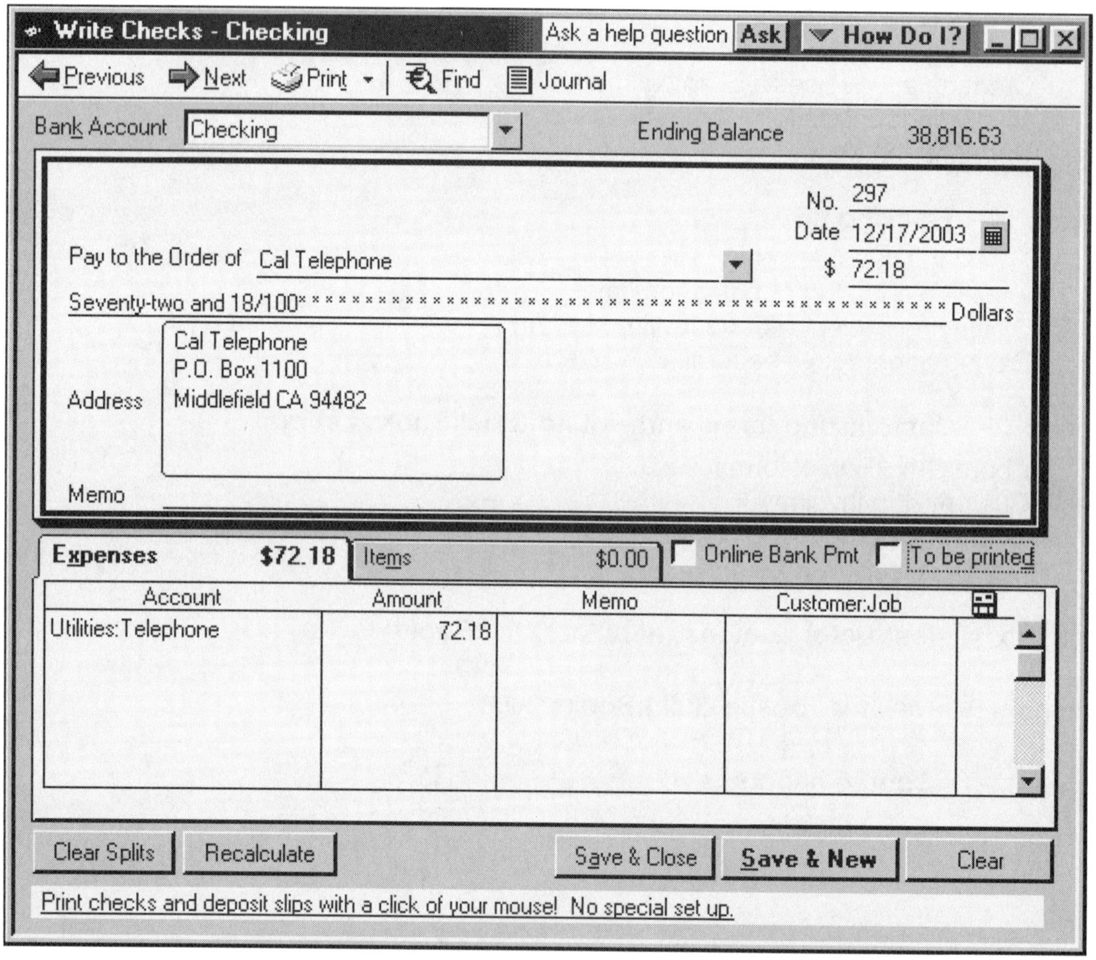

You fill out most forms by choosing from lists.

Handout 3

Information stored in the Customer list

Here's an example of the information stored in customer records in the Customer:Job list.

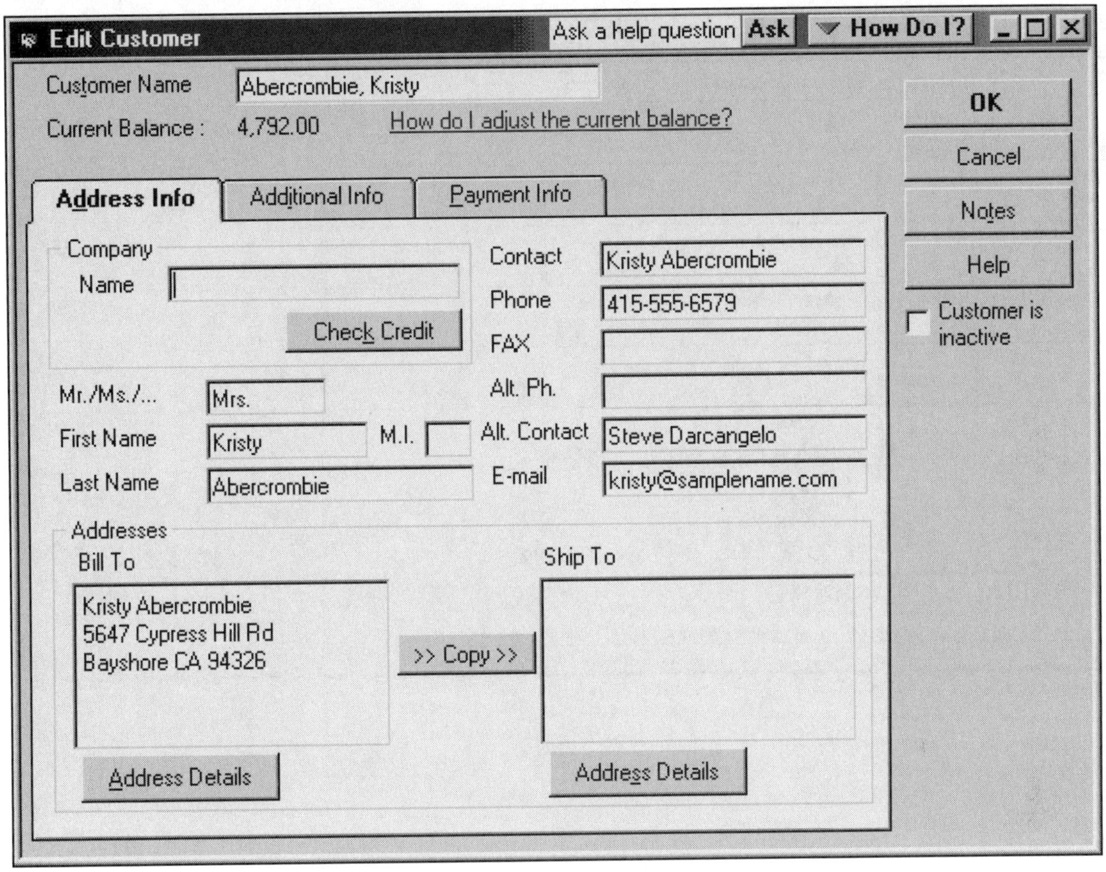

Handout 4

Register for an accounts receivable account

Registers show all the activity in one account.

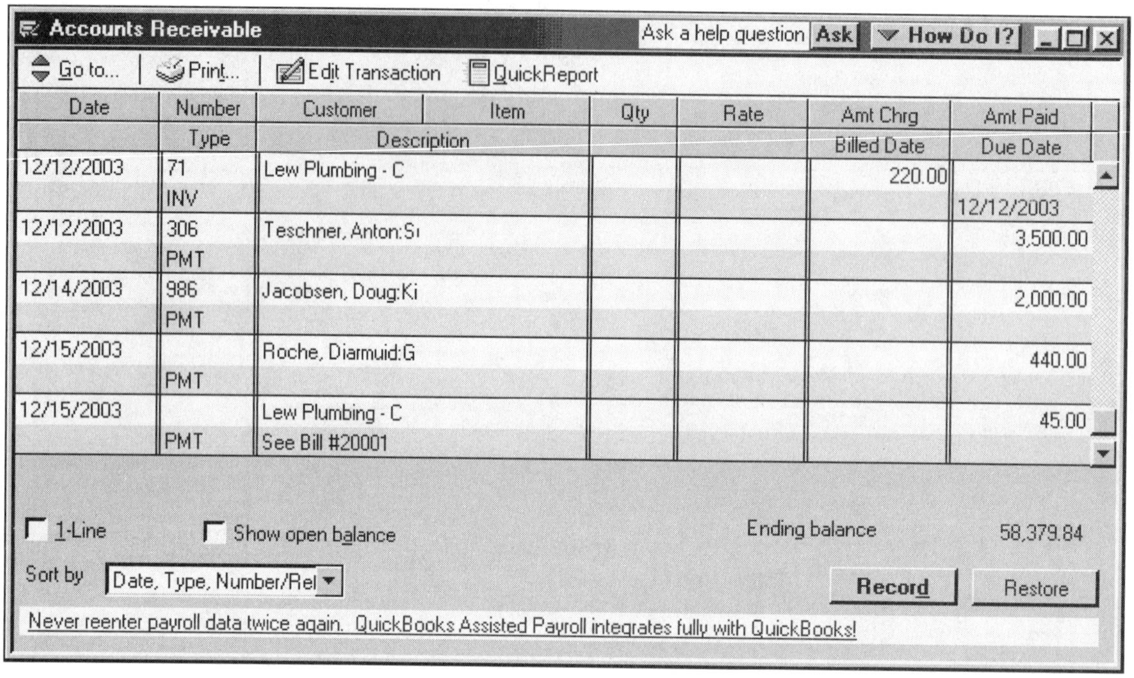

Date	Number / Type	Customer / Description	Item	Qty	Rate	Amt Chrg / Billed Date	Amt Paid / Due Date
12/12/2003	71 / INV	Lew Plumbing - C				220.00	12/12/2003
12/12/2003	306 / PMT	Teschner, Anton:S					3,500.00
12/14/2003	986 / PMT	Jacobsen, Doug:Ki					2,000.00
12/15/2003	PMT	Roche, Diarmuid:G					440.00
12/15/2003	PMT	Lew Plumbing - C / See Bill #20001					45.00

Handout 5

The QuickBooks chart of accounts

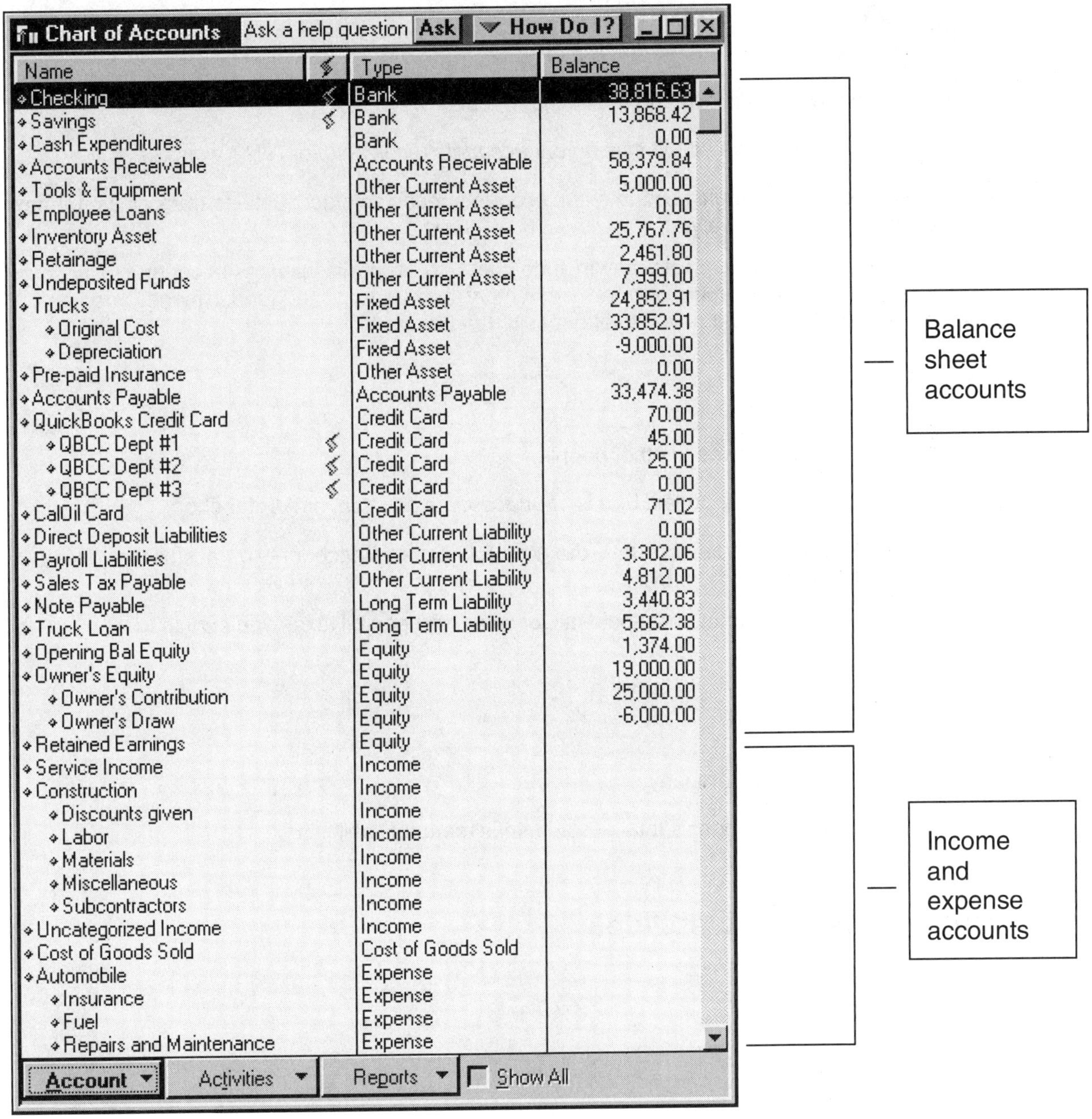

Name	Type	Balance
Checking	Bank	38,816.63
Savings	Bank	13,868.42
Cash Expenditures	Bank	0.00
Accounts Receivable	Accounts Receivable	58,379.84
Tools & Equipment	Other Current Asset	5,000.00
Employee Loans	Other Current Asset	0.00
Inventory Asset	Other Current Asset	25,767.76
Retainage	Other Current Asset	2,461.80
Undeposited Funds	Other Current Asset	7,999.00
Trucks	Fixed Asset	24,852.91
Original Cost	Fixed Asset	33,852.91
Depreciation	Fixed Asset	-9,000.00
Pre-paid Insurance	Other Asset	0.00
Accounts Payable	Accounts Payable	33,474.38
QuickBooks Credit Card	Credit Card	70.00
QBCC Dept #1	Credit Card	45.00
QBCC Dept #2	Credit Card	25.00
QBCC Dept #3	Credit Card	0.00
CalOil Card	Credit Card	71.02
Direct Deposit Liabilities	Other Current Liability	0.00
Payroll Liabilities	Other Current Liability	3,302.06
Sales Tax Payable	Other Current Liability	4,812.00
Note Payable	Long Term Liability	3,440.83
Truck Loan	Long Term Liability	5,662.38
Opening Bal Equity	Equity	1,374.00
Owner's Equity	Equity	19,000.00
Owner's Contribution	Equity	25,000.00
Owner's Draw	Equity	-6,000.00
Retained Earnings	Equity	
Service Income	Income	
Construction	Income	
Discounts given	Income	
Labor	Income	
Materials	Income	
Miscellaneous	Income	
Subcontractors	Income	
Uncategorized Income	Income	
Cost of Goods Sold	Cost of Goods Sold	
Automobile	Expense	
Insurance	Expense	
Fuel	Expense	
Repairs and Maintenance	Expense	

Handout 6

About assets, liabilities, and equity

Assets

- Include both what you have and what other people owe you.
- The money people owe you is called your *accounts receivable*, or A/R for short.
- QuickBooks uses a single account—the accounts receivable account—to track all the money that different people owe you.

The rest of your company's assets may include checking accounts, savings accounts, petty cash, fixed assets (such as equipment or trucks), inventory, and undeposited funds (money you've received from customers but haven't yet deposited *in the bank).*

Liabilities

- What your company owes to other people.
- The money you owe for unpaid bills is your *accounts payable,* or A/P for short.
- QuickBooks uses a single account—the accounts payable account—to track all the money you owe different people for bills.

A liability can be a formal loan, an unpaid bill, or sales and payroll taxes you owe to the government.

Equity

- The net worth of your company.
- Equity equals the company's total assets minus the total liabilities.

Equity = Assets - Liabilities

Handout 7

Sample balance sheet

Rock Castle Construction

3/31/03 **Balance Sheet**

As of March 31, 2003

ASSETS	
Current Assets	
Checking/Savings	29,454.55
Accounts Receivable	94,246.05
Other Current Assets	93.19
Total Current Assets	123,793.79
Fixed Assets	43,900.00
TOTAL ASSETS	167,693.79
LIABILITIES & EQUITY	
Liabilities	
Current Liabilities	
Accounts Payable	44,118.16
Credit Cards	1,129.36
Other Current Liabilities	2,655.72
Total Current Liabilities	47,903.24
Long Term Liabilities	8,470.96
Total Liabilities	56,374.20
Equity	111,319.59
TOTAL LIABILITIES & EQUITY	167,693.79

Handout 8

Sample profit & loss statement

Rock Castle Construction

04/01/03 **Profit and Loss**

January through March 2003

	Jan - Mar '03
Ordinary Income/Expense	
Income	
Labor income	46,935.00
Markup income	4,865.46
Materials income	7,976.18
Sales income	12,000.00
Subcontractor income	32,319.00
Total Income	104,095.64
Expense	
Legal	125.00
Office Supplies	11.87
Payroll Expenses	45,751.23
Reimbursable Expenses	44,572.18
Rent	1,150.00
Telephone	103.76
Truck	293.18
Worker's Comp	4,518.00
Total Expense	96,525.22
Net Ordinary Income	7,570.42
Other Income/Expense	
Other Income	
Interest Income	45.87
Total Other Income	45.87
Net Other Income	45.87
Net Income	7,616.29

Handout 9

Setting up QuickBooks

After installing the QuickBooks program, follow these steps to set up QuickBooks for your company:

1. Choose a QuickBooks start date, and set up your company with the EasyStep Interview.
2. Fine-tune your chart of accounts and enter historical transactions.
3. Finish entering payroll information (add new payroll items, finish entering employee payroll information, and so on).
4. Complete customer and vendor information.
5. Complete the Item list.

Handout 10

How to choose a start date

If today is close to the end of your fiscal year, the last day of your fiscal year is an excellent start date. You'll probably have an accurate balance sheet to enter in QuickBooks.

If today is midway in your fiscal year, ask yourself whether you really want to enter all transactions from the beginning of the year.

- **If the answer is no**, choose a more manageable start date, such as the end of the last quarter or the end of last month.
- **If the answer is yes**, choose the end of your last fiscal year as your start date. You will then have complete records in QuickBooks for the current fiscal year.

Handout 11

QuickBooks balance sheet accounts

This account type...	*Tracks...*
Bank account	Checking, savings, and money market accounts. Add one bank account for every account your company has at a bank or other financial institution. (You should also use this type for petty cash.)
Accounts receivable (A/R)	Transactions related to the customers who owe you money, including invoices, payments, deposits of payments, refunds, and credit memos. Most companies have only one A/R account.
Other current asset	Assets likely to be converted to cash or used up within one year, such as notes receivable due within a year, prepaid expenses, and security deposits.
Fixed asset	Long-term notes receivable and depreciable assets your company owns that aren't likely to be converted into cash within a year, such as equipment or furniture.
Accounts payable (A/P)	Transactions related to the vendors to whom you owe money, including your company's outstanding bills, bill payments, and any credit you have with vendors.
Credit card	Credit card purchases, bills, payments, and credits.
Current liability	Liabilities scheduled to be paid within one year, such as sales tax, payroll taxes, accrued or deferred salaries, and short-term loans.
Long-term liability	Liabilities such as loans or mortgages scheduled to be paid over periods longer than one year.
Equity	Owner's equity, including capital investment, drawings, and retained earnings.

Handout 12

Registers associated with QuickBooks windows

You can display the register associated with a window by choosing **Use Register** from the Edit menu.

While you have this window displayed:	***You can display the register for this account:***
Create Invoices	Accounts Receivable
Enter Bills	Accounts Payable
Write Checks	The account you have displayed in the Bank Account field on the check form
Receive Payments	Accounts Receivable
Make Deposits	The account you have displayed in the *Deposit To* field, or Undeposited Funds if that option is selected
Enter Sales Receipts	The account you have displayed in the Deposit To field
Create Credit Memos/Refunds	Accounts Receivable
Enter Credit Card Charges	The account you have displayed in the *Credit Card* field

Handout 13

Using the keyboard to move around a register

To do this:	*Press these keys:*
Move up or down one transaction at a time	↑, ↓
Move up or down one screenful at a time	PgUp, PgDn
Move to beginning of previous or next month	Ctrl+PgUp, Ctrl+PgDn
Move to beginning of register	Ctrl+Home
Move to end of register	Ctrl+End

Handout 14

Determining the value of a fixed asset

Fixed asset: Equipment or property your business owns that is not for sale (for example, a computer system or a company vehicle).

Because fixed assets wear out or become obsolete, their value declines constantly from the day you purchase them. The amount of this decline in value is **depreciation**.

The value of a fixed asset equals

the Original Cost

minus

the Accumulated Depreciation
(the total amount of depreciation
since the asset's purchase)

Handout 15

Tracking asset cost and depreciation

1 Create a fixed asset account for each asset (or group of assets) you want to depreciate.

2 Add two subaccounts to each asset account you created. One subaccount tracks the cost of the asset, the other tracks accumulated depreciation. If you acquired the asset after your QuickBooks start date, you enter 0.00 as the opening balance for both accounts.

3 Create an expense account to track depreciation expense. Give the account a name like "Depreciation Expense."

4 When it's time to enter an asset's depreciation, enter the depreciation amount as a decrease in the asset's Accumulated Depreciation account.

5 When you take out a loan to pay for the asset, create a long-term liability account to track the loan (with an opening balance of 0.00).

6 Enter the amount of the loan as an increase in the asset's Cost account. Assign the transaction to your loan liability account.

Handout 16

Understanding QuickBooks equity accounts

Equity = Assets – Liabilities

If you sold all of your assets today, and you paid off your liabilities using the money received from the sale of your assets, the money you'd have left would be your equity.

QuickBooks equity accounts

QuickBooks adds these accounts for you:

Opening Bal Equity

When you set up your QuickBooks company file as of a particular start date, you may already have company assets and liabilities as of that date. As you tell QuickBooks the opening balances of your assets and liabilities, QuickBooks automatically tracks the amount of equity in the Opening Bal Equity account.

Retained Earnings

This account tracks your company's net income from previous fiscal years. QuickBooks automatically transfers your profit (or loss) to Retained Earnings at the end of each fiscal year.

Handout 17

Create Invoices window

In QuickBooks, an invoice is a form on which you record details about a sale to a customer who owes you money.

An invoice lists the services you are providing or the products you are selling. It also shows the quantity and price or rate of each item (unless you choose an invoice design that does not show them).

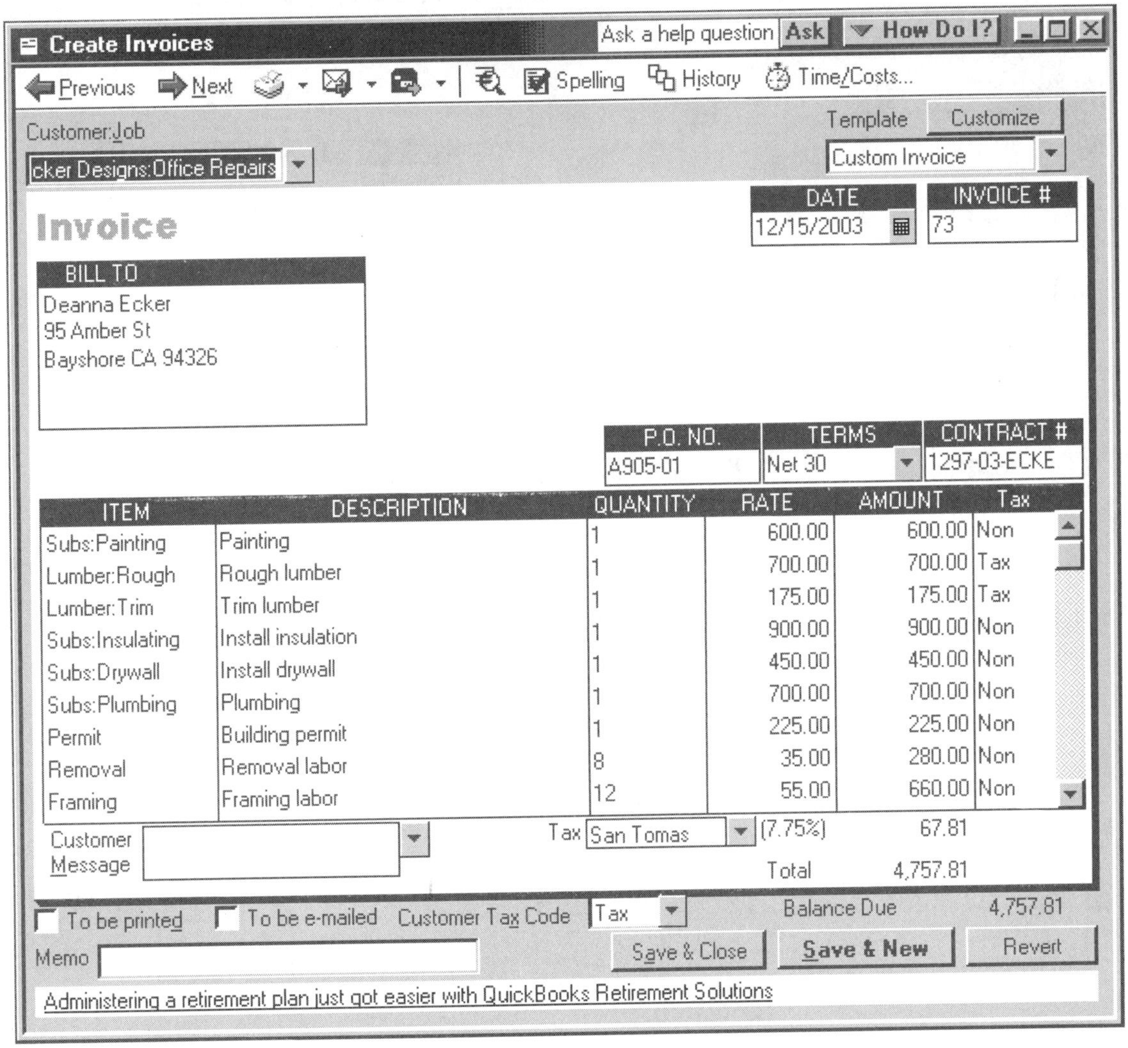

ITEM	DESCRIPTION	QUANTITY	RATE	AMOUNT	Tax
Subs:Painting	Painting	1	600.00	600.00	Non
Lumber:Rough	Rough lumber	1	700.00	700.00	Tax
Lumber:Trim	Trim lumber	1	175.00	175.00	Tax
Subs:Insulating	Install insulation	1	900.00	900.00	Non
Subs:Drywall	Install drywall	1	450.00	450.00	Non
Subs:Plumbing	Plumbing	1	700.00	700.00	Non
Permit	Building permit	1	225.00	225.00	Non
Removal	Removal labor	8	35.00	280.00	Non
Framing	Framing labor	12	55.00	660.00	Non

Handout 18

Enter Sales Receipts window

To record what you sold and received full payment for at the time of sale, use the Enter Sales Receipts window.

You can print the form to use as a customer receipt if you wish.

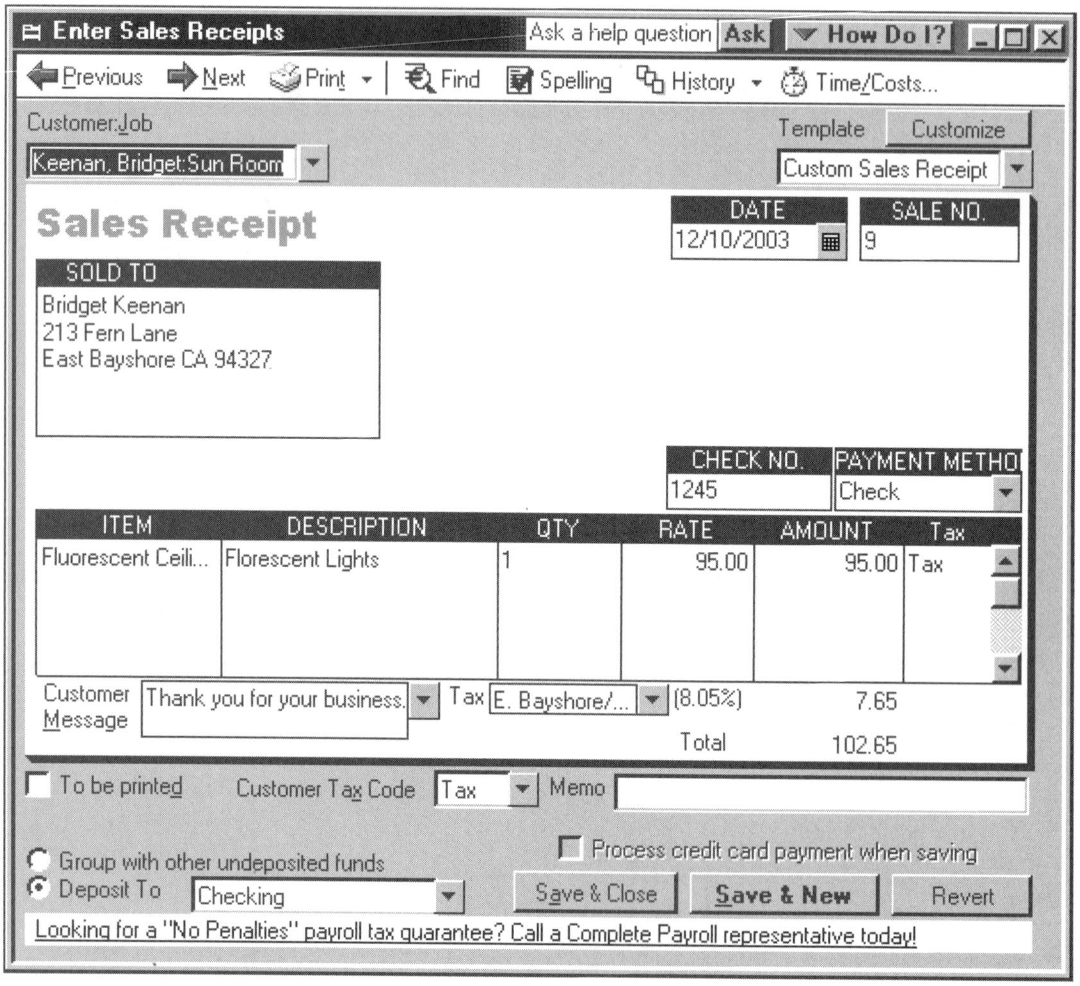

Handout 19

Choosing a format for sales forms

Use this format . . .	*If you . . .*
Service	Primarily sell services but occasionally sell goods.
Professional	Sell services and need a lot of room for descriptions of your services.
Product	Sell parts or products and need fields relevant to shipping.
Custom	Want to tailor a form to your type of business.

Handout 20

Types of QuickBooks items

Whether you're recording a sale or a purchase, you use items from your Item list to fill out the form quickly. When you choose an item in the **Item** field on the form, QuickBooks fills in the description, rate or price, and then calculates the amount.

	Items for things you sell or purchase
Type	***Use when recording sales for***
Service	Services you charge for or services you purchase.
	EXAMPLES: Professional fees, labor
Inventory Part	Items you purchase, track as inventory, and then resell.
	EXAMPLES: Electrical outlets, T-shirts
Inventory Assembly	Items you buy or produce, track as inventory, and resell.
	EXAMPLES: Pre-assembled door kits, bicycles
Non-inventory Part	Items you sell but do not purchase; items you purchase but do not resell; items you purchase and resell but do not track as inventory.
	EXAMPLES: Custom-made slipcovers, pizza, office supplies
Other Charge	Other charges on a sale or a purchase, such as freight or finance charges.
	EXAMPLES: shipping charge, delivery charge
Group	Fast entry of a group of individual items already on the list.
	EXAMPLES: Group of services and lab fees for office visits, group of services and food items provided by a caterer

	Items that calculate
Type	***Use for***
Subtotal	Calculating a subtotal before calculating a discount or charge that covers several items.
Discount	Calculating an amount to be subtracted from the total.
	(To discount several items, use a Subtotal item first).
Payment	Payment received at the time of invoicing so that amount owed on invoice is reduced.
Sales tax item	Calculating a single sales tax for a sale.
Sales tax group	Calculating two or more sales taxes grouped together and applied to the same sale.

Handout 21

Receive Payments window

Use the Receive Payments window to record payments from customers. If you billed a specific job for a customer, be sure to apply the payment to the job (not just the customer name).

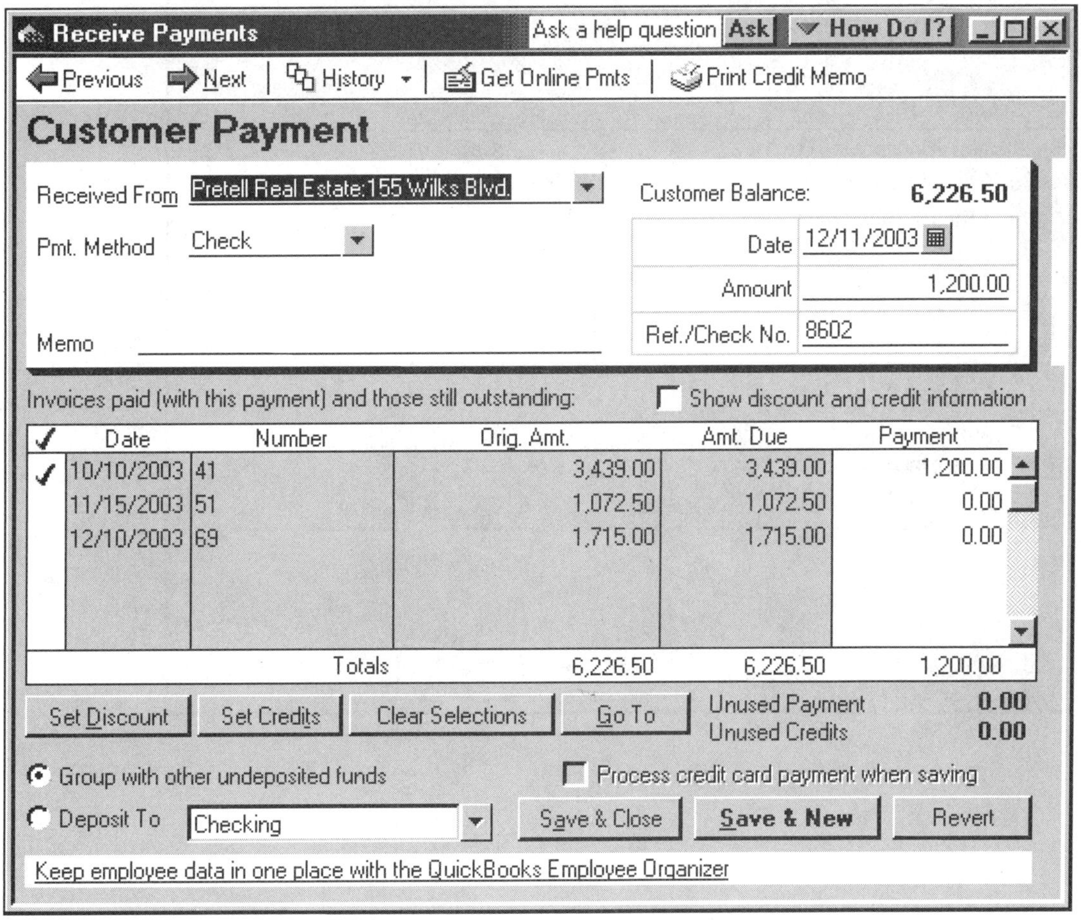

To open the Receive Payments window, choose Receive Payments from the Customers menu.

Handout 22

Make Deposits window

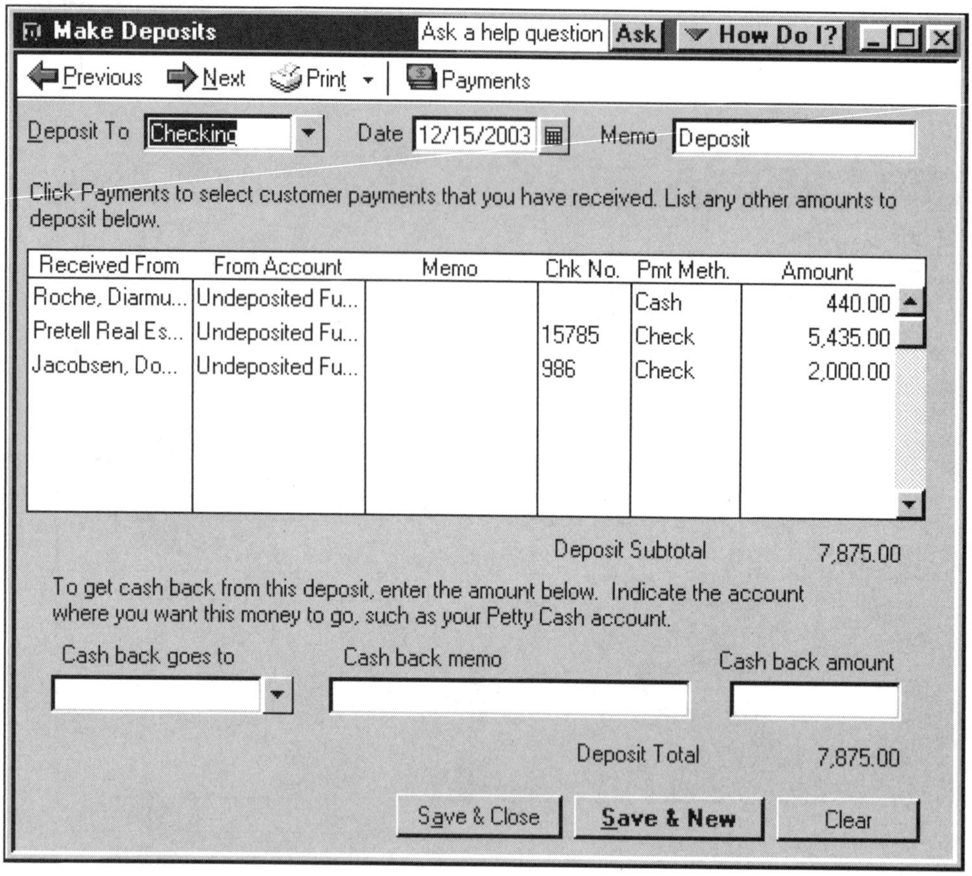

Handout 23

Handling expenses in QuickBooks

Do this:	*When:*
Write a check manually *or* pay with a credit card	You need to purchase an item and pay for it on the spot.
Write and print a QuickBooks check	You receive a bill from a vendor that you want to pay immediately.
Use accounts payable in QuickBooks	You receive a bill from a vendor that you want to pay later, and you want to track the total amount you owe to vendors.

Handout 24

Creating a QuickReport from a list, register, or form

When you're in...	*The QuickReport shows you...*
A register (with a transaction selected)	All transactions in that register for the same name
A form (invoice, bill, or check)	All transactions for that particular customer, vendor, or payee
A list (with an item or person selected)	All transactions for that item or all open transactions for that person

Handout 25

Preset report types in QuickBooks

Company & Financial reports include the following:

- **Profit and loss reports** give you a global view of your company's income, expenses, and net profit or loss over a specific period of time.
- **Balance sheet reports** show the financial position of your business by listing assets, liabilities, and equity.
- **Cash flow reports** show the net change in your cash during a period.
- **Customers & Receivables (accounts receivable) reports** give you information about the "receivables" side of your business: which invoices are due (or overdue), how much each customer owes your company, and so on.
- **Sales reports** give you information about what you have sold and to whom.
- **Jobs & Time reports (QuickBooks Pro and Premier only)** give you information on job profitability, item profitability, how your estimates compare to actual costs, and how much time you and your employees are spending on various projects.
- **Vendors & Payables (accounts payable) reports** give you information about the "payables" side of your business, including which bills are due, your sales tax liability, and your current balance with each vendor.
- **Purchases reports** give you information about your purchases.
- **Inventory reports** give you information about the status (such as the quantities you have on hand or on order) and the value of your inventory.
- **Employees & Payroll reports** give you information about your payroll expenses and liabilities.
- **Banking reports** include check detail, deposit detail, and missing check reports.
- **Accountant & Taxes reports** include income tax summary, income tax detail, general ledger, trial balance, journal, transaction journal, and audit trail reports.
- **Budget reports** show how your income and expenses compare to the budgets you have set up.
- **List reports** give you a way to display information from your QuickBooks lists.

Handout 26

Seeing more of an onscreen report

Click...	*To do this...*
Hide Header	Hide everything in the report header (company name, report title, date range, today's date, etc.). This button does not affect the printed report.
Show Header	Display the report header you previously hid.
Collapse	Hide subaccounts, jobs, and subclasses; by summarizing their amounts under the main heading. This button affects both the onscreen and printed report.
Expand	Display the subaccounts you previously hid.

Handout 27

QuickInsight graph types

- An income and expense graph shows your income and expenses for the period you specify.
- A sales graph shows your company's sales income for the period you specify.
- An accounts receivable graph shows how much your customers owe.
- An accounts payable graph shows how much you currently owe your vendors.
- A net worth graph shows changes in your company's net worth.
- A budget vs. actual graph lets you see the variance between your budgeted amounts and the actual amount you earned or spent.

Handout 28

Inventory in QuickBooks

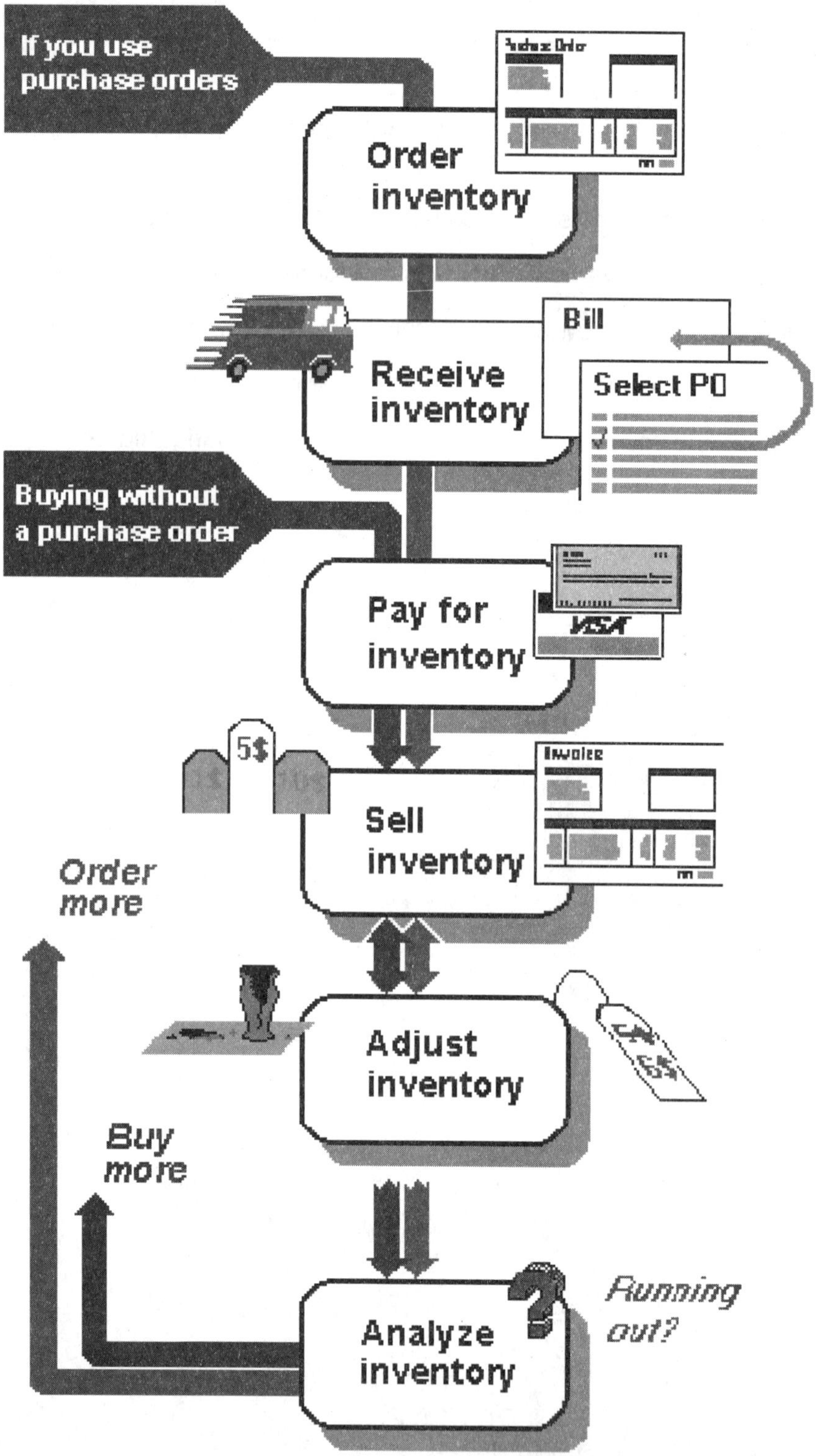

Handout 29

Paying for inventory items

If…	*You pay by…*
You're making an over-the-counter purchase	Entering a check or credit card receipt.
You've entered an item receipt for inventory, but the bill hasn't arrived yet	Entering the bill when the item receipt arrives. (Choose Enter Bill for Received Items from the Vendors menu.) You then pay the bill just like you would any other QuickBooks bill.
You've entered a bill for inventory you've received	Paying the bill just like you would pay any other QuickBooks bill. (Choose Pay Bills from the Vendors menu.)

Handout 30

Sales tax in QuickBooks

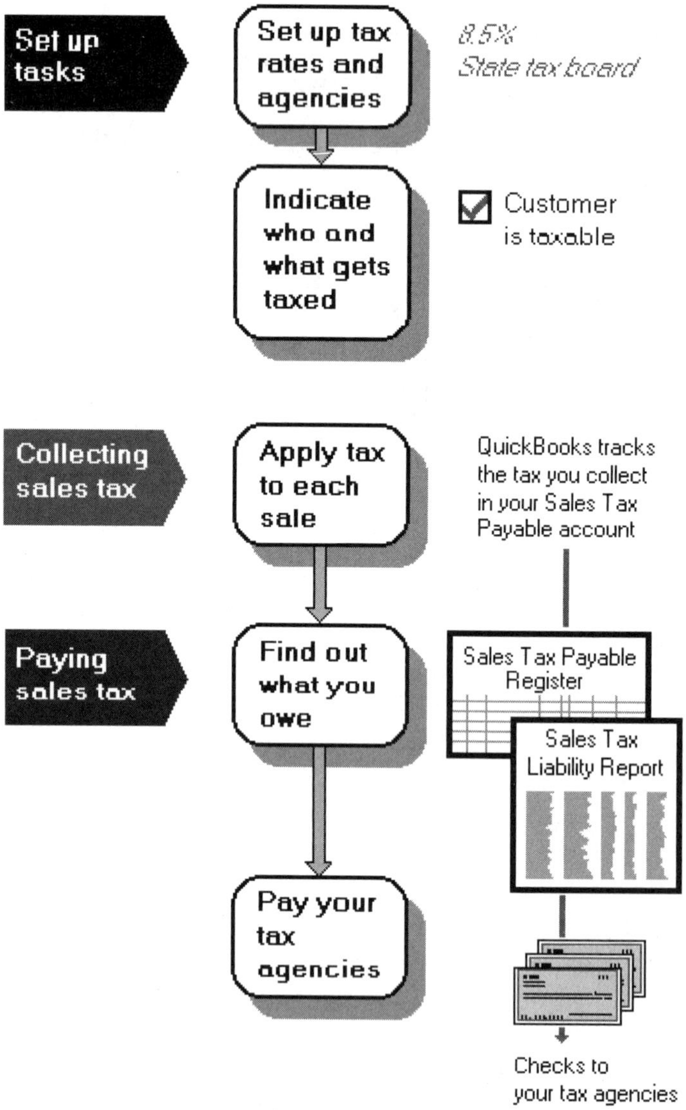

Handout 31

When to use a sales tax group

Example

When you report the tax you've collected to your state, they require that you show your taxable and non-taxable sales for each county, *and they expect you to report the state tax you've collected separately:*

- **County X at 2%,**
- **County Y at 2%, and**
- **State at 6%**

If your reporting situation is like this, you need to create *separate sales tax items for each county and the state*, since you report on each separately.

Then, for your customer's benefit, you can create group tax items, one for each county, which includes that county's tax and the state tax:

- **Group 1, called County X ... 8%**

  includes items for County X: 2% and State: 6%

- **Group 2, called County Y ... 8%**

  includes items for County Y: 2% and State: 6%

This way, your customers see one overall tax, but QuickBooks can still report on each county and the state separately.

Handout 32

Viewing your sales tax liability

Use this method...	*When you want to...*
Sales tax liability report	See a summary of how much you have billed (or collected) on behalf of each sales tax agency, *and* see how much you owe each tax agency.
Sales Tax Payable register	Scan the tax-related transactions QuickBooks has recorded in your Sales Tax Payable register.
Pay Sales Tax window	See how much you owe each tax agency. Pay the sales tax your business owes.

Handout 33

Overview of payroll tracking

Employer responsibilities:

1 Calculate gross pay for employee.

2 Calculate federal withholding.

3 Calculate state withholding.

4 Calculate FICA.

5 Calculate Medicare.

6 Calculate federal unemployment.

7 Calculate state unemployment.

8 Add any other deductions.

9 Withhold taxes and deductions from employee's paycheck.

10 Write a check for the net pay to the employee.

11 Submit tax reports and pay taxes to government.

12 Pay any other withheld deductions.

Handout 34

Items on the Payroll Item list

A **payroll item** is anything that affects the amount on a paycheck. The QuickBooks sample company has the following items for wages and federal taxes:

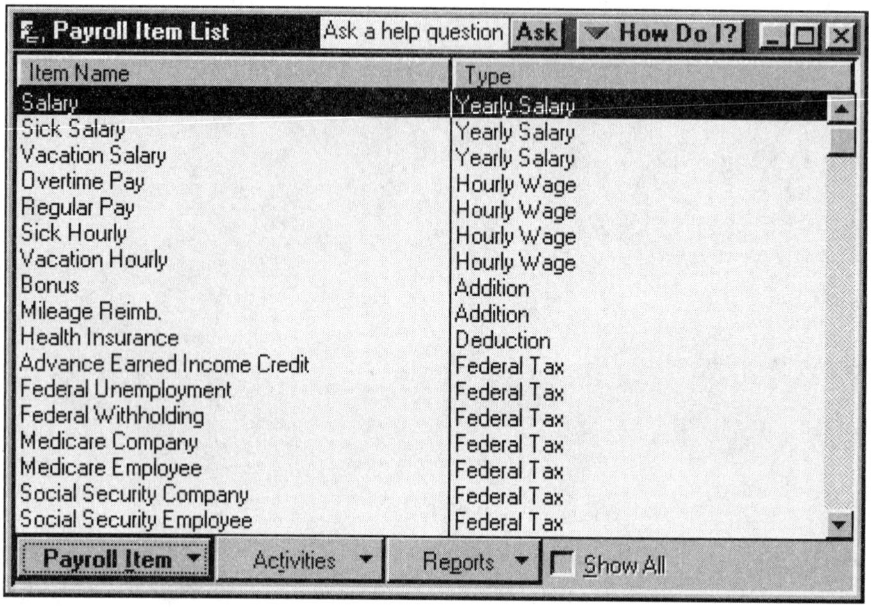

You can add other items to the list as you need them.

Handout 35

Tracking payroll expenses and payroll liabilities

Payroll Expenses

Employees' gross pay

Employer payroll taxes:

- Social security (FICA)
- Federal unemployment insurance (FUTA)
- Medicare
- State unemployment insurance (SUI)—*if paid by employer*
- State disability (SDI)—*if paid by employer*

Payroll Liabilities

Taxes you've withheld from paychecks for:

- Social security (FICA)
- Federal unemployment insurance (FUTA)
- Medicare
- State unemployment insurance (SUI)
- State disability (SDI)
- State income tax
- Federal income tax

Handout 36

Creating an estimate

An estimate is a description of work, or products, you propose to sell to a current or prospective customer. After you create an estimate, you can use it to create one or more invoices.

Estimates are not available in QuickBooks Basic.

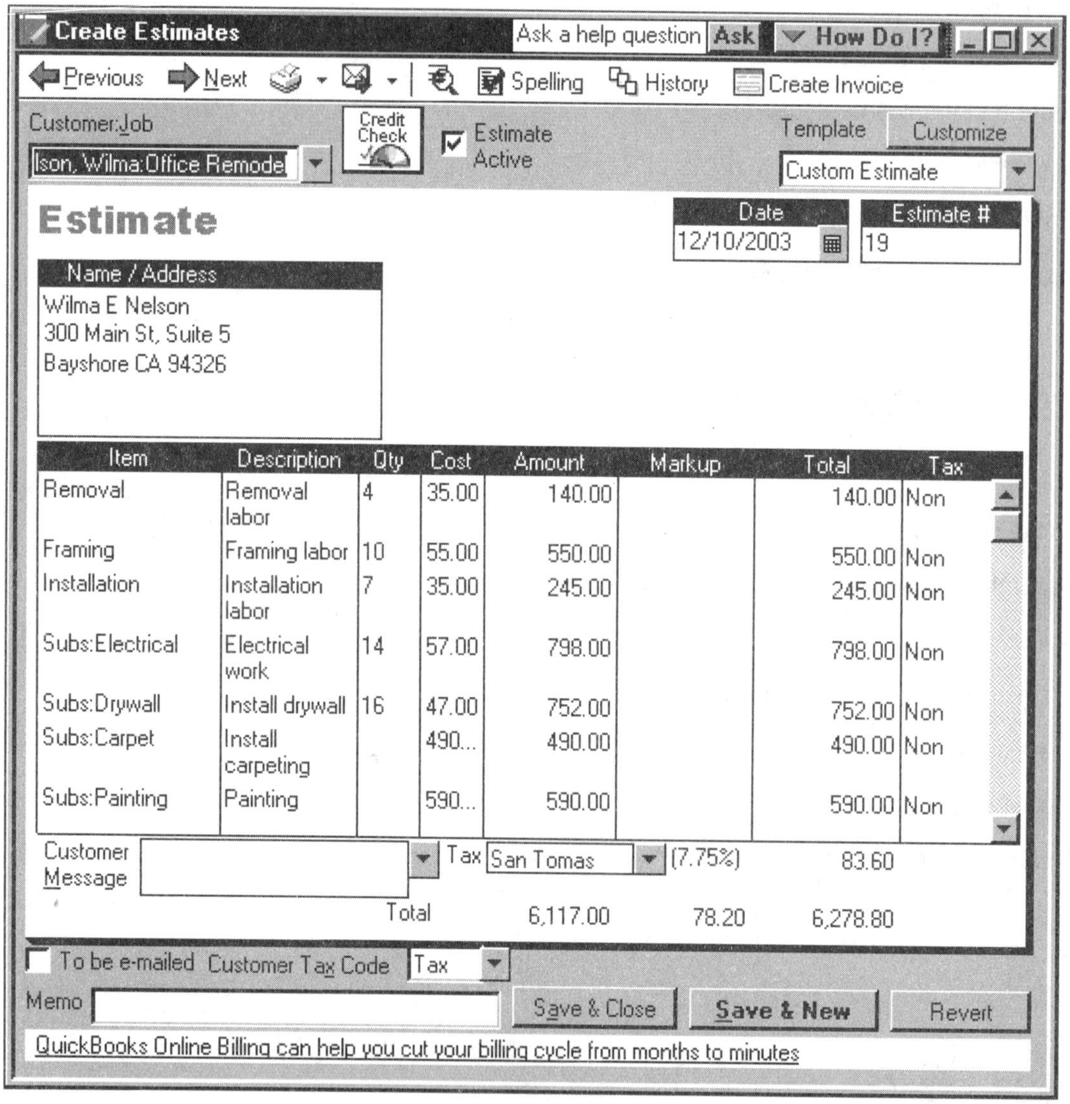

Handout 37

Creating invoices from an estimate

After you create an estimate, you can use it to invoice the customer.

QuickBooks Pro and Premier let you do the following:

- Create an invoice for the entire estimate (100%).
- Create an invoice for a percentage of the entire estimate (for example, 33.33% if you want to invoice for one-third of the estimate).
- Create an invoice for selected items or for different percentages of each item.

Handout 38

Invoicing customers for time worked

To invoice a customer for time worked, click Time/Costs in the Create Invoices window. Then, click in the Use column to select the time entries you want to want to include on the invoice to that customer.

In this example, all of the time worked in November on Anton Teschner's sunroom will be added to his invoice.

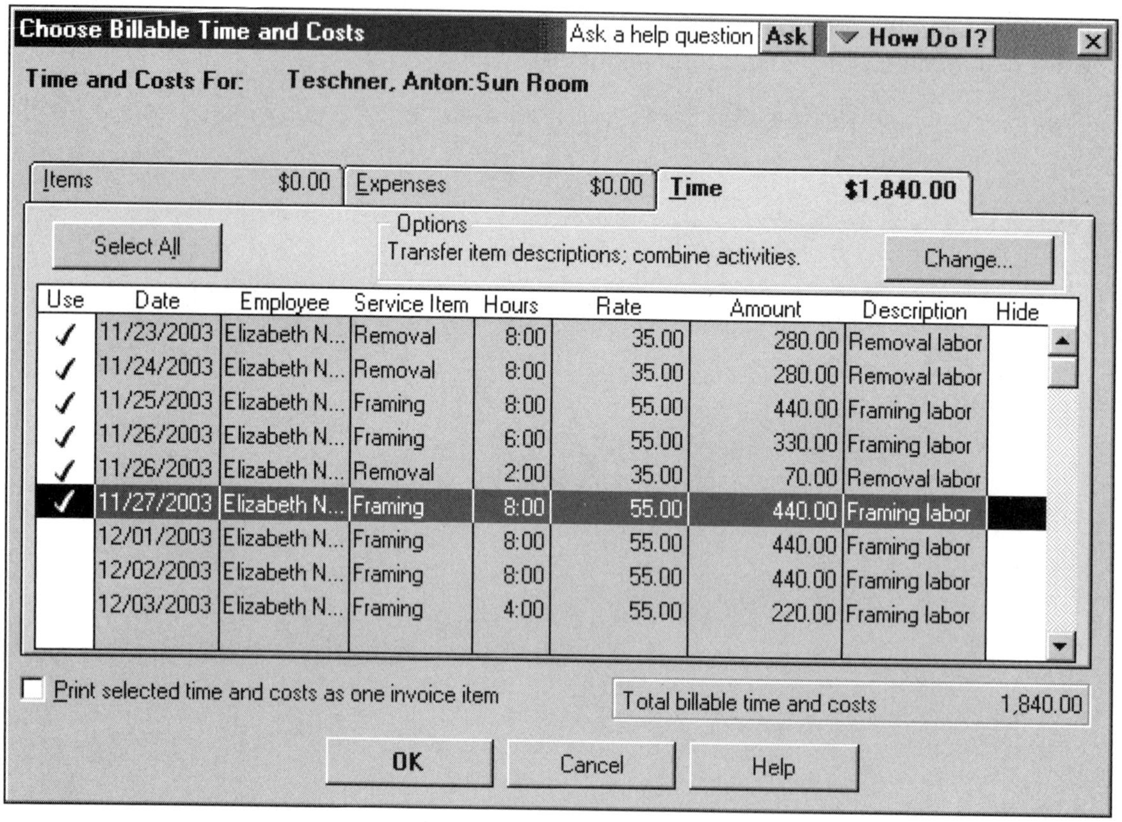

Notice that QuickBooks created two line items for time worked: one for all billable time for Removal (18 hours), and one for Framing (22 hours).

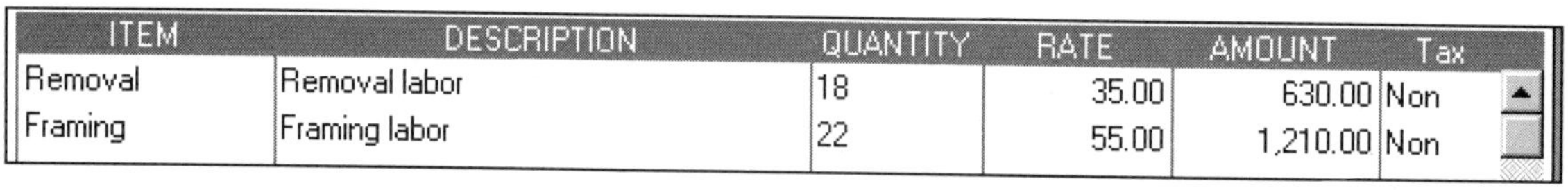

Handout 39

Types of QuickBooks forms you can customize

- **Invoice**
- **Sales receipt**
- **Credit memo**
- **Statement**
- **Purchase order**
- **Estimate (QuickBooks Pro and Premier only)**
- **Sales orders (QuickBooks Premier only)**

For each form, you can decide which fields and columns to include, what they are called, and where to place them.

Once you have created your forms, you can save the new layouts as “templates”—to use again and again.

Handout 40

QuickBooks Layout Designer

The Layout Designer lets you move, change the size, change the fonts, and turn on/off the borders for all fields. You can also import your logo, place it anywhere you want, and resize it in the Layout Designer.

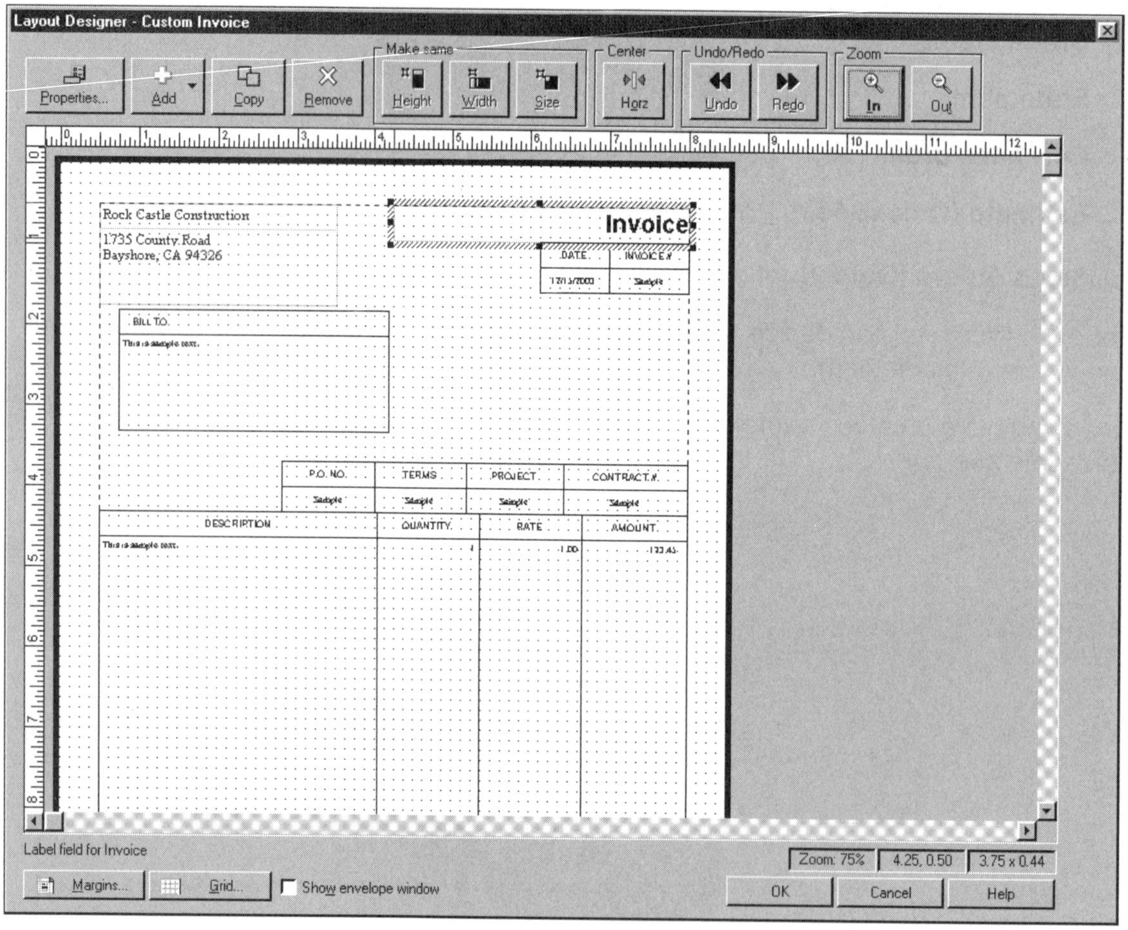

Index

I

J

L

M

N

O

P

Q

R

S

T

U

V

W

Instructor's Guide Evaluation

QuickBooks in the Classroom 2003

____

Instructor Name

____

Organization Name

____

Date

MAIL TO:
QuickBooks in the Classroom
Intuit MS 2475
P.O. Box 7850
Mountain View, CA 94039

OR FAX TO:
1-650-944-3133

Objectives	**Success Level** low 1	2	3	4	high 5
The guide covered all the topics and features you wanted	☐	☐	☐	☐	☐
The information was organized in a logical manner	☐	☐	☐	☐	☐
The file on the exercise disk was accurate and helpful	☐	☐	☐	☐	☐
The lessons and topics were easy to find	☐	☐	☐	☐	☐
The step-by-step format was helpful	☐	☐	☐	☐	☐
The screenshots were accurate and helpful	☐	☐	☐	☐	☐

Please indicate the class level: (circle one)

K-12 Community College University Adult Education ________________

What did you like most about the guide? What section or handouts were the least helpful?

____

____

What aspects of the guide could be improved? What topic is missing or needs more clarification for your students?

____

____

What other examples would be helpful to your students?

____

____

What other teaching materials, if any, do you use to teach this course?

____

____

What is the name of your course, and what is the course length?

____

____

Training Skill Evaluation - Before Class

This class is designed to meet the following objectives. To ensure that you receive the most effective training, rate your confidence performing each objective now, using the numbered scale on the right. Using the information you provide helps to determine whether the objectives of the course have been met.

Objectives	never attempted 0	low 1	2	**Success Level** 3	4	high 5
Create a QuickBooks company	☐	☐	☐	☐	☐	☐
Add and edit information in company lists	☐	☐	☐	☐	☐	☐
Modify one of the QuickBooks preset chart of accounts	☐	☐	☐	☐	☐	☐
Customize QuickBooks forms	☐	☐	☐	☐	☐	☐
Create customer invoices	☐	☐	☐	☐	☐	☐
Receive payments from customers and make bank deposits	☐	☐	☐	☐	☐	☐
Write checks, assigning the amounts to specific expense or bank accounts	☐	☐	☐	☐	☐	☐
Enter and pay bills	☐	☐	☐	☐	☐	☐
Assign reimbursable expenses to customers	☐	☐	☐	☐	☐	☐
Open/use registers for QuickBooks balance sheet accounts	☐	☐	☐	☐	☐	☐
Reconcile a QuickBooks checking account	☐	☐	☐	☐	☐	☐
Track credit card transactions	☐	☐	☐	☐	☐	☐
Work with QuickBooks asset and liability accounts	☐	☐	☐	☐	☐	☐
Create and customize QuickBooks reports and graphs	☐	☐	☐	☐	☐	☐
Track and pay sales tax	☐	☐	☐	☐	☐	☐
Manage inventory with QuickBooks	☐	☐	☐	☐	☐	☐
Run payroll with QuickBooks	☐	☐	☐	☐	☐	☐
Create estimates, track time and do advanced job costing	☐	☐	☐	☐	☐	☐
Export a QuickBooks report to Microsoft Excel	☐	☐	☐	☐	☐	☐
Write a letter using the QuickBooks Letters feature	☐	☐	☐	☐	☐	☐

____

Your name

____

Your organization

____

Your instructor's name

____

Date

Training Skill Evaluation - After Class

This class is designed to meet the following objectives. Please rate your confidence performing each objective now, using the numbered scale on the right.

Objectives	never attempted 0	low 1	2	3	4	high 5
Create a QuickBooks company	☐	☐	☐	☐	☐	☐
Add and edit information in company lists	☐	☐	☐	☐	☐	☐
Modify one of the QuickBooks preset chart of accounts	☐	☐	☐	☐	☐	☐
Customize QuickBooks forms	☐	☐	☐	☐	☐	☐
Create customer invoices	☐	☐	☐	☐	☐	☐
Receive payments from customers and make bank deposits	☐	☐	☐	☐	☐	☐
Write checks, assigning the amounts to specific expense or bank accounts	☐	☐	☐	☐	☐	☐
Enter and pay bills	☐	☐	☐	☐	☐	☐
Assign reimbursable expenses to customers	☐	☐	☐	☐	☐	☐
Open/use registers for QuickBooks balance sheet accounts	☐	☐	☐	☐	☐	☐
Reconcile a QuickBooks checking account	☐	☐	☐	☐	☐	☐
Track credit card transactions	☐	☐	☐	☐	☐	☐
Work with QuickBooks asset and liability accounts	☐	☐	☐	☐	☐	☐
Create and customize QuickBooks reports and graphs	☐	☐	☐	☐	☐	☐
Track and pay sales tax	☐	☐	☐	☐	☐	☐
Manage inventory with QuickBooks	☐	☐	☐	☐	☐	☐
Run payroll with QuickBooks	☐	☐	☐	☐	☐	☐
Create estimates, track time do advanced job costing	☐	☐	☐	☐	☐	☐
Export a QuickBooks report to Microsoft Excel	☐	☐	☐	☐	☐	☐
Write a letter using the QuickBooks Letters feature	☐	☐	☐	☐	☐	☐

Success Level

____
Your name

____
Your organization

____
Your instructor's name

____
Date

continued on the next page

Training Skill Evaluation - After Class (continued)

Please answer the questions below.

What sections or handouts were the most helpful?

____

____

____

What sections or handouts were the least helpful?

____

____

____

What did you like most about the course?

____

____

____

What aspects of the course could be improved?

____

____

____

Other comments:

____

____

____